JEFFERSON'S NEPHEWS

JEFFERSON'S NEPHEWS

•

A FRONTIER TRAGEDY

BOYNTON MERRILL, JR.

PRINCETON UNIVERSITY
PRESS

Copyright © 1976 by Princeton University Press

Published by Princeton University Press, Princeton, New Jersey
In the United Kingdom:
Princeton University Press, Guildford, Surrey

All Rights Reserved

Library of Congress Cataloging in Publication Data will
be found on the last printed page of this book

This book has been composed in Baskerville
by Science Press, Ephrata, Pa.

Printed in the United States of America
by Princeton University Press, Princeton, New Jersey

"How are the mighty fallen! Tell it
not . . . , publish it not in the streets. . ."

II Samuel, 1:19–20

To THOSE who consider themselves above the common man, the loss of wealth and reputation is a grievous, deep, and secret pain. It becomes nearly intolerable if the downfall occurs in full public view.

Among the Colonial Virginia gentry there existed a social structure similar, in many ways, to that of English royalty. Its influences and attitudes lingered for many decades after the American Revolution. One such aristocratic family, that of Charles Lewis of Albemarle County, brother-in-law to Thomas Jefferson, having lost most of its patrimony, emigrated to the western frontier of Kentucky in 1808, taking little with them except their pretensions. There on the frontier, where others thrived, the Lewis family experienced heartbreaking misfortunes, and at last met ruin in an incredible climax of horror, bloodshed, and natural upheaval.

The great forests, rivers, and rich lands; the frontier lawmen, merchants, settlers, slaves, and outlaws; all these set the scene for the final tragedy that inexorably unfolded, first in a kitchen cabin, then a rough log courtroom, and finally in a graveyard at the top of a steep hill.

To Marian

PREFACE

LATE IN THE year of 1811 a crime of singular depravity was committed in the west Kentucky frontier county of Livingston. The two men charged with the murder were nephews of Thomas Jefferson. In the century and a half or more since the murder, most of the facts have been distorted or lost, and indeed, the crime itself has been nearly forgotten, even though it was widely known in Kentucky at that time.

About ten years ago I came into the ownership of a portion of the plantation where this crime occurred. Becoming interested in discovering the truth about the legends, I spent increasing time with old records, letters, and books, until, five years ago, the search for the true story became a full-time occupation, and has been ever since. Although at times I felt like a secondary victim of the tragedy, the understanding I have gained about our heritage has been somberly rewarding.

This book is a reconstruction of the crime, its consequences, and the circumstances that led to its commission. The social, religious, and governmental institutions of that time are discussed, as are the family and friends of the accused, Lilburne and Isham Lewis. Their family traced its beginnings far back into the colonial period of Virginia. For nearly sixty years the Lewises were neighbors of Thomas Jefferson's family in Albemarle County, Virginia, and for three successive generations these two families were bound together by intermarriages. Jefferson's connection with this branch of the Lewis family is discussed herein at length for the first time.

In the years since the murder, slavery and the frontier have both disappeared, and governmental structures have been drastically altered. The old-time patterns of plantation and family life have nearly ceased to exist, and the doctrines and purposes of certain religious denominations have changed so much that the sects are scarcely recognizable. None of the families, customs, and institutions, not even the land and rivers, are the same today as they were then, yet they are with us still.

ix

ACKNOWLEDGMENTS

THROUGH SEVERAL of the years this book was in preparation, I was fortunate to have the help of a tireless and perspicacious research assistant, Mrs. Clara Lee Whitt, of Marion, Kentucky. Although her contributions were not limited exclusively to Kentucky and Mississippi, much of the new information gathered in those states was her discovery. Assisting me in an extended search for pertinent old documents and records in Virginia, Mr. David L. Thomas, graduate assistant at the University of Virginia Library, rendered skillful and much appreciated service.

Out of the legion individuals who have helped me in this work, special thanks are due to a few whose contributions were integral and particularly generous: Mr. James A. Bear, Jr., Charlottesville, Virginia; Dr. Julian P. Boyd, Princeton, New Jersey; Mr. Littleton Groom, Princeton, New Jersey; Mr. and Mrs. Gabe McCandless, and Miss Reba Smith, of Smithland, Kentucky.

The librarians, curators, and staffs of the institutions where much of this work was done were without exception friendly, cooperative, and efficient. These people made my work a pleasure. Among those to whom I am especially indebted are Dr. Jacqueline Bull and her staff of the Wilson Library, University of Kentucky, Lexington; Mr. Alexander M. Gilchrist, Margaret I. King Library, University of Kentucky; Dr. Dumas Malone, Mr. William G. Ray, Mr. Gregory A. Johnson, and the staff of the Manuscripts Department, Alderman Library, University of Virginia, Charlottesville; Mr. James R. Bentley and the staff of the Filson Club, Louisville, Kentucky; Mrs. Ruth W. Lester, The Papers of Thomas Jefferson, Princeton, New Jersey; Mrs. Frances H. Stadler, Missouri Historical Society, St. Louis; Miss Julia Neal, Kentucky Library, Bowling Green, Kentucky; Miss Sarah Winstead, Henderson Public Library, Henderson, Kentucky; and Mrs. Margaret V. Henley, Goochland, Virginia.

In addition to the people and organizations named above, the staff members of the following institutions were most helpful to me in my use of their collections, archives, and records: the state historical societies of Kentucky, Virginia, Massachusetts, Missouri, Tennessee, Wisconsin, and Albemarle County, Virginia; The Presbyterian Historical Society in Philadelphia; The Thomas Jefferson Memorial Foundation, Charlottesville, Va.; The Virginia State Library, Richmond; The National Archives and The Library of Congress, Washington, D.C.; Yale University Library, New Haven; Moravian College Library, Bethlehem, Pennsylvania; Lexington Theological Seminary, Lexington, Kentucky; Margie Helm Library, Western Kentucky University; the law libraries at the University of Kentucky in Lexington, and the Kentucky Court of Appeals in Frankfort; the medical, geological, and Margaret I. King libraries at the University of Kentucky; the public libraries of the Kentucky cities of Lexington, Louisville, Henderson, Paducah, and Marion; the public libraries of Evansville, Indiana; and the George Armstrong Library in Natchez, Mississippi; the United States Bureau of the Census; the Mississippi State Land Office; the offices of the United States Geological Survey in Charlottesville, Virginia, and Lexington, Kentucky; the United States Department of Agriculture, A.S.C.S. office in Asheville, North Carolina; the United States Army Corps of Engineers, Louisville and Cincinnati; the circuit and county courts of Boone, Henderson, Livingston, and Union counties in Kentucky; the circuit and county courts of Albemarle and Goochland counties in Virginia, Adams County, Mississippi, and Gallatin County, Illinois.

For valuable help in the study of the Lewis family genealogy I am indebted to Mrs. Marilyn J. Martin, Newtown Square, Pennsylvania; Dr. Michael J. Moore, Roanoke, Virginia; and especially to Mrs. Grace Lewis Santti, Warren, Michigan.

For their interest, helpful interviews, and correspondence I wish to thank Mr. and Mrs. Schuyler Marshall and Mr. and Mrs. Stephen Sweeney of Albemarle County, Virginia; Mr. Bernard Peyton Chamberlain, Charlottesville; Mr. E. Holcombe Palmer and the Rev. George J. Cleaveland, Diocese of Virginia, Richmond; Mr. Arthur D. Engle, Bloomingburg, Ohio; Mr. Albert W. Dickey, Sun City, Arizona; Mrs. May Fleming Howell and Mr. and Mrs. Richard H. Peek of Livingston County, Kentucky; Dr. James F. Hopkins, Dr. Thomas D. Clark, Mr. J. Winston Coleman, Jr., and Dr. Lawrence S. Thompson, Lexington, Kentucky; Hon. John S. Palmore, Frankfort, Kentucky; and Dr. Lester McAllister, Indianapolis.

The author and publisher are grateful to the following for permission to quote extracts from copyright works: The

American Philosophical Society for Edwin M. Betts's *Thomas Jefferson's Garden Book;* The Evansville (Ind.) *Sunday Courier and Press* for William C. Greer's "Terror of 1910: Halley's Comet"; Princeton University Press for Edwin M. Betts's *Thomas Jefferson's Farm Book* and Julian P. Boyd's *The Papers of Thomas Jefferson;* Wendell H. Rone, Sr. for his *An Historical Atlas of Kentucky and Her Counties;* The Thomas Jefferson Memorial Foundation for Sarah N. Randolph's *The Domestic Life of Thomas Jefferson;* the University of Missouri for *The Family Letters of Thomas Jefferson* by Edwin M. Betts and James A. Bear, Jr.; and the University Press of Kentucky for Frank L. McVey's *The Gates Open Slowly.*

For permission to quote from documents, manuscripts, letters, and other works under common-law copyright, the author and publisher are grateful to the following: Mrs. Lee L. Davis, Hilton Head, South Carolina; The Filson Club, Louisville, Kentucky; The Kentucky Historical Society, Frankfort; The Kentucky Library, Bowling Green; The Library of Congress; The Massachusetts Historical Society, Boston; The Missouri Historical Society, St. Louis; The Presbyterian Historical Society, Philadelphia, Pennsylvania; The State Historical Society of Wisconsin, Madison; Dr. Hambleton Tapp, Versailles, Kentucky; The University of Virginia Library (Manuscripts Department and Tracy W. McGregor Library), Charlottesville; and The Virginia State Library, Richmond.

My special thanks are due Mrs. Dorothy H. Gibbs, Lexington, Kentucky, my typist, who is an infallible speller, and a wise and meticulous craftsman of words; and Mrs. Margaret Case, my editor, another rare person who has these talents.

Among the many who have waited patiently and given me encouragement, Mr. Jonathan Daniels stands out in my mind. Foremost of these, however, is my wife who, for ten years in our home, has been a gracious and understanding hostess to the disturbed ghosts of Lucy Lewis's family.

While I extend my appreciation to all these generous people for their help, I must reserve for myself the entire responsibility for any shortcomings this work may have.

CONTENTS

CONTENTS

LIST OF MAPS AND FIGURES

MAPS

FIGURES

xv

JEFFERSON'S NEPHEWS

·1·

COLONIAL DAYS

THE FOUNDER of the Lewis family in Virginia, Robert Lewis, settled near the coast during the earliest years of the colony's history. Lewis had been a Welsh lawyer. Attracted by the challenge of the new world, he arrived in Virginia twenty-six years after the first representative government was established at Jamestown in 1619. In the same year that this government was formed at Jamestown, the first indentured blacks came in bondage to the English colonies in North America.[1]

Robert Lewis lived in Gloucester County, and it was there that his son built the imposing plantation house called Warner Hall. As land along the coast and rivers was taken up, successive generations of Virginians moved inland to the west, a trend that eventually only the Pacific coast could stop. So it was with the Lewises, who were to become one of the more influential and prolific families of Virginia. The great-grandson of Robert, named Charles, settled in Goochland County near the James River about forty miles upstream from Richmond. His plantation home was called the Byrd and, because Charles Lewis was a common name at that time in Virginia, he identified himself as Charles Lewis of the Byrd.[2]

There were ten children in the family of Charles Lewis of the Byrd and his wife, Mary. For those fortunate people, like Charles of the Byrd, who owned sizable tracts of land and numerous slaves, raising a large family was not an economic problem. As the sons reached maturity, however, their prosperity and prestige depended upon acquiring enough additional land so that each of them could establish himself as a planter in his own right. Traditionally the father provided his sons with land and slaves. This was routinely done by the wealthy gentrymen in colonial Virginia.

England's primary interest in her American colonies was profit, which, in the case of Virginia, was mainly derived from tobacco. England controlled both the market and the price. As the Virginia tobacco industry developed and the stream of wealth began to flow into British hands, steps were taken to increase the production of this valuable weed. Britishers were

3

encouraged to emigrate to Virginia where, it was presumed, if settlers were given land, they would grow tobacco.

During the 1600s certain emigrants to Virginia were given grants or patents of land on which to live and in 1705 the statutes were revised so that it became lawful for "any person to take up and plant land" in the unoccupied parts of the colony. The grantee could patent up to 500 acres in each grant at a cost of approximately one and one-half cents per acre. In order for the patent to be valid the tract selected had to be vacant or previously unclaimed. It was then surveyed by the official surveyor of the precinct, and the description was recorded in the local court records. In addition to this, the grantee was required to "improve" the land within three years by erecting certain buildings, clearing, fencing portions of it, or by making other specified improvements.[3]

By 1720 there was a provision in the land patent law that gave a marked advantage to wealthy people like Charles Lewis of the Byrd. If a grantee owned fewer than five slaves, his patent was limited to 500 acres, but if he owned more than five slaves, he could patent an additional 200 acres for each slave he owned, up to a total of 4,000 acres in a single patent.[4] The Virginia colonial law was made by the aristocracy, and it favored aristocrats. Those with influence could obtain large grants of land even though they were not immigrants, and those who had money enough could buy outright from the people who had obtained their grants at an earlier time.[5]

In 1731 Charles Lewis of the Byrd paid six pounds and received a patent for 1,200 acres of land on the Rivanna River near the mouth of Buck Island Creek (see Map 1). This grant, and the properties later added to it, were called Buck Island. It is located approximately eight miles southeast of Charlottesville. About 800 acres of this patent lay on the north side of the Rivanna River in Fredericksville Parish, and the rest was directly across the Rivanna, on the south bank, in St. Anne's Parish.[6] This was one of the earliest patents obtained in this part of Virginia, a section which was then wilderness country. Although several much larger grants were made in Albemarle, the average land grant from 1727 to 1745 was just over 800 acres. As the county became more populated, the size of the grants decreased markedly.[7] It is doubtful that Charles of the Byrd moved to Buck Island to oversee the opening of the plantation, for his

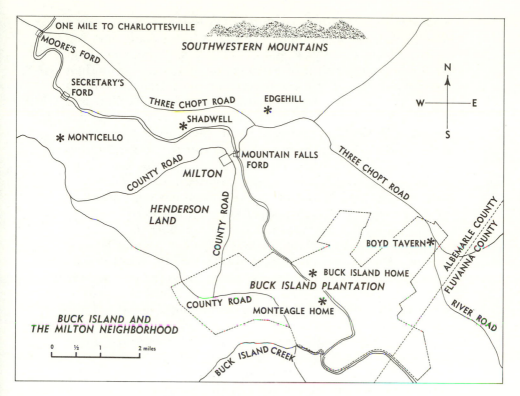

ONE MILE TO CHARLOTTESVILLE
SOUTHWESTERN MOUNTAINS
MOORE'S FORD
SECRETARY'S FORD
THREE CHOPT ROAD
EDGEHILL
*
SHADWELL
*
* MONTICELLO
COUNTY ROAD
MILTON
MOUNTAIN FALLS FORD
THREE CHOPT ROAD
N
W   E
S
HENDERSON LAND
COUNTY ROAD
BOYD TAVERN *
ALBEMARLE COUNTY
FLUVANNA COUNTY
* BUCK ISLAND HOME
BUCK ISLAND PLANTATION
COUNTY ROAD
MONTEAGLE HOME
*
RIVER ROAD
BUCK ISLAND AND
THE MILTON NEIGHBORHOOD
0   ½   1   2 miles
BUCK ISLAND CREEK

Map 1. *(Map by Thomas E. Clark)*

regular residence was in Goochland, and it was there at the Byrd that he lived in later years.[8]

The second son of Charles Lewis of the Byrd was also named Charles, and was distinguished from his father by the use of "Jr.," and the further identification of "Buck Island." It was probably this son who moved to Buck Island at the age of nineteen, perfected his father's patent to the land, and opened the plantation. Charles Lewis, Jr. built his home there on the 800-acre tract on the north side of the Rivanna. In 1744, when he was twenty-five years old, Charles Lewis, Jr. married Mary Randolph. In the following year their first child was born, a son

5

whom they named Charles Lilburne Lewis. In time a second son was born, Isham, and then over the years six daughters followed. About a year before Charles Lewis, Jr. married, and no doubt anticipating this marriage, his father had given him control and use of the 1,200 acres at Buck Island.[9] Charles Lewis, Jr. had far more land than the average farmer, and through it, access to farming on a commercial scale and, in turn, wealth and local prominence. Soon afterward he became a magistrate and member of the country court. This small group of men administered the business and minor judicial affairs of the county. Locally it was a most important office. Regardless of their origin, the early Albemarle magistrates were members of the aristocracy of wealth, which is to say they were owners of sizable tracts of land.[10] Nearly half of the Buck Island tracts were bottom land, level and rich fields, certainly among the most productive in the county. Along the Rivanna the lands sloping down to the bottoms were less productive, and the hilly ground was poor farmland indeed. The top soil was thin, scarcely covering a sandy subsoil conglomerate containing some gravel and loose rock.

Transforming a wilderness tract into a plantation was an arduous undertaking. Some of the trees were cut and hewn or whipsawed to make the buildings, and others were split for fence rails, but the land cleared by the removal of timber for these purposes was insignificant. Where labor was scarce or time was pressing, the trees were left in place but deadened by removing a narrow strip of bark completely around the trunk. If the trees were girdled in late summer they seldom sent up troublesome sprouts from the roots in later years, and although they might put out a weak and spindly growth of leaves the next season, the trees would soon stand skeletal and bare against the sky. Meanwhile the underbrush was burned off or dug out with grubbing hoes, the soil was scratched with plows, and the first crop was planted under the canopy of dead branches. Eventually the limbs fell, and then the trunks. These were usually burned where they lay.

If the planter owned many slaves or could hire labor, the trees were cut off at waist height and the branches were rolled together so they would burn. The stumps sent up sprouts for several years, but if the shoots were cut off regularly with axes or grubbing hoes, in time the stump would die and rot away. Occasionally when new ground was cleared the stumps were dug out or cut off below plow level.[11]

As the new ground of Albemarle was cleared for crops, its riches were quickly extracted and the fertility of the soil declined rapidly. The traditional practice was this: a field was cultivated in tobacco four or five successive years; the land then lay fallow for a year or so, after which the process was repeated.[12] Although tobacco was the main cash crop of the county in the early days of its setlement, it was certainly not the only product of the plantations. Practically all of the food, as well as the cotton, flax, and wool for cloth had to be grown and processed at home. This required an amazing diversity of crops and skills, all dependent on slaves at some point. It is unlikely that any significant changes in farming practices took place at Buck Island during the lifetime of Charles Lewis, Jr. The tools, the crops, the livestock breeds, and the methods of planting, harvesting, processing, and storing changed very little from one generation to the next.

By 1745 Albemarle was emerging from the wilderness. There were about a hundred white residents in the county, and nearly twice that number of slaves. In the following decade the population more than doubled. Over ninety-five percent of the people were engaged in agriculture, but a few still made their living by hunting. There were a few lawyers in the county, a doctor or two, and an occasional schoolmaster to serve the children of the wealthier planters. In time some of the plantation owners built sawmills, flour and grist mills, ferries, warehouses, trading posts, and taverns. In the time of the early settlement, there were few independent craftsmen, but many of the larger plantations were fairly well equipped with tools and slaves who could do carpentry, blacksmithing, tailoring, and other crafts on a functional if not artistic level.[13]

About a mile to the north of the Buck Island plantation the Three Chopt Road twisted from Albemarle eastward toward Richmond. When first laid out, this road was a mere trail blazed by three notches on nearby trees, but it became the main thoroughfare for east-west traffic in Albemarle. In 1749, four years after receiving the deed of tenancy from his father, Charles Lewis, Jr. bought a tract of 400 acres that lay between the Three Chopt Road and the northern line of his plantation, thus giving Buck Island frontage on the two east-west arteries of transportation in the area, the Rivanna River and the Three

7

Chopt Road. Two years later he bought another several hundred acres adjoining this last tract.[14]

By 1776 Charles Lewis, Jr. had lived at Buck Island for twenty-one years, holding in his name the deed of tenancy but not, however, the full title to the plantation. In that year, when he was forty-five years old, his father, Charles Lewis of the Byrd, gave him full title to the 400 -acre tract of land south of the Rivanna, and not long afterward gave him a full title deed to the 800 -acre tract north of the river, where Charles Lewis, Jr. and Mary had lived for two decades. Immediately after receiving the first of these deeds, he conveyed back to his mother and father a life interest in the property. This legal device assured the son that when his parents died the Buck Island property would be his, and that, meanwhile, his parents would neither sell it, give it away, nor leave it to another child. In turn it guaranteed to Charles of the Byrd and his wife a measure of security in that they could claim the profits from the plantation if they needed or chose to do so.[15]

Charles Lewis, Jr. had been in a favorable position from the time he had first moved to Albemarle as a youth. In the beginning he had access to 1,200 acres of land, and later he acquired hundreds of acres more. He could ship his crops to Richmond, a marketplace with access to the sea. Across the Atlantic the merchants of England provided not only a market for Virginia tobacco, but also credit for lean years against promised future deliveries. An inventory of Charles Lewis, Jr.'s possessions gives a fair picture, not only of the wealth he eventually achieved, but also of his operation of the Buck Island plantation.[16]

By the time he died, Charles Lewis, Jr. had acquired fifty-seven slaves. He had plows, sleds, harnesses, and other pieces of gear for his eleven horses and two oxen. He was well equipped with hand tools; nearly forty hoes of various types, sixteen reaping hooks or long sickles for harvesting small grain, several kinds of axes and iron wedges, and numerous other implements for carpentry and farming. In addition to these, he had all the apparatus necessary to manufacture clothing: a cotton gin and cotton wheels, a flax wheel, looms, and heckles, which were used to comb and dress the hemp and flax.[17]

Even though his implements were rudimentary, Charles Lewis, Jr. was able to produce impressive corps. At the end of 1782 he had an inventory of 15,750 pounds of loose tobacco, worth $400; "two hhds. tobacco, 2,000 pounds prized up," worth $50; 332 barrels of corn, worth over $550; 280 bushels of rye; 166 bushels of oats; and 30 bushels of wheat. There were bundles of flax and hemp, various seeds, fodder for the livestock, 65 gallons of vinegar, and 125 gallons of cider.

The value of the corn listed in this inventory does not necessarily indicate that corn was as important as tobacco as a source of income. Corn was used more often than it was sold. The customary basic ration for adult slaves in the antebellum south was a peck of corn meal and three or four pounds of bacon or salt pork per week.[18] The diet of the Lewis slaves no doubt contained other items, but corn was basic. Dr. George Gilmer, a local physician in Albemarle, thought that the health of the slaves would be better if milk were substituted for meat in their diet. In a speech to the citizens of Albemarle he said: "Let us only inquire in this Colony which are the most robust and hearty, calculating everything, the white and the negroe. Certainly the latter; and where they are kindly used and plentifully fed with good hoe-cake and milk, they live as long, look as well and get as many children."[19] In general, the plantation economy at Buck Island was this: part of the corn was fed to the hogs; the corn and pork were fed to the slaves; and the slaves grew the tobacco, which was then sold for cash or credit.

The list of livestock completes the farm portion of the plantation inventory; 86 head of cattle, 12 sheep, 140 assorted hogs, and several litters of pigs. The inventory of Buck Island, including the household furnishings, was appraised at over $11,500. This figure did not include the value of the buildings, land, and the considerable amount of gold and silver that Charles Lewis, Jr. owned at his death.[20]

Shortly after Charles Lewis, Jr. had begun to open the Buck Island plantation, a family by the name of Jefferson had moved to the neighborhood. Peter Jefferson, the head of that household and a skilled surveyor, was then thirty-five years old. Jefferson built his home, Shadwell, three miles upstream from the Lewis home at Buck Island. There were two young daughters in the Jefferson family, and in 1743, the same year they moved to Shadwell, Jefferson's wife gave birth to a son, Thomas.

Two years later, the county court of Albemarle was established, and Peter Jefferson, like his neighbor, Charles Lewis, Jr., became one of the first magistrates. Jefferson was present in court on the day that Charles Lewis, Jr. recorded the document from his father, Charles of the Byrd, which gave the young man the legal right to use and control the Buck Island plantation.[21]

Jefferson's wife, Jane Randolph, was the oldest daughter of Isham Randolph of Dungeness, a member of one of the richest Virginia families. Isham Randolph owned hundreds of slaves and nearly 12,000 acres of land. About a month after Buck Island was given to Charles Lewis, Jr., Peter Jefferson moved his family away from Shadwell to care for the family and estate of a devoted friend who had just died. Ten months after the Jeffersons left Shadwell, Charles Lewis, Jr. married Jane's younger sister, Mary Randolph. For the rest of their lives Mary and Charles Lewis, Jr. lived at Buck Island.

The Jeffersons stayed away for seven years before returning to Shadwell, but thereafter Mary and Charles Lewis, Jr. were neighbors of the Jeffersons. By that time there were five children in Jefferson's family, and another child, Lucy, was born in the fall of 1752. The oldest son, Thomas, was nine years old, and except for vacations, he remained away from Shadwell at school. With characteristic energy, Peter Jefferson improved the buildings at Shadwell; a larger home to replace the old cabin, a mill, barns, and out-buildings were erected. These projects, his service in the House of Burgesses, and other community duties occupied him until his premature death in 1757 at the age of forty-nine.[22]

It is not known how close Peter Jefferson and his brother-in-law, Charles Lewis, Jr., were personally. They had been neighbors for only five years, Peter was thirteen years older than Charles Lewis, Jr. and, although they had married sisters and lived near each other, Jefferson did not choose Charles Lewis, Jr. to be an executor of his will nor a guardian of his children. Lewis had been appointed to serve as an appraiser of Jefferson's bountiful estate, but that was an action of the court and the task involved only a limited amount of time and routine business judgment.[23]

Peter Jefferson's estate was adequate to provide for the widow Jane and her children. As the younger Jefferson children reached school age they were sent to Buck Island, where Mr. Benjamin Snead was employed as tutor by Charles Lewis, Jr. During the years of 1764 and 1765, Randolph Jefferson, Peter's youngest son, boarded with his aunt and uncle at Buck Island during school sessions.[24] Snead's demands upon his students were probably not too rigorous, if the later correspondence of some of his pupils is any indication. At that time Randolph's older brother, Thomas, having had far better preparation, was a student at William and Mary College in Williamsburg. The younger children of Peter Jefferson and Charles Lewis, Jr. knew each other well before they reached school age, and through their common school experience at Buck Island they became very closely associated. Eventually there would be several marriages between the children of Shadwell and Buck Island. This became a trend, in fact, for the Lewis and Jefferson families intermarried for three successive generations.

· 2 ·

THE FIGHT FOR FREEDOM

DURING THE decade just prior to the Revolution, the children of Shadwell and Buck Island reached their maturity. The oldest Jefferson son, Thomas, completed his education and was admitted to the bar. In 1769, he began his illustrious political career, when he was chosen to be a member of the House of Burgesses. In that same year, Charles L. Lewis, the oldest son of Charles Lewis, Jr., married Thomas Jefferson's sister, Lucy. Lucy was seventeen and Charles L. Lewis was twenty-two. If the ceremony was held at Shadwell, it was one of the last festive occasions in the old Jefferson home, for five months after the wedding, Shadwell burned to the ground. Thomas Jefferson's home, Monticello, had not been completed at that time, and Lucy's mother, Jane, may have stayed, for a while at least, at Buck Island with her sister, Mary Lewis. The newlyweds, Charles L. Lewis and Lucy, eventually established their home on the section of the Buck Island plantation which lay south of the Rivanna River.

These were years of increasing tension between Virginians and their British rulers. At issue were economic as well as political and religious freedoms. Of all the patriots in Albemarle before and during the Revolution, the men of the Lewis family were among the most zealous. For reasons of health or age, Charles Lewis, Jr. of Buck Island was evidently not involved in military service at this time, but both his sons, Charles L. Lewis and Isham, volunteered, and at least three of his sons-in-law served as well.

Following the Boston Tea Party, the Virginia Assembly expressed its sympathy for Bostonians by setting aside a day for the colony to fast and pray. The governor, Lord Dunmore, in a fit of choler, dissolved the assembly, which promptly reassembled in a tavern and agreed to sample public opinion to see if Virginians would support a governmental association. The result was the formation of the Virginia Convention a few months later. In each county a committee was elected to enforce the resolutions of the convention. The popular support of the committeemen enabled them to function as an effective local government during the time between the fall of colonial rule and the establishment of state government. The members of the local committee were in most cases gentrymen who had previously proved themselves as social and political leaders.[1]

Among the fifteen committeemen elected for Albemarle in 1775 was the fiery and patriotic Dr. George Gilmer, who owned a large tract of land adjoining the plantation of Charles Lewis, Jr. of Buck Island. Gilmer was not content with the deliberate actions of the Albemarle committee, and harboring "suspicion of the most dredful nature" against the British, proceeded to raise an independent company of volunteer minutemen. This company of twenty-six men and three officers was "composed of men of reputation and character" who were to operate "under the strictest military discipline." In their enlistment oath the volunteers swore to obey the commands of the elected officers; to muster four times a year, or oftener if necessary; and to provide a gun, shot-pouch, and powder-horn. The duty uniform was a hunting shirt. Gilmer was chosen to be one of the lieutenants. The brothers of Buck Island, Charles L. Lewis and Isham, were members of the company.[2]

This troop, and others like it in Virginia, was under the general command of George Washington, who was given command of the American Continental army a few months later. At the end of April officers of the first Independent company wrote to Colonel Washington saying that they were angered and alarmed that Lord Dunmore had seized the powder from the magazine at Williamsburg. They said they were ready to march to Williamsburg and retake the powder or die in the attempt.[3]

The company was evidently spoiling for a fight, an attitude which was aggravated by the rumor current in Virginia that Lord Dunmore planned to provoke a slave rebellion.[4] Convincing themselves that they were needed, and without further orders from Colonel Washington, the volunteers marched for Williamsburg on May 2, under the command of Col. Charles Lewis of North Garden, Albemarle County, a brother-in-law of Charles L. Lewis. While they were en route, Washington replied to their letter, applauding their spirit but advising them that the situation was under control and their presence was not needed.[5] The volunteers discovered this themselves by the time they were halfway to Williamsburg, for they met another company of volunteers returning with the news that the British had evacuated their troops and there would be no battle. The cap-

13

tain of that company, Patrick Henry, made an eloquent speech of thanks, and the companies disbanded.[6]

After being dismissed, the volunteers returned to Albemarle, where they received a mild admonishment from the Albemarle Committee, which had passed resolutions to the effect that the companies were "not to be led to duty without the voice of the committee." Undaunted by this, the company immediately wrote to their fellow volunteers in Williamsburg, pledging support if it were ever needed.[7] One Albemarle citizen who was in Williamsburg a month or two later wrote to his wife that Dunmore's seizure of the powder and his other activities had alarmed the citizens of Williamsburg far less than it had the excitable residents of far-off Albemarle.[8]

By mid-June the company had grown to more than seventy-five volunteers, and on the seventeenth a muster was held. Lt. George Gilmer exhorted his troops at length, urging them to "rouze up every spark of defensive courage" or else "be deemed timid, contemptible mortals." "We'll bleed to the last drop," he said, and pointed out that they must put aside private interest and join in a united purpose for "We are now destitute of every article necessary for our immediate defense." More than a year would pass before the Declaration of Independence was written, but Gilmer criticized those who still maintained a personal relationship with anyone in the British service. "Altho civility in declared enemies sometimes may justify a social intercourse, we are so situated as to forbid hospitable feelings."[9] In spirit, Gilmer was the Sam Adams of Albemarle. Charles L. Lewis, present at the muster, heard this speech—which was delivered while, far to the north, in Boston, on that same day, the Battle of Bunker Hill was in progress.

About a month later George Gilmer marched again, but this time with orders. "On an Application of the Mayor Recorder and Treasurer for assistance as 1st Lieutenant to the 1st Company . . . I have Marched to Wmsbg. with 28 Chosen Riffle Men, . . . a very respectable set of Volunteers, who do give our County credit." Charles L. Lewis and his brother, Isham, were among this small group of Albemarle's elite firebrands. They left on July 11 and arrived three days later in Waller's Grove, on the east side of Williamsburg, where volunteer companies from other counties were assembling.[10] Captain Charles Lewis of North Garden did not lead this march, as he had the first one.

His presence was required at the more important job of representing Albemarle County at the impending session of the Virginia Convention, which was to meet in St. John's Church in Richmond on July 17, where he acted as an alternate for Thomas Jefferson, who was in Philadelphia at the Continental Congress. In Lewis's absence the over-all commander of the Albemarle Volunteers was Capt. Charles Scott.

The impatient and impulsive Lt. George Gilmer was irked by the situation that developed at Waller's Grove. He wrote to Jefferson complaining that for some time all of the assembled troops had been totally inactive except for their misconduct. "Capt. Scott our commander in chief, whos goodness and merit is great, fear[s] to offend, and by that many members are rather disorderly. We appear rather invited to feast than fight. Anderson and Southall's entertain elegantly the first in the best manner by far."[11]

The dozen or so company commanders at Waller's Grove soon realized that the behavior of their troops in camp would bring no credit to the command. They fell back on the last resort of officers who were elected by their own troops: they issued resolutions that henceforth the privates would have to attend roll call, and when on duty must obey orders. They could not go to sleep, desert a post, or be absent without leave. Violators were to be reprimanded and on the third offense the volunteer would be expelled. For firing a gun without permission the soldier was to "be taken into custody by the Officer of the Guard and there kept two hours without victuals or drink."[12]

Gilmer, who was still "determined to bleed to the last drop in the defense of the American Cause," next turned his attention to what remained of the British funds in Virginia. This money was in the hands of the receiver-general, naval and customs officers, and lesser fee and tax collectors. Their loyalty to America was suspect. Because of reports that sizable amounts of these funds were being turned over to the British, Gilmer "proposed laying hands on all his Majesties money immediately," and went into action. He confiscated some of the money and, with threats, administered loyalty oaths to the ex-British functionaries, until he was advised by the Virginia Convention that this unauthorized proceeding could not be approved.[13]

After this reprimand, the officers at Williamsburg stopped functioning as a vigilance committee. They returned the money

15

to the officials and made obeisance to the convention in a dispatch that begged the convention to lay down some guidelines for them, lest in excessive zeal they bring on calamity.[14] It was an incident full of chaos and excitement. There was much posturing and fury, which left no doubt that Gilmer and his detachment of Albemarle patriots were anxious to chastise the British. Shortly afterward, Gilmer's minutemen were disbanded and the Lewis brothers returned home.

Prompted in part by the misdirected enthusiasm of the volunteers at Waller's Grove, the convention realized that there would have to be a more manageable and comprehensive military organization in Virginia. It was hoped that the militia, with its compulsory service, would provide the answer. In October of 1776 the convention "totally dissolved" all the then-organized minutemen companies in the state and transferred the pesonnel to the militia.[15]

In actual practice, the militia system did not work well. The militiamen were expected to provide their own arms and to appear at periodic musters or training sessions held at some convenient place in the county, usually near the county seat. The militia was customarily not called out for duty except to meet specific emergencies, and then only for as long a time as the campaign was expected to last, generally a few months at most. Few companies were fully armed, and in none of these were their arms standardized. The supply or quartermaster system was haphazard, where it existed at all. During the war there were chronic shortages of lead, powder, and food, and the soldiers were poorly trained and frequently demonstrated an irresistible urge to see how the family and crops were getting along at home. When there was no enemy threat to an area, or when a campaign was not impending, the militia musters became social functions for the men, at which orders and speeches were shouted by the voluble, peach brandy and "cyder" were downed by the convivial, and the martially oriented uproar was enjoyed by everyone except the few officers who knew something about war.[16]

During the Revolution, when the militia was called out the term of service was seldom for more than two months, and even during that short period desertions were often epidemic. There was little provision for the safety and health of the women and children left at home, and the absence of the father during crop seasons might mean the following winter would be one of poverty and hardship. In the field the militia usually proved to be ineffectual. For campaigns and offensive operations that were planned in advance, every attempt was made to raise volunteer troops, since their morale and performance of duty were more dependable.[17]

In September, anticipating action in the coastal area of Virginia, the convention ordered a volunteer regiment to be organized from Albemarle. Training was completed by December 1775, and the next March the regiment had been called into service on the coast of Virginia. This regiment was deployed in the Hampton area in late May and June, and on the Potomac in July. Charles L. Lewis served with the Albemarle regiment during this tour of duty, and probably had trained with the regiment at Rockfish Gap the previous fall. Sickness among the troops of this regiment was severe in the swampy coastal areas.[18] By early fall of 1776 the Albemarle regiment had returned home and was preparing to join the expeditions against the Cherokee Indians, who were marauding on the frontiers. It appears that Charles L. Lewis did not go on this campaign against the Cherokees, but instead performed other military service in Albemarle.[19]

During the first year of hostilities Charles L. Lewis had served in the field as a volunteer and was away from Albemarle much of the time. After that tour of duty ended, he joined the Albemarle militia and eventually became the county lieutenant, or commanding officer of that unit. There can be no doubt that Charles L. Lewis and the other men in the Lewis family were dedicated to the fight for freedom from England.

In the matter of religious freedom, the Lewises were equally vehement. During the colonial period the Episcopal church had been the official church of the colony of Virginia. At first no other denominations were permitted, but in time a measure of tolerance was exercised and dissenting churches were permitted to hold services. Nevertheless, members of all denominational affiliations were taxed for the support of the Anglican church.[20] The controversy developed along denominational lines, with the Presbyterians and Baptists in the forefront of the dissenters' ranks. Among the most vociferous of those who opposed the special status enjoyed by the Episcopal church were the Lewises of Buck Island. They were staunch Presbyterians.

17

Presbyterian worship services were conducted at Buck Island over the years by at least six different Presbyterian ministers. The first resident Presbyterian minister in Albemarle County, Samuel Black, settled there in 1747, but his church was far removed from Buck Island and from other isolated Presbyterian homes. As a result, small groups of Presbyterians gathered in private homes to worship together.[21] When they could, the ministers attended the Lewises, but usually the family conducted its own services with the help of religious books from the library of Charles Lewis, Jr. Among these were several Bibles, a prayer book, Watts's hymnbook, and six volumes of various sermons by Davies, Whitefield, and Gillie.[22]

Enjoying a modest guaranteed income from the government, the Episcopal clergymen, in many cases, became indolent in their ecclesiastical duties. The clergy of other denominations, zealous through necessity, were resentful, if not envious. One angry Presbyterian wrote that while there were a few worthy and respectable Episcopal clergymen, the great majority were vicious, grossly immoral, and unfit company for any gentleman. He added that because no spiritual discipline was exercised by the church, profane athiests, diests, drunkards, and debauchees of every kind were admitted to the clergy whenever they made application.[23]

In a more objective observation, Thomas Jefferson recalled the background of the religious controversy:

> In process of time, however, other sectarisms were introduced, chiefly of the Presbyterian family; and the established clergy, secure for life in their glebes and salaries, . . . found employment enough, in their farms and schoolrooms, for the rest of the week, and devoted Sunday only to the edification of their flock, by service, and a sermon at their parish church. Their other pastoral functions were little attended to. Against this inactivity, the zeal and industry of sectarian preachers had an open and undisputed field; and by the time of the revolution, a majority of the inhabitants had become dissenters from the established church, but were still obliged to pay contributions to support the pastors of the minority. This unrighteous compulsion, to maintain teachers of what they deemed religious errors, was grievously felt during the regal government, and without a hope of relief.[24]

For several years before the Declaration of Independence, petitions from groups of dissenters had been sent to the colonial legislature, asking not only for toleration, but also for other freedoms in religious matters. This issue came before the Virginia legislature in the fall of 1776, accompanied by a flood of petitions from dissenters as well as petitions from the Anglicans, who were "still violent for a re-establishment of the Episcopal Church."[25]

The Lewises appear to have been instrumental in preparing at least one of the several dissenters' petitions that were circulated in Albemarle.[26] The first signature on this petition was that of Charles Lewis, Jr. It was closely followed by the names of his two sons, Charles L. Lewis, Isham Lewis, and by the names of his three sons-in-law. Seventy-one other petitioners signed this request. If this petition did not actually originate at Buck Island, it certainly had the fervid support of the whole family. A week before, an almost identical petition had been endorsed by 169 citizens. Again near the head of the list were five members of the Lewis family.[27]

In the issue of religious freedom, the Buck Island Lewises held opinions very similar to those of Thomas Jefferson, although the interests of the petitioners probably were more parochial than those of Jefferson. He championed religious freedom in the Virginia legislature, motivated by a sense of justice and a desire to establish complete intellectual freedom. He noted that while the majority of the citizens were dissenters, more than half of the legislature was composed of men sympathetic to the Church of England. This situation, he said, "brought on the severest contests in which I have been engaged." The issue would not be completely resolved until ten years had passed.[28]

·3·

A COLONEL IN THE MILITIA

AFTER THE first year of the Revolution, Charles L. Lewis served in the Albemarle militia. Whether his duties took him out of the county or not is unknown, but one document does confirm that he was in Albemarle in 1777. In June the general assembly of the state passed an act which required all free men over sixteen to take an oath to renounce allegiance to the king, to swear loyalty to Virginia, to protect her freedom and independence, and to reveal to a justice of the peace "all treasons or traitorous conspiracies" which he might discover. One list of signatures of Albemarle men contained Charles L. Lewis's name. First on the list, as might be expected, was the signature of George Gilmer, among whose papers a copy of this document was found. It is likely that Gilmer was the justice of the peace who administered the oath.[1]

At the beginning of the Revolution, there was no public mail service in Virginia. It became imperative to establish a dependable communication system and in the early stages of the war, fifty-two Albemarle patriots pledged themselves to ride eighty miles to Fredericksburg to pick up and deliver papers and letters for the subscribers. Even though the service was voluntary, each subscriber who failed to perform or hire the duty done when his turn came, was subject to a penalty of five pounds. The route was run once a week and each subscriber was responsible for the trip once a year when his turn came around. Jefferson, Gilmer, Mazzei, the Walkers, and many other prominent and wealthy members of the gentry were among the volunteers. Charles L. Lewis and his father, Charles Lewis, Jr. of Buck Island, were also on the list of voluntary subscribers.[2]

In Albemarle the year 1779 began with some local excitement, for a prisoner-of-war camp was established just outside Charlottesville at a place since called the Barracks. The British and German prisoners captured at Saratoga were to be kept there because the location was thought to be beyond the reach of his Majesty's soldiers. Four thousand prisoners marched more than six hundred miles from Massachusetts, and arrived early in January during a long period of terrible cold.

20

In order to guard the British prisoners, a six hundred-man regiment was enlisted from Albemarle and the neighboring counties. To many young men of Virginia this guard duty seemed preferable to being drafted into the Continental army, a thing they feared, for it would take them far from home. Enlistment in the Barracks guard regiment entailed one or two years' service, which was to be limited to the area of the Barracks. Service in the guard regiment was not entirely a soft berth, for there were frequent shortages of food, clothing, and pay; however, in general the guards got what they were worth, for during the two-year stay in Albemarle nearly half of the four thousand prisoners escaped, and there was fear on one occasion that the guard regiment itself would mutiny.[3] In mid-June of 1780, four hundred militia men, two hundred of them from Albemarle, were alerted to be "held in the most Perfect readiness to march at the shortest Notice" to reinforce the guard regiment at the Barracks.[4] That fall the British invaded Virginia and the British prisoners at the Barracks were evacuated to Maryland, where it was felt they would be beyond the reach of rescue by Cornwallis.

Charles L. Lewis may have been serving with the guard regiment, but it is more likely he was in the Albemarle militia. By this time he had risen to the rank of major, and there are several records of his presence in Albemarle during 1779.[5] In the course of that year six jury inquests were held in Albemarle regarding the property of persons who were British sympathizers, and in each of the "inquisitions" the property was confiscated in the name of the state of Virginia. The total property seized amounted to at least 4,450 acres, 2 city lots, and 52 slaves. Refusal to take the oath of allegiance was tantamount to forfeiting one's property. There were thirteen men on this jury of implacable Albemarle patriots. Among them were Charles L. Lewis and his brother, Isham.[6]

At this time Charles L. Lewis was thirty-three years old, and his family was increasing in size. His oldest son, Randolph, was six. Jane, his eldest daughter, was next in age, then came the second son, Lilburne, a child of three. Like his family, Charles L. Lewis's fortunes were increasing as well. A few years before he had bought nearly one thousand acres adjoining the five-hundred-acre tract his father had given him on the south bank of the Rivanna.[7] The sixteen hundred acres his father owned north of the Rivanna were certain to come to him when Charles

Lewis, Jr. died. Charles L. Lewis no doubt realized that he was becoming an increasingly important person in the county.

It was a tradition of long standing in Virginia for well-to-do gentrymen to offer their political talents to the state. "No school of leadership was more creative than the colonial tobacco plantation. Although consistently outnumbered by the small planters, the men of property took as their natural right positions of authority in society, religion and politics. They dominated the parish vestries, county courts, local militia, Governor's Councils, and obtained a large number of seats in the lower house of the colonial assemblies. They played the role of the English county squires, whom they instinctively imitated."[8]

Charles L. Lewis's father and grandfather both had accepted roles of leadership during colonial days. In mid-April of 1781, Charles L. Lewis sought to continue the tradition by running for a seat in the Virginia legislature. Two seats from Albemarle were vacant, and four candidates put themselves forward. Of the four men who ran for the legislature, Lewis appears to have been the most prosperous and closest to the type of person usually chosen for the legislature; nevertheless, he was disappointed.[9] George Gilmer sent the outcome of the election to Governor Jefferson in a few acerbic and depreciatory sentences:

13 April 1781 Charlottesville

Dear Sir:
    Revolutions indeed. Yesterday George Twyman, C. L. Lewis, James Marks, and Issac Davis mounted the rostrum, the two latter were returned delegates for the once favored County of Albemarle. . . .
    Happy the man who can feal himself adequate to the rapid changes in his sphere of life, this day moving in the Congregation of groans, the next wishing to become a Legislature. The two [who] had Confederated to blend their forces together had the In't [Interest?]. Twyman and C. L. L. would have been returned but they could not hang together.[10]

Evidently Marks and Davis ran as a team and won the election, while Lewis and Twyman competed when they should have cooperated. Gilmer did not appear to be enthusiastic about the candidates, and felt that the once honorable pattern of public service by competent people had degenerated into petty local politics.[11]

In the same month that Charles L. Lewis was defeated in the

election, there was a local dispute that threatened Lewis's advancement in the militia. The county lieutenant, who commanded the Albemarle militia, and his second in command had resigned their offices. In filling such vacancies the county courts were required to recommend the new officers, and these promotions then had to be ratified by the Council in Richmond; as, indeed, they usually were. In this situation, however, the Albemarle court broke tradition, and did not recommend promotion for the officers who were next in rank, Lt. Col. Reuben Lindsay and Maj. Charles Lilburne Lewis, but instead recommended Capt. John Marks and Capt. Thomas Walker, Jr. As Gilmer wrote to Jefferson: "The courts failing to promote in the line will occasion numberless resignations."[12]

It must have been a bitter blow to Charles L. Lewis. On April 12, he had been defeated in a political election by James Marks, and on the next day, Capt. John Marks, the brother of James, had been nominated for promotion over Lewis's head to the rank of colonel. Governor Jefferson was angry too, but apparently more because he disliked both Marks and promotions that violated seniority, than because he especially favored his brother-in-law, Charles L. Lewis. In a letter to the leader of the council Jefferson hastily intervened in the affair on behalf of Lindsay and Lewis. He enclosed a resolution that he had written. It was adopted by the council that same day, and sent on to Lindsay: "John Coles County Lieutenant and Nicholas Lewis Colo. of Albemarle having resigned their commissions, the board advise that Reuben Lindsay the present Lt. Colo. be appointed County Lieutenant and Charles Lilburne Lewis the present Major be appointed Colo. of the militia of the said county."[13]

In this affair of militia promotions in Albemarle, Jefferson had acted too quickly, for Colonel Lindsay had not been passed by for the top position of county lieutenant, but rather had refused to serve, and had himself proposed Captain Marks for the job because Marks had been "recommended by a great majority" of the members then present. Lindsay wrote to Jefferson, thanked him for the promotion, and said he would serve until he could be replaced. He noted that he had given Major Charles L. Lewis the commission promoting him to lieutenant colonel.[14]

Unanswered in this exchange of letters is the question of why Reuben Lindsay and the "great majority" of the members of the county court recommended Capt. John Marks to be promoted over Maj. Charles L. Lewis. There must have been something about Lewis that offended the members of the county court. It may have been nothing more than local politics, or it may have been that Lewis had personal shortcomings which made him unacceptable to the court. One can only speculate, but it is certain that, whatever Jefferson's motives were, his timely intervention was responsible for the promotion of his brother-in-law.

Charles L. Lewis, now a colonel, would soon be tested in his new command. Five weeks after this incident, British Lt. Col. Banastre Tarleton, in a lightning raid from seventy miles away, came crashing out of the night into Albemarle County with 250 mounted British troops.

Cornwallis had invaded Virginia in January of 1781, and in May, the General Assembly, fearful of being captured, temporarily moved the seat of state government from Richmond to Charlottesville and ordered the large stocks of military supplies then at Richmond to be dispersed to several places far upstream from the capital city. One depot was at Point of Forks, where the Rivanna joined the James River. Other supplies were hastily moved farther on to Albemarle and stored, some in Charlottesville, some in the old courthouse near Scottsville, and some at Bennett Henderson's tobacco warehouse on the Rivanna River at Mountain Falls, about two and a half miles upstream from the Lewis home at Buck Island. Among the supplies held at Bennett Henderson's warehouse were 256 barrels of powder, an item of great importance to the American Revolution at that time, despite the fact that the powder had been somewhat damaged by water because the canoes that brought it up the river had not been properly clamped together.[15]

Tarleton's orders were threefold: to destroy all military stores or other American resources he could find; to capture Thomas Jefferson, whose term as governor had expired a day or two before; and to capture or disperse the members of the assembly in or around Charlottesville.[16] Tarleton's raid was a stunning achievement and might have been completely successful had it not been for the extraordinary nighttime ride of Jack Jouett, the Paul Revere of Albemarle. Jouett detected Tarleton's troops while they were forty miles from Charlottesville and, suspecting their purpose, mounted his horse and thundered away through the darkness, using back roads and short-cuts not known to the

British. Coming to the Rivanna just before dawn, he crossed the Mountain Falls Ford at Henderson's, where the powder was stored.[17] Jouett continued on to Monticello, arriving at 4:30 A.M. with the warning that enabled Jefferson and his family to escape capture. Jouett then went on to Charlottesville to rouse the legislators. They held a hasty session, adjourned to meet a few days later in Staunton, where they felt they would be safe, and scurried off to the west. Jouett's warning, which gave the citizens three hours' time before the British arrived, did not defeat all of Tarleton's purposes, but it robbed him of a complete success, which would have been a severe blow to the Americans.[18]

Tarleton and his mounted troops galloped down from Louisa Courthouse on the road which lay along the eastern side of the Southwestern Mountains. Near Shadwell, where Jouett had turned south to ford the Rivanna at Mountain Falls, Tarleton turned west onto the Three Chopt Road. After he had crossed the river at Secretary's Ford, three miles above the ford at Mountain Falls, Tarleton detached Captain McCleod and some troopers to Monticello with orders to capture Jefferson.[19] Tarleton missed the 256 barrels of powder at Bennett Henderson's warehouse because he took the wrong turn, and at Monticello missed taking Jefferson captive by ten minutes.

Apparently there was no significant defense of Charlottesville made at the Rivanna; neither was a stand made elsewhere in the county: "Captain John Martin . . . was stationed in the town with two hundred men. . . . But the suddenness of the alarm, the uncertainty respecting the numbers approaching, and the widespread terror of Tarleton's name, probably led Captain Martin to think that the most prudent course was to withdraw from the scene."[20]

Charlottesville was left undefended, as were the state legislators, Thomas Jefferson, and the precious military stores. Tarleton wrote a report about the fate of these supplies. "A great quantity of stores were found in Charlottesville and the neighborhood; one thousand new firelocks that had been manufactured at Fredericksburg were broken: Upwards of four hundred barrels of powder were destroyed: Several hogsheads of tobacco, and some continental clothing and accoutrements shared the same fate."[21] Others have claimed that Tarleton exaggerated and that much of the powder and all of the lead escaped seizure by the British.[22]

As for the capture of the Virginia legislature, Jouett had spoiled Tarleton's hopes. The record is not clear, but it appears that of the dozen or so people taken captive there were only four legislators. One of these was a junior representative from the Kentucky district named Daniel Boone. The prisoners were treated reasonably well. Some were paroled at once, and others were marched thirty miles to Point of Fork and released there.[23]*

Tarleton had been unopposed in his raid, yet he failed in some of his objectives only because of Jack Jouett. The nonappearance of the Albemarle militia is puzzling. In the many accounts of the raid, neither the militia nor its commanding officers have been criticized. The failure of the Albemarle militia in June is an example of the disorder which was characteristic of all militia troops in Virginia at that time. For five months at least, chaos had been the rule among the troops levied from the counties for service with Steuben, whose regiments were far under strength as a result of desertions and forged discharges.[24] Indicative of the general disorder was Jefferson's command of January 19 to the county lieutenants, directing them to return a count of the actual strength of their units, as their duty required. They were six months delinquent in this routine task, and Jefferson warned that their "inattention" would not again pass unnoticed. The British added to the confusion by placing on parole every man in the counties through which they had marched. These oaths, if honored, would keep large numbers of Virginians out of action.[25]

Invaded, suffering a disastrous inflation, with her men at

*Daniel Boone, who at that time was a rather unimportant junior representative from Fayette County in the Kentucky district, had tarried in Charlottesville to help Jack Jouett and others load the public records and supplies on wagons so they could be removed to safety. When the British entered the town they took Boone, whom Jouett inadvertently identified as a captain, and led him off to The Farm, the plantation of Nicholas Lewis, which Tarleton was using as headquarters. Boone was held that rainy night in a barn where charcoal was stored, and "where an insulting soldiery with apparent reluctance administered . . . a scanty portion of nourishment." The next day, June 5, Tarleton and his troops withdrew from Charlottesville via the Three Chopt Road, taking Boone and a few other captives with them to Point of Fork, where they extracted paroles and released the prisoners. Within two weeks Boone was back in the legislature, which was still meeting in Staunton. On June 21, Boone presented a "petition from Sundry inhabitants of the county of Fayette . . . praying that the town of Lexington, in the said county, may be established a town, by act of Assembly."

arms inexperienced, often without supplies or weapons, taking false parole, or deserting, Virginia was nearing military ineffectiveness. Governor Jefferson did not even know how many troops he had in his command. The fire that had burned so brightly in the spring of 1775 cast far less heat in the spring of 1781. This was the condition of the Virginia State Militia as Tarleton crossed the Rivanna into Charlottesville. Of the Albemarle militia, probably more than half, and surely the best and most willing soldiers of them, were serving elsewhere. The two hundred troops in Charlottesville, under the immediate command of Captain Martin, "prudently withdrew from the scene" when Tarleton arrived. The rest of the militia who were not mustered, were scattered in the county at their homes, some as far as thirty miles away. To call them all to arms and assemble them would have been more than one day's work.

The better known accounts of the raid do not mention Colonel Lewis, so his actions at that time may be only surmised. The county leadership undoubtedly realized that effective armed resistance to Tarleton's 250 veteran troopers was impossible under the circumstances. The only thing left to be done was to carry off or hide as many of the military supplies as possible before Tarleton got to them. Apparently Tarleton did not get to Henderson's warehouse, for it was not burned. Perhaps it was here that Col. Charles L. Lewis spent June 4 and 5, safeguarding the powder or moving it into a better hiding place. He could have accomplished nothing by venturing into Charlottesville which, on June 4, was totally controlled by the British.

What Lewis did do those two days is unknown, but he cannot be blamed exclusively for the failure of the militia. The largest and best part of his men had probably been levied out from under his command, the remainder were poorly armed, and scattered all over the county. This was no fault of his, nor was he to blame that he had less than three hours warning—if, in fact, any at all—when three days would have been scant time to prepare effective resistance.

The British invasion of Virginia dominated the most personally distressing period Jefferson ever endured. Near Point of Fork, Cornwallis destroyed Elkhill, one of Jefferson's plantations. Crops, barns, fences, and livestock were laid waste, and thirty slaves were carried off to die of pestilence.[26] As governor and military commander-in-chief of the state, Jefferson had to cope with disorganization, inflation, and apathy while bound by

27

a state constitution that overly restricted the executive branch. His attempts were earnest but largely ineffectual, and his retirement from the governorship on June 2, as he felt was required by the constitution of Virginia, came at a time of extreme emergency brought on by Cornwallis, Simcoe, and Tarleton. Because the legislature had fled from Tarleton and did not elect a new governor until June 12, Virginia, at the time of her greatest peril, was without a governor for ten days.[27] Casting about for a scapegoat for the disgraceful situation following the British invasion, Jefferson's political enemies, Patrick Henry among them, accused him of deserting the government. The House of Delegates adopted a resolution requiring an inquiry to be made into Jefferson's conduct during the previous twelve months. This was the lowest point in Jefferson's lifetime of public service. Six months later, the committee reported a resolution which exonerated Jefferson's "ability, rectitude, and integrity," and thanked the former governor for his "impartial, upright, and attentive administration whilst in office." The assembly adopted the resolution unanimously.[28] This should have ended the matter, but in later years Jefferson's enemies elaborated on his flight from Tarleton's troopers and drove him to distraction with false charges of cowardice. The injustice is clear, for the assembly and the soldiers, who retired with far less aplomb, were not held up to such ridicule as Jefferson suffered.[29]

From that time on Jefferson's antipathy toward Patrick Henry in partiuclar, and the British in general, became more bitter.[30] Had it been possible for Col. Charles L. Lewis to muster his militia and defeat Tarleton, this chapter of Jefferson's life would have been less trying; however, there is no indication that Jefferson ever felt or expressed any disappointment in his brother-in-law for his actions on June 4 and 5.

Within ten days after the raid, the remaining militiamen of Albemarle and eleven other counties were called into the field by a resolution of the legislature.[31] Four months later, the French and American victory at Yorktown ended the fighting in Virginia. Col. Charles L. Lewis continued his services in the Albemarle militia for at least another year, during which period he held the position of County Lieutenant.[32]

· 4 ·

PROSPERITY

DURING THE Revolution there had been chaos in the American economy. One of the most distressing problems was the severe inflation in paper money, which became acute as the war dragged on. Scarcity of goods was one factor and the over-printing, of nearly forty million pounds worth, of continental dollars was another. Equally important was the huge counterfeiting operation run by the British. The bogus bills were given away gratis in immense sums at New York to anyone who was greedy enough to run the risk.[1]

At that time in Virginia the exchange rate was five hundred paper dollars for one gold guinea, an inflation factor of at least one hundred times.[2]

The farm economy in Albemarle was also in a state of upheaval during the Revolution. The English market for tobacco had disappeared, and Virginia's primary source of income had gone with it. General shortages of food and fiber dictated that farm production be shifted away from tobacco in favor of food and cloth, even though this change involved the loss of a certain prestige to "planters," who grew tobacco, as opposed to "farmers," who raised food products.[3] At the very time when wheat was most needed, for three successive years, from 1777 to 1779, the Albemarle crop was nearly destroyed by weevils.[4]

The people of Albemarle, who at first had objected to the arrival of the four thousand British prisoners at the Barracks because they feared a local famine, realized before long that the prisoners were an economic asset to the area. During 1779 a supply system was set up for the prisoners and guards and, even though shortages appeared during the next year, there is little doubt that Albemarle was comparatively prosperous during the two years that the prisoners were there. Farmers, tradesmen, merchants, and, in fact, anyone who had anything to sell to the prisoners or the guard regiments, profited from this sizable nearby market. The prisoners could testify to this, for they felt unanimously that the prices charged for food were outrageously high.[5] The people of Albemarle were quite willing to supply the troops and guards with provisions on credit. Although in some

29

cases payment was never made, and in others the payment came only after court action, the final result was that, because of the prisoners, Albemarle enjoyed a local economic boom for the two years of 1779 and 1780, while other parts of Virginia languished.[6]

For most of this period, Col. Charles L. Lewis was in Albemarle, and although he held high rank in the militia this would not have hindered the operation of his plantation or the sale of his farm produce to the troops at the Barracks. At the same time, his father, Charles Lewis, Jr., assisted by the colonel's younger brother, Isham, and an overseer, ran a productive and diversified farm operation.[7] Records made during this time of inflation show that in addition to his numerous slaves, cattle, and other possessions, Charles Lewis, Jr. owned a sizable amount of specie.[8] He may have been one of those who traded with the prisoners for hard cash.

From 1781, when the prisoners left Albemarle, on through the Confederation period until the Constitution was signed, there was extreme hardship in Albemarle. During 1783 the sheriff was unable to collect taxes, and money was so short that there were almost no bidders for delinquent property.[9] In spite of this, Col. Charles L. Lewis was able not only to pay his taxes, but also to consolidate his properties and expand into various profitable business ventures. This decade from 1782 to 1792 was to be a prosperous one for Col. Charles L. Lewis.[10]

In 1782, Charles Lewis, Jr. died at Buck Island at the comparatively young age of sixty-one.[11] Although Col. Charles L. Lewis did not realize his share of his father's wealth at that time, he was one step closer to it. His father left him the remaining fifteen hundred acres of the Buck Island plantation, but specified that the land and the income from it were reserved for the use of his wife, Mary, for the rest of her life.[12] Col. Charles L. Lewis now owned title to, but not the entire use of, nearly three thousand acres. His mother and his younger brother, Isham, continued to reside in the old Buck Island home north of the Rivanna.

Isham had not married, and even though he owned land elsewhere in the county, he lived with his parents.[13] When his father, Charles Lewis, Jr., died, Isham took over the management of the northern section of the Buck Island plantation, which his mother held in trust.[14] This arrangement continued for about eight years, until Isham's death in 1790. Shortly after losing Isham, his mother leased her interest in the Buck Island tract to her other son, Col. Charles L. Lewis, who already held title to the land.[15] The term of the lease was for the remainder of her life, during which she was to receive twenty pounds rent annually. She reserved for her own use "the dwelling house and other houses belonging thereto together with fifty acres adjoining the said house." Of her twenty-nine slaves she kept seven, and she kept two of her ten horses. With this indenture, Col. Charles L. Lewis obtained nearly full control of all the family land on the Rivanna. He owned about forty adult slaves, an adequate number for the profitable farming of his three thousand acres. At his mother's death he would inherit one-eighth of the remainder of his father's estate.

In addition to the wealth he had inherited and the income from his plantation, Col. Charles L. Lewis had received revenue from other business ventures. One was a real estate promotion in which he joined his brother-in-law, Bennett Henderson, in establishing the town of Milton on Henderson's land at Mountain Falls, where the warehouse and mill stood. The state legislature vested the land in seven trustees, among whom were Col. Charles L. Lewis, his brother-in-law, Edward Moore, and his cousin, Howell Lewis.[16] The town was established in 1789, flourished, and became the commercial center of the county for the next twenty years. Twenty lots were sold in the first decade.[17] Considering Bennett Henderson's interest in the town, and the family ties of the trustees, it might be said that Milton was very nearly a Lewis family venture. Of the other trustees who were not Lewises, two were or had been in the legislature and no doubt helped obtain the enabling act for Milton, one had been acting sheriff and a magistrate, and another would become a magistrate and member of the state legislature.[18]

At this time, Col. Charles L. Lewis was also involved in two other business ventures, a stage line and a tavern. In the early 1790s Lewis owned and paid taxes on four of the sixteen stage wagons in the county. During this time he also owned twenty horses.[19] These stage wagons may have carried freight, or passengers, or both; it is not known. The shift in agriculture, in which wheat replaced tobacco as the leading cash crop of the county, would have created a brisk demand at this time for cartage service to and from Milton or Richmond. The Three Chopt Road, which ran through the north corner of Lewis's

Buck Island plantation, was the main road from Albemarle to Richmond. Where it crossed Lewis's land there was a junction with the River Road, which ran south along the Rivanna.[20] At this point stood Watson's Old Ordinary, which was later run by Thomas D. Boyd under the name of Boyd's Old Tavern.[21] The land where the tavern stood was owned by Col. Charles L. Lewis, who had obtained a tavern or "ordinary" license in 1790. He built the tavern and rented it to others, first Watson and then T. D. Boyd, who moved to Albemarle in 1803. The location of this tavern at the Three Chopt Road and River Road junction would have been convenient for Lewis's stage line to use as a way station.[22]

During these years, Col. Charles L. Lewis became a rich man. The state of his fortunes was recognized by Thomas Jefferson, who wrote to a friend, "C. L. Lewis my brother-in-law is becoming one of our wealthiest people."[23] As his prosperity and his family both increased, Colonel Lewis evidently felt that he and Lucy needed a more stately home. Since their marriage in 1769 they had lived on the 500-acre tract south of the Rivanna in a hewn log house covered by weather-boards. This house had two rooms on the ground floor and two on the second. At each end of the house stood a large brick chimney which served fireplaces on both floors. At the rear of the house was a two-room ell with loft rooms overhead.[24] This old house was typical of the time, and was probably similar to the old Buck Island homestead north of the Rivanna. A visitor to Albemarle in 1779 described such buildings, which were commonly seen on plantations.

> The face of the country appears an immense forest, intersperced with various plantations, four or five miles distant from each other; on these there is a dwelling-house in the center, with kitchens, smoke-house, and out-houses detached, and from the various buildings, each plantation has the appearance of a small village; at some little distance from the houses, are peach and apple orchards, &c. and scattered over the plantations are the negroes huts and to-bacco-houses, which are large, built of wood, for the cure of that article.
>
> The houses are most of them built of wood, the roof being covered with shingles, and not always lathed and plastered within, only those of the better sort that are finished in that manner, and painted on the outside; the chimneys are often of brick, . . . the windows of the better sort are glazed.[25]

Colonel Lewis and Lucy located their new home on a bluff

that rose 150 feet above the south bank of the Rivanna. Between the foot of the bluff and the river, 500 feet away, lay a narrow strip of bottom land. From the home site there was a beautiful view of the Rivanna Valley, with hills and the Southwestern Mountains in the distance. Monticello, six miles away by road, was clearly visible. Across the Rivanna to the north, and just one-half mile away, was Buck Island, Lewis's childhood home, where his mother still lived.

The new home, which was a large one for the Piedmont area, was named Monteagle (see Figure 1).[26] It did not compare in size, grandeur, or workmanship with the splendor of the colonial plantation homes of the Tidewater, nor did the Rivanna have the majesty of larger rivers. Built of brick, the house had two stories and a cellar, all of which were laid out on the same plan. Each floor had four rooms sixteen feet square, two on each side of a ten-foot-wide hall that extended the full depth of the house. The stairway to the second floor at the east end of the hall, near the back door, had two flights and a landing, flat hand rails and rectangular balusters. The effect was clean and functional, rather than ornate. There were four large chimneys, two on the north side and two on the south, so that each of the twelve rooms could be heated by a fireplace. In the north and south walls of the house there were no windows, but every room in the house had two windows on either the east or west side. The floors were sawed pine planks of varying widths, some quite wide. The basement had a brick floor, which was about four feet below ground level. The basement windows, instead of having two sashes, had only one. The front entrance to the home was a double door reached by wide wooden steps leading up about five feet to a wide one-story wooden porch with a roof supported by four square columns. There was a similar porch on the west side of the house. The side lights of the door held four panes on each side, and the transom contained six panes, giving a simple functional impression to the entrance.

On the first floor, the ceiling was nine feet high, but in the cellar and on the second floor the ceilings were a little over seven feet high. The house had a hip roof, unusually shallow, and was covered with split shingles. The interior walls and ceilings of all three floors were of hair plaster applied over hand-split lathing.

For the time and place, Monteagle was a fine home, a twelve-room brick structure on a hill with a lovely view, overlooking most of the 3,000 acres Lewis owned. Except for the brick

33

Figure 1. Monteagle, the Lewis plantation home in Albemarle.
This building has been restored since this picture was made in 1937.
(Courtesy of The Virginia State Library, Richmond.)

cornices there was little ornateness about the home. The generally square floor plan, common hardware, and simple stairway and entrances, did not indicate that Col. Charles L. Lewis was a man of extraordinary wealth or imagination. Colonel Lewis had traveled widely in Virginia and had certainly seen more impressive homes than Monteagle. It was the home of a gentryman, but not one of unlimited wealth or sophisticated taste;[27] nevertheless, Colonel Lewis had built a far better than average plantation home. Considering the large supply of slave labor available to Colonel Lewis, the actual cash outlay for the home would not have been great. The timber would cost him nothing, and neither would the sawing of beams and planks, or splitting the shingles and lathing. The windows and door frames were hand-tooled on the plantation.[28] The brick was probably burned at home; thus, all that might have to be paid for was the glass, nails, and perhaps hardware, or the labor of a few highly skilled craftsmen.

By 1785 there were five dwellings and fifteen other buildings on Lewis's plantation.[29] In addition to the Monteagle home and the older dwelling where he and Lucy had lived earlier, there were three identical slave houses. They were more spacious and better built than the usual slave quarters or cabins of a later period. In each one there were two downstairs rooms, twelve by sixteen feet in size, and over them two loft rooms under the steep, shingled roof. There was a huge central brick chimney in each of the cabins, which served back-to-back fireplaces that heated the two downstairs rooms. The loft stairway was steep and narrow, making a right-angle turn in three steps, thus taking up little space in one corner of the room. At both ends of the slave houses there were two windows, one on each floor.[30]

As soon as they were built, the spacious rooms of Monteagle were filled with Lewis children. By 1791, when Colonel Lewis was forty-four and Lucy was thirty-nine, there were nine children in their family. The youngest son had been named Isham after his uncle, and the three youngest daughters were Lucy B., Martha C., and Ann M.[31] Early in that year Randolph, the oldest son of Colonel Lewis and Lucy, married his second cousin, Mary Howell Lewis. Jefferson's daughter relayed the news of the event to her father, "A cousin of ours Randolph Lewis is lately married to Miss Lewis of the *bird*. The bridegroom was 18 and she 15."[32]

It was a pattern in the Lewis family for the sons to join their

father in business as they reached the age of sixteen. Randolph
had been so occupied during the two years prior to his marriage,
and continued the arrangement for another year afterward.[33]
When Randolph had been married for about a year, Colonel
Lewis gave him 750 acres of land and seven slaves.[34] The land
bestowed on Randolph was approximately half of the Buck Island tract north of the Rivanna, and included the house and
buildings where Randolph's widowed grandmother, Mary R.
Lewis, lived. She still had the lifetime interest in the house and
land, but had rented the land to her son, Randolph's father. She
may have welcomed Randolph and his bride into the Buck Island home to live with her. As long as she lived, however, Randolph could not sell and give possession to the farm, nor could
he exercise any claim on the house.

Because he owned so few slaves and only three horses at that
time, Randolph could not take up the traditional plantation life
which had been the source of wealth and power for his forebears
for more than three generations. He would have to find other
means of livelihood. The day of huge land grants in Virginia was
over. The frontier had moved west across the Appalachians into
Kentucky, where the Revolutionary soldiers of Virginia had
received tracts of that rich wilderness as pay for their services.
Those who did not want to emigrate often sold their warrants,
which then entered the turbulent whirlpool of land speculation.

Randolph's great-grandfather had divided his huge estate
holdings among five sons, and they all achieved the wealth of
gentrymen. Land, the measure of wealth, was easy to obtain in
his generation. In the next generation, by means of inheritance,
patent, and purchase, Randolph's grandfather had acquired at
least 4,500 acres, which he later divided among three of his
children.

In the same way Randolph's father, Col. Charles L. Lewis, had
put together holdings of 3,000 acres by the time Randolph married, but meanwhile two things had happened slowly but inexorably. The once rich virgin land of Virginia, which had
brought prosperity and power to its first owners, was becoming
"farmed out" and exhausted; and, as the Piedmont of Virginia
filled up with settlers, the grants of new land decreased in size
and value and became more difficult to obtain.[35] Fortunes could
no longer be amassed by the easy acquisition of huge tracts of
unspoiled Virginia land. The tide of Virginia gentrymen had

swirled up against the mountains, leaving behind it a depleted and washed-out land.

In spite of this change, the old family patterns remained, and when Col. Charles L. Lewis gave his son part of Buck Island "for his better maintenance and support," he was repeating the actions of his father and grandfather before him. But this time there was a difference. Randolph's land had been cruelly and wastefully farmed for fifty years, and there was no other unclaimed land nearby that he could acquire. His father, too, although unable to obtain new ground, nevertheless diminished the size of his plantation by gifts of land to his sons. Colonel Lewis was following the family pattern which, through repetition, had become a vain obligation.

· 5 ·

THE VIRGINIA PLANTER

THERE IS little reliable information about the personalities of Col. Charles L. Lewis and Lucy, or about the way they lived. The few existing scraps of information about Colonel Lewis indicate that, like most gentrymen, he took an interest in the pedigree and breeding of horses.[1] The records indicate that all of the men and women in his family were literate, and the estate inventories of several generations of Lewises show that they had some concern for books. Their collections were modest, but on several occasions they borrowed books from Jefferson's fine library at Monticello.[2] In spite of this interest, it is doubtful that any of Colonel Lewis's sons went to college. As they reached the age of sixteen, Colonel Lewis took them into partnership with him, and probably assigned them some responsibility for his business and plantation affairs. This, and the fact that the sons married early, ruled out advanced education for them.[3]

It is certain that the Lewises were not intellectually deficient. For the most part, they took their place in community affairs. They served eagerly in the military and local government organizations, and were active in the fight for religious freedom.

These few facts reveal very little about the personalities and customs of this family. Their social affairs, recreation, daily routines, and attitudes cannot be described with assured accuracy. Few of their letters survive, and no diaries or pictures of them are known to exist. The Lewises were, however, members of the wealthy slave-owning class of Virginia plantation owners, and that particular group has been described many times, and in some detail, by interested and literate observers who visited in Virginia, both before and after the Revolution. Whether or not their comments and generalizations could be applied to the Lewises must remain conjecture.

Prior to 1800 most of the books supplying information about Virginia and her citizens were written by Europeans.[4] Some of these writers were military men, while others were ministers, doctors, or philosophers. In general, these travelers looked down on Americans, and believed that the Western Hemisphere was inferior in most ways to western Europe. Their reports were somewhat biased and were widely resented by Americans.

Nevertheless, the accuracy of many of their observations has been established.[5]

One of the earliest of these traveling commentators was Rev. Andrew Burnaby, an Anglican minister who toured America twenty-five years before the Revolution. Of Virginia he recorded these impressions:

> It will not be difficult to form an idea of the character . . . of its inhabitants. The climate and external appearance of the country conspire to make them indolent, easy, and good natured; extremely fond of society, and much given to convivial pleasures. In consequence of this, they seldom show any spirit of enterprise, or expose themselves willingly to fatigue. Their authority over their slaves renders them vain and imperious. . . . Their ignorance of mankind and of learning exposes them to many errors and prejudices, especially in regard to Indians and negroes, whom they scarcely consider as of the human species. . . . The display of a character thus constituted, will naturally be in acts of extravagance, ostentation, and a disregard of economy; it is not extraordinary therefore, that Virginians outrun their incomes. . . . They are haughty and jealous of their liberties, impatient of restraint, and can scarcely bear the thought of being controuled by any superior power. . . . There are but few of them that have a turn for business, and even those are by no means expert at it.[6]

Speaking about the ladies of Virginia, Burnaby found them to be "generally speaking, handsome." He said they had but few advantages, and consequently were seldom accomplished; which made them reserved. They were immoderately fond of dancing, and chiefly spent their time in sewing and taking care of their families. In addition, they seldom read, or endeavored to improve their minds; however, they made as good wives, and as good mothers, as any in the world.

At the time of the Revolution, a German officer named Du Roi more or less agreed with what Burnaby had said about the Virginia ladies. Du Roi found them to be industrious, polite, better mannered than Yankee ladies, and more courteous to strangers. The women were more industrious than the men, for while women worked about the house, the gentlemen worked nowhere. Continuing his comments, the German said that gambling for large stakes was a notable fault of Virginia planters.[7]

During the Revolution the English officers held as prisoners in Albemarle were given permission to travel within a 100-mile radius of Charlottesville. One of these officers, Lieutenant

39

Anburey, observed and wrote about the Virginians and their way of life. As might be expected of an Englishman, he divided the white citizens into classes, but noted that since the war had begun, class lines were becoming indistinct. In general, he found that planters consigned their slaves to an overseer because they thought it beneath their dignity to superintend their own affairs, and in addition were "abominably lazy." The best of the planters had liberal educations, a thorough knowledge of the world, and were gracious in their manners and conversation. Most of these families had fine silver services, carriages, and all, without exception, kept their own studs. Of the middle- and lower-class Virginians, Anburey had fewer good things to say:

> The second class [is] . . . hospitable, generous, and friendly; but for want of a proper knowledge of the world, and a good education, as well as from their continual intercourse with their slaves, over whom they are accustomed to tyrannize, with all their good qualities, they are rude, ferocious, and haughty, much attached to gaming and dissipation, particularly horse-racing and cockfighting; in short, they form a most unaccountable combination of qualities and principles directly opposite and contradictory, many of them having them strangely blended with the best and worst of principles, the most valuable and most worthless, many possessing elegant accomplishments and savage brutality, and notwithstanding all this inconsistency of character, numbers are valuable members of the community, and very few deficient in intellectual faculties.
>
> The third class, which, in general, composes the greatest part of mankind, are fewer in Virginia, in proportion to the inhabitants, than perhaps in any other country in the world; yet even those who are rude, illiberal, and noisy, with a turbulent disposition, are generous, kind, and hospitable. We are induced to imagine there is something peculiar in the climate of Virginia, that should render all classes of so hospitable a disposition.
>
> The lower people . . . are averse to labor, much addicted to liquor, and when intoxicated, extremely savage and revengeful. . . . Their amusements are the same with those of the middling sort, with the addition of boxing matches, in which they display such barbarity, as fully marks their innate ferocious disposition. . . . Previous to the combatants falling too, they enter into an agreement, whether all advantages are allowable, which are biting, gouging, and (if I may so term it) Abelarding each other. If these three preliminaries are agreed upon, they instantly fall to.[8]

The foregoing opinions may have been prejudiced, the Reverend Burnaby's perhaps by a religious sense of propriety, and Anburey's by the fact that he was describing his wartime enemies. At about the same time that Lieutenant Anburey was writing down his observations in Virginia, another man with less cause for prejudice was also making notes. He was the Marquis de Chastellux, a man of science and ability, a member of the French Academy, and a major general in the French army that fought for America under Rochambeau.

Chastellux noted the difference between the character of the Virginians and that of the people of the northern colonies, tracing these differences back to the founders. The first colonists in Virginia were soldiers and gentlemen who were favorably disposed to the prejudices of nobility and hereditary rank. Even though the government of Virginia might become democratic in form, said Chastellux, the character and spirit of the Virginians would remain aristocratic; another cause, slavery, was operating to produce a similar result. It was not because slave ownership was a mark of distinction or special privilege, but rather that owning slaves corrupted the master into vanity and sloth, which two vices went well together with aristocratic inclinations. Chastellux said that New Englanders, who owed their origin to religious enthusiasm, revolted against England through reason and calculation, but that Virginians took the same action from motives of pride. Chastellux frequently remarked the indolence of Virginians, and stated that it was limited only by their cupidity, as their avarice, in turn, was moderated only by their laziness.

Chastellux said that a free negro in Virginia was little better off than a slave; and yet, in justice, he declared that many Virginians treated their negroes with great humanity, in general seemed grieved at having slaves, and talked of abolishing the institution and finding other ways to work their land. The motives for this varied: the more thoughtful considered justice and human rights; whereas those with economic interests complained that slaves were inefficient and expensive to maintain, and that an epidemic among the slaves could bankrupt the master.

The Frenchman noted that Virginians were known for their hospitality, and received strangers willingly and well. Because of the scarcity of towns, society revolved around visits to the homes, where Virginians were able to live nobly because of the numerous domestic slaves who performed the household tasks. Virginians were proud of their furniture, silver plate, and linen; they read little and sometimes dissipated their fortunes through gambling, hunting, and horse races. The women had little share in the men's amusements, were coquettish and prudish before marriage, and dull afterward.

Chastellux said he wanted to speak generously of the virtues of the Virginians but was able, in truth, to mention only magnificence and hospitality. He said he wished he could add generosity to the list, but he could not, for he thought Virginians were too much attached to their own interests.[9]

The marquis' book was published in 1786, and was received in Virginia with very little enthusiasm.[10] Thomas Jefferson was one of the very few Virginians who agreed with Chastellux. After reading the Frenchman's book, he wrote the following letter to the marquis:

Paris Sep. 2, 1785.

Dear Sir

You were so kind as to allow me a fortnight to read your journey through Virginia. . . . With respect to my countrymen there is surely nothing [in it] which can render them uneasy, in the observations made on them. They know that they are not perfect, and will be sensible that you have viewed them with a philanthropic eye. You say much good of them, and less ill than they are conscious may be said with truth. I have studied their character with attention. I have thought them, as you found them, aristocratical, pompous, clannish, indolent, hospitable, and I should have added, disinterested, but you say attached to their interest. This is the only trait in their character wherein our observations differ. I have always thought them so careless of their interests, so thoughtless in their expenses and in all their transactions of business that I had placed it among the vices of their character, as indeed most virtues when carried beyond certain bounds degenerate into vices. I had even ascribed this to it's cause, to that warmth of their climate which unnerves and unmans both body and mind. While on this subject I will give you my idea of the characters of the several states.

In the North they are	In the South they are
cool	fiery
sober	Voluptuary
laborious	indolent
persevering	unsteady
independant	independant
jealous of their own liberties, and just to those of others	zealous for their own liberties, but trampling on those of others
interested [tight fisted]	generous
chicaning	candid
superstitious and hypocritical in their religion	without attachment or pretentions to any religion but that of the heart.

42

These characteristics grow weaker and weaker by gradation from North to South and South to North, insomuch that an observing traveller, without the aid of the quadrant may always know his latitude by the character of the people among whom he finds himself. . . . I think it for their good that the vices of their character should be pointed out to them that they may amend them; for a malady of either body or mind once known is half cured. . . . I have the honor to be with very sincere esteem Dear Sir Your most obedient & most humble servt.,

Th: Jefferson[11]

In nearly every instance, foreign visitors agreed with Jefferson's opinions about the character of Virginians. They were unanimous in the opinion that the Virginia slave owners tended to be hospitable, generous, and outgoing and yet, at the same time, they were lazy, hedonistic, fiery, and unsteady.[12] It cannot be claimed, on the basis of known facts, that all these traits were characteristic of the men in the Lewis family. It does appear, however, that most of the Lewises' social peers did fit in this category and, indeed, the Lewises themselves may well have been people of this sort.

· 6 ·

THE SHIPWRECK OF
THE FORTUNES

ALTHOUGH Col. Charles L. Lewis's prospects appeared to be bright in 1792, there were bad times ahead for him, as there were for most Virginians. Economic depressions, crop failures, business, and probably personal errors as well, combined over a ten-year period to bring about what Jefferson would describe laconically as "the shipwreck of the fortunes" of the Lewis family.[1]

That spring there was a stock market collapse that affected the entire nation. This panic followed a two-year speculative boom in purchases of the government debts.[2] As a whole, Virginians were not responsible for this crash, even though they felt its sting. Virginia had only a few private banks, which deserved little confidence, and after the crash Virginians experienced a great shortage of sound bank notes in circulation.[3] Most of the speculation took place in the mercantile circles of the Northeast, while Virginians in general, and Jefferson in particular, looked on in rage at the result of the Federalist policies.[4] No evidence has been found to indicate that Colonel Lewis was involved in this speculation himself, but as a business man and farmer he would have been indirectly affected by it.

There was a general business recovery beginning in 1793, when France declared war on Britain and Holland, and the warring nations bought great quantities of American food and raw materials.[5] This prosperity was followed by a sharp depression in 1798, traceable to our disputes with France, and another in 1802, following the peace of Amiens.[6] Apparently Colonel Lewis was very much affected by these last two depressions. In 1799 the number of slaves he owned dropped from twenty-seven to ten, and in 1802 he lost not only all his remaining slaves, but also all of his horses.[7] He never recovered financially after this, and was dependent on his children for the remainder of his life.

Another situation that unquestionably contributed to Lewis's decline was the exhaustion of the soil in Albemarle, which resulted from the reckless farming practices used by generations of Virginians.

The hoe and the spade were the tools used in the cultivation of tobacco.... Hoes and spades merely scratch the surface of the
ground instead of breaking it deeply. This sort of cultivation
invited erosion, which cut deep gullies across the tobacco fields.
The soil was further exploited by the ignorant apprentice laborer
and negro slave worked by the ruthless overseer who, paid with a
portion of the crop he raised, was anxious to make the most of his
opportunities by "skinning" the soil of its resources for the present
gain.... The soil was exhausted for present returns and thus
ruined in utter disregard for the future. Fresh lands were
constantly cleared and expended to satisfy the insatiable demands
of growing tobacco.[8]

By 1780 Jefferson was aware of the evils of an agriculture
based on tobacco as the primary crop. He thought that
eventually other states farther south would be able to undersell
Virginia, and would force Virginians to abandon the raising of
tobacco altogether. He looked forward to that day, recognizing
the harm that had been done to the state. "It is a culture Productive of infinite wretchedness. Those employed in it are in a
continued state of exertion beyond the powers of nature to support. Little food of any kind is raised by them; so that the men
and animals on those farms are badly fed, and the earth is
rapidly impoverished."[9]

Within a decade, as Jefferson had hoped, wheat had by and
large replaced tobacco as the primary cash crop of Albemarle. In
1796, the Duc de La Rochefoucauld-Liancourt of France visited
Albemarle County and recorded his observations. He found
that, although wheat culture had generally replaced tobacco,
farming practices were as bad as ever. The fields were planted
year after year in wheat or corn, never receiving the least bit of
manure, until they were exhausted and abandoned. If the
abandoned land grew up in weeds or was used as pasture, then
in eight or ten years the farmer returned to the old field and
repeated the cycle. If the abandoned field lay bare of cover, then
a twenty-year rest was not sufficient to restore productivity. The
usual yields were five to six bushels of wheat and ten or fifteen
bushels of corn to the acre.[10]

Three years after the duke's visit, a county resident noted that
the land in Albemarle was "worn out, washed and gullied, so
that scarcely an acre could be found in a place fit for cultivation."
He said the land had been butchered by tobacco, and "there was
not a good plough in the entire county."[11] Another observant

45

man in Albemarle noted that the wealth of Albemarle had run down its rivers; after a rainstorm the waters came down from the mountains with great "impetuosity," overflowed the banks of the Rivanna for many miles, and "washed away the earth, which being of a red cast, appeared like a torrent of blood." The damage done by floods was compounded by forest fires. "During the summer months these fires are very frequent, and at Charlottesville I have seen the mountains on a blaze for three or four miles in length, they are occasioned by the carelessness of waggoners who, when night approaches . . . make a large fire to warm them when they sleep, which on pursuing their journey the next morning, they neglect to extinguish."[12]

Exhausted land was not the only problem facing plantation owners in Albemarle. Extremes of weather, plant diseases, insects, and erratic market prices combined to make the 1790s a decade of difficulty for farmers in the Milton neighborhood. There were three crops of vital importance: wheat; tobacco, which provided most of the planters' cash or credit; and corn, which was the primary source of food for slaves. Corn was also important in the production of pork. The loss or substantial reduction of any one of these crops would have been a serious matter. In the eight years from 1792 to 1800, there were only two years in which crops were harvested and sold without the occurrence of some calamity. In 1792, the crops were good, but after the harvest of the previous year weevils had destroyed practically all of the wheat. In 1793, there was a severe drought in August, and the corn crop was reduced by a third. In 1794, the wheat crop was "miserable."[13] In midsummer of 1795 Jefferson wrote to Thomas Mann Randolph describing the farm prospects for that year. "I mentioned in my last letter the ravages committed by the rains. Since that we have had still worse, I imagine we never lost more soil than this summer. It is moderately estimated at a year's rent. Our crops of corn will be much shortened by the prostrate & drowned condition of the plants. . . . Tobacco has fired excessively. Many have cut their crops green."[14]

In the fall of the same year, the weevils again attacked the wheat. George Washington wrote to Jefferson in sympathy. "I am sorry to hear of the depredation committed by the weavil in your parts. It is a great calamity at all times, and this year, when the demand for wheat is so great, and the price so high, must be a mortifying one to the farmer."[15]

The crops in 1796 were very good, but during the early part of the year there was an extreme shortage of corn in the area as a result of the poor yields of all grains the year before. Jefferson said corn could not be bought at any price, and that his situation was threatening beyond anything he had ever experienced. He summarized the situation, saying, "we shall starve literally if I cannot buy 200 barrels, & as yet I have been able to find but 60."[16]

In 1797 the wheat crop was a total failure, having been killed by five degrees below zero temperature in mid-winter. In 1799 there was an extreme shortage of tobacco plants in Albemarle. Most of the planters lost practically all of their plant beds, and in some cases the failure was complete.[17] During the same year, the tobacco market in Richmond collapsed. A tobacco agent reported, "Tobo has become more dull than ever, scarcely any-one appears inclined to purchase at any price. . . . I fear it has fallen never to rise again." When the short tobacco crop of 1799 from Albemarle reached the market in 1800, the price was still exceedingly low. Jefferson referred to it as "the tragedy by which we have . . . lost so much."[18]

In Albemarle the eighteenth century ended in a decade that was disastrous for plantation owners. Jefferson had predicted their downfall in a letter to his daughter:

> The unprofitable condition of Virginia estates in general leaves it now next to impossible for the holder of one to avoid ruin. And this condition will continue until some change takes place in the mode of working them. In the mean time, nothing can save us and our children from beggary but a determination to get a year before-hand, and restrain ourselves vigorously this year to the clear profits of the last. If a debt is once contracted by a farmer, it is never paid but by a sale.[19]

Only by the most rigorous stewardship and economy could a plantation owner stay solvent in such times. It is not known whether Col. Charles L. Lewis's character tended toward such self-control, or whether he was one of the more typical Albe-marle residents referred to by Jefferson as "lazy and hospitable," and described by some less charitable persons as indolent, ex-travagant, and given to drinking and gambling.[20] The times were such that even the most industrious of men could fail at farming. Lewis was not alone. Woods's *History of Albemarle* lists nearly four hundred families and individuals that emigrated from Albemarle County to other states. Many of them left during or shortly after this decade.[21]

The property tax rolls of Albemarle give a clear picture of the decline of the Lewises of Buck Island and Monteagle after 1792. For the first few years of this period, Colonel Lewis was in partnership with his second son, Lilburne. At first there were nearly forty slaves, twenty horses, four stage wagons, and a tavern license. By 1794 Colonel Lewis had given 750 acres of land and seven slaves to his oldest son, Randolph, and he had sold or somehow disposed of the stage line wagons and seven of the horses. During that year he also gave up the tavern license.[22]

During 1796, Colonel Lewis and Lilburne were joined in their partnership by young Charles, the third son, who had just turned sixteen. The year had been a bad one for them. The inventory of Colonel Lewis's slaves went from thirty-nine to seventeen, and five horses were sold, leaving only seven. There were just over two thousand acres left in the plantation. The Lewis family had had a severe setback. They had sold all the slaves under sixteen years of age, and fourteen of the slaves over the age of sixteen.[23] If some of the seventeen remaining slaves served as domestics, Colonel Lewis owned too few field hands to pay the expense of an overseer, since the labor of at least twenty slaves was necessary to offset the cost of this prestigious luxury.[24] During the time that Lilburne was in partnership with his father, the Lewises did not have an overseer. Presumably Lilburne or his father supervised the field labor, a task not performed by the gentry in most cases.

In September of 1797, Lilburne married his second cousin, Elizabeth Jane Woodson Lewis, the sister of Mary, who had married his brother Randolph five years before.[25] Elizabeth's father, Robert Lewis of the Byrd, was the uncle of Lilburne's father. After his marriage, Lilburne left the family partnership, but continued to live in Albemarle. The nature of his business is not known, and although he owned no land at the time of his marriage he was taxed for six slaves, two horses, and "two chariot wheels."

During 1798 and 1799 the fortunes of Colonel Lewis and young Charles appeared to be improving gradually, for they had acquired a few more slaves and hired an overseer. While Lilburne had been working with the family, slave management did not appear to be a problem, but within a year after Lilburne left, an overseer had been hired. The reason for this is not clear. Perhaps young Charles was unwilling, or unable to control the field hands. The few existing records of young Charles's life indicate that he may have been somewhat irresponsible. A few years after this time, Charles wrote to thank his uncle Thomas Jefferson for a favor, "Be assured, that however thoughtless I may have been heretofore, it shall be my constant study . . . to do that which be most to my interest, and the interest of those by whom I have been promoted."[26] Concerning this promise of Charles's to mend his ways, his mother Lucy wrote, "A positive asshearance from . . . Charles of his constant application, to his present occupation, has given the family great pleasure."[27] During 1799, the year the overseer was hired, a mulatto baby named Matilda was born to one of Randolph's slaves. Young Charles was the father of this baby. Charles's act of miscegenation must have distressed the Lewises, for although such conduct was evident among some of the upper class in Albemarle, it was not typical of the gentry.[28]

Another possible reason for the employment of an overseer was the often-mentioned indolence and pride of some Virginia plantation owners. It is not known that the Lewis men were "abominably lazy" or "unwilling to expose themselves to fatigue," as other plantation owners had been described. They may have been, but having an overseer did impart a certain prestige to planters. An overseer would have given young Charles and Colonel Lewis time for other activities of business, or pleasure, if they preferred.[29]

Even though the reasons for having an overseer may have appeared sound to them, the Lewises would have been financially better off without him. During the following year, 1800, Colonel Lewis and Charles sold off all but eight adult slaves, no more than barely enough hands to provide food, service, and clothing for the family. Debts were accumulating with local merchants, and Colonel Lewis had further reduced his land holdings by 830 acres, which he had given to Lilburne. This tract lay along the north bank of the Rivanna, next to the land owned by Randolph.[30]

At a time of financial crisis, when he needed every asset in order to survive, Col. Charles L. Lewis had yielded to the family tradition by which the father provided his sons with land. Colonel Lewis now owned about seventeen hundred acres of land, most of it poor or exhausted, and too few slaves to farm the areas that were fertile. He was appearing more frequently in court in suits regarding money and his father's estate, and once was fined eight dollars for a contempt of court occasioned by not answering a summons.[31] Colonel Lewis was past the point of recovery and, although he held on for a year or two longer, by the end of 1803 he had lost all of his slaves, including the house servants, all of his horses, and had left only fourteen hundred acres, useless to him now, except for sale.[32]

In 1802, one year before the final crash of Colonel Lewis's fortunes, Isham, the youngest son, became sixteen, and joined his father and brother Charles in the collapsing family partnership. It was an arrangement in name only, for, excepting the land, there were no assets, credit, or other means of providing income. There was little left for the sons and only disgrace for the father. Young Charles left home in 1803, and Isham did the same the next year. They probably moved in with their older brothers or with some of their numerous aunts or uncles. Extended family visits were common among the gentry.

Having no other assets in 1802, Colonel Lewis began to dispose of parts of his land. His debts were pressing, but as he sold off his land he still clung to a desire for his children to own part of the ancestral property. "The Virginia system had been made for caste society; the landed aristocracy was as much a caste as that in England—minus the titles. They had the same love of land, the same obsession that the alienation of any part of their possessions was treason to the family."[33] By circumstance, Colonel Lewis was able to sell most of his land and still kept it in the family, for the sales were made to Craven Peyton, a young man who had become Lewis's son-in-law a few years before.

Although Craven Peyton came to the Colonel's rescue, he suffered in this relationship. Peyton was two years younger than Colonel Lewis's oldest son, Randolph. He had settled in Milton with his two brothers, and the three of them had been successful in various business enterprises. When the two Peyton brothers died unmarried, Craven inherited their interests in Albemarle County, and in 1795 married Jane Lewis, the colonel's oldest daughter.

In 1802, in the first of the forced sales of his land, Colonel Lewis sold Peyton 400 acres of land for $1,000.[34] Colonel Lewis's distress at losing this land may have been mollified by the fact that it became the property of his daughter and her husband. Still, having established a pattern of giving property to his sons as they reached maturity, the colonel must have felt obligated to his two younger sons, Charles and Isham. They, in turn, would have regarded their father with some expectancy. Torn on one hand by pride and the family custom of giving one's sons a life-time sinecure, and on the other hand by debts and the impending loss of all he owned, Colonel Lewis evidently chose to favor his sons over his creditors.

In July 1802, Colonel Lewis and Lucy deeded to their son, Charles, one-half of the 1300-acre tract of land on which their home, Monteagle, stood. The half of the Monteagle tract that was given to young Charles contained about 200 acres of excellent bottom land lying on Buck Island Creek and the Rivanna, and 450 acres of upland timber.[35]

The other half of Monteagle, which was not conveyed to young Charles in this deed, may have been intended for Isham, but, as it turned out, he never received it, for Colonel Lewis's necessity to meet his debts intervened. By 1803 the Buck Island dynasty had fallen apart. Colonel Lewis owned no slaves or horses, and his land was worth less than his debts. The only chance he had for some income was to sell his remaining land, or to sell, before he received them, the slaves he would inherit from his father's estate when his mother died. He did that on October 20, 1803, just eleven days before the old lady's death at the age of seventy-eight.[36]

Again it was Craven Peyton who came to Lewis's rescue.

This indenture of bargain and sale made this twentieth day of October in the year eighteen hundred and three . . . witnesseth. That whereas Charles L. Lewis by the will of his father is entitled to a portion of Sundry Negroes upon the death of his mother . . . and whereas the said Craven Peyton has paid and assumed to pay a considerable sum of money for the said Charles L. Lewis to wit, to Gamble and Temple Seven hundred dollars to Brown and Reves & Co. Twelve hundred Dollars and to William Galt five hundred Dollars. Now This instrument bears evidence that for and in consideration of the sums of money thus paid and settled for the said Charles L. Lewis, he the said Charles L. Lewis has bargained and sold and . . . doth . . . transfer to and forever invest . . . Craven Peyton with all . . . claim which he the said Charles L. Lewis may Possess in the before recited estate . . . . Craven Peyton is in all respects to stand in the shoes of the said Charles L. Lewis in relation to this estate. . . . In witness the said Charles L. Lewis hath put his hand and seal the Day and year above written.[37]

One of the witnesses to the signing and delivery of this document was Isham Lewis. The only one of the four Lewis sons who had not received part of the family property was given, instead, the doleful duty of officiating at the final loss of his father's inheritance.

Colonel Lewis received twenty-four hundred dollars credit on his debts by selling his shares in his father's estate.[38] All he had left was 650 acres of land south of the Rivanna and 600 acres north of the river. His desperation was such that, incredibly enough, he sold one piece of land that he himself did not own, and, what is more astonishing, the victim of this fraud was his own son-in-law and benefactor, Craven Peyton. The property involved in this fraudulent sale was the 650 acres which Colonel Lewis had given young Charles in 1802.

The wording of the original deed from Colonel Lewis to young Charles was clear. Charles was to have the 650 acres "during his natural life, free and clear from the claim or claims of all and every person." If Charles should marry in the future, then his ownership of the land was to change from a lifetime interest to a fee simple title, and the land could pass on to Charles's heirs. If Charles were to die without having married, then, the deed specified, the 650 acres would automatically become the property of Charles's sisters.

About two years after receiving this land from his father, Charles sold all his own interest in it to Craven Peyton for fifteen hundred pounds, approximately five thousand dollars.[39] At the time Peyton bought the land from young Charles, he evidently had not seen the deed in which Colonel Lewis transferred the land to Charles, for they lied to Peyton about its contents. They did not tell Peyton about the specification that Charles's sisters could claim the land in the event of Charles's death. In addition to this, they convinced Peyton that Colonel Lewis still held a claim to the land, and would continue to do so until Charles married. This was not true, for Colonel Lewis no longer held any legal claim or interest whatsoever in that particular 650 acres. Peyton did not know this, however, and mistakenly believed that Colonel Lewis still owned the land because Charles was still single. At this point, having bought out Charles's interest, Peyton actually owned the tract entirely, for no one else had any legal claim to it except for the possible claim of Charles's sisters in the event Charles should die.

In the erroneous belief that Colonel Lewis still had a claim on the land, and wishing to consolidate his own possession of it, Peyton bought from Colonel Lewis the nonexistent interest in the land, which was actually Peyton's all the time. It cost Peyton another five thousand dollars to be so grossly cheated by his father-in-law. The deception is apparent in the deed from Colonel Lewis to Peyton, where the tract is described as "containing six hundred and fifty Acres, it being the land the said Charles L. Lewis conditionally conveyed to Charles L. Lewis Jr., and which the sd. Peyton has since bought of the said Lewis, Jr."[40] The true "condition" was that if Charles married, his lifetime deed would then become a fee simple deed. The false condition, of which the Lewises convinced Peyton, was that Colonel Lewis would continue to own a claim in the tract until Charles married.

There is no indication at this time that Peyton knew he had been defrauded. On the other hand, Colonel Lewis knew it and young Charles knew it. Randolph may not have known of the deceit, but he witnessed and recorded the deed to young Charles in 1802 as well as the one to Peyton in 1804.

Eight months after the fraudulent sale, Peyton bought another tract of land from Colonel Lewis. It contained 387 acres, and lay adjoining and north of the lands Lewis had given Randolph and Lilburne. The purchase price was one pound per acre, approximately $1,290 altogether. This tract was hilly and very rough. Evidently Peyton did not want the land, but bought it as a favor to Colonel Lewis, for within two years he had resold it to another party.[41]

In September of 1805, Colonel Lewis made his final sale of land to Craven Peyton. This was the last piece of the original grant patented by Charles Lewis of the Byrd three generations before. Peyton paid Col. Charles L. Lewis five thousand dollars for this land, just exactly half of the amount the colonel and young Charles together had fraudulently collected for the same-sized tract.[42] The brick plantation manor, Monteagle, stood on this section of land, and Colonel Lewis reserved it, with six acres of ground and the outbuildings nearby, for his and Lucy's use during their lives. This was not an unusual provision for deeds at that time, but there was another provision interlined into the document which reveals the apprehensive mental state of Colonel Lewis at that time.

> I do hereby oblige myself my heirs exetrs or assigns not to dispose of the within mentioned 550 acres of land during the life of Colo Charles L. Lewis & his wife without their entire consent, neither lease or rent it to bad or unprincipled [word unclear] men that would treat Colo Lewis family amiss. Given under my hand and seal the 10th Sep 1805.
>
> C. Peyton (Seal)[43]

Shortly after this sale was transacted, Colonel Lewis gave his son, Isham, the last remaining property he owned, 230 acres of poor ground on the Three Chopt Road. The mere ownership of a few hundred acres of thin land in Albemarle did not make Isham well off, by any means. This property apparently had been rented out. It was described as being "in the possession of Thomas D. Boyd," the keeper of Boyd's Tavern and store.[44] Isham did not keep the 230 acres long enough for it to appear in his name on the tax rolls. He transferred it to his sister, Ann M. (Nancy), who resold it a few years later. For tax purposes this tract was valued at $138.[45]

Of all the sons, Isham, the youngest, had been given the least; and now neither he, nor young Charles, nor their father owned title to one thing of value—slave, horse, or plot of ground.

Craven Peyton had paid Colonel Lewis a total of nearly fifteen thousand dollars, a huge sum in those times, and had paid the son, Charles, five thousand dollars more, all in three years time, and the money was gone as soon as gotten, very likely to pay debts. By the end of 1807 Colonel Lewis did not even own enough furniture to set up housekeeping. There was nothing left for Isham, and his cup of bitterness ran over. A few years later Isham wrote to his uncle, Thomas Jefferson, asking for a job, and said that the necessity to ask for help was brought on, as he expressed it, "not from my own imprudences, but [rather] those of an unfortunate father, whose promises of wealth and neglect to bring me up in any useful pursuit" had caused the troubles.[46]

The personal role that Craven Peyton played in the Lewis family is puzzling. Peyton and Jane had been living at Monteagle since 1802 and, according to his mother-in-law, Lucy, he was the acting head of the whole family. Lucy wrote to her brother, who was then the president:

> I have seen more happiness, for the last five years hear, [at Monteagle] thin I evar saw the hole time before since my having a family, for in the last five years there was nothing that I wanted or that eather of my Daughters wished for but what was got, and I do declare to you that Mr. Peyton has been to me as the most dutiful child and to my Daughters as long as they were undar his guidence, as the most just and affectionate farthar.[47]

Lucy was appreciative, but if Colonel Lewis or his daughters were grateful to Peyton for his generosity and concern for them, they left no record of it.

54

· 7 ·

CRAVEN PEYTON,
THOMAS JEFFERSON, AND
THE HENDERSONS

DURING THE same period that Col. Charles L. Lewis's financial fortunes began their final plummet, three of his in-laws became embroiled in a triangle of business intrigue that lasted for more than ten years and ended in animosity and the loss of thousands of dollars to one of them. Colonel Lewis was not directly involved in the episode, but the three people concerned had all played vital roles in his own business affairs. It was as though Colonel Lewis, for once in his life, stood in the calm eye of a hurricane that raged around him.

One of the people was Colonel Lewis's son-in-law and benefactor, Craven Peyton; the second was Lewis's sister, Elizabeth, the widow of his close associate, Bennett Henderson; and the third was Lewis's brother-in-law, Thomas Jefferson. At the heart of this controversy was an attempt to gain control of the businesses that handled and transported a large part of the agricultural products of Albemarle County. At stake, also, was the milling industry at Milton.

In Albemarle, agriculture was the basis of nearly all business. As is still the case today, there was more money to be made in the processing, handling, and resale of farm products than in the actual growing of them. The key to this situation was transportation, that and the simple fact that in rural areas, where crops were grown, there was not enough population to provide a significant consuming market. Because certain manufactured items and luxuries could not be bought with whiskey, pelts, or personal notes of credit, some crops had to be sold for cash, and it was over sixty miles from Albemarle to Richmond, the nearest sizable market. Moving crops in bulk was a formidable project because the roads were unmarked and unimaginably poor.

During this time Jefferson wrote to a friend who intended to visit Monticello and warned him to change his route. He said that the Three Chopt Road was so badly cut by wagons that it would soon become impassable.[1] Col. Charles L. Lewis's four stage wagons had not helped that situation. When wagons could no longer pass over a road, the farmers sometimes put an axle on their hogsheads and rolled them to Richmond behind their horses.

The Lewises were probably among the first Albemarle residents to use the Rivanna for transportation. In 1763, when he was twenty years old, Jefferson took a canoe down the Rivanna from the Mountain Falls. He recalled that, in earlier years, "a canoe, with a family in it, had passed and repassed several times between Buck island creek in Albemarle and the Byrd creek in Goochland."[2] This family may well have been that of Charles Lewis, Jr. traveling back and forth between Buck Island and the Byrd.

After his trip, Jefferson realized the potential of the Rivanna and became interested in using it to transport farm products. He saw that, if the Rivanna were cleared, it could be used to transport grain, flour, hemp, and most important of all, tobacco. At Jefferson's urging, the colonial legislative assembly at Williamsburg commissioned eleven prominent men of the Rivanna neighborhood as trustees to receive private subscriptions, let contracts, and arrange for the removal of rocks and other obstacles to shallow draft boats. The river was to be widened to a minimum of fifteen feet and cleaned out to a depth of at least twenty-one inches. Col. Charles L. Lewis's father and Thomas Jefferson were two of these trustees.[3] By 1772 at a cost of two hundred pounds, the river was opened, and subscription fees were being accepted to maintain the work that had been done. This system of maintenance continued sporadically for at least twenty-five years, and probably until the founding of the Rivanna Navigation Company in 1805.[4]

Jefferson described the success of these efforts to clear the Rivanna: "The river is regularly boatable about 7. or 8. months from the beginning of November (not obstructed by ice once in 2 years & then only a few days) and in the Summer months the boats always hold themselves in readiness to catch the accidental tides from showers of rain, so that a great deal is done that season: and there is rarely any accumulation of produce for want of a tide."[5]

Prior to 1800, there had been no serious attempt to improve navigation above the Mountain Falls, or Milton Falls, as they came to be known. At that time, most navigation stopped here, and transportation proceeded by land. From the Milton Falls it was over thirty miles down the Rivanna to its junction with the James and, except in times of drought or flood, the current was swift and shallow. The canoe was an ideal boat for such waters— speedy, light, and of shallow draft. The inherent instability of the canoe was overcome by lashing two of them rigidly together, side by side, with poles across the gunwales. On this sort of crude platform hogsheads or other goods could be loaded and carried rapidly and almost without effort to Richmond. On the return trip, the boatmen poled the canoes upstream with far less effort than would have been required for other types of boats.[6] As early as 1775, batteaux were in use on the Rivanna. These were flat-bottom boats about fifty or sixty feet long, which tapered in width from four feet at the bottom to six feet at the gunwales. A boat of this size carried eleven hogsheads of tobacco and drew thirteen and one-half inches of water.[7]

In addition to improving roads and rivers, another measure was used to facilitate the journey of crops to market; farm products could be partially processed in order to reduce their bulk before they were transported. This had the added benefit of increasing their value as well. Tobacco leaves were tightly pressed, or "prized," into a large wooden barrel, or drum, nearly five feet in height and about three and a half feet in diameter. The drum was called a hogshead, and when full weighed from one thousand to two thousand pounds, depending upon the type of tobacco and size of the hogshead. Hemp was processed into fiber and baled. The price of grain in bulk would little more than pay for the trip to Richmond; it was, moreover, liable to be damaged by rain showers or leaking boats. Converted into whiskey or flour, however, these grains, shrunken in volume and enhanced in value, traveled safe from the weather in kegs and barrels.[8] The same applied to peaches and other fruits that were converted into brandy or cider.

The opening of the Rivanna to navigation was to have important effects on Albemarle County and its residents, especially those who lived near the falls. Bennett Henderson was one of those who was so affected. Henderson had been active in the fight for freedom in Virginia, and had served in the same units with Charles L. Lewis during much of the Revolution. They were together on the two marches to Williamsburg, and in the Volunteer Albemarle Regiment that fought in the coastal area of Virginia in 1776. Three years later Lewis and Henderson were members of the jury that confiscated the property of British sympathizers in Albemarle. They were both signers of the petitions for religious freedom. They had much in common.

By the end of the Revolution, Henderson had risen to the rank of colonel in the Albemarle militia, and shortly thereafter Virginia paid him for his service with a land grant in Kentucky.[9] At about this same time, Henderson became a magistrate, or justice of the peace, for Albemarle County.[10]

Henderson owned more than twelve hundred acres on the south side of the Rivanna, both up and down stream from the falls. Controlling the southern approaches to this important location, Henderson realized that he had a rare opportunity to make money from the people who came to ship their produce by river. He built a flour mill, a distillery, a tobacco inspection warehouse, and a storehouse. To Henderson's location came wagons from all over the county, and even from the Valley of Virginia across the mountain range.[11] Of the variety of goods they carried, tobacco was by far the most important prior to 1790, not only because it was the principal cash crop, but also because it served as a medium of exchange through the use of warehouse receipts. When delivered to the warehouse, the tobacco was weighed and inspected and a receipt was given to the grower. These receipts then served as currency and were honored throughout the state.[12] Henderson's warehouse gave shelter to a variety of other farm and commercial products. At one time during the Revolution it was the repository for 256 barrels of gunpowder.[13]

Henderson owned what was, in effect, the port of the county, and he was influential in a good part of its business: shipping, distilling, warehousing, milling, and storage. In 1789 Henderson and Col. Charles L. Lewis ventured into real estate development. At the end of that year, an act of the Virginia legislature created the town of Milton on a section of Henderson's land that was located on high ground a few hundred yards back from the river. Milton was laid out to cover seventy acres, and was surveyed off into lots.[14] The town rapidly flourished as businessmen opened profitable firms there. Peyton & Price, Brown Rives & Co., Henderson & Conard, Rives & Co., and others were able to acquire wealth from the busy commerce of Milton.

About four years after Milton was established Bennett Henderson died, while still a comparatively young man. Within two years after his death there was nothing left of his fortune except the real estate. His widow was Elizabeth Lewis, the sister of Col. Charles L. Lewis. Jefferson described the Henderson family as "being absolutely pennyless." How Henderson's fortune was lost within two years after his death is unknown, but Col. Charles L. Lewis, as executor of the estate, could not, or did not, help the situation. Henderson left debts for which is sons were liable and had not paid eight years after he died. His widow and children, even with Colonel Lewis's help, were unable to manage the businesses at a profit, although they evidently tried, for in 1795 they were raising the level of their mill dam and had borrowed money against its future earnings to finance the construction. Even in this effort they were finally thwarted.[15] Six years later, Henderson's 1,234 acres of land at Milton were divided into parcels of equal size and distributed among the children by lottery. Commissioners were appointed by the court to make the division because Henderson had died without leaving a will.

This, then, was the situation in Albemarle County before the fall of 1801: the most potentially valuable business complex in Albemarle was to be broken up and divided among a family of a dozen people who had no money, who were unable to continue the businesses, and some of whom were still children. If someone else could acquire and reassemble all the parts of the Henderson interests at Milton, and put them under careful management, he would own what was then the commercial key to Albemarle.[16] There was a man who wanted to do just that. By the time the Henderson land was divided, this man, Thomas Jefferson, had become president of the United States.

Eight years before this, in the same year that Bennett Henderson died, Thomas Jefferson had resigned as secretary of state. Discouraged by the political bickering in the administration and anguished over the increasing influence of Alexander Hamilton, Jefferson intended and believed that he would never again serve in public office. He returned to Albemarle and to private life eagerly, perhaps hoping that through careful management of his properties he could earn enough to offset some of the large amounts of his own money he had spent in the service of his country.[17]

For three years Jefferson led the life of a country squire, managing his farms, setting up a small nail manufactory, working on his yet-unfinished Monticello, and digging a canal for his mills. He laid his political pen aside for a while, or claimed to have, and happily lost himself in the bucolic activities of the planter's life. Then a lifetime's habit became too strong. His letters to old friends and political comrades indicated his continuing concern that the American government was becoming no more than a corrupt copy of the "despotic, monarchical, and aristocratical" British government. Jefferson was drawn back into politics in spite of his expressed wishes.[18] In 1797 he became vice president, and four years later, president. For twelve years, beginning in 1796, Jefferson would be in Albemarle only on visits, and certainly not often or long enough to make his business interests profitable. Jefferson's plantations were left in the care of managers, and the income from them was small indeed. From the large tract Jefferson owned next to Henderson's land, firewood could be cut and sold to the residents of Milton, and some of Jefferson's farms were rented to other men.[19] Nevertheless, these and other income sources, even with his president's salary, were insufficent to keep him out of debt.

For a long time Jefferson had realized that there was potential profit in the commercial milling of flour. At Shadwell he owned a site that was suitable for a large mill, provided a mill race or canal were built. In 1776 he began to dig a canal three-fourths of a mile long, much of it through solid rock, which was blasted out. The work continued intermittently for twenty-seven years, and was finally completed in 1803 at a cost of twenty thousand dollars. The flow of water in the canal proved inadequate, and a four-hundred-foot dam had to be built across the Rivanna to raise the water level. At the same time, the construction of the mill itself was begun. The mill was forty by sixty feet, five floors high, and by the time it was finished in 1806, had cost Jefferson an additional ten thousand dollars. The whole undertaking was a disaster. He rented it out for twelve hundred dollars per year, or an equal value in flour, but the venture was seldom out of trouble. Bad management, floods that washed out the dam, high maintenance cost, and fluctuating markets were some of the things that combined to make this project a torment for him.[20]

In 1800, however, Jefferson was hopeful about the future of his mill. He still wanted the Henderson properties at Milton, and to get them he needed a partner or an agent, an active and experienced businessman, preferably one who had money, who could act for him as agent and not be suspected. He found that man in Craven Peyton.

Craven Peyton and his two brothers, Robert and John, had

moved to Milton from Loudon County, Virginia. They were from an enterprising family and were associated with their uncle, who had been a supply officer during the Revolution. The three brothers were single when they came to Milton sometime before 1793. In 1795 Craven married Jane Lewis, the eldest daughter of Col. Charles L. Lewis. She was eighteen years old, and the groom was twenty at the time of the marriage.[21]

The exact nature of the Peyton business is not known, but it is said that the firm of Peyton and Price at Milton laid the foundation for a large fortune. Evidently part of the enterprise was contracting to supply food to the troops. Peyton's brothers died when they were young and still single, and Craven inherited their estates, and very likely also that of his uncle, who had died unmarried. Before he was twenty-five, Craven had become financially well-to-do and had married into a prominent family. He had not bought or speculated in land prior to 1800, but had confined himself to other types of business.[22]

Peyton's and Jefferson's correspondence began around 1800, but they had probably known each other for several years before that, certainly for the five years that Peyton had been his nephew by marriage. Their friendship appears to have been cordial and marked by mutual respect during the thirty years it continued— primarily a business relationship in which Peyton represented some of Jefferson's interests. Peyton was diligent in Jefferson's behalf, and occasionally they met on a more sociable level: once, at least, in the dining room at Monticello, to enjoy the early spring peas that were Jefferson's pride.[23]

In the fall of 1799, Jefferson evidently realized that he could not, or would not, separate himself from national politics and might become president. Meanwhile, his best opportunity for commercial success lay at Milton, in the hands of the widow Elizabeth Henderson and her children. Not only was the Henderson property valuable in its own right, but also the Henderson mill would be in competition with the new flour mill that Jefferson proposed to build upstream at Shadwell. In order to consolidate all these properties Jefferson and Peyton joined together in an agreement in which Peyton was to be the publicly acting member and Jefferson the secret partner.

Jefferson himself gave what is probably a reliable summary of his and Peyton's relationship: "While I was living out of the state, he [Peyton] was so kind as to act for me in the purchase . . . [of land] . This he did voluntarily and faithfully, but that trouble, I

61

had no right to continue on him after I returned home to live and to act for myself. During the eight years elapsed since that time, I have been my own sole agent in this business."[24] That the working arrangement between Jefferson and Peyton was a secret one is confirmed in another of Jefferson's letters. Peyton had asked Jefferson if he could pay some obligations to Jefferson in corn rather than in money. Jefferson replied that it would be "as convenient for me that Mr Bacon should receive corn from you as money; but you must be so good as to inform him . . . that it will remain in account between you and me, for he knows nothing of the existing trust."[25]

At the very beginning of their association, Jefferson reminded Peyton that the property must be bought "in your own name."[26] The need for secrecy was twofold. First was that Jefferson, as a high-ranking political figure, had suffered some of the most vituperative personal muckraking ever known in the politics of this nation. His religion, his personal conduct, his business affairs—in short, everything about him—was used as a target for the scathing Federalist slander. If he were trying to buy and reestablish a business complex in Albemarle, he certainly did not want the Federalists to know about it, even though his intentions and conduct were entirely legal. The second reason for secrecy was his relationship with the Henderson family.[27]

There is little record of friction between Jefferson and the Bennett Henderson family prior to 1793. Bennett and his older brother, John, had many things in common with Jefferson: friendship with Philip Mazzei, similar views regarding politics, religious freedom, and service to the American cause.[28] There was, however, one area in which their interests collided: that of competition in the milling business. Bennett's water grist mill, located just downstream from Shadwell, was serviced by a mill dam Bennett had built across the Rivanna without legal authority.[29] Not only did the mill compete with Jefferson's for business, but the dam was an obstruction to Jefferson's full use of the Rivanna for transportation. By 1793 both Bennett and his brother had died, and Bennett's widow, Elizabeth, was left with eleven children, all of whom were under age, except for John, the eldest, who was appointed guardian over his brothers and sisters. From that time on the relations between the Hendersons and Jefferson deteriorated. There is not much doubt that the Hendersons, especially John and his mother, grew to hate Jefferson, and, as the years of continuing dispute went by, Jefferson's attitude toward them turned from patience to near vin-dictiveness.[30]

In 1795, the Hendersons began to raise the height of their dam, one result of which would have been to ruin or "drown" Jefferson's mill location. Jefferson countered with a suit that eventually resulted in having the dam destroyed (at the begin-ning of the litigation Jefferson had offered to advance them money for their lawyer, since he did not want it thought that he was taking advantage of their poverty).[31] On the south side of the Rivanna Jefferson's property adjoined the Henderson land, which occasioned continuing disputes over trespass and the cut-ting and selling of firewood to the residents of Milton.[32]

With such hostile feelings between them, Jefferson realized the Hendersons would not sell him their land; or else, out of resentment, they would demand more than its worth. If they had known that Craven Peyton was acting for Jefferson in buy-ing the property, the result would have been the same. Con-sequently their arrangement was kept secret.

Jefferson's and Peyton's first business association began in late 1799 with the rental of part of Shadwell, the 400-acre farm and home where Jefferson had been born. Jefferson's anxiety to rent his farms was extreme, for he realized he could not supervise them properly in his absence and he needed whatever income they would bring.[33] The rental contract for Shadwell was to run for five years, and Peyton agreed to pay a dollar an acre per year for 160 acres. A crop rotation plan for wheat, corn, and rye was agreed upon, in which each of the fields was to be rested two out of the five years. Tobacco was not to be grown. At the end of two years Peyton and Jefferson were discussing the rental of Shadwell to a third person, because Peyton planned to move from Shadwell to Monteagle, the Lewis family home.[34] Jef-ferson's records show that Peyton was given credit for rent as the tenant at Shadwell for only two years, 1800 and 1801. During the time Peyton lived there, he built the west end and repaired the east end of the dwelling house. He owned six slaves at this time, not enough for large-scale farming, although he certainly could have hired more from other men.[35]

Peyton's residing at Shadwell was an effective camouflage for the secret agreement between Peyton and Jefferson. Their meetings and correspondence would not stir up suspicion in the neighborhood if their relationship were thought to be that of landlord and tenant, nor would Peyton's buying up the Henderson lands be suspect if he were apparently expanding his own business operations in Milton to include farming. Letters between Peyton and Jefferson in the fall of 1801 mention almost everything except farming: mills, bank notes, sale of firewood, the division of Henderson's land, and other business matters. As usual, Peyton asked for Jefferson's approval. "You will please let me know how you approve of the proceedings." Peyton was far more to Jefferson than merely his tenant at Shadwell.[36]

In 1801, Jefferson's first year as president, the plan to buy the Henderson lands was put into action. The county court had appointed commissioners to divide the twelve hundred acres among the ten Henderson children. The widow, Elizabeth Lewis, owned a dower of 277 acres, and dower rights in all the other land. The property was laid out in four general areas, and each of these areas was split into ten equal parts and given a number from one to ten. Lots were then drawn in the children's behalf so that each child would have four parcels, one in each of the four areas.[37] The fact that some of the lots contained dwellings or other buildings was left to chance, and the child who drew those lots would own the buildings, except for the warehouse and mill, in which each heir owned one share. A letter indicates that Peyton and Jefferson had been buying some of the inheritance rights and the widow's dower rights even before the division of the land, and the financial record that Thomas Jefferson kept of the Henderson transactions lists these purchases.[38]

Following the drawing of the lots, Peyton wrote to Jefferson from Shadwell, saying that one of the Henderson children, whose inheritance they had previously bought, drew the lot that contained Henderson's mill seat. Peyton urged Jefferson to build his commercial mill at Milton rather than at Shadwell, since it would cost him only a third as much. Having spent twenty thousand dollars on the canal to the mill location at Shadwell, Jefferson declined Peyton's advice and built the mill at Shadwell. He should have listened to Peyton.[39]

The structure of the Jefferson-Peyton agreement was this: Peyton was to buy all the parcels of the Henderson property near Milton in his own name and was to manage that property while he held it. After Jefferson left public life and returned to Albemarle, he was to take the land off of Peyton's hands.[40] During the time that Peyton was acting for Jefferson there was a frequent exchange of letters that kept Jefferson aware of

Peyton's progress and problems, and gave Jefferson's directions and wishes to Peyton. The tone of these letters shows that Peyton was a conscientious man who was most anxious to please Jefferson. On one occasion, discussing one of the Henderson tracts Jefferson wanted to buy, Peyton wrote: "I wish you to say how far I may bid." Obviously Jefferson was calling the shots, not Peyton, and a later letter clearly indicates that Peyton was acting for Jefferson. "I shall be glad to learn from you whether the right of Lewis & Henderson has been purchased; it being interesting to me to have that property all consolidated in my own hand."[41]

Jefferson kept careful records of his affairs with Peyton. As Peyton bought the property, Jefferson recorded the purchase and the price. From time to time, in order to balance their account, Jefferson sent Peyton sums of money, and paid bills for him. The income from the land that Peyton bought for Jefferson derived mostly from the sale of firewood and the rental of houses and farms. This money was received and kept by Peyton, but in the accounts it was deducted from the money that Jefferson owed Peyton. From year to year these accounts were kept in fairly close balance, so that it was actually Jefferson's money that made the purchases, while Peyton arranged the purchase of the land, managed it, and held title to it.[42]

Jefferson, through Peyton, spent just under eight thousand dollars for the Henderson properties, most of which were purchased between 1801 and 1804, during Jefferson's first term. About two thousand dollars of the total went to other persons who had bought parcels from the Hendersons and resold to Peyton. In 1801 Mrs. Henderson had moved to Shelby County, Kentucky, taking with her the five children who were under twenty-one years of age. In September of 1802, Craven Peyton made a trip to Kentucky to buy the remaining unsold parcels. Understandably, after the Hendersons moved away the rate at which Peyton bought their land slowed down. During this same time, Peyton himself was experiencing distress from his involvement in the failing business affairs of his father-in-law, Col. Charles L. Lewis.[43]

By 1807 Peyton was in such financial straits that he wrote Jefferson that he was compelled to sell part of his own land and offered it to him at "a sacrifice of several hundred pounds," and for Jefferson's accommodation offered to make the payments "very easy." This land was not part of the Henderson property.

Jefferson replied that it was quite out of his power to be a purchaser of additional land. "Nobody is more puzzled to make both ends meet, and I fear at the close of my office I shall find I have not done so."[44] Jefferson assumed that there was enough money in the "trust" with Craven Peyton to continue buying the Henderson tracts, but evidently he underestimated the effect of the impending embargo. Peyton told Jefferson that the warehouse money was nearly gone, and that the merchants were pressing him for orders because they thought he owned the property.

A shortage of funds was not Peyton's only anxiety, for, during most of the years that Peyton acted as Jefferson's agent, he was involved in legal proceedings against the Hendersons. The legal documents and evidence in the court records fill more than one hundred pages.[45] In essence, what happened was this: Peyton had paid for all the rights of the widow and her minor children in September of 1802, having gone to Kentucky for that purpose. John Henderson, the eldest son, had remained in Albemarle, living in the Henderson home, which he rented from Peyton. Following the destruction of the old mill dam, John decided to relocate the family mill further downstream and dig a millrace, or canal, that would bring water to turn the mill wheel. John faced two problems in this project; the two-acre mill seat he intended to build on had previously been bought by Peyton, and the land through which the canal had to run was a fifteen-acre section of the dower lands that Peyton had also bought. He paid in cash for both, but this did not seem to trouble John, who began the construction of the new mill and had the 380-foot canal almost completed before Peyton obtained an injunction from the county court to stop the work. In his answer to Peyton's charges, John claimed that he owned the two-acre mill site, not Peyton. He also claimed that his mother had given him permission to dig the canal across her land before she sold the property to Peyton, and that this permission was understood to be implicit in the deed of sale she made to Peyton. When John was requested to prove his claims with documentary evidence, he said that "he verily believes it was either lost or mislaid, so that since that time it could not be found, and cannot now be had."[46]

The battle seesawed on through several years. Peyton's injunction to halt the work was "dissolved" in 1804. Answers were made, depositions taken, the case was continued, dismissed, and

66

then appealed. In 1805, the case was heard before George Wythe, a close personal friend of Jefferson's and a justice of the Superior Court of Chancery in Richmond. Jefferson's name appeared nowhere in the testimony, although it was he who personally organized and wrote the early drafts of Peyton's lengthy petition in the Bill of Complaint against John Henderson.[47] At stake were Peyton's reputation and Jefferson's money. One weak point in Peyton's case was that when he had bought the rights and property of the Henderson children who were underage, he had dealt with James L. Henderson, who did not have the proper authority to act in behalf of his brothers and sisters. The decision went against Peyton and Jefferson, but later they appealed the case. The decision of the Court of Appeals found no error in the previous decree, and to all effects the plans of Peyton and Jefferson for the Henderson land at Milton could go no further at that time.[48]

The bitterness of this controversy is worth noting. In the Bill of Complaint that Jefferson wrote for Peyton he referred to some of the Hendersons as "certain evil minded persons" and said they were using "artifices and influence" as well as nonexistent deeds or "pretended conveyances." Depositions were taken from other persons in an attempt to discredit the character of John Henderson. One deponent, Richard Price, stated that John Henderson had, and intended to use, an altered and interlined legal document, and added that he had known Henderson for twelve years and such an act would be characteristic of his principles. He went on to say that the general widespread opinion of Henderson was that in his other dealings with men he was not fair, and had had "a good many" disputes with most men he had dealings with.[49] Mr. Price may have been right. For several years the income of Henderson's tobacco warehouse had been declining because of the injustice with which the Milton dealers treated the planters. About one thousand hogsheads of tobacco each year were diverted from Henderson's and sold to a warehouse thirty miles away at Columbia.[50]

In the answer to Peyton's complaint, John Henderson replied in kind, saying that Peyton's conduct toward the Hendersons had "been marked by the most insatiable avarice, and that every artifice and skill, that the complainant could make use of (and he is sorry to say . . . too much low cunning) . . . had been practiced in order to circumvent and defraud the poor unsuspicious widow and orphans." Near the end of the argument, and with fine rhetorical outrage, Henderson called the court's attention to Peyton's "grasping and nefarious inclination. Oh tempore: Oh Mores."[51]

Jefferson's bitterness against the Hendersons lingered for years. Writing to Peyton at a later time, Jefferson said that Elizabeth Henderson was guilty of "sheer falsehood" and that her son James "might evade giving . . . of his testimony as there is not one grain of honesty in the . . . [manuscript torn] ."[52]

It is difficult to see how Col. Charles L. Lewis could have stayed completely out of this argument. He was a trustee of Milton, was the brother of Elizabeth Henderson, and was the executor of her husband's estate. Even though he had no personal financial investment in this affair, it would seem reasonable for him, as Henderson's executor, to advise Elizabeth in the matter, at least until she moved away to Kentucky. Nevertheless, his name does not appear anywhere in the lengthy record of the controversy.

By mid 1809, a few months after Jefferson returned from Washington for good, Peyton had had enough of their "partnership" and wrote Jefferson:

> If it is entirely agreeable to you, & it can be done without throwing any obsticle in the way of obtaining those rights now undar age, I shall be glad for you to receive the proparty, for several reasons. Several persons have been pushing me for the warehouse money, togethar for other rents when they become due. My refusal makes them beleave I am unwilling to pay my debts, howevar I am quite willing to encountar anything in any way whatevar to render you the least service in my power, & am in hopes no inconvenience can arise from the transfer being made. Any day that will suite your convenience I will come up.
>
> with great esteem
> C. Peyton[53]

This plaintive request from the admiring and loyal Peyton was not granted until two more years had passed. In August of 1811, Peyton recorded the deed by which he sold to Jefferson 1157½ acres for approximately $7,660.[54] The deed states that this sum had been paid to Peyton "at divers times preceeding the present date," and Jefferson's accounts verify this.[55] Consequently, no money changed hands then, and the sale was less a sale than a transfer of title from Peyton to Jefferson which revealed and ended their secret partnership of ten years' standing. Peyton was now free from the burden and the embarrassment that had gone with it.

Peyton's reasons for acting as Jefferson's secret agent are somewhat obscure. It is natural to assume that Peyton was paid for his work and worries, but strangely enough, in all the carefully kept records of these transactions, there is no clear and specific reference to remuneration for Peyton's services. There are a few entries that may have concerned Peyton's pay. In his account book Jefferson made the following entry in 1812: "June 18. purchased of Craven Peyton 20. lots in Milton, being all he holds there under the Hendersons . . . the consideration 150. D. to be credited to his acct."[56] Twenty years before, these lots were being sold for about fifty dollars each.[57] Thus the twenty lots should have been worth one thousand dollars. If the "consideration" Jefferson mentioned was the purchase price, then the lots had fallen to fifteen percent of their former value, but if the "consideration" of $150 was Peyton's profit or agent's fee for the transaction, and the value of the lots had not fallen in the previous twenty years, then Peyton received a fifteen percent commission in this sale. This may or may not have been the basis on which Peyton was paid.

A year later Jefferson wrote a note to Peyton, and remarked that he owed Peyton $550 and would make arrangements to have it paid on a certain day. This may or may not have been in payment for Peyton's services. If so, it is seven percent of the purchase price of Henderson's land, but Jefferson may have paid Peyton other sums previously for this service.[58]

In 1817 Jefferson stated that Peyton had bought the Henderson lands for him "voluntarily and faithfully." One wonders if by "voluntarily," Jefferson meant "without pay." Sixteen years earlier Craven Peyton had bought the first parcel of land for Jefferson. In his notes that summarized the purchases from the Hendersons, Jefferson commented that in this first transaction Peyton was "to run the risk and be at the expense of procuring the deed etc. no consid'n expressed." At the time Jefferson could not pay for the first tract, but he arranged to repay Peyton a month or two later. Peyton had offered to use his own money for this transaction, and Jefferson accepted Peyton's favor, adding that this accommodation would add to his obligation.[59]

69

At this time, apparently, no agreement had been expressed between them as to a "consideration" for Peyton's efforts. Beyond these two comments of Jefferson, no trace of a cash or property payment to Peyton was found in the documents used to prepare this discussion. One can at least hope that Peyton's decade of assistance to Jefferson was somehow rewarded. Jefferson was sixty-eight and Peyton was thirty-six when their partnership ended.

The later part of Jefferson's presidency was a discouraging time for him. His foreign policies had failed, and as a result, the national economy was crippled. Instead of exerting strong leadership to the very end, Jefferson, in effect, threw up his hands and abdicated his authority.[60] The reasons for this are not entirely understood, but it is certain that the chaotic state of his personal business affairs in Albemarle caused him much anxiety, and usurped his time and energy during this period of crisis for the United States.

Although the Jefferson-Peyton partnership had finally ended in 1811, the two men remained more or less financially involved for at least ten years longer. It was over a year before they finally settled their accounts in the Henderson property, and after that they sold each other produce from their farms from time to time. Once, as a special favor, Jefferson ground plaster for Peyton, and another time offered to sell him slaves. Jefferson's financial affairs continued to deteriorate for the remaining fifteen years of his life, during which he was constantly in Peyton's debt.[61]

· 8 ·

JEFFERSON AND THE
LEWISES

THOMAS JEFFERSON'S feelings about his Lewis relatives at Buck Island and Monteagle are somewhat shadowed and concealed, in part by time, and perhaps by Jefferson's intention. He never directly discussed his relationship with the Lewises, but enough letters exist to indicate the disparity of their interests and achievements, and to indicate some of the personal reservations he held about them.

One factor in the remoteness between the Lewises and Jefferson was his frequent if not perennial absence from Albemarle during the years the Lewises lived there. When Jefferson was two, his parents moved the family away from Albemarle for seven years, returning to Shadwell in 1752. Soon afterward, Jefferson was placed under the tutelage of Rev. William Douglas in Goochland County, and remained there for most of the next five years. From 1758 to 1760 Jefferson boarded at Rev. James Maury's School a few miles from Shadwell, and came home only on weekends and vacations. The next four years were spent in Williamsburg, first at William and Mary College, and then studying law under George Wythe. Of his first twenty-one years, Jefferson had spent almost all his time away from the Shadwell-Buck Island neighborhood. While he was receiving a fine classical and legal education, his younger brother and sisters had a far less impressive education at a school that was held nearby, at the Buck Island home of their cousins, the Charles Lewises. Mr. Benjamin Snead was the tutor. Randolph, Thomas's younger brother, boarded at Buck Island for two years.[1]

Rev. James Maury noted that sons of the gentry seldom extended their schooling for as long as their twentieth year, being distracted by early marriages, children, and the management of their large estates.[2] This was the pattern in the Lewis family; Charles L. Lewis was twenty-one and Lucy Jefferson was seventeen when they married. Their two oldest sons, Randolph and Lilburne, married brides who were only fifteen years old when they themselves were not yet twenty. Jefferson commented indirectly on the typical product of this Virginia pattern of indifferent education and early marriage. He said that he wanted his daughter to be well read, since the odds were fourteen to one that when she married, her husband would be a "blockhead" and that the education of the children would become her responsibility.[3] During his formative years, Thomas Jefferson had only occasional contact with his Lewis cousins, and developed very few interests in common with them.

During the forty-odd years between Jefferson's twenty-first birthday and his retirement to Monticello in 1809, he was gone from Albemarle for extended periods, serving in the House of Burgesses, Continental Congress, Virginia House of Delegates, and then as governor of Virginia, minister to France, secretary of state, vice-president, and finally president. While the Lewis interests were parochial and largely confined to their property in Albemarle, the reach of Jefferson's intellectual curiosity was universal and diffuse.

This difference in outlook is clearly illustrated by a letter which Jefferson wrote to Col. Charles L. Lewis from France:

Paris, Jan. 10. 1789.

Dear Sir

My apology for not having written to you before is the great distance I am from you, and the little interest you would probably take in the occurrences of this part of the world. We have indeed at times been threatened with wars, which might in the long run come round to us. . . . Our system should be to meddle not at all with European quarrels, but to cultivate peace within and without, pursue agriculture, and open all the foreign markets possible to our produce. There will be an immediate and vast demand here this spring for our flour so that that article should sell well in Virginia. I do not foresee any circumstance which may favor the price of tobacco. France, which takes near half of what we make, is at present fully stocked. I hope to see yourself and my sister in the course of the next summer. I have asked of Congress a leave of absence for six months and if I obtain it in time I propose to sail in the Spring and return in the fall. This will allow me to pass about two months at Monticello and to enjoy during that time the company of my antient friends which I shall ever prefer to all others, as I do my own country to all I have yet seen. My daughters retain the same affection for their native land and connections, and are impatient to find themselves among their relations. They join me in an affectionate recollection of my sister and yourself. In our country where man and wife make one, I may hope she will consider this letter as written to her also. Be so good as to assure her of my love, and to accept yourself the sentiments of cordial esteem with which I am Dear Sir Your sincere friend & servant.

Th: Jefferson[4]

Although Jefferson mentioned the affectionate recollections he had of Colonel Lewis and Lucy, and assured Lewis of his cordial esteem, there can be no mistake that Jefferson thought that Colonel Lewis would not be interested in international affairs except as they affected farm prices. The phrase, "the little interest you would probably take in the occurrences of this part of the world," was to be used by Jefferson again the very next day in a letter to his brother Randolph, a letter which Bernard Mayo has used to illustrate Jefferson's awareness of the "striking intellectual disparity" between Jefferson and his younger brother.[5]

Except for the mention of farm prices in the letter sent to Colonel Lewis, these two letters are remarkably similar in content and tone.[6] The same friendly regard was also present in a letter that Jefferson wrote Charles L. Lewis's mother a year later, after he had returned to Albemarle from France:

Monticello Jan. 10. 1790.

Dear Aunt

I am much obliged to you for your kind offer of the bed; and would avail myself of it as freely if I had the occasion, but the goodness of my neighbors with some little provision of our own has placed us at our ease as to that article. I accept with due sensibility your friendly congratulations on my return, and it would be the wish of my heart that it were to remain here, where all my affections are. But that not being as yet my destiny, I shall go again with the hope that neither my absence will be so long nor your time so short but that we shall meet again and again. Neither your health nor your age admit reasonable doubts on your part. I shall certainly do myself the pleasure of seeing you at Buck-island before my departure, together with my daughters, who join me in assurances of esteem for you, and am Dear Aunt yours affectionately,

Th: Jefferson[7]

It is evident that there was a mutual regard between Jefferson and his aunt, Mary Randolph Lewis. In addition to this respect, this letter expresses an affection greater than was required by the formalities of kinship or the manners of that time. Apparently more or less the same feelings existed between Mary's

73

husband, Charles Lewis, Jr., of Buck Island, and Jefferson. When Charles Lewis, Jr. had written his will in 1782, he specified that "my friend, Thomas Jefferson," was to be one of the five executors.[8] Twenty-four years earlier, Charles Lewis, Jr. had performed a similar service for the Jefferson family in making the inventory of the estate of Peter Jefferson, Thomas's father.

In the next generation of Lewises, that of Col. Charles L. Lewis and Lucy, there was an air of equal warmth to Lucy, but a courteous reserve between Jefferson and Col. Charles L. Lewis, a coolness which was to become more marked in later years. Until Jefferson became president in 1801, the correspondence between Colonel Lewis and Jefferson dealt mainly with a few business affairs, but also included some items of a more personal nature. In 1790, on the day before he accepted the position of secretary of state, Jefferson sent to Colonel Lewis a settlement of the family estate in which Lucy was one of the beneficiaries. At the end of the letter Jefferson included the following personal remarks: "—I send you the pedigree of the horse Caractacus also the only two I have of the books your son desired. The others I either have not or are lent out. . . . Some of our neighbors are to come and dine with us tomorrow: we shall be very happy if you and my sister will be of the party."[9] Three days after the dinner party at Monticello, Jefferson left again, this time to fill the newly created office of secretary of state.

In one of his return visits to Albemarle a year or so later, he transacted a real estate sale in which Col. Charles L. Lewis was involved. Jefferson wrote of the affair to his Italian friend, Philip Mazzei. An excerpt from this letter reveals some information about both the fortunes and personality of Colonel Lewis. The subject of the letter was Jefferson's attempt to oblige Mazzei in selling Colle, a farm Mazzei owned in Albemarle.

> I sold Colle, when last in Virginia, to a Mr. Thomas. . . . I was made very happy by being able to get £250. for it, when I really had not expected more than £100. you can have no conception of the ruinous state in which it is. He [Thomas] has credit till Octob. next, but as I knew he was not to be depended on, I took a security as solid as can be desired, C. L. Lewis my brother in law. I gave both of them notice at the time that if the money was not paid at the day I should sue them: and I expected at the time I should have to sue, which will force a credit of another year. Still I thought it worthwhile to submit to that to get so advanced a price. C. L. Lewis is becoming one of our wealthiest people.[10]

One wonders why Jefferson expected to have to sue Thomas and Colonel Lewis in order to get his money. Jefferson said that he knew Thomas was not to be depended upon, and implied that Lewis was not reliable either, even though he was wealthy. Jefferson clearly expected his brother-in-law to try to avoid paying Thomas's note when it came due, despite his signing it as security for Thomas, a legally binding action. Perhaps Jefferson thought that Colonel Lewis was the sort of man who, in spite of his riches, would pay off his legal obligations with law suits. The matter was not quite that simple, in fact, for there were other financial claims against Mazzei's estate which might have cast doubt on the validity of the deed to Colle.

Nevertheless, Jefferson was right about Thomas and Lewis. It was four years before Jefferson got the money for Colle. In the meantime, Thomas and Lewis had sold the property to another man, realizing a profit of £125. The sale of Colle, which Jefferson reported to Mazzei with evident satisfaction in 1792, had turned into a wrangle during which Jefferson was forced to sue Colonel Lewis, and in turn be sued by another person who was also involved in the dispute.[11]

This was a situation that normally would not have enhanced friendly feelings, but it nevertheless appears that Jefferson did not become bitter or spiteful with his brother-in-law. He kept his distance from the Lewises, but he helped Colonel Lewis and the other members of his family whenever he could. An example of this concern is a letter Jefferson wrote to Craven Peyton at a time when Lewis was deep in financial trouble:

> In my letter of Oct. 8 covering a Columbia bank note for 1248[d]. 27[c] I recommended to you to dispose of it without delay. I had more reasons for this than would have been proper then to mention. That bank is now in a crisis which may end mortally. If that note is still in your hands or any where else so as not to have cleared us of all responsibility for it, if it be sent to me by return of the 1st or 2d post after you receive this, I shall be able to excuse it. Otherwise it will not be in my power. If you are entirely clear of it, let it go, unless it be in Colo. C. L. Lewis's hands, on whose account I would meet the inconvenience it would cost me to get it covered. I shall be glad to hear from you on this subject by return of post, as I have considerable anxiety about it.[12]

Peyton replied, in effect, that Jefferson's "considerable anxiety" was unnecessary, for he had passed the dubious note on to someone else. "Those notes which you mention was dispos[d] of

immediately aftar they were recev^d. & in case of failure in the bank it appears that the holder of the note must be the sufferer. It was requisite for me to put my Name on them."[13]

That same fall Jefferson had done a smaller favor for the Lewis family. This time it was for young Charles, the third son, who wished to borrow some books from Jefferson's library. In his request young Charles mentioned that Jefferson had previously made efforts to promote Charles's interest. Such efforts by Jefferson in reply to requests from the Lewis family became a repeated task. In nearly every communication between them after 1800, the Lewises asked Jefferson for various favors, which, in each case, were granted over the years in turn to Charles, Randolph, and Isham. Charles's letter reveals the limitations of his education. "It has been my wish for some time past to place myself in a situation for reading. In my endeavours to do this, I have ever found a difficulty in not having that scholastic knowledge necessary, but having devoted some time past to that purpose, and feeling myself as to that, in some degree prepared to prosecute my end; another difficulty arises, the want of books, to remove which, I am induced from necessity, though with gratitude in full recollection of your past endeavours to promote my interest, which perhaps ought to forbid it, to request your favor in the loan of such as I cannot otherwise procure."[14] When Jefferson's permission returned two days later, young Charles sent a slave boy to Monticello to get the books.[15]

One of the few known times when the Lewis family attempted to return Jefferson's favors they were nearly rebuffed. Their gesture was accepted reluctantly, if not with embarrassment. The incident involved an offer by Lucy and her daughters-in-law, the wives of Randolph and Lilburne, to knit some socks for Jefferson. The letter mentioning this affair was written by Martha, Jefferson's beloved and possessive daughter, who had married Thomas M. Randolph.

> Edgehill June 19 1801
> In an absence of 3 months I blush to think that this is the first time I have written to My Dear Father. . . . Your stockings are at last disposed of, but not to my satisfaction because I am sure they will not be so to yours. Aunt Carr after many ineffectual efforts to put them *out* acceded at last to the united and importunate entreaties of Mrs. Randolph and Mrs. Lilburne Lewis to let them knit them for you; and Aunt Lewis dining with me a few days after

and hearing of the failure of the means upon which I had counted in accomplishing my part of the under taking, insisted in a manner baffled resistance upon my letting her and her Daughters take them home and do them. It is a disagreeable piece of business, but not one to have been fore seen in the first instance and not to be avoided afterwards with out hurting the feelings and perhaps giving offence to those ladies. . . . Believe me with ardent affection yours.

M. Randolph[16]

Following her mother's death, and for the rest of Jefferson's life, Martha was closer to her father than any other member of the family. Her sense of duty to him and anticipation of his wishes are puzzling in their intensity.[17] There is no doubt that she knew his feelings. Martha's blunt comments that this affair of the stockings was a "disagreeable piece of business" and that it was "not to my satisfaction because I am sure they will not be so to yours," is a clear indication that Jefferson had deep reservations about accepting this personal favor from Lucy and her daughters-in-law. It may have been that Jefferson's sense of reticence about his personal affairs was a factor here. On the other hand, the situation may have arisen because he and Martha wanted to have as little to do with the Lewises as possible.[18]

More light can be thrown on this Jefferson-Lewis family relationship by noting some of the things that Jefferson did not do. When he went to France for five years, he did not leave his two young daughters at Buck Island, but rather with his sister-in-law, Elizabeth Wayles Eppes. When, from time to time, it was necessary to delegate the management of his farms and other business interests, he did not choose any of the Buck Island Lewises for these positions of trust, nor was Jefferson ever involved in any joint business ventures with them, other than the occasional sale of a slave or minor farm products. Other than the one dinner party mentioned, it is doubtful that there was much socializing between Monticello and Monteagle.

The memoirs of Isaac, one of Jefferson's Monticello slaves, mentions Jefferson's brother, all of his sisters, and all of their husbands, with the exception of Lucy and Charles L. Lewis.[19] Equally puzzling is the lack of any mention of the Buck Island Lewises in Sarah N. Randolph's book, *The Domestic Life of Thomas Jefferson*. A third book, containing the reminiscences of Edmund Bacon, Jefferson's farm manager, also makes no mention of the

77

Lewises of Buck Island. None of these three books is entirely objective in viewpoint. The memoirs of Isaac and Edmund Bacon were written long after the events took place; and, while Sarah Randolph had many of Jefferson's papers available for her use, her selection of them and their use in the text is somewhat biased. Nevertheless, one must conclude that the members of the Charles L. Lewis family were not frequent visitors at Monticello, nor were they members of the inner circle of Jefferson's family.

Jefferson's correspondence mentions many visits back and forth between the families of his sisters and daughters, some of them rather lengthy stays, but there is only one known instance in which such a visit was made to Buck Island after that generation was grown. Anna Scott Jefferson, Thomas's sister, had been living with her widowed sister, Martha J. Carr, while Jefferson was in France. Although Anna was somewhat "intellectually deficient," definitely roly-poly, and at the age of thirty-two an old maid, she appears to have been sweet-spirited, for she was beloved by Martha Carr and Jefferson.[20] In the spring of 1787, Anna visited the Lewises at Buck Island, apparently to help them with a siege of illness. Martha Carr reported the results of the interlude to Jefferson:

> A S J left me last spring to make a charitable visit to Buck Island with a promise of being back in a few weeks. She was not as good as her word. I grew uneasy at the length of her stay, wrote letter after letter pressing her to return but to no purpose. Toward the last of October I was surprised with the news of her Marriage with Mr. Hastings Marks. As he has been for some years an Inhabetant of Charlottsville you may perhaps know him. I do not but what Information I have been able to get by hearsay I will give to you. He is said to have led a very Irregular life, has little or no fortune but is very capable of book keeping and has been of late extremely industreous. I heard she had no intention of visiting me, poor Girl. I suppose she did not expect she could have my approbation to the step she had taken, but so far from my feeling aney resentment or not wishing for her society, I find compasion added to my tenderness for her.[21]

In response to this news, Jefferson wrote two very warm and cordial letters of congratulation to Anna and her bridegroom, Hastings Marks. He did not mention Martha Carr's dismay, nor the Lewises of Buck Island.[22]

There were many other times in letters to the various

members of his family when he might naturally have mentioned Lucy or her family, but did not. One such letter he wrote to Anna from England the year before her marriage. He ended the letter by asking her to remember him to his two sisters, Martha Carr and Mary Bolling, and their families.[23] He did not ask to be remembered to his only other sister, Lucy, or her family. Buck Island was not so far that Anna could not have passed on the word of such a remembrance.

Jefferson was not as close to Lucy Lewis's family as he might have been, nor was he favorably impressed with some of the Lewises' other kinfolk. He heartily disliked Colonel Lewis's sister, Elizabeth Henderson, and her family. Speaking of a certain brother-in-law of Colonel Lewis, Jefferson said, "I knew he was not to be depended on."[24] Another of Charles L. Lewis's brothers-in-law, because of unfortunate habits, became "overwhelmed with debt, stripped of his property, declared insane . . . and was placed in the asylum." For a period of over five years Jefferson had tried unsuccessfully to collect a small debt from this man.[25]

On another issue, Jefferson and the Lewises held opposing attitudes. For much of his life, and certainly after 1780, Jefferson felt that the Presbyterian church, and especially its clergy, was intolerant.[26] In later years this viewpoint hardened into the opinion that of all clergymen the Presbyterians were the "loudest" and the most "tyrannical and ambitious."[27] In his old age, Jefferson noted that there was a "cloud of fanaticism" in the atmosphere of the country. He said, "This must be owing to the growth of Presbyterianism. The blasphemy and absurdity of the five points of Calvin, and the impossibility of defending them, render their advocates impatient of reasoning, irritable, and prone to denunciation."[28] Although the Lewises were staunch Presbyterians, it is unlikely that Jefferson had them in mind when he wrote this condemnation, for his spleen was primarily directed at the doctrine and clergy of this sect.

In general, Jefferson's relationship to the family of his sister Lucy did not appear to be enthusiastic. His scanty correspondence with them was always correct, warm to Lucy, but more often quite matter-of-fact with the men of the family. One letter is typical. Apparently Colonel Lewis had dunned Jefferson about the settlement of Peter Jefferson's estate, from which Lucy would receive five pounds. Jefferson replied with veiled exasperation, "You may rest assured that yours shall be of the first monies he [the executor] pays." And while on the subject of money, Jefferson continued, bringing up a five-year-old debt owed him by the Buck Island plantation: "I am sent back again to you by Mr. Edward Moore for the amount of the smith's work entered in my books in the name of Isham Lewis, but done in fact as he says for the plantation at Buckisland of which Isham had then the direction. The amount is 3-9-9 with interest from the year 1785. If you can settle between yourselves who is to pay it I shall be satisfied so that somebody does it."[29] Jefferson ended the letter with his customarily courteous closing, "I am Dear Sir your affectionate humble ser[t]." Jefferson may have felt a twinge of irony as he wrote it, but his patience, which is evident in this letter, was characteristic of other dealings he had with the Lewises. In many of his contacts with them, he played the role of protector or did them certain favors. For Charles L. Lewis he salvaged a colonel's commission and tried to save him from a bad bank note. At Randolph's request Jefferson bought a slave family at a time when he could not afford it. For Charles he did several favors, among them lending him books and money. He would do as much for Isham in the future. No written record has yet been found to prove that Jefferson did any special favors for Lilburne. There is no doubt, however, that they were well acquainted.[30]

In trying to ascertain Jefferson's opinion of his relatives, the Lewises, the factor of genetic inheritance cannot be avoided. The inbreeding that resulted from a succession of first-cousin marriages in the Lewis family is notable. These marriages mixed and remixed the Lewis family with the Randolphs and the Jeffersons. Even though Jefferson's mother and father were not consanguine, their children were not uniformly capable. Of Jefferson's one brother and six sisters who reached maturity, none of them even remotely approached his intelligence, except Jane, who died in her mid-twenties. One sister, Elizabeth, was markedly retarded. His younger brother, Randolph, although not as deficient as Elizabeth, was simple-minded, and Randolph's twin sister, Anna Scott Jefferson, was "deficient in intellect."[31] It is as though, through a quirk of inheritance, he possessed all of the portions of brilliance that might have fallen to his brother and sisters.

In his own children as well, Jefferson was unfortunate, for out of five that were born, three died in infancy. Modern medicine might well have saved them to live normal lives, but it is a speculative possibility that genetic traits played some part in their untimely deaths. Jefferson himself was a victim of severe recurring headaches, and his grandson, Francis W. Eppes, suffered seizures that were described to Jefferson by his daughter, Martha. "Little Francis is doing well but it is in the best health allways that he has been attacked with those dreadful fits; I cannot help but fearing them to be epileptic. The noise in the throat the foaming at the mouth and drawing back of the head certainly bear a much greater resemblance to that than convulsions which My aunt's children have been subject to."[32]

There is no record of genetic flaw in the ancestry of Jefferson's father, Peter, but his mother, Jane Randolph, was from a lineage of mixed distinction and tragedy. The Randolph family of Virginia was one of the largest, oldest, wealthiest, and thoroughly intermarried dynasties of the colonial aristocracy. Jefferson's competent and respected daughter, Martha, married Thomas Mann Randolph, a young man of promise who in later years became increasingly temperamental until, before his death, he had lost his reason.[33] Martha made cryptic reference to certain Randolph traits in her son: "I see enough of the Randolph character in him to give me some uneasiness as to the future."[34] Thomas Mann Randolph's second cousin, John Randolph of Roanoke, was a man of unquestioned but erratic brilliance. His physical impotence was probably brought on by an endocrine imbalance.[35] He lived alone for long periods and suffered fits of intense depression that he sought to relieve with alcohol and, in later years, morphine.[36] At times his sanity was suspect.

At an earlier time these two tragic cousins had been close observers of an affair that brought disgrace on the Randolph family when it was revealed in full detail to a pleasantly scandalized southern society. A brother of John Randolph, Richard, had married a sister of Thomas M. Randolph, and another sister had gone to live with the couple. In time the unmarried sister bore a child sired by Richard, her brother-in-law. This couple, regarded as incestuous, was accused and tried for the murder of the child. The case was not proved against them, and Richard died shortly thereafter, a victim of poisoning.[37] Jefferson's daughter, Martha, testified as a witness at this trial of her sister-in-law.

Jefferson, who himself had Randolph blood, was thrown with others of that family all his life. That the Randolphs were social aristocrats there can be no doubt, but whether they all possessed the "virtue and talents" of "natural aristocrats" is questionable.

Jefferson was perceptive. Speaking of his mother's family, he implied that their prestige was based on wealth and birth. "They trace their pedigree far back in England and Scotland, to which let everyone ascribe the faith and merit he chooses."[38]

Jefferson's relationship to his mother is a mystery. In the incredible profusion of written material that he left, there is scarcely a mention of her. In his autobiography, which he wrote at the age of seventy-seven, he recorded the date of her marriage and the sentence quoted above regarding her pedigree. When Jefferson was thirty-three, his mother died. Near the end of a newsy letter to a member of the family he casually mentioned the fact in the following lines: "The death of my mother you have probably not heard of. This happened on the last day of March after an illness of not more than an hour. We suppose it to have been apoplectic."[39] He had also noted her death in his account book, saying only that she had died at eight o'clock that morning in her fifty-seventh year.[40] If Jefferson ever spoke or wrote more about his mother's death, none of it is known. Seven years before, his mother's house at Shadwell had burned to the ground. Jefferson referred to the fire as "my late loss," lamenting the destruction of his papers and library. He did not mention any inconvenience his mother might have suffered.[41]

Except for the business details of Jefferson's management of his mother's affairs, the few items mentioned above compose nearly all that is generally known about the relationship between Jane and her son, Thomas. Dumas Malone has stated that Jefferson probably did not place a very high value on her advice, and that the scarce mention of her was due to the consistent reticence he maintained in all his personal affairs.[42] John Dos Passos believed that Jane's education was probably limited to the subject of household management, and added that there was "something strangely frigid about the scanty references to his mother that may betoken real dislike."[43] In contrast to this, Jefferson's love for his sister Jane and his wife was deep and rich, and his grief at their deaths was profound. His emotional attachment to his daughters, especially Martha, was almost obsessive.

One wonders how much of "the Randolph character" was evident in Jefferson's mother, and also if his coolness toward her might have been a result of characteristics he associated with the Randolph family, traits that perhaps he thought were heritable. As a scientist Jefferson was well aware of the principles of selective breeding, and lamented in a letter that "man, who while with his domestic animals he is curious to improve the race, by employing always the finest male, pays no attention to the improvement of his own race, but intermarries with the vicious, the ugly, or the old, for considerations of wealth or ambition. . . . Experience proves, that the moral and physical qualities of man, whether good or evil, are transmitted in a certain degree from father to son."[44]

If Jefferson were secretly worried about the Randolph blood in his own family he would have been aware of its presence in the Charles L. Lewis family, for Lewis's mother, Mary, was the sister of Jefferson's mother, Jane. It was through these sisters that the Randolph blood was first introduced into the Lewis and Jefferson families. In the next generation the Lewis and Jefferson families were joined by two first-cousin marriages: Charles L. Lewis married Jefferson's sister, Lucy, and Anna J. Lewis married Jefferson's brother, Randolph. The Randolph blood, and perhaps the "character" as well, was prominent in the children of these unions.

That Jefferson placed any importance on the presence of Randolph blood in his own and the Charles L. Lewis family is speculation. On this question Jefferson was silent. On other occasions as well, Jefferson did not express his opinion. One of Jefferson's grandsons noted this trait in a reminiscence. "He spoke only of the good qualities of men, which induced the belief that he knew little of them, but no one knew them better. I had formed this opinion, and on hearing him speak very favorably of men with defects known to myself, stated them to him, when he asked if I supposed he had not observed them, adding others not noted by me, and evincing much more accurate knowledge of the individual character than I possessed, observing 'My habit is to speak only of men's good qualities.' "[45]

The times when Jefferson mentioned the Lewises in his letters were so rare that the full range of his feelings about them is difficult to ascertain. He did, however, comment on aristocratic families, like the Lewises, whose wealth was based as much on birth as on natural talent. "I agree with you that there is a natural aristocracy among men. The grounds for this are virtue and talents. . . . There is also an artificial aristocracy, founded on wealth and birth, without either virtue or talents; for with these it would belong to the first class. The natural aristocracy I consider as the most precious gift of nature, for the instruction, the trusts, and government of society. . . . The artificial aristocracy is a mischievous ingredient."[46]

·9·

THE PLAN TO EMIGRATE

WHEN Colonel Lewis lost his fortune, his two youngest sons, Charles and Isham, shared the disaster with him. The land that Colonel Lewis had given Charles could have provided the young man with a modest livelihood, but he had sold it for five thousand dollars, which he soon spent. The Colonel's gift of land to Isham was little more than a token, and, like young Charles, Isham soon lost possession of his portion of the old Buck Island plantation. The education of these two sons appears to have been mediocre. They had no occupational skills, and their training and experience in business was limited to observing their father lose his fortune. The prospects for the future of these young men were not encouraging.

Charles was a little better off than Isham, however, for in 1806 Jefferson gave young Charles a commission as a lieutenant in the army. The story of Charles's army career is found in five letters from Jefferson's correspondence. The first was sent to Jefferson by Charles while the new lieutenant was in Baltimore waiting transfer to his first duty assignment.

Baltimore 29 Apl 1806

Dear Sir

At the request of my Mother I have purchased for her in this place a few articles, and knowing the uncertainty of their being safely conveyed in the mail, I have taken the liberty, (for which I hope you will pardon me) to send them to Washington by Col° Berbeck, with a request that you will let your servant carry them to Monticello, to which place I imagine you will shortly go. Uninteresting as it may be to you Sir, I cannot avoid presenting to your acceptance my respectful thanks for the commission with which you have lately honored me, and be assured that however thoughtless I may have been heretofore, it shall be my constant study so long as I continue in the U. S. service, to do that which will be most to my interest, and the interest of those by whom I have been promoted.

I am Sir respectfully
Y^rObt. Servt.
Ch. Lewis[1]

Why did young Charles feel he had to assure Jefferson that he would mend his ways? Charles may have felt guilty about his financial irresponsibility, or, on the other hand, he may have referred to an earlier incident in his life, his siring of the mulatto slave girl, Matilda.[2] Matilda, who was six years old by this time, was owned by Randolph, Charles's oldest brother, which indicates that Matilda's mother belonged to Randolph.[3] The flimsy structure of slave society was generally matriarchal in pattern, and in the absence of a recognized or legal father, the children stayed with the mother, and became the property of the mother's owner.

For a white man to have intercourse with a slave woman, though not unique or illegal in Virginia, and not uncommon in Albemarle, nevertheless would have been regarded as unsuitable for a person of Charles's class.[4] Matilda was born at about the same time that young Charles was preparing to marry his first cousin. Jefferson had noted the impending nuptials in a letter: "Nancy Jefferson is said to be about marrying Charles Lewis."[5] Matilda's birth may have been one reason the marriage never took place.

Two days after Charles first wrote to Jefferson from Baltimore, he wrote again, asking to borrow thirty dollars, and promised that the ever-obliging Craven Peyton would refund it.

Baltimore 1st May 1806

Dear Sir

Before I left Albemarle, I was not apprised of the expense attending a military dress &c, nor did I expect to have been detained here until monday next, it being the day appointed to sail, by the Capt of the vessel in which I shall go to N. Orleans, which will make the fourteenth day since my arrival at this place. I must therefore Sir reluctantly ask of you the loan of $30 until you get to Monticello, at which time it will be faithfully refunded by Mr. C. Peyton to whom I will write so to do, should you be disposed to favor this request, which would be thankfully accepted by Sir

Y^r. Obt. Servt.
Ch Lewis[6]

The three letters that follow reveal the final events of Charles's army career.

Monticello May 26. 06.

Dear Sister

I received lately by post from your son Charles, then at Baltimore, the packet which I now send you and hope it will get safely to hand. I believe he was destined to New Orleans, altho it is more probable he will go to some of the more healthy stations; perhaps Fort Adams, where the main body of our troops are by this time, and will probably remain.

I intended to have rode down to see you this week, but have been taken with a lameness in the knee, which scarcely permits me to walk out of the house. Whether it will leave me before I must set out for Washington is uncertain, as that must be within a week. I hope your health is better than it has been, altho you are approaching, as I am already arrived, at the age where firm health is not usually our lot, still mine is good. Present my friendly respects to Col° Lewis and my salutations to the family, and be assured yourself of my constant and tender affections.

Mrs. Lucy Lewis   Th: Jefferson[7]

Monteagle May 26. 06.

dear Brothar

The receipt of your lettar to day, gave me much real pleasure, but your presents hear much more, if your health woud of permitted, which I hope will, before you leave us, as to mine I enjoy more perfect health, thin I have done for many years past. The packett you was so kind as to send from Charles to gethar with a positive asshearance from him of his constant application to his present occupation, has given the family great pleasure, and has laid them undar perpetual obligations to those whom have placed him in his presant pleasant situation. Mr. Lewis begs you will accept his worm respects. And be leav me to be with real esteem

Lucy Lewis[8]

Washington Oct. 7, 06.

Dear Sir

To me has fallen the painful duty of communicating to you intelligence which came to me by the post of yesterday evening. In a letter from Mr. Parmelee Commissioner of land claims in Orleans, dated Opelousas Aug. 28. is the following paragraph. 'Charles Lewis, a Lieut. in the US. army came to this place the latter part of July last, on his way to Natchitoches. The fore part of this month he was siesed with a severe inflammation in his head, of which he died the 12th instant. I am induced to make this communication by being informed that he was your nephew.' In another letter from Govʳ. Claiborne dated Natchitoches Aug. 28 he says 'in addressing you at this time I have to announce an event, which, unpleasant as it may be, is nevertheless proper to acquaint you of. Lieut. Lewis of the army who I learn was your nephew, died a few days since at Camp Hamilton in the county of Opelousas. He had lately joined the army, & was on his arrival in good health, but was soon hurried into another world by a violent fever. During his illness he had the best medical assistance which the country afforded, and experienced all the friendly attentions which a benevolent society could render. Lieut. Lewis promised to make an excellent officer, & his death is sincerely lamented.' These paragraphs contain every word I have received on the subject, so that it is not in my power to add a single detail to them. Experience in the school of affliction has taught me that words give no consolation: that time & silence are the only medicines for grief. From them alone, yourself & my afflicted sister can receive alleviation; and praying you to present her by tenderest affections, I offer you my friendly salutations & assurances of great regard.

Col° Charles L. Lewis   Th: Jefferson[9]

Young Charles had died unmarried and without lawful issue. This, according to the deed Colonel Lewis had written four years before, gave 650 acres of land to Charles's sisters. However, since that deed had been written in 1802, both Charles and Colonel Lewis had sold their claims in the land to Craven Peyton. These conflicting claims were still unsettled eleven years later.

Young Charles's death was not the only source of grief for the Lewis family that fall. Elizabeth, one of Lucy's younger daughters, died just a month after Charles. Craven Peyton, who was to the Lewis girls "as the most just and affectionate farthar," wrote the news to Jefferson from Pennsylvania. "Two of Col° Lewis daughtars & myself was attacked with the fevar about 15 days ago.—Betsy Lewis whom I carried to Bethlehem to school, with my little Daughtar, was not receaved by the Director because she was two years Oalder than their rules admitted of. She expared on the twelvth day, her sustar & myself are both very low now."[10]

Even though 1806 was a sad year in many ways for the Lewises, the two oldest sons, Randolph and Lilburne, were somewhat better off than the other members of the family. During the period that saw Colonel Lewis's wealth and property dwindle away, Randolph and Lilburne both managed to keep and even increase their modest wealth. In the ten years since Randolph had married, he had more than doubled his holdings in slaves and horses. At the same time, Lilburne, whose 830-acre section of land adjoined Randolph's, owned eight slaves and five horses.[11] Although Lilburne owned slightly more land than Randolph, his land was rougher and had fewer acres suited for cultivation. It was appraised in the tax rolls at about two-thirds the value of Randolph's tract. Both Randolph and Lilburne were well established in Albemarle County in 1803; Lilburne was well up in his twenties, and had three children, while Randolph was thirty, and having been married longer, had at least four children. Both brothers had served the county as jurors, and Randolph on several occasions had been assigned by the county court to lay out or supervise new roads. The brothers were familiar with business procedures and community affairs. They had survived a decade of agricultural disaster that had ruined not only their father but also many other wealthy plantation owners. That Randolph and Lilburne were able to make a living on their plantations speaks well for their ability, for if their land was typical of Albemarle as a whole, the fields had been badly used and were nearing exhaustion. Randolph and Lilburne may have had sources of income other than their farms. Information about them is scanty, but it is apparent that they were not wholly satisfied with their lives in Albemarle.

The will of their grandfather, Charles Lewis, Jr. of Buck Island, specified that their grandmother, Mary, should hold a lifetime interest in the land that their father had given them. Randolph and Lilburne owned every legal right to the land except that of selling it during their grandmother's lifetime. At the end of October 1803, Mary died at the age of seventy-eight, having outlived her husband by twenty-one years. Randolph and Lilburne were now free to sell their farms if they wished, and Lilburne wasted no time. Within six weeks of Mary's death he had sold all his land, and shortly afterward moved away from Albemarle County. The timing of this sale indicates that Lilburne had planned the sale and move earlier, and had been waiting for the old lady to die. The buyer of Lilburne's farm was Hugh Nelson, a prominent and wealthy lawyer who had recently moved to Albemarle. The purchase price is not known, but when Nelson resold the property twelve years later, he received $13,500 in payment.[12]

Lilburne's residence for the next four years was Hanover County, Virginia. The records of that county were destroyed during the Civil War, making it difficult to learn much about this

period in Lilburne's life. Exactly where or how he lived is unknown, but he spent some time in Richmond, and made one trip
to Kentucky. Elizabeth bore him two more children, a daughter
in 1804 and, in 1807, a son, their fifth child. Whatever his occupation was, Lilburne was able to make a living from it, for in
1807 he bought property in Kentucky worth over eight thousand dollars. Evidently he had been able to save some of the
money he had received from Nelson four years before.

Randolph continued to live at Buck Island for two years after
Lilburne moved away in 1803, but it was a period of declining
fortune for him. In 1804 he borrowed nearly $900 from the
Carr family.[13] They carried some of Randolph's other expenses
on an open account until September 1805, when his debts were
due. By then Randolph owed them nearly $1,500. Randolph's
financial situation was beginning to resemble that of his father a
few years before. In 1805, Randolph sold nine of his fifteen
slaves, and the day after his debt to Carr was due he sold to one
David Michie all of his eight hundred acres of land "called and
known by the name of Buck Island." Randolph did not sell the
family burial plot, "one quarter of an acre around the old graveyard between the garden and the mill pond." Michie, an enterprising lawyer and merchant in Milton, had invested in real
estate in several parts of Albemarle County. He made Buck Island his home, became sheriff in 1812, and in later years became
involved in lengthy legal disputes with Jefferson over property
at Milton in which they both claimed an interest. Michie paid
Randolph nearly $14,000 for this last sizable piece of the Lewis
family property in Albemarle.[14] Randolph and Mary then
moved to her parents' plantation, the Byrd, in Goochland
County, where they lived for two years.

Unlike his father, Randolph had sold out before going under
financially. Presumably he paid his debts in Albemarle, perhaps
spent some of the money he received from Michie for living
expenses, and still had $9,100 left in 1807, for he spent that sum
to buy land in Kentucky. He and Lilburne had decided to take
their families and emigrate to this reputed Garden of Eden west
of the great mountains. Fertile land at a low cost was scarce in
Virginia by 1807, but in Kentucky the opposite was true; great
areas of rich virgin land were open for sale at cheap prices.
There were huge forests of fine timber, unlimited wild game,
and an established water transportation system to carry farm
products down the rivers to New Orleans and the markets of the

world. The natural wealth of Kentucky had been widely discussed in Europe and America after the publication of John Filson's history of Kentucky in 1784, and had been a matter of common knowledge in Virginia for at least three decades before that time.[15]

Following the close of the Revolution, emigration to the west was given impetus by the state of Virginia which, short of cash and possessing tremendous quantities of land, paid off many of her soldiers with grants of land. These land grants touched off a wave of migration into this western wilderness. Many grantees whose ties with eastern Virginia were too strong for them to want to move put their Kentucky grants up for sale on a speculative market that was wildly active.

When Randolph and Lilburne decided to emigrate to Kentucky with their families, this westward movement of settlers had been going on for more than two decades. What had been a few settlers on horseback or afoot in 1780, two decades later became a flood of 20,000 people a year in wagons, barges, on horse, and afoot. During the ten years ending in 1800, the population of Kentucky increased from 7,000 to 221,000.[16]

Kentucky was no longer a wilderness devoid of people. Many of her new citizens were from Virginia and had known each other in the old dominion. Woods's history of Albemarle contains a partial list of over three hundred heads of families who moved to Kentucky from that one Virginia county. The total number of individuals must have been well over a thousand. The decision of the Lewis brothers to emigrate to Kentucky was not remarkable in any way; it was a choice being made by many Virginians. When Randolph and Lilburne arrived in Kentucky, they would find acquaintances and close kin scattered all across the state.

It is not known which of the two brothers first decided to emigrate to Kentucky, nor can we tell when it became definite that they would go together. It is probable that Randolph had decided to go to Kentucky before he sold Buck Island. That he moved in with his in-laws at the Byrd does not suggest a permanent arrangement. Early in 1806, Lilburne made a trip from Virginia to western Kentucky, apparently to inspect the property the brothers intended to buy. He reached his destination on the Ohio River in west Kentucky in January of 1806, and returned to Albemarle within two months.[17] By the end of March 1806, it was general knowledge among their acquaintances in Virginia that the two brothers intended to emigrate to Kentucky.[18]

In the spring of the next year Randolph's and Lilburne's preparations for the move increased in tempo. The date for the departure was tentatively set. Randolph wrote to his Uncle Jefferson asking him to buy a slave family that would be split up if Jefferson did not buy the wife and children:

> Dear Uncle   Byrd April 20th 1807
> The purport of this is from a solicitation which your man Moses was desirous I should make known to you, of my removing the 1st of October next to the State of Kentuckey on the Ohio River five miles from the junction of the Cumberland River, I am persuaded that there is a very great regard and esteem existing with Moses and his wife, and my wish is, for them to be accommodated by some method of remaining in this country as husband and wife; I have no doubt but what this is your wish also, that they should be gratified and indulged in this pleasure, the only method by which this gratification can be produced is by your approbation in the purchase of this Woman her age is 27 years, she is extremely healthy and faithful, she has too children both males, the first is six years old last Month, the other is four years old last February, and the Woman is now pregnant, the too boys I can assure you are large and healthy my object is not to acquire an extravagant sum for those Negroes, if your conclusion is to make a purchase of them, no difficulty will take place in fixing the value of them, this may be obtained by whatever arrangement you may conceive is right. Your answer will be readily received from the Post-Office of Columbia in Fluvanna
>
> > I am Dear Sir with great esteem your
> > Randolph Lewis
> > Goochland[19]

It was a rare thing for Jefferson to buy slaves. He owned a large number of negroes, and from time to time was forced to sell some of them to pay his debts.[20] Jefferson's reluctance to buy these three slaves from Randolph is evident in Jefferson's reply to Randolph's request.

> Dear Sir   Monticello Apr. 23. 07.
> Yours of the 20th is received, nobody feels more strongly than I do the desire to make all practicable sacrifices to keep man & wife together who have imprudently married out of their respective familes, & I had accordingly told Moses that if it should be your pleasure to sell his wife, reasonably, I would buy her when I could with convenience; for I assure you that nobody is less able to make

purchases than myself, or more pressed for money, or time for its paiment. The epoch of your departure would find me illy able to meet any considerable *new* engagement, but if you will be so good as to say to me in one word, what is the lowest sum you will take for the woman & her children, I will in like manner say in one word, yea or nay. I prefer deciding for myself on the price I may consent to pay, rather than leave to valuers to fix one which may be beyond my convenience or approbation. I would ask you also to fix what times of paiment would be necessary, as, to avoid disappointments, I must take them into calculation. You may perhaps leave some debts to be paid after you are gone, which may bring the object more within my compas. I suppose you would prefer that the delivery of the persons should be about the time of your departure when I shall be probably here, as I expect to be here during the months of August & September. With every wish for your success and happiness I salute you with friendship and esteem.

Mr. Randolph Lewis   Th: Jefferson[21]

During the next week or two Randolph and Jefferson continued negotiations. They set the price of Mary and her children at about $500, and since Randolph owed that amount, if not more, to a certain Walter Key, Jefferson agreed to obligate himself to Key for $500 worth of Randolph's debts.[22] The transaction was finally completed, and the president noted it in his account book. It was a paternalistic duty that Jefferson could not conveniently afford.[23]

About two months after the sale of the slave Mary and her sons to Jefferson, Randolph and Lilburne met with George Pickett in Richmond, Virginia, to complete the purchase of the land in Kentucky, where the two men intended to live for the rest of their lives. At fifty-four years of age, Pickett was one of the most influential and prosperous businessmen in Richmond. He was a member of the firm of Pickett, Pollard, and Johnson, and dealt extensively in public securities and the buying and selling of western lands.[24] Pickett's business agent in Kentucky was George Trotter of Lexington.

Pickett sold the Lewis brothers two tracts of land that fronted on the Ohio about three miles above the junction of the Cumberland and Ohio rivers. For his home place, Lilburne bought the southernmost tract of 1,000 acres, and Randolph and Lilburne together bought a second tract of 1,000 acres that lay a mile and a half upstream from Lilburne's farm. The brothers divided this northernmost tract, each taking half. Randolph was to live on one of these two 500-acre tracts. Randolph also purchased three separate tracts of land, which were located an average of fifty miles from the place where he intended to live in Livingston County.[25] These three tracts were not adjacent to each other; two of them contained 1,000 acres each, and the third was 1,333½ acres in size. Randolph intended to sell some of this land as soon as he could, for with only seven slaves, he could not possibly have farmed it, even if it had been located next door. Randolph's reason for buying these three parcels is unknown. Pickett may not have been willing to sell the Lewis brothers the lands on the Ohio without unloading the other three tracts on them; or, on the other hand, it may have been that Randolph took the initiative and, believing he could make a profit in a resale, willingly bought the tracts for speculative purposes, as Pickett himself had done.

All of the land the Lewis brothers bought had originally been military land grants. Pickett bought three of the tracts from the original grantees, another from the second man to own it, and of the last tract Pickett was the fourth successive owner.

Lilburne paid over $8,300 for the 1,500 acres in his two farms, and Randolph paid nearly $9,100 for the 3,833⅓ acres he bought. Of the $9,100 Randolph had spent, $7,400 were invested in the three tracts he hoped to resell. It was money tied up in speculation, money frozen in one of the least liquid of all assets, land.

Randolph had sold his hard-used Buck Island plantation with its improvements at the rate of $17.60 per acre. In west Kentucky he bought virgin land without improvements for an average of $2.38 per acre. Lilburne had paid an average of $5.50 per acre for land that was generally superior and better located than Randolph's.

By the time the brothers had bought the land in Kentucky, their parents had evidently decided to go with them. Craven Peyton, realizing that Colonel Lewis was soon to leave Albemarle for good, became distressed at the complexity of his unsettled business affairs with his father-in-law. Early in August, Peyton wrote to President Jefferson, who was then at Monticello, asking Jefferson to mediate and help settle the accounts between Peyton and Colonel Lewis.[26] Jefferson's reply clearly shows the tremendous pressure that Jefferson was under at this time. Just a few weeks earlier, the British frigate, Leopard, had violated American neutrality by raking the American warship, Chesapeake, with cannon fire until she lay helpless. The British then boarded her and carried off four sailors they claimed were British deserters. The nation was enraged. During this same time, the treason trial of Aaron Burr was in progress in Richmond.

Not only was the pressure of Jefferson's official duties extreme, but, as he had mentioned in his letter to Randolph four months before, his own financial affairs were in bad condition. Unknown to Jefferson then, he would never again be entirely free from the threat of personal financial ruin. Jefferson's reply to Peyton is a masterpiece of tact, for, in spite of Jefferson's disclaimer, he was experienced in business accounting, and was a lawyer as well. Jefferson's reluctance to become involved in the Lewis family troubles is obvious if unexpressed.

Dear Sir   Monticello Aug. 10.07.
I was so much engaged in preparing for a post that I could not answer by your servant the letter he brought, requesting me to settle the accounts between Col° Lewis & yourself. I might state as a good reason for declining it, that I am by no means sufficiently versed in matters of account to undertake that office with the necessary consciousness that I could properly discharge it. But independant of this, my excessive occupations render it quite impossible. In addition to the ordinary duties of the government which are heavier on me here, alone, than when at Washington with my associates, the extraordinary occurrences in the Chesapeake, the state of things that brings on, & the correspondence produced by the volunteer conscriptions, really occupy my pen through the day & my mind through the night, insomuch that tho' I am here, I cannot pay the least attention to my own affairs lying directly around me. Under these circumstances I hope Col°. Lewis & yourself will see the impossibility of my undertaking what you desire. I salute you with great esteem & respect.
Mr. Craven Peyton   Th: Jefferson[27]

Not all the Lewises were going west. Jane remained with Craven Peyton at Monteagle, and her sister Mary stayed behind to marry her double first cousin, the president's namesake nephew, Thomas Jefferson, Jr. Isham stayed behind in Virginia, too, but all the rest were leaving, three separate families: Randolph's; Lilburne's; and the colonel, Lucy, and their three daughters. Randolph and Lilburne were self-sufficient heads of

94

households, but their father and Lucy and their three daughters, the third family, was destitute. They had been dependent on Craven Peyton for the previous four or five years and, even though they were now moving to Kentucky, they still turned to Peyton for some of the basic necessities they needed to take with them for their comfort and survival.

Peyton agreed to let them have four aging slaves, three beds, a clock, two silver tankards, and a looking glass. Because of his involvement in Colonel Lewis's financial troubles, Peyton himself was having difficulty paying his own obligations. Consequently Colonel Lewis promised to pay Craven Peyton forty-two pounds (approximately $140) a year rent for the slaves and furniture.[28] The indenture was drawn up and signed six days before the journey was to begin, and on the day of departure, November 20, Isham's name was added to the document as the security for his father, pledging to pay Peyton the rent if his father did not.

It is clear that four aging slaves, three beds, a clock, looking glass, and two tankards did not comprise in themselves what Lucy described as "everything to make us comfortable." Lucy and the colonel undoubtedly had some of the many other tools and articles that they would need for frontier housekeeping. Perhaps Peyton gave them some free of cost, or their sons intended to provide them in Kentucky. No doubt on the eve of their departure all of the Lewises felt their prospects were favorable. Over five thousand acres of new land waited for them in Kentucky, and in it lay bright hope for the family wealth, prestige, and happiness. Lucy was optimistic when she wrote her letter of farewell to Jefferson.

Monteagle November 19th, 1807

My dear Brothar

I now take up my pen to bid you a dieu, supposing I nevar shall have the pleasure of again seeing you tomorrow we shall be on our way to the Mouth of the Cumberland Rivar, you may think very strange that Oald people take so great a Journey. Nearley all my children remove to that place and their desire for their parents to go appears very great. This is my only inducement to go, for I have seen more happines for the last five years hear, thin I ever saw the hole time before since my having a family, for in the last five years there was nothing that I wanted or that eathar of my Daughters wished for but what was got, and I do declare to you that Mr. Peyton has been to me as the most dutiful child and to my Daughters as long as they were undar his guidence, as the most just

95

and affectionate farthar, therefore you will see I have no othar reason for moving thin a wish to be with the bulk of my children, and aftar gitting to Cumberland my prospects are very bright, for a suppoart for Mr. Peyton, has furnished us with every thing to make us comfortable, but land and that the boys has promissed to give us. I feal much hurt at leaving two Brothears, for evar, and not seeing eathar, I wish you all the happiness that can possibly be expressed by an affectionate Sustar

Lucy Lewis[29]

·10·

THE TRIP TO KENTUCKY

THERE WERE two routes open to the Lewises for the trip west, both of which were in general use in 1807. One choice would have been to go southwest from Albermarle, following the valleys of the Allegheny Mountains to the southwest tip of Virginia, and then cross over the mountains into Kentucky at the Cumberland Gap or one of the other mountain passes. From there, the Wilderness Road led northwest into central Kentucky, where it connected with other trails going further west.[1] These so-called roads and trails were appallingly bad, in many places being little more than a blazed footpath or, where "improved," they were obstructed by stumps and rocks that had not been cleared away. There were no bridges. The streams were crossed by fords, and the rivers by primitive ferries. Paving of any sort, even gravel, was nonexistent, and the surface of the road, which in dry weather was ankle-deep in dust, became a river of mud when rain fell. The best time to depart on this route was early or midsummer, and the worst possible time to start would have been early winter, the time the Lewises chose to leave Albemarle.

The other choice open to the Lewis family was to make the trip by boat down the Ohio River. The roads leading from Albemarle north and then west to Pittsburgh were bad enough, but at least they were superior to those over the mountains and into Kentucky. By this river route it would be a trip of nearly 1,180 miles, 160 miles overland to Pittsburgh and 920 miles by river to the mouth of the Cumberland River in Kentucky. Travelers using the river route to the west usually scheduled their trip so that their boats would reach the falls, or rapids, at Louisville, during the months when the water level was high, and they could float over the falls in comparative safety.[2] Usually the water was high from late fall through the spring, and was lowest during the summer and early fall.

The removal of the Lewises from Albemarle on November 20 would have enabled them to reach their departure point on the river by wagon, embark on their flatboat, and float down the Ohio in time to clear the falls on the crest of the winter and spring rise. This same high water would have lessened the

97

danger from rocks, snags, and shoals that were a peril in some other places on the Ohio during periods of low water. The Lewises would have known that under ideal conditions they could float from Pittsburgh to the falls at Louisville in ten days,[3] and reach their new homes five days later, averaging about fifty miles a day.[4] They would have enjoyed comparatively good shelter, for most barges were roofed over and enclosed along the sides. In this way, if all went well, they could transport their entire party, and all their belongings and supplies for the trip, without undue hardship. Upon their arrival in Livingston County, if their new homes were yet to be built, they could continue to live in the boats until their homes were ready. They could tie the boats directly to the river frontage of their own farms, and when they were through with the barges they could use the timbers from the boats to help construct outbuildings.

The problems of moving the three Lewis families to Kentucky must have been immense, for theirs was a sizable party of people. Assuming that they all went west together, there were six adults and fifteen children ranging in age from infancy to the late teens, and there were at least twenty slaves—close to forty people in the party, all requiring food and shelter.[5] There was livestock, as well, which had to be fed on the trip. Although cattle, hogs, sheep, and horses could have been bought after the arrival in Kentucky, it was customary for emigrants to take some of their animals with them to provide meat and milk during the trip, and to provide breeding stock after they reached their new homes.[6] Certainly the best horses would have been taken, for the pride that Virginians took in their blooded horse flesh is well known.

In addition to the people and livestock, there was a small mountain of baggage to be moved. A partial list of the possessions of just Lilburne's family indicates the magnitude of transporting the goods and baggage of all the Lewises to Kentucky. Lilburne had six bedsteads, three trunks, two bureaus, five tables, twelve chairs, ten crocks, two kettles, ten meat tubs, a whiskey barrel, linens, mirrors, clothes, farm equipment, small tools, tableware, and many other items of lesser size.[7] In addition to this baggage there was that of Randolph's family, of Colonel Lewis's family, and that of the slaves. It was well known that mountain trails could not compete with the Ohio River when household goods and supplies were to be transported, and it seems almost impossible to believe that the

Lewises would have left Albemarle so late in the fall if they intended to make the entire trip overland by wagon. That route was harrowing enough in summer, but the prospect of spending December and January on the trail, exposed to the winter storms and mountain wilderness with no shelter, is unthinkable when there was a better alternative. No evidence has been discovered to indicate that the Lewises traveled to west Kentucky by land. There is some indication, however, that they did make the trip by river.[8]

There was one inexpensive but vital item that the party would require for the trip, a small book published in Pittsburgh, called *The Navigator*. This river guide book was compiled and printed by Zadok Cramer, who sold it at the cost of one dollar at his bookstore on Market Street. Lilburne owned a copy. *The Navigator* contained detailed maps and written directions for travelers on the rivers. It described the channels, bars, islands, rocks, currents, and warned against places where danger existed. It listed the distance between landmarks on the river, as well as the mileage from these locations to Pittsburgh. With this book a cautious traveler could be his own river pilot. To have attempted the trip without either this guide book or previous experience would have been foolhardy. *The Navigator,* which was first published before the turn of the century, continued to be printed and revised by Cramer for two decades, after which it was copied and sold by other publishers for more than thirty years.[9]

Lilburne's copy of *The Navigator* gave the following advice about selecting a departure point for a downstream trip:

> The principal places where families ... prepare for embarkation, are Brownsville, (or Redstone) Pittsburgh, and Wheeling. There are people in each of those places, that make it their business to accommodate strangers descending the river, with every article they may want either in provisions, farming utensils, boats or other crafts, etc. at a cheap and reasonable price. There are large boatyards at each of these places, and their boats are generally well made and strong, the price of which varies according to their make, length and strength; one convenient for a family—between 30 and 40 ft. in length, costs from 1 dollar to 1 dollar and 25 cents per foot, making perhaps 35 dollars for a comfortable family boat, well boarded up on the sides, and roofed to within seven or eight feet of the bow: exclusive of this expense is the price of cable, pump, and fire-place, perhaps ten dollars more. . . .

The number of embarkations, and their conveniences, which take place at Brownsville, Pittsburgh, and Wheeling, depend much on the different stages of the water in the different seasons. . . . Boats can go from Pittsburgh at a much lower state of water than they can from Brownsville. . . . Pittsburgh is preferred as a place of embarkation to Wheeling, when boats can descend from it, for two reasons: first, it is about 45 miles nearer Philadelphia or Baltimore; and secondly, merchants and travelers say they are better accommodated here with storage for their goods, and all other conveniences they may stand in need of than they could be at Wheeling; therefore, they seldom go there, except in cases of very low water embarking either at Brownsville or Pittsburgh.[10]

Which one of these cities the Lewises chose for their port of embarkation is unknown, but Pittsburgh had better conveniences and was more often used by travelers than were the other two river towns.

The citizens of Pittsburgh manufactured or handled most of the goods needed by the residents of the Mississippi and Ohio valleys. There were warehouses, shipyards, hardware, glass, and shoe factories; publishing firms and bookstores; dealers and retailers of almost every article in use at that time.[11] Pittsburgh was the beginning, and New Orleans the end, of one of the great commerce and transportation systems of America, the river route of the Ohio and Mississippi. The volume of traffic and commerce on these rivers was immense. In 1807 New Orleans handled over five million dollars worth of western produce.[12] The greater part of the flow of the goods was downstream, although some products were carried upstream to market in keelboats that were towed or pushed against the current by manpower alone. Almost all the products manufactured east of the Allegheny mountains that were to be sold in the west were funneled through Pittsburgh, where they were loaded on several types of boats, to be floated down the Ohio to their destinations along the shores of the "western waters." To these finished products from the east were added the riches of the farms and forests—food, fiber, timber, fur, hides, and tobacco—which were bound for New Orleans and the markets of the world. Pittsburgh was actually an inland seaport that supplied most of the people who lived west of the Alleghenies.

The ship-building industry was one of the major elements of the thriving economy of Pittsburgh. Although the most skilled workmen had come there from the Eastern coast, all of the raw materials were local. Large forests of black walnut and white oak were nearby. Iron fittings were produced from ore in Pittsburgh; and hemp, which had become one of the leading cash crops in the Ohio Valley, supplied the numerous rope walks of Pittsburgh and other cities downstream. Pittsburgh did not have a monopoly on building boats and ships, for they were constructed in many locations: at Marietta, Ohio; Elizabeth, Pennsylvania; Cincinnati, Ohio; and as commerce increased, boatyards appeared at cities and towns all along the rivers. As the number of western emigrants grew, so did the demand for barges and boats. Pittsburgh became favored as a place of embarkation, and its boatyards prospered.[13]

There were three different types of boats built in these yards. The simplest were those used by families like the Lewises, who were going west with all their possessions to make a new home. Theirs was a one-way voyage, downstream, with no return intended. They required a boat with stability and great carrying capacity, one on which they could build cabins in which to live, and shelters to protect their baggage and livestock. They did not need a mobile boat, or one with sleek lines, designed to be maneuverable. Cost was a factor, and the construction, if solid, did not need to be complex. Once the settlers' barge had drifted to its destination, there was no possible way to get it back upriver to be resold. Most often these boats were broken up and the timbers used for other purposes.

Boats of this general type were called flatboats. This category included the boats used by the settlers, known as broadhorns or Kentucky boats, and the huge barges used for trade and commerce, which were variously called arks, flatboats, or New Orleans boats. All of these were flat-bottomed, with sides from 2 to 6 feet high. They were rectangular in shape, except for the ark, which sometimes had a pointed bow. They varied in length from 20 to 120 feet, and in width from 10 to 25 feet. When these commercial boats reached New Orleans and delivered their cargoes, they were sold for lumber, and the crews usually walked or rode home over the outlaw-plagued Natchez Trace.[14]

The shelters built on flatboats were of great variety. The New Orleans boats were, as a rule, covered over from front to back with a slightly arched roof that protected the cargo and provided a platform for the oarsmen at the long steering sweeps. The shelter of the broadhorns varied from a cabin at one end to a complete roof. The two long steering oars of the broadhorn were mounted, one on each side of the roof, and extended outward into the water, giving the vague impression of the horns of an animal; hence the figurative name. Usually there was a third steering sweep at the back of the boat.

Flatboats in their many sizes and designs were by far the most common boats on the river, but keelboats were also used in great numbers. These were the greyhounds of commerce, thin and long of line, manned by colorful crews of incredibly tough and rowdy men who were by their own boast "half horse and half alligator." They rowed the keelboats downstream and brought them back up against the current, laden with cargo both ways. The upstream trip was accomplished by the superhuman efforts of the crew, occasionally aided by a sail. When the water was low enough and the banks were clear, a cordelle, or rope, sometimes as long as one thousand feet, was stretched out to the bank. With this device the boats were dragged upstream by the crew, which struggled along the shore. "The immensity of this undertaking can hardly be realized at this time, but in early days before the introduction of steam, men cordelled heavily laden barges, unconscious of the enormity of the undertaking, and plodded along in quite good humor."[15] More often than using the cordelle, the crew pushed the keelboat upstream with long poles. Each of the crewmen would take his place in line at the front of the boat, brace his pole against the bottom of the river and, leaning against it, walk to the back of the boat along a narrow runway. He would then return to the bow and repeat the effort, time after time, all day long. Ninety percent of western riverborne freight went downstream with the current. The other ten percent was carried upstream in keelboats.[16]

Keelboats varied in length from 30 to 75 feet, and in width from 7 to 18 feet. Because of the curving lines of the hull, with its pointed bow and stern, and the cabin running the full length of the boat, the construction of the keelboat was more complicated than the flatboats, and its cost was higher, varying from $2.50 to $3.00 or more per running foot. On the downstream run the keelboats customarily carried a crew of nine or ten men who manned oars during the day, and at night the boat was allowed to drift. In this fashion 100 miles a day could be navigated. In contrast, the flatboats usually tied up to the shore at night, and their speed of travel, limited to the rate of the current, seldom exceeded three and a half miles an hour, or forty-two miles in a twelve-hour day. For the return trip the keelboat crew was approximately tripled in number but, even then, the best efforts yielded only ten or twenty miles progress a day against the flow of the river. In addition to freight, the keelboats frequently carried paying passengers.[17]

The third type of boat built in the shipyards of Pittsburgh and other river cities was a deep draft, ocean-going vessel, designed for trade on the high seas. A partial list of the seagoing craft built at Pittsburgh and the other shipbuilding cities of the upper Ohio, for the twelve years following 1800, included at least forty brigs, barks, schooners, armed galleys, and gunboats. "No little wonder was expressed in European ports by the advent of some of these vessels whose home ports lay so far in the interior of a continent."[18] After the hulls were built, they were loaded with cargo and floated to New Orleans, where the masts, sails, and rigging were installed. The ships were then ready for the sea. Some of these ships were as large as 450 tons, and drew from eight to twelve feet of water.

If the overland part of the Lewises' journey went smoothly they should have been able to reach their point of embarkation and been ready to cast off by mid-December. As Cramer pointed out, the fall navigating season usually began in October and continued until the first of December, when the ice began to form and travel stopped on the upper sections of the Ohio. In favorable years the river was not closed until the end of December. Usually the ice did not break up in the river until the middle of February, when the four-month spring navigating season began. Even if the river were not frozen over completely in December and January, it was likely that great floating slabs of ice drifted in the current and threatened the safety of the Lewis party. *The Navigator* was explicit in warning against this danger, which seemed to be the greatest when the boat had run aground or was tied up to the bank for an overnight stop or to obtain provisions.

> Prevent yourself being caught on the river among floating ice if possible, unless indeed, when it is very thin and thawing very fast: and even in this case it would be better to detain unless the river is clear of ice. And as frequent landing is attended with considerable loss of time and some hazard, you should contrive to land as seldom as possible; you need not even lie by at night provided you trust to the current, and keep a good look out: When you come to, the strength of your cable is a great safeguard. A quantity of fuel, and other necessaries should be laid in at once and every boat

ought to have a canoe or skiff along side to send on shore when necessary, or as a relief in case of accident. . . .

One other precaution perhaps is necessary in case you are on the river in time of ice, which above all other seasons is certainly the most perilous. If at any time, you are obliged to bring to on account of ice, great circumspection should be used in the choice of a place to lie in. There are many places where the shore projecting to a point throws off the cakes of ice towards the middle of the river, and forms a kind of arbour below. By bringing to, in such a situation and fixing your canoe above the boat, with one end strongly tied to the shore, and the other out in the stream sloping downwards so as to drive off the cakes of ice, which would otherwise accumulate, and tend to sink or drive your boat from her moorings, you may lie with a tolerable degree of safety.[19]

Cramer's warning was sound. In February of 1805 the *Lexington Gazette* reported that "upwards of 200 crafts of various sizes . . . passed the mouth of the Kentucky in the cakes of ice, some of them bearing persons in board frozen to death."[20]

Although the greatest danger the Lewises faced was the icy river itself, from time to time Indians fired at boats on the river. Among the previous generation of Kentucky settlers there had been constant terror of Indian massacres, captivity, and thefts. In 1808 this fear was largely gone, except in Livingston County, and while these horrors still occurred in the upper Indiana Territory, the Indians had become little more than an occasional nuisance along the Ohio. As late as 1811, Indians threatened river voyagers from the right or northern bank, but the Lewis family would not have needed to turn their broadhorn into a floating fort.[21] Thirteen years earlier, the keelboat packet service between Pittsburgh and Cincinnati had good cause to reassure its customers with a newspaper advertisement. "No danger need be apprehended from the enemy, as every person on board will be under cover made proof against rifle or musket balls, and convenient portholes for fireing out of. Each of the boats are armed with six pieces carrying a pound ball; also a number of good muskets, and amply supplied with plenty of ammunition: strongly manned with choice hands and the master of approved knowledge."[22]

The need for such elaborate defenses had ended a few months after this advertisement was run. The last large-scale invasion of Kentucky by hostile Indians took place in 1782, but smaller raids and bloody attacks on boats continued along the

Ohio River until "Mad" Anthony Wayne's victory in 1794, after which harassment by Indians was more of a rarity.[23]

The best hope the Lewises had for their safety and health was their boat. It was possible to make this trip in comparative comfort if the living quarters were large enough and well constructed. Aaron Burr made such a journey in ease and safety on the Ohio in the spring of 1805. "His boat was a rude floating house, or ark, sixty feet long and fourteen wide, containing four apartments, a dining room, a kitchen with fire-place, and two bed-rooms, all lighted by glass windows, and the whole covered by a roof, which served as a promenade deck. The cost of this commodious structure, he found, to his astonishment, was only a hundred and thirty-three dollars."[24]

The Lewis broadhorn must have been larger than Burr's boat and their voyage was begun in midwinter, not spring. If they had prepared well and their boat was not frozen in, there was little need for them to suffer except from confinement and dampness from leaks. Against this threat, voyagers were cautioned to take a pump as well as oakum, a caulking iron, and mallet, but even these precautions could not have eliminated the persistent dampness of the cold air and the threat of illness.

There are only two known fragments of writing still in existence that contain information about the progress of the family journey. They indicate that the Lewises endured considerable hardship. In a letter to Jefferson his granddaughter briefly mentioned Lucy's troubles. "Poor Aunt Lewis I believe had a dredful journey. Mr. Peyton received a letter from them after they had been gone ten weeks and they were 4 hundred miles from the place to which they were going."[25]

The letter that Lucy wrote to Craven Peyton has not been found, and it is doubtful if it still exists. Without it one can only guess at the nature of the things that made the journey so "dreadful." If the trip had gone well, with proper planning and no delays, the Lewises should have been able to travel from Buck Island to their point of embarkation in three weeks and drift downstream to the mouth of the Cumberland in another fifteen or twenty days. Instead of the ideal five weeks, they had spent ten weeks in mid-winter on the road and the river, and had finally been forced to tie up their boat and delay their trip while only a little over halfway to their new homes. An old memoir recalls that it was in Gallatin County, Kentucky, where this lengthy layover occurred, probably at the mouth of the Kentucky

River.[26] The settlement of Port William, incorporated fourteen years before, was located there, but had not yet grown to the status of a village.[27] Three years later a traveler described Fort William as "a small place consisting of about fifteen families. . . . We were informed that some of the country people still retain their vicious propensity for fighting, biting and gouging, and that they had lately introduced stabbing, a practice which had been learned at New Orleans; but the laws being very severe against these vices, the lawless were kept in check, and the state of society was improving."[28]

If Lucy or some of the others in the party had been so sick that they required help this would have been the place they chose to stop. About sixty miles up the Kentucky River, in the neighborhood of Frankfort, lived Colonel Lewis's sister, Elizabeth, the widow of Bennett Henderson.[29] Her home was established and medical help was available nearby in Frankfort. If illness was not the cause of their stop in Gallatin County, it may have been that they were caught there by ice or low water in the river, and they chose to tie up and visit their relatives until it was safe to travel again.

Whatever the cause of their stop in mid-voyage, they could have avoided the inconvenience and much of the discomfort if they had left Albemarle on the first of October, as Randolph had originally planned, instead of seven weeks later. Better yet, they could have waited until early spring.

When the Lewises finally cast off from the mouth of the Kentucky River in the spring for the last part of their trip, they would pass only one more good-sized town, Louisville. Behind them were Steubenville, Wheeling, Marietta, Cincinnati, and other lesser towns. It was an easy two-day float, scarcely seventy miles, from Gallatin County to the head of the rapids. Bear Grass Creek flowed into the river at Louisville, forming a deep and safe harbor that was free from the treacherous currents found just below this anchorage.[30] Here the pilots were picked up. For a fee of two dollars they guided the boats through the rapids. These pilots were county officials, and were experienced in their work. The act establishing the office of Falls Pilot mentioned certain abuses that had caused grief for many travelers a few years before. "Great inconveniences have been experienced and many boats lost in attempting to pass the rapids of the Ohio for want of a Pilot, and from persons offering their services to strangers to act as Pilots, persons who were by no means

106

qualified for this business."[31] Unlicensed persons posing as pilots were fined ten dollars.

One articulate traveler passed through the rapids in a keelboat a few years later and left this description of the experience:

> As you approach the head of the rapids, the mighty stream rolls on in a smooth unbroken sheet, increasing in velocity as you advance. The business of preparation creates a sense of impending danger: the pilot, stationed on the deck, assumes command; a firm and skillful helmsman guides the boat; the oars, strongly manned, are vigorously plied to give the vessel a *momentum* greater than that of the current, without which the helm would be inefficient. The utmost silence prevails among the crew; but the ear is stunned with the sound of rushing waters: and the sight of waves dashing, and foaming, and whirling among the rocks and eddies below, is grand and fearful. The boat advances with inconceivable rapidity to the head of the channel—"takes the *Chute*"—and seems no longer manageable among the angry currents, whose foam dashes upon her deck, but in a few moments she emerges from their power, and rides again in serene waters.[32]

This voyager had the advantage of riding in a keelboat, which had a moderate amount of steerage way. The Lewises, however, were in a flatboat, which was almost unmanageable in critical situations. It could make a successful transit of the rapids only if it entered swift water at exactly the right place, or if the water were high enough in flood to clear them over or around the worst of the rocks. This man shot the rapids at the end of April. It is probable that the Lewises passed the falls two months earlier, when the water was usually at a higher stage. As *The Navigator* stated: "The Rapids of the Ohio are hardly to be perseived by a navigator in times of high freshes, unless by the superior velocity of the boat. When the water is low the greater part of the rock becomes visible and it is then that the passage becomes dangerous."[33]

If the Lewis party took the time to go into Louisville when they were at the falls, they would have found a town of about a thousand white males over sixteen years plus their families, over two thousand blacks, and eleven retail stores. Many of the houses were built of brick and contained three stories. On Wednesdays and Saturdays nearby farmers brought their produce to a busy central market house. The city also boasted a two-story courthouse, a theater, and a newspaper.[34]

In spite of this progress the city was stamped with the roughness of the frontier. Louisville lacked the prim piety and order of the settlements of New Englanders at Marietta and Gallipolis, or the industriousness of the citizens of Cincinnati. A petulant acquaintance of John James Audubon remarked of Louisville that "science or literature has not one friend in the place." This was not entirely true, for Audubon mentioned the names of many cultured and hospitable families who were friendly to him during his three-year residence in Louisville.[35]

Despite some signs of refinement, the city had found it necessary in 1806 to pass a law forbidding the citizens to throw firewood, kitchen wash, dead animals, stable manure, and shavings into the public highway. This law also prohibited the practice of making bricks out of clay from the streets and firing them in kilns that blocked the roadway. It was not until three years after the Lewises made their trip that stores were required by law to close their doors on Sunday.[36] Prior to the passage of this law, a newcomer to Louisville who had opened a store and closed it for the Sabbath, was reproached by a citizen who claimed no one had ever closed a store before on Sunday, and that the Sabbath had not yet come over the mountains. The newcomer replied that he had brought Sunday with him from Virginia.[37] The livelier citizens probably felt that he was welcome to it as long as it did not interfere with their rightful entertainments. What they did in private is not known, unless it was there that they recuperated from their public festivities. Self-righteous European travelers were common at this time on the frontier, and in many cases, having enjoyed the hospitality and friendship of the westerners, they returned to the Continent to write accounts of their travels that were critical of their benefactors. Some of these commentators were themselves practitioners of plagiarism and theft.[38] They did, however, record the pleasures that some of the Kentuckians of Louisville took for granted in 1808: widespread gambling and drunkenness, billiard rooms and taverns, numerous fights in which eyes were gouged out and noses and ears bitten off, horseracing and target shooting with rifles on public roads, and the enchanting custom of using the streets of Louisville as the place where stallions served at stud for public contemplation, the enrichment of their owners, and the improvement of the breed.[39]

The European visitors couldn't seem to get into the proper spirit of things and, with their writing, created the still-surviving suspicion that nowhere in the world is the common man as devotedly and persistently common as he is in Kentucky; and that even the privileged Kentuckian is secretly dedicated to genteel hedonism.

Downriver from the falls at Louisville to the mouth of the Cumberland, a distance of 310 miles, cabins were few and far between. There were only two small villages: Henderson at the Red Banks, with less than 150 inhabitants; and Shawneetown, which consisted of a few cabins. Shawneetown was used as a landing place for the saltworks on the Saline River in back of the village.*[40] In spite of the scarcity of houses and towns, the Lewises would not have been lonesome on the river. That year two thousand commercial flatboats and keelboats reached New Orleans from the Ohio River. If the boats of the multitude of settlers were added to this number, it can be estimated that when the river was open an average of more than fifteen boats a day came downstream. The dangers and hardships these travelers shared bound them together in a brotherhood of need, and those few who broke the iron-clad rule of the inland waters and passed by a boat in distress without giving aid, were regarded as brigands of the lowest order.[41]

A few miles below Shawneetown was the Cave in Rock, a famous landmark of the lower Ohio. The mouth of this cave stood just above high-water level, 60 feet wide and 25 feet high, and led into a room 180 feet deep. The cave was in a massive rock cliff that rose steeply from the Indiana shore of the river along a distance of half a mile. Prior to 1808, the cave had been used intermittently by outlaws and travelers alike for shelter. From time to time in the next thirty years it provided headquarters and refuge for murderers, pirates, whores, counterfeiters, and at one time was even used as a tavern that dispensed food, liquor, hired passion, robbery, and murder.[42]

From the Cave in Rock it was only thirty-five miles down-

---

*In December 1816, the Illinois Territorial Legislature granted a bank charter to John Marshall of Shawneetown. Marshall began this banking service in a room of his residence, which is still standing. Tradition has it that a few years after the opening of this bank, a group of men came from the Lake Michigan area to borrow $10,000, which was to be used in the development of a village they proposed to call Chicago. After listening carefully to their pleas, the directors of Marshall's bank retired to discuss the advisability of the loan. They returned shortly to the waiting group with their reply: "Gentlemen, we have carefully considered your request and do not feel justified in making the loan to you. You are just too damn far from Shawneetown to ever amount to anything." (*Herrin* [*Illinois*] *Egyptian Republican,* September 26, 1926).

stream to the Lewises' new homesites. On their left now lay Livingston County. From the river bank, the flat bottom lands in most places stretched back half a mile or more to the foot of the steep timbered slopes that led up to the higher ground. The Lewises passed the tricky "S" shaped entrance to the channel at the head of Hurricane Island. This was one of the most difficult islands on the Ohio for boats to pass. The channel was on the south, or Kentucky side, of the island, and there were sand bars above the island that made the current treacherous. In crossing from the north side of the river into the channel, boats were often thrown onto the head of the island or drawn into the water on the north side, which was full of rocks and snags.[43] Marooned in this manner, some boats had been plundered and the owners had vanished mysteriously. Wise travelers went armed.

Ten miles below, the Lewises came to a massive bluff around which the river turned to flow south. The next bluff, eighteen miles downstream, stood on the river frontage of land owned by Randolph and Lilburne. From this hill could be seen one of the most beautiful views of the lower Ohio River. Downstream for six miles from this bluff to the mouth of the Cumberland, lay a strip of rich bottomland almost a mile in depth. A small upper corner of these bottoms lay in Randolph's farm, and two miles below lay the thousand acres where Lilburne would live. Behind the bottomlands a series of hills rose 250 feet or more above the flat ground. In the middle of the river in front of Randolph's farm lay Stewart Island, containing several hundred acres. The main channel of navigation was on the far side of Stewart Island from the Lewis property, but the family would have had no difficulty landing at the farm on the Kentucky side.[44] From the hill on Randolph's land the river was in full view for miles in both directions and, while the view was not ruggedly spectacular, there was a placid grandeur to it.

·11·

THE LAND AND TOWNS

IN Livingston County most of the countryside was unevenly rolling high ground, a plateau that in ages past had been eroded into myriad narrow valleys. In the upland areas, grass-covered barren lands could be found, spotted with groves of large cedar trees; but covering most of the land grew the dense, primal, hardwood forest. Along the rivers, where mist gathered in the mornings, lay the flat, highly fertile bottomlands. Where it had not been cleared, this ground supported dense canebreaks and magnificent stands of trees—pecan, sycamore, cypress, oak, maple, chestnut, cottonwood, poplar, walnut, and other varieties in abundance. In the creek bottoms and ravines the trees reached astonishing size. Favored by moisture and sheltered from the wind, they thrust their trunks straight up, often seventy or more feet to the first limb, as if striving to put their leaves in the sunlight. In the glens under the leaves of the trees it was dusky; noon sunlight did not enter these hollows until the leaves fell in autumn. The roads and trails, for the most part, were laid out along the high ground, generally following the ridges to secure natural drainage and avoid too many stream crossings.

West Kentucky was also a land of many rivers that were used extensively for transportation, even though the water level varied widely from season to season. The spring rains and the melting snows upstream brought a rise each year. Between the banks ran swirling muddy water that carried limbs and even whole trees along with it. Sometimes the rivers overflowed the banks and flooded the bottoms. During the summer the water fell, exposing sand bars, beds of rock, and hard-baked, waffle-cracked mud flats. In dry periods the river was scattered with bars, rocks, and sawyers, and the water was confined to a more tortuous and constricted channel. Often there was little or no current, and in the sloughs and bayous the water lay still, disturbed only by the sinuous passage of a moccasin, the feeding of summer ducks, or the occasional splash of a fish.

A year or so after arriving in Livingston, Colonel Lewis wrote to Jefferson describing the abundance of fish to be found there.

111

My fealings has not as yet discovered any difference in the climate here & Virg. except cooler nights both winter & summer. You would be delited with the rivers in this countra par[ticularly?] the Ohio . . . [manuscript blotted]. Viewing it you would be astonised at the number size and diferent kinds of fish in the Western waters. [I] have seen a fish since coming here that I never herd of til geting to this place. They are very large which is called the shovell. They have a shovel that projects from the nose several feet in length which is composed of a hard grisel, entierly strate, immouvable but with the hole body. They are not a fish of pray. They have a very larg mouth in shape of that of shad. They are from six to eight feet in length, including the snout or shovel, have no scales, the skin and colour nearly the same of a cat [fish], have no bones. Instead of a bone in the back it is a hard grisel, not any appearance of a rib. They are very fine fish. I am told they feed on their back with the mouth wide open runing the shovel in thick muddy bottoms or bancks. The buffelow [fish] and carp can be caught in any season in abundence, the weight from ten to thirty pounds. With the double hook I have caught 200 lb. in the day. There can be no doubt the Western contra the finest in the world.

I am Dear Sir Yrs. Affectily.
Chas L. Lewis[1]

Natural wild life was so profuse in west Kentucky that a hunter with health enough to walk seldom needed to go hungry. The dense canebrakes were literally full of wild animals. Settlers had grown accustomed to the ready supply of meat and fish, but people newly arrived from the east were surprised at its plenty. Of all wild meat venison was preferred, and ammunition for the flintlock rifles was seldom wasted on smaller game, which was trapped, or caught in pens, in the case of turkeys and partridges. The taking of wild game for food was routine, but the hunting of wolves, bears, and panther was far more purposeful and exciting. The marauding forays of these beasts were a trial to livestock owners, and occasionally a threat to the isolated family. In 1813, in a neighboring county, a slave was torn to pieces and eaten by a pack of wolves, and two years later, in Muhlenberg County, a panther was shot that measured eleven feet from its nose to the tip of its tail. Encounters with bear were common, and sometimes a victim was forced into a fight for his life with only a knife to aid him. One hunter was horribly mangled in such a battle in Union County, but the bear was finally stabbed and cut to death.[2]

Although wild meat was easily obtained, pork and beef were

generally preferred, and were an important part of western commerce. It was not practical to fasten up the stock at night for protection from predators, because immense labor was involved in building split-rail fences around large tracts of meadow and pasture land. Hogs and cattle usually ran wild and covered a wide territory in search of forage, mast, and roots. Most of the stock wintered in the canebreaks. It was difficult to establish the ownership of the animals after they had ranged free for several months and had gathered in random flocks. This problem was solved by a form of branding in which each livestock owner cut certain identifiable notches or croppings in the ears of his animals. These were called "stock" or "ear" marks. Each stockman's name and a clear description of his earmark was recorded in the county court records, along with all the other official business entries. For example, in Livingston County the following stock-marks are on record:

> July 4th, 1808—John Gray's stockmark—a split in the right ear and under bitt off the left.

> Jan. 2nd 1809—John Jones stockmark—a swallow fork in the left ear and a crop in the right.

> Robert Woodside stockmark—one bitt cut out of the under edge of both years and a crop off the left ear and a nick in the upper edge of each ear.

> Aug. 26th 1811—On motion of James Johnson it is ordered that his ear mark be recorded which is a swallow fork in the left ear.[3]

Killing predatory animals was a matter of concern to everyone in the community. Wolves were especially troublesome. In the springtime the bitches howled at evening, giving away the location of their dens. The mothers were killed and the whelps were dug out of the dens and destroyed. No bounty hunter who knew the location of a den would disturb it before the bitch had whelped. It would have been throwing money away. There was a two dollar cash bounty paid for killing adult wolves, and a one dollar cash bounty for wolves less than six months of age. This bounty could be claimed by presenting the wolf's scalp or head to a magistrate and giving a statement under oath that the wolf had been destroyed and that the scalp was in fact the scalp and not a patch of hide from somewhere else on the carcass of the wolf. This oath was required because some enterprising men had counterfeited wolf scalps, claiming several bounty payments from one animal. In 1808, over forty wolf bounty claims were paid by the court of Livingston County. One typical entry reads, "To Josiah Ramsey for two wolf skulps—$4.00."[4]

Other species of animals and birds were troublesome, as well. In the fall, when the corn had dried in the field or stood in the shocks, the squirrels were attracted to it and came in great numbers to strip the rows nearest the woods and then extend their voracious thievery further and further into the field. Raccoons were also guests at this free banquet. The unfortunate farmer would send a boy to stand ineffectual guard with a gun, and then hasten to gather the crop before it was destroyed completely.

Another pest equally aggravating, though of great beauty, was the parrot or Carolina paroquet. The young ones were of solid emerald green color, and as the birds matured their necks and heads became a brilliant scarlet and yellow. When full grown the paroquets were a full fourteen inches in length, with wings just under two feet from tip to tip. The strong rounded beak could inflict a deep and painful wound. Although they never ate corn, there was little else they did not feed upon or wantonly destroy. They gathered in flocks of hundreds and stripped the unripe fruit from trees, or assailed the stacks of wheat until the shocks seemed to be covered with a moving, iridescent, green and yellow blanket. At such times the parrots could be killed easily, for the single discharge of a shotgun would finish as many as fifteen or twenty of them. The others swirled away in flight, shrieking, only to return greedily in a few minutes to be slaughtered in the same place. The parrots squawked constantly when in flight.[5]

The flesh of these birds could be eaten, but it did not compare to the delicate dark meat of the young passenger pigeon. The pigeons gathered in flocks so immense that it is difficult to believe or to describe. A flock migrating to new forest feeding grounds was often so huge that it took two days to pass overhead, flying at the speed of a mile a minute. Beneath this dense concentration the sunlight was attenuated to dusk, and the droppings fell like white rain.

The pigeons stayed in a district as long as there was ample food, mostly beechnuts, pecans, or acorns. There they roosted and nested in season, but left when the mast was exhausted, perhaps not to return for several years. When roosting at night, the birds were killed in multiplied hundreds by men who used poles to knock them off the tree limbs. So densely did the birds pack themselves on the branches that limbs frequently broke under the load and in falling crushed many birds beneath them. Hogs were fattened on the dead birds beneath such roosts. The wild pigeons returned to the chosen place to roost night after night, but during the day many fed as far as fifty or one hundred miles away. In nesting seasons the squabs, two in each nest, were highly prized for food, and were gathered by knocking the nests down or by cutting down the taller trees.

A few years after the Lewises arrived, the wild pigeons were in the Livingston vicinity. The negro slave hands at the salt works near Shawneetown became exhausted from killing the birds that week after week flew in and alighted to drink the brine from the salt wells as it flowed from the pipes. The pipes carried the brine from the salt wells to the edge of the forest, where there was firewood to stoke the evaporating kettles.[6]

When the Lewises arrived in Livingston County, it covered far more territory than at present. Its boundaries were in the shape of a rough square forty miles on a side, with a panhandle fifteen miles wide that stretched south to the Tennessee line. The Ohio flowed along the north and part of the western sides, while the course of the small Tradewater River was the eastern boundary. The southwestern boundary of the county followed the Tennessee River. The panhandle lay between the Tennessee and Cumberland rivers, including most of the land now known as "the land between the rivers" (see Map 2).

The division of Kentucky counties began in colonial Virginia, long before Kentucky became a state in 1792. As settlers poured in, new counties were formed. This process of dividing counties continued in Kentucky until no county seat was so far from a citizen's home that one could not go on horseback to the courthouse in a day.[7]

Lying to the southwest of Livingston County was the huge territory between the Tennessee and Mississippi rivers now called the Jackson Purchase. By treaty, all this area belonged to the Chickasaw Indians. No one settled there, for the Chickasaws were uncompromising in defense of their claims. The hunting grounds were rich in game and good land.[8]

In the spring of 1808 there were only four towns in Livingston County. Some early western settlements came into being more or less spontaneously at places where people gathered for purposes of trade or transportation, at the mouth of the rivers, at ferries, where traces or roads crossed each other, or at mill sites

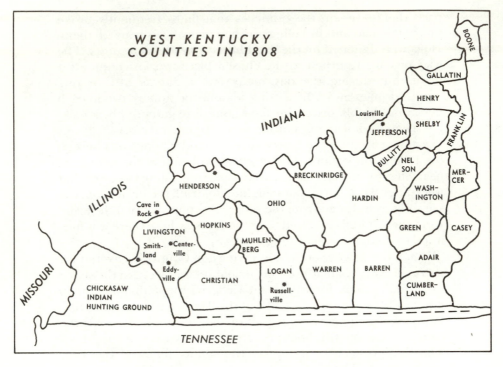

Map 2. *(Map courtesy of Wendell H. Rone, Sr.)*

and fords. Other towns were planned communities, and had been established as seats of government for newly formed counties, as real estate promotion schemes, or as home towns of people who had certain religious or economic interests in common. The citizens of communities like this often came west in a group.

One such town in Livingston County was Eddyville. It was by far the largest town in the county in 1808 and was, in fact, the second largest town on the Cumberland River—Nashville, Tennessee being first. Eddyville had been planned and built on the land of the extraordinary businessman and statesman, Matthew Lyon. In 1799, Lyon had bought a large tract of land on the Cumberland, having been advised to do so by his friend, Andrew Jackson.[9] At that time Lyon, a prosperous businessman, lived in Vermont and represented that state in Congress. He would become one of the most important and consistent supporters of Jefferson's policies in Congress. Lyon cast the crucial vote that broke the stalemate and made Jefferson president in 1801. Lyon's arbitrary and cruel imprisonment by the Federalists under the terms of the Sedition Act had helped to solidify western public opinion behind Jefferson.[10]

After buying the land in Kentucky, Lyon returned to Vermont and, with customary energy, organized a party of about fifty people that included his married sons and daughters, eight or ten skilled tradesmen, and all of their families. Inside of six months they were in Livingston County, building the town that was named for two large eddies in the river near the town site.[11] Two years later, in 1801, Lyon had served out his term in Congress as representative from Vermont. He sold his extensive properties in that state and moved to Eddyville with his wife and a second party of about seventy industrious Vermonters. They traveled by wagon to Pittsburgh, where they built their own boats and continued down the Ohio to the mouth of the Cumberland, then forty-five miles up that river to Eddyville.

Lyon's fame and popularity were such that within six months after his arrival he had been elected to the Kentucky legislature, and a year after that had been picked to return to Congress, this time to represent his new homeland, the western district of Kentucky. He served in that capacity for eight years following his election in 1802.

Under Lyon's competent leadership, industries soon sprang up in Eddyville; brick kilns, a grist mill, paper mill, hemp packing plant, wool and cotton card manufactory, distillery, and sawmill. These were followed shortly by the mining of iron and its processing into hardware, a tannery and leather goods factory, and finally, the largest enterprise, a shipyard of impressive size in which seagoing vessels of 150 tons were built in 1805.[12]

In its earliest days Eddyville served as the seat of government for Livingston County, but in 1804 the county seat had been moved from Eddyville fifteen miles northward to Centerville, a crossroads town with a more central location in the county.[13] It was here that the Saline Trace divided, one fork going north to cross the Ohio at Cave in Rock, and the other proceeding northwest to cross the Ohio at Yellow Banks (now Golconda), Illinois.[14]

The Centerville neighborhood and town of 1808 was a good example of a frontier county seat village. In 1797 the Reverend Terah Templin, a Presbyterian of some fame, had brought his parishioners from Washington County to the Centerville (now

117

Fredonia) area, where they established the Livingston Presbyterian Church.

A church historian, Littleton Groom, states that this church and its members had a stabilizing effect on the community for many miles around, and that Centerville did not become a "rougue's harbor" like Russellville in Logan County, or the Cave in Rock area in Illinois. The generally low state of morals in America at that time gave much concern to established churches. In a pastoral letter sent to all its churches in 1798, the Presbyterian General Assembly lamented that "profaneness, pride, luxury, injustice, intemperance, lewdness, and every species of debauchery and loose indulgence abound."[15] It appears that in spite of the Reverend Terah Templin, Centerville was not entirely populated by saintly people. Mr. Groom notes that careful parents did not permit their sons to visit or loiter in the village. A search of the court records reveals the reason. Centerville was known for certain unecclesiastical activities which seem to have revolved around one James Ivy.

By 1808 Centerville had a population of about forty whites and six slaves. It had been the county seat for four years, and yet the stray pound, for confining horses on court day, had still not been built, nor had the whipping post and pillory been erected. The stray pen and stocks were required by law for county seats, and in 1808 the grand jury indicted the justices of the peace of the county for this failure.[16] There was a log courthouse and a jail of sorts, to which the jailer objected "as being insufficient."[17] Centerville also had two taverns, one of which was run by James Ivy and his wife, Ruth. The other tavern was owned by a certain Enoch Hooper, who was not on the best of terms with Ivy. The presence of two taverns in such a small town can be explained by the fact that Centerville was the county seat. When the county court or the circuit court met there for the scheduled sessions, the residents of Centerville were far outnumbered by the visiting lawyers, petitioners, litigants, plaintiffs, defendants, witnesses, and onlookers, many of whom wanted food, lodging, and entertainment.

James Ivy was somewhat of an entrepreneur in business. In 1806 he had rented "a 52 kettle pit at the Saline Lick, with sufficient quantity of wood and water for the purpose of making salt in said pit."[18] Ivy was to pay $100 per month for the lease, and agreed to deliver all the salt he recovered to the U.S. agent stationed at the pit, which was located in Illinois. It appears that

Ivy never operated the pit himself, for inside of two months, he had rerented the operation to one James Bruff. Bruff sued Ivy for lying about the productivity of the operation. Ivy then disappeared temporarily, so Bruff could not reclaim his losses. In time Bruff went to Louisiana, where he got "chills and fever," and was not able to come back to Centerville and press his case. This earliest mention of James Ivy in the court records is a fitting introduction to his character.[19]

His tavern appears to have reflected his personality. Many of the numerous indictments for profanity found in the court records were based on conversations that took place at Ivy's. The profanity indictments did not state what it was that had provoked such a flow of blasphemy, but it may have been Ivy's amazon wife, Ruth. She and Ivy deserved each other. One indictment against her proclaimed that "Ruth Ivy, wife of James Ivy, tavern-keeper, of said county on the first day of January 1808, at the house of said James Ivy, by force and arms did make an assault on one William Griffin . . . and him did then and there beat, wound, bruise and ill treat."[20] This assault was brought on by the theft of two drawer locks costing twenty-five cents each. The thief was Abraham, a slave owned by William Griffin. Abraham took the stolen locks to James Ivy, who fenced them and was subsequently indicted. Ruth took out her wrath on Will Griffin, Abraham's owner. Ruth was not only a violent avenger but, like Abraham, was a thief as well. Another true bill indictment issued just a month after she beat up William Griffin alleged that she stole a freemason's apron worth fifteen dollars from the estate of a man who had died shortly before.

Enoch Hooper, the innkeeper of the other tavern in Centerville, was somewhat upset by his competition, and in 1808 began keeping a record of the profanity of Ruth and James, which he subsequently presented to the grand jury. Hooper's list was impressive. Against Ruth he furnished information for twenty-seven separate indictments, which contained from one to twenty-two oaths each, ranging from "By God" and "By Jesus" to one supplication which may well have been granted, "I'll be God almighty damned." Against James Ivy, Hooper presented information for at least as many indictments, containing in excess of seventy-five profane oaths.

Hooper, a captain in the militia, seems to have been a somewhat more reliable person than James Ivy.[21] When the county court approved the construction of the stock and whipping post on the public square at Centerville, Enoch Hooper was one of the three trustees approved to let the contract for twenty dollars. The contract called for a platform eight feet long and four feet wide to be erected seven feet off the ground, "and pillory thereon." The whipping post was to be "twenty inches in diameter of good strong white oak and a pair of clamps placed on said post at a proper height for whipping."[22]

Hooper's motivation for presenting information against Ruth and James Ivy is unknown; he may have wanted to harass his competition, or he may have had a genuinely outraged sense of decency. If so, he had good cause for, prior to the indictments for profanity presented by Hooper, James Ivy had been indicted on two counts for bad debts, once for defamation of character, twelve times for assault and battery, and fifteen times for drunkenness.[23]

It is no wonder that John Gray, the commonwealth's attorney, finally concluded that James Ivy was running a disorderly house, and brought him to trial with a true bill charging that James Ivy

did keep & maintain, and yet doth keep & maintain, a certain common, ill governed and disorderly house: and then . . . there unlawfully and wilfully did cause & procure certain evil disposed persons, as well men, as women of evil name and fame; as well black as white, and of dishonest conversation, to frequent and come together in the said house for his own lucre and gain: and unlawfully and willfully did permit, and yet doth permit, the said men & women & negroes, in the said house at unlawful times, as well in the night as in the day, then & the said other times there to be & remain, drinking, tipling, whoring, and misbehaving themselves; to the great damage & common nuisance of the Citizens of this commonwealth aforesaid and town of Centerville.[24]

After the trial had ended, the foreman of the petit jury wrote the verdict on the outside of the indictment. "We of the jury find the defendant not guilty."

The God-fearing parishioners of the Reverend Terah Templin lost that round, but without their presence and influence in 1808, the neighborhood of Centerville might well have become a genuine "rogues harbor."

The third town in Livingston County was Kirksville, a small place of fewer than twenty-five people, one of whom was a slave. Beginning in 1800, an official inspection station for flour, hemp, and tobacco was operated at "the Forks of Hurricane Creek" next to Kirksville.[25] Kirksville lay twenty miles northwest of Centerville, on the banks of the Ohio opposite the head of Hurricane Island.[26] It was only five miles from Kirksville upriver to Cave in Rock, the pirate lair. Kirksville and Cave in Rock were connected in crime by the person of James Ford, one of the cleverest and most ruthless of American criminal masterminds. Although his nefarious career did not reach its zenith until twenty years after the Lewises came to Kentucky, by the time they arrived, Ford owned Hurricane Island and a five-hundred-acre plantation, where he made his home on the river near Kirksville.[27] This was the site of the treacherous passage at the head of Hurricane Island, where there was real danger of being drawn into the rocky northern channel or being grounded on the head of the island.[28] Pilots were available to guide travelers through this dangerous spot, but the pilot was often a masquerading outlaw who deliberately wrecked the boat on Hurricane Island, where it was plundered at leisure. There was a ferry across the river at Hurricane Island controlled by Ford, who, by 1808, had been justice of the peace, and had influenced the establishment of ferries and roads that led the innocent to their ruin. Although all the residents of Kirksville could not have been involved in the murder and robbery ring, they must have known that Hurricane Island was used as a depot for stolen horses and livestock, and that boats had been deliberately wrecked and looted there. Ford's role as master planner of this gang was probably not widely suspected until a decade or more after 1808.[29]

The fourth town of Livingston County was Smithland, located on the west side of the county at the mouth of the Cumberland. Smithland was about thirty miles distant by road from Kirksville, and over twenty-five miles from Centerville. Lilburne's farm was located about four miles up the Ohio from Smithland, and Randolph's home property was a mile above Lilburne's.

The town of Smithland had been planned and established as a profit-making real estate venture by William Croghan, Sr. of Locust Grove, near Louisville. A brother-in-law of Gen. George Rogers Clark, Croghan was a gentleman of widespread influence in Kentucky. After the purchase treaty of July 1805 had extinguished the final claims of the Chickasaws to land east of the Tennessee River, the land between the rivers was opened for settlement. Croghan had applied to the Livingston County Court to establish the town of Smithland on land that Croghan owned at the mouth of the Cumberland.[30] Before Croghan founded Smithland on this new location, an insignificant settlement bearing the same name had existed for a few years a mile or two below the mouth of the Cumberland. By 1808 it was "dwindling away to nothing," as Cramer noted. Croghan's petition was granted, and by the time the Lewises arrived three years later, lots had been laid out and sold, and Smithland was ready to grow.

In the fall of 1807, about the same time the Lewises left Virginia, a traveler named Christian Schultz visited Smithland and left this record of his impressions:

> At the mouth of the Cumberland—likewise known by its more ancient name of Shawanese River—is a small settlement called Smith Town, consisting of only five houses. The situation, however, is extremely eligible for further improvement. . . . Most of the boats descending to New Orleans and Memphis generally make a halt here, either for hams, provisions, boats or repairs. . . . It appears to be a kind of *inland port,* where runaway boys, idle young men, and unemployed boatmen, assemble to engage as hands on board of any boats that may happen to call.
>
> An amusement has already been introduced at this place, which, although excusable in large towns and cities, yet in a new country, and especially in an infant settlement like this, cannot be too much condemned. You will scarcely believe, that in a place just emerging from the words, which, although advantageously situated, can prosper only by dint of industry and care, and where the girdled trees which surround its houses threaten with every storm to crush the whole settlement,—you will scarcely believe, I say, that a billiard table has been established, which is continually surrounded by common boatmen, just arrived from the Salt Works, St. Louis, or St. Genevieve, who in one hour lose all the hard-earned wages of a two months' voyage.[31]

In May of the next year another traveler reported that the inhabitants of Smithland depended on what they could make by their trade with the boatmen, and were not inclined to grow more corn than their horses required, for there were only thirty acres of poorly cleared cropland around the town. There were two ferries at Smithland, one on the Ohio and the other crossing the Cumberland.[32]

By 1810 there were about twenty heads of households in Smithland, and a total of just one hundred people, including the slaves. Religious services were held in homes, for Smithland had no church and there was not much likelihood for one in the near future. The interest of communities like this centered mainly on extracting profit from the river men who, in turn, seemed willing to buy or take whatever diversion was at hand.[33]

·12·

HOUSES AND CROPS

THE NEW LIFE Randolph and Lilburne were beginning in Kentucky would be similar in many ways to that of their grandfather, Charles Lewis, Jr. of Buck Island, when, as a young man nearly seventy years before, he had opened his plantation on the Rivanna. The land was new ground, more fertile than it would ever be again, but it had to be cleared before its riches could be exploited. When the needs of the family and slaves had been met, if there was a surplus from the farm it could go to market by river boat. Although there were small settlements in the county, they were not nearby, and a visit to town required a ride of several hours over trails that were usually impassable for wagons. The plantations and home places were at first isolated, no more than clearings miles apart in a sea of forest.

There were, however, some differences between the situation of Randolph and Lilburne and that of their grandfather. He had been a member of the colonial gentry and had received his land at small cost through his father's influence. He had more slaves and more capital available than his grandsons and, in the culture of tobacco, had a cash crop that was more or less in steady demand. He was a member of the upper class in a society that generally imitated the English social structure, which was based on family blood lines, inheritance, and rigid class stratification.

Randolph and Lilburne, on the other hand, had paid substantially for their land in Kentucky, and did not have a single dominant cash crop on which they could depend for income. The Embargo of 1807 had destroyed any temptation to grow large crops of tobacco in Livingston County. In colonial Albemarle, being a member of the gentry was a tremendous advantage in acquiring a fortune, whereas in west Kentucky two generations later, one's family connections were less important than one's political influence. Competence, industry, cleverness, and motivation: these things brought wealth on the frontier, where what a man could do was more admired than his surname, and self-styled aristocrats were mistrusted, when not resented. Certainly the Lewises' close kinship to Jefferson, who

123

was much admired in Kentucky, would have aroused local curiosity, but in Livingston County in 1808 it would have been difficult for the Lewises to convert curiosity into the cash they needed so badly.

The cash crop system of the huge plantations of the south had not yet come into being in the west in 1808. That system was based entirely on slave and overseer labor, and a typical owner usually produced only one or two of the five staple crops: cotton, rice, hemp, sugar, and tobacco. Frequently these large plantations raised little food of their own, but bought it from producers further north to feed their numerous slaves.[1]

In Livingston County the pattern was different. The largest holder of slaves in the county in 1810 owned seventeen negroes. Only fourteen men in the county owned more than ten slaves.[2] If the numbers of male and female slaves were about equal, the fourteen largest slaveholders had an average of only five or six prime men able to do hard physical labor. It is doubtful that there was any farm operation in Livingston that was run by an overseer, so the direction of slaves and management of the farms had to be handled by the owners. Those who owned few slaves joined in the labor, and those who owned none and tried to farm lived a life of hardship and fatigue.

Of the fourteen slaves who belonged to Lilburne in 1810, four were prime hands: Carter, Frank, Isaac, and Archer. Randolph owned seven slaves, of whom three were men, and only two, Andrew and Adam, were fit for field work.[3]

In the beginning, Randolph and Lilburne were faced with two fundamental tasks, to build their homes and to clear and plant their land. Planting season would not wait, whereas the Lewises could have continued to live in the cabins on their broadhorns until there was time to build houses.

The work of opening a farm in Livingston on new ground was a huge job, as it had been for their grandfather in Albemarle, and it was done the same way. Although they could have felled their trees at once and burned them or hauled them off, this procedure had serious drawbacks. It was a time-consuming, if not extravagant, use of labor, and the stumps that remained would have stayed alive for several years, sending up vigorous sprouts each spring. The alternative method of preparing forest ground for cultivation was to grub out the underbrush and girdle the trunks of the trees by cutting off a two- or three-inch strip of bark all the way around the tree. The trees starved and died, and stood barren until they fell or were burned down later.

124

The first crop was planted among these dead and dying trees and, as successive seasons went by, the dead roots, and finally the stumps themselves, either rotted away or were pulled out in the process of farming.[4]

Such extensive preparation was not required for the livestock. The animals were allowed to forage for themselves. The milk cows and horses were tethered or hobbled so they could not wander away, and the hogs and sheep were earmarked and let run free. The production of food for the animals was unnecessary. "They had a wonderful range for stock. Pea-vines were knee-high over much of the county, vast canebrakes stood in many places, and there was always an abundance of mast. On all these the horses, cattle and hogs fared exceedingly well."[5]

Cane, which grew only in rich wet lands, sometimes reached a height of twenty feet, and grew so densely that it formed an almost impenetrable thicket. The canebrakes were valuable to the local inhabitants as a source of forage. Even after the country had been settled for many years, the settlers drove their cattle to the cane in the autumn and left them there without attention until the next spring. Livestock ate it greedily and thrived on it.[6]

Corn, wheat, and buckwheat were the most important grain crops grown by the Lewis brothers. The varieties of vegetables they raised are unknown, but the soil and climate of west Kentucky are suitable for any vegetable that does not require a tropical habitat. Fruit trees suited to temperate zones would grow here too, but the Lewises could not have had time to establish their own orchards. No doubt they made use of the wild plums, grapes, pawpaws, and the endless supply of nuts and berries that grew in the forests.

Preserving food in the home required knowledge and skills long out of use today. Fruits and vegetables were dried in the sun, and corn and wheat were ground into meal and flour. The following devices were used to preserve and process their food: churns, crocks, jars, kettles, barrels, hand millstones, and meat tubs. The heavier work involved in killing and putting up meat was performed by the men. Meat was preserved by salting or smoking, or it was pickled in brine. An old recipe gives instructions for these processes:

Bacon and Pork

One bushel of salt to £1000 [1000 pounds of meat]—in three weeks hang it in smoke—dip it strong [brine] boiling hot once in March and once in July and hang it up as before.—Cut yr pork in

125

pieces 4 inches square—salt on floor in three days pack it Bll [in a barrel] filling it wt pickle so strong as to bear [float] an egg—1802.

Jas Gay[7]

Making cloth was a burdensome task for the Lewis women. Cotton was raised for the looms and to stuff quilts, and it is likely they also grew flax to make the linen that settlers combined with wool in the fabric called mixed cloth, later known as linsey-woolsey. They cleaned, sorted, spun, and wove the threads into cloth. The cotton gin, cards, spinning wheels, reels, and looms that Randolph and Lilburne owned were about equal in value to their farm tools.[8]

The production of cloth was regarded as women's work, and demanded a great deal of their time, far more, evidently, than the men spent in their traditional tasks outside the home. Colonel Lewis described this division of labor on the frontier:

I think the richness combined with the immence quantaty of fertile lands in the western contra will be a means of establising a great deal of indolance. I find how the blacks and whites are very much so of the mail [male]. The labour of the woman to precure clothing is much the hardest labour done. They are constantly employ[d] of both colours. Were I in the same situation as a number of the pore are in Virginia I should prefer to be a Slave in Kentucky than a freeman in Virginia & to labour on their pore land as hard as they do. The situation of the slave here is far parferable. The males of every discription here dont work more than one fourth of their time notwithstanding every man has more corn thin they know what to do with as well as meat.[9]

The farming equipment that the two brothers owned seems hopelessly inadequate today. With no more than forty-five dollars' worth of farm tools between them, these men had every reason to expect to feed and clothe their families and slaves, and reap some small profit in addition. The three most important tools were the hoe, the axe, and the plow. The brothers together owned four plows worth only about a dollar each, for the metal mouldboard plow was not yet in use. They had seven axes, seven hoes, and a few other implements: sheep shears, wedges, beam scales, harness and gear for the horses, a hammer, clivis, grindstone, mattox, and two sleighs. The sleigh, also called ground sled or landslide, took the place of the wagon in frontier life. It was a simple box or platform built across two timber runners. Anything too heavy or bulky to be hauled on a horse was skidded over the ground on a sled pulled by a horse.

The Lewises did not own any wagons in Kentucky.[10] The public roads did not run near the Lewis farms, and even if they had, wagons would not have been dependable transportation because of the execrable condition of the roads. Had the Lewises come west by wagon instead of by boat, they would have had to cut at least three miles of wagon road before they could even reach their own farms.

Once the Lewises had planted the crops, they could have turned their full attention to completing their homes. No description of their houses exists, but the legends are unanimous in stating that the Lewis residences were larger than the usual house built at that time in western Kentucky. The list of Lilburne's furniture roughly indicates the minimum number of rooms in his house. This list contains only the house furniture which would take up space, and omits kitchen equipment, pictures, mirrors, bed clothes, and other small items: 6 bedsteads and one trundle bed, 3 tables, 12 chairs, 2 spinning wheels and a reel, 1 bookcase and about 50 books, 1 backgammon table, 1 dressing box, 3 trunks, and 2 bureaus.[11]

At the very least, Lilburne's house must have had two or more bedrooms, a dining room, parlor, and kitchen. During that period persons who had servants usually built a separate one-room building for the cooking, so the odors, heat, noise, and mess of preparing food and cleaning up after meals would not disturb the family. The kitchen was attached to the house by a walkway that was called the dogtrot. Sometimes the dogtrot was covered over for shelter. At a discreet distance from the house the privy would be located, and at a somewhat greater distance the slave quarters and corn crib were built. When time permitted, a barn or stable for the horses may have been added to these buildings.

The lists of Randolph's furniture are less detailed than Lilburne's, but they indicate that Randolph had about the same amount of furniture as Lilburne, and there were, in addition, two more children in Randolph's family than in Lilburne's. It appears that Randolph's house was at least as large as his brother's.

The farm on which Lilburne built his home was nearly in the form of a square, and contained one-thousand acres (see Map 3). The slightly longer side faced the river for a distance of one and a third miles, while the back line of the property was one and a quarter miles from the river. The section of the farm that adjoined the river was bottom ground, flat and fertile, although

127

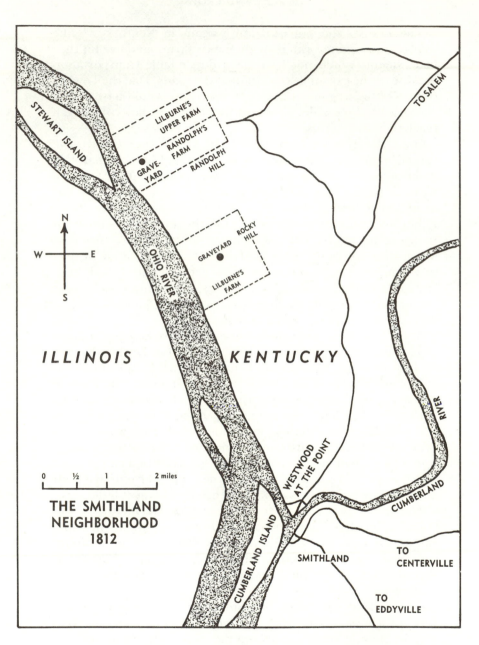

Map 3. *(Map by Thomas E. Clark)*

it contained a few areas that were poorly drained. On the back half of the farm the southern, or downstream, side was creek bottom, more or less level ground lying between higher rolling terrain on the south, and a steep-sided rocky hill that covered the north rear quarter of Lilburne's property.[12] Lilburne located his buildings on the ten or twelve acres of gently sloping ground on the top of this hill and, following the pattern of Virginia plantation owners, gave his home a name, Rocky Hill. Although the brow of the hill facing the west was half a mile from the river, the view was restful and expansive, for the elevation was more than two hundred feet above the low ground that surrounded the homesite on three sides. Beyond Lilburne's east, or rear, line, the hill sloped gradually back into a large valley. The other approaches to the hill were extremely steep, a jumble of grey, lichen-covered rocks and boulders among which grew a dense stand of hardwood timber.

Even though the approaches that led to Lilburne's home were steep and inconvenient, there were good reasons for locating a house on high ground. In rainy seasons the water drained off quickly. The fields and garden plots that stood on high ground dried out and warmed up sooner in the spring, allowing the farmer to plow and plant at the most favorable time, and the horses and livestock suffered less from foot diseases when they did not stand in mire. Settlers found it less of a task to clear high ground, for usually the trees were smaller and the undergrowth less rank. In the early 1800s the flood crests were not as high as they are today, but nevertheless it was not uncommon for the bottom lands to be covered by water in the winter or spring. This alone was reason enough to build on high land, but the desire for personal comfort was also a factor. Midsummer in west Kentucky can be brutally hot, and those who live on hilltops are frequently cooled by breezes that do not blow through the bottoms or valleys. These breezes also helped to blow away the insects, gnats, and especially the mosquitoes that are legendary in the Ohio Valley.

James Hall, who traveled the Ohio Valley in 1820, reported that mosquitoes were active from the earliest warm weather until frost. He claimed that visitors to the country were more troubled by the insect than were the natives, who somehow became acclimated to the bites. Hall was explicit when he described a certain "English lady, not remarkably ugly before, who became

129

absolutely hideous in consequence of the vile pimples left by these venomous creatures."[13]

At that time, when malaria was common along the Ohio, the relationship between the mosquito and the disease was unknown. There was, however, a widespread superstition that tended to keep people out of low wet areas where mosquitoes bred. It was the belief that night air, fog, and especially the mist that rose from swamps and low marshes were apt to cause illness. People who built their dwellings away from low ground not only escaped the imagined danger of the miasma, but also found freedom from the mosquitoes that swarmed in such fantastic numbers near swampy land.

The place where Randolph located his home is not known exactly. From court commissioners' reports we know it was somewhere on his five-hundred acre farm, which lay about a mile up the river from Lilburne's Rocky Hill. Randolph's farm was long and narrow, fronting on the river for only one-half mile, but extending back almost two miles. There was little river-bottom land on this property, but a broad shallow valley ran back more than halfway through the farm. Along most of the southern property line stood a wooded ridge that reached its greatest height near the back corner of the farm. Today this hill is called Randle Hill, a time-frayed alteration of its original name, Randolph Hill. Directly on the river at the northern corner of the farm was another spot of high ground, the downstream end of a bluff that ran along the river for nearly half a mile. Although the highest point of this bluff was not on Randolph's farm, from his portion of this hill one of the loveliest views of the lower Ohio could be seen.[14]

Lilburne owned the land on the north side of Randolph's farm. This second tract of Lilburne's was the same shape and size as Randolph's. The contours were different, however, for the front part of the farm on the river was high and rough, whereas the back portion, being creek bottom, was better suited to agriculture. Lilburne owned more land in his Rocky Hill plantation than he could clear and farm with his few slaves. It is unlikely that he tried to clear or cultivate this upper tract. It had cost Lilburne over sixteen hundred dollars, an investment that brought him no income.

In most cases, building a settler's home was a community affair of shared labor and socializing. The cabin was made from the materials at hand: green timber, rocks, and mud. "When a settler had determined upon building a house, he gave notice to all his neighbors of the fact. People then were considered within neighborly bounds if they lived within twenty miles of the proposed new house. Most of the invited folks were slave owners, and they were supposed to bring their entire available male force, bound and free, to the house 'raising.' . . . It required one day, generally, to prepare the materials for the house, and sometimes the foundation was laid on the first day. The 'raising' proper, occupied the second day which . . . sufficed for finishing the roof, and sometimes the floor was completed upon this day. The finishing touches were given to the domicile on the third day by a few carpenters who smoothed off the floor, made a door-shutter, a bedstead, a table and some stools."[15]

The houses Randolph and Lilburne built for themselves certainly were more elaborate than a one- or two-room cabin. The sawed and seasoned timbers of which the Lewis broadhorn was built may have been used in the houses. If more lumber was needed, it could have been bought from Matthew Lyon's sawmill in Eddyville, or could have been cut with a two-man whipsaw.[16] The market value of sawed poplar planking was one and one-half cents a board foot; for example, a plank ten feet long and a foot wide was worth fifteen cents.[17] The use of sawed timber in their houses would have required the use of nails, which, along with window glass, they could have bought as they passed through Pittsburgh or Louisville the previous winter.

Building houses like Randolph's and Lilburne's was not a two- or three-day project, and, while some of their neighbors may have helped them, it is more likely that the Lewises hired laborers and carpenters to assist and direct the slaves in the work. In the detailed lists of the possessions of the brothers there is no mention of carpenter tools.

The location of Lilburne's home on Rocky Hill has been established. The exact site of Randolph's home buildings on his farm is more uncertain, and as for the place where Colonel Lewis, Lucy, and their three daughters lived, there is little chance of discovering its precise location. When Lucy wrote her farewell letter to Jefferson in 1807 she mentioned the "suppoart" from Craven Peyton and the land "that the boys has promised to give us." If Lucy, Colonel Lewis, and their daughters had intended to live as a part of Randolph's household they would not have needed the four aging domestic slaves they rented from Peyton, nor would they have needed land. It is clear that they intended to establish a household separate from those of Randolph and Lilburne. There is evidence that they lived, at least for a while, somewhere on Randolph's farm, and not on Lilburne's.[18]

There are two locations on Randolph's farm where very old log homes once stood. These houses were remembered clearly by a keen and charming lady, Mrs. May Fleming Howell, who was eighty-three years of age in 1970. She lived most of her life at Birdsville, on what was once Randolph's property. She described the two houses, first the smaller one that stood near the top of the high bluff overlooking the Ohio River:

> The house was big, very old, made of wide hewed logs, and was located just down the hill from the graveyard where the mimosa tree stands now. It had three rooms, a loft, and a front porch. The room in the back was a kitchen and it had a small back porch. It had old fashioned small windows, small panes, one window in each room and no shutters. The hewed logs had clay chinking, or plaster chinking. Two of the rooms were large. The house had an immense fireplace and did not have a hall. There was a cistern for water. Up where the entrance to the cemetery is now there was a log barn. The house was real, real, old when I was a child in the 1890s. It has been down at least twenty years, since before 1950.
>
> My uncle, Dr. Furnace, lived there in 1890. He was a surgeon, a hip and spine specialist. My father was James J. Fleming and Mother was Emmalena Hibbs. Mother's parents were James Lacey Hibbs and Emmalina Branch who were married in 1847.
>
> There was another house on the back of the farm that was older than the one by the graveyard. We called it the Cowper house. It was just above Cowper spring. It was a two-story log house with a hall, bigger than the other house by the cemetery.[19]

The road that runs up the hill at Birdsville and then straight back from the river for more than a mile follows the property line between Randolph's farm and the upper tract of five-hundred acres that Lilburne owned. This road jogs slightly where it crosses Phelps Creek. The two-story Cowper house was located a short distance south of this crossing at the foot of Randolph Hill. Cowper Spring is nearby at the edge of Phelps Creek, and has been almost filled in by time and trampling cattle. It is over a mile in a straight line between the sites of these two houses. They were each about two miles away from Rocky Hill, where Lilburne lived. Mrs. Howell's statement that the two-story house was older than the house on the hill by the river may have been based on a difference in the condition of the two houses during her childhood. It is quite possible that the houses were about the same age, and it is also possible that Randolph built one or both of them in 1808. With no more evidence at hand, one is tempted to guess that Randolph, Mary, and their seven children lived in the larger house by Cowper Spring and that Lucy, Colonel Lewis and their three daughters lived at least for a while in the house overlooking the river on the "land the boys has promised to give us."

Despite having a house, domestic help, and available land, the survival of Lucy's small family would have depended on a steady supply of food, firewood, wool, and cotton if not cloth, and also enough money to buy other necessities. It is unlikely that the aging and bankrupt colonel, even with the help of his daughters and house servants, could have grown enough food and fiber to meet all their needs. Colonel Lewis and Lucy would have required help from their sons if they were to be comfortable and secure.

·13·

THE SMITHLAND
NEIGHBORS

THE SECTION of Livingston County where the Lewises lived was called the Smithland neighborhood. Except for the residents of Smithland town, the families of the district were comparatively isolated, often living several miles from the nearest homestead. One such neighbor of the Lewises was Amos Persons, who had moved to the vicinity from Georgia about a year before the Lewises arrived. Although he was two years older than Randolph, he had been married for only two years. Person's "extensive" farm was located on the Ohio River at the mouth of Bayou Creek,[1] about two miles up the river from Randolph's property. The owner of nine slaves, eight horses, and a grist mill, Persons was a prosperous and respected man.[2] He was a conscientious friend and good neighbor of Randolph's family.

A closer neighbor of the Lewises was Jonah Hibbs, a native Pennsylvanian who had come to Kentucky about ten years before the Lewises.[3] Following his arrival, Hibbs had acquired over 1000 acres of land in the county, and had established his farm, home, and orchard on a 600-acre tract of land that joined Lilburne's Rocky Hill farm on the north and east sides. Hibb's home farm did not front on the Ohio, but lay a mile or more back from the river in the broad undulating valley below and to the east of the property of the Lewis brothers.[4] Since Hibbs's house was about a mile from Rocky Hill, Jonah probably was Lilburne's nearest neighbor. The east fork of Cypress Run flowed out of Hibbs's farm and meandered through the back part of Randolph's farm on its way to the river.[5]

Hibbs appears to have been a steady sort of citizen. His family consisted of his wife and four children. He owned three slaves and three horses. He was appointed a justice of the peace in 1809, and was promoted to the rank of major in the militia that same year. Evidently he was an abstemious man for, that fall, he presented another neighbor, Jonas Menser, to the grand jury for retailing one-half pint of whiskey without a license. There is

134

little indication that Jonah Hibbs and the Lewises were close friends.

Smithland town was the center of commercial activity in the county. There were only five houses there in 1807, but in two years' time it had increased to twenty households, a growth spurred by the commerce that the two rivers brought to its waterfront. Chief among its businessmen was Joseph Woods, who kept a combination store and warehouse. Businesses such as Woods's operated under some handicaps. Where it was necessary for firms, courts, and individuals to keep financial records, documents reveal that the accounts were sometimes kept in British pounds, shillings, and pence, and, just as often, in dollars and cents. The lack of a standard monetary system was confusing, since the conversion of values from one system to the other involved a certain amount of inconvenience and room for error or controversy. Conversion tables were available, however. One such table indicates that, at that time, a cent was slightly less valuable than a British penny; eleven cents being equal to ten pence. The shilling was worth thirteen cents, and the British pound, containing twenty shillings, was worth $2.60.

This situation was further complicated by the fact that there was no standard coin or paper money. The coins of every nation in Europe, and Arabia and India as well, circulated in Kentucky, and a coin's value, in cases of doubt, was ascertained by weighing it in balances. The Spanish dollar, known as a piaster, was regarded as the standard of value in this chaos of coinage. It was also called a "piece of eight" because it was frequently cut into eight pieces in order to make change. Some blacksmiths or merchants had grown so sharp that when they had an occasion to cut a Spanish dollar they made five quarters or ten bits out of the piaster. As for paper money, the notes of the Bank of the United States and the first Bank of Kentucky occasionally circulated, but they contributed little or nothing to west Kentucky in the way of financial service. More highly trusted than bank notes were tobacco warehouse receipts and land warrants issued by the state treasurer. These papers were assignable and passed readily from one person to another. They were a popular and reliable form of paper money.[6]

Barter was often resorted to, with salt, tobacco, gunpowder, pelts, lead, whiskey, and other goods used for exchange. Credit was arranged on a person-to-person basis, for the most part, and the personal notes, drafts, and letters of credit that recorded these transactions were often used as negotiable paper in spite of the financial risk inherent in them.

In addition to these difficulties, Joseph Woods's business was further complicated by the necessity for him to act as a banker. R. T. Durrett described this aspect of the merchant's life on the frontier.

> In the midst of such a jargon of coins, and paper money, and produce and peltry, there was need of banks and bankers. . . . The merchants were generally the bankers, and out of the confusion of coins and paper money and produce and peltry that went as money, they wrought the best order they could. . . . In these stores were kept all the kinds of merchandise that were bought by the pioneers. Groceries and dry goods, hardware and medicine, books and liquors, implements and furniture, fire-arms and jewelry were sold over the same counter. These merchants, moreover, bought and sold coins and paper money and produce and peltry of the country and were practically the bankers of the times.[7]

The retail portion of Woods's business was probably less comprehensive than that described above. More important to him were his shipping and wholesaling enterprises on the Ohio and Cumberland rivers. He was part of an industry that transported and handled an astonishing volume of goods. As early as 1800 the following items passed by Smithland on the rivers: 22,714 barrels of flour, 1,017 barrels of whiskey, 12,500 pounds of pork, 18,710 pounds of bacon, 75,814 pounds of cordage, 3,650 yards of country linen, 700 bottles, and 700 barrels of potatoes. Engaged in this trade in 1800 were 515 flat-boats, barges, and keelboats, and by 1808 the number had grown to over 2,000.[8]

A typical ship in this trade was the Monongahela Farmer, built at Elizabeth on the Monongahela River. She made her downstream trip seven years before the Lewis family made theirs. This ship left the upper Ohio in May of 1800, carrying 700 barrels of flour and 500 barrels of whiskey. After being attacked by Indians, she was delayed for three months at Louisville waiting for high water to carry her over the falls. Henderson was passed two days out of Louisville, and the ship continued on to Fort Massac, Illinois, located twenty-two miles below the mouth of the Cumberland. At Fort Massac the ship added 2,000 bear skins and 4,000 deer skins to her cargo. Her cargo was sold in New Orleans upon arrival there, and the

Monongahela Farmer was then fitted out in full rigging and entered the regular New Orleans and West Indies trade.[9]

The mouth of the Cumberland was a natural transfer point for goods going up or downstream on both rivers. Cargoes produced at Nashville and other places in the Cumberland watershed were floated to the mouth of the river, where they waited for a boat headed for New Orleans. One such boat was the Louisiana, of 300 tons, launched at Pittsburgh in 1804. She sailed in ballast to the mouth of the Cumberland, where she loaded a cargo of cotton, and eventually delivered it to Liverpool, England. Several other Pittsburgh- and Marietta-built ocean-going ships of this period loaded their full cargoes at the mouth of the Cumberland and carried them directly to England, thus avoiding the charge for reshipping at New Orleans.[10]

The state of Kentucky maintained some control over the weights, measures, and quality of the goods shipped from her ports. Tobacco, hemp, flour, and preserved beef and pork were some of the items that were inspected regularly at official stations, where they were sampled and weighed; the barrels, hogsheads, or bales were then branded or stamped if they were up to standard. In 1804 the legislature of Kentucky established an inspection station for beef and pork at the mouth of the Cumberland, very likely in Joseph Woods's warehouse.[11] The inspector's duties were described in the act.

> Sec. 3. *And be it further enacted,* That every barrel so salted and inspected, shall contain not less than two hundred pounds nett weight of pork or beef; that beef of the first quality, consisting of the best pieces, being free from necks and shanks, be denominated mess beef; that barrels consisting of an equal proportion of each quarter, shall be denominated prime beef; . . . and the inspector shall brand each barrel in at least two places, one on the head and the other on the side, with the words "mess beef," or "prime beef," "mess pork," or "prime pork," as the case may be.[12]

The inspector was paid twenty-five cents for each barrel he inspected, and was subject to fines if he did not do his job properly.

The location of Smithland was made to order for an entrepreneur such as Joseph Woods. After he established his business there it thrived for a number of years, even though some of his transactions were on the shady side. In a three-year period Woods was indicted six times for tippling; in one case for selling two gallons of cider without license and "letting it be 'drank' in

137

his storehouse."[13] During this same period, in almost every term of circuit court he either sued someone or was sued himself. The details of these cases indicate the scope and nature of his business. In 1809 Woods sued David Caldwell for not delivering 2,000 pounds of lead that Woods had paid for. In that same session Woods was sued by Richard Ferguson, who had agreed to rent Woods's keelboat for "the purpose of freighting goods, wares, merchandise and other produce." The suit arose when Woods failed to hand over the keelboat, claiming that Ferguson would not pay the rent previously agreed upon. The case was later settled out of court. In another deal Joseph Woods, "for value received," had promised to deliver to Natchez "109 gallons of good whiskey and 100 pounds of good bacon," and was hauled into court for not delivering the goods, a failure that cost him $44.50.[14]

Another example of Joseph Woods's style of doing business was his involvement in the sale of a certain quantity of tobacco, presumably in hogsheads, in which some of the tobacco had been taken out and replaced by cotton. This adulterated tobacco was then "sold for more than it should have been." James McCawley, a friend of Woods, was indicted by the commonwealth's attorney for perjuring himself while testifying as a witness in this case in Woods's behalf. McCawley's bail was set at $1,000. Joseph Woods signed the bond as McCawley's security, and McCawley, standing trial in 1811, was found not guilty by a jury whose foreman was another very close friend, Lilburne Lewis. Even though Joseph Woods was one of the original four trustees of the town of Smithland, an aggressive merchant and the owner of nine slaves, nonetheless he seems to have been the type who would manage to get five quarters out of a Spanish dollar.

Joseph Woods may have had a few rough edges but, compared to his friend James McCawley, he was a cultured gentleman. McCawley ran the other business establishment in Smithland, the tavern with the billiard table that had so horrified Schultz because the common boatmen gambled away their wages there. McCawley renewed his tavern license with the county court every year, as the law required, posting a £100 bond that had to be signed by a second person as his guarantor or security. Joseph Woods stood as his security one year, but more often the co-signer was Richard Ferguson, another Smithland resident. The rates McCawley charged at his tavern were set by the county court, the same tavern rates that prevailed all over the county. In 1810 the tavern rates were listed in multiples of the Spanish half real, worth six and one-quarter cents, or one-half of a twelve-and-a-half-cent one-bit piece.

Dinner, supper or breakfast	25¢
Lodging per night	6¼¢
Corn or oats, per gallon	12½¢
Horse to hay or fodder together with corn or oats; twelve hours	37½¢
Whiskey per half pint or peach brandy[15]	12½¢

At this time McCawley's household, where he kept his tavern, was composed of one woman, two young children, three slaves and McCawley himself.[16] Unlike James Ivy in Centerville, McCawley ran his tavern and pool hall in a more or less orderly fashion, or so it appears from the court records, which indicate that McCawley was seldom presented to the grand jury for profanity, drunkenness, theft, or other lesser crimes, nor did he fail each year to be granted a renewal of his tavern license.

But even if McCawley was not given to petty evils, there is no doubt that he was a person of violent nature, who was capable of brutal cruelty. McCawley appears to have preferred favorable odds when assaulting his victims. He and his friend, Richard Ferguson, were members of a four-man gang that beat up a certain William Barker so severely that "his life was dispaired of," and on the same day, this time the gang having increased the odds to eleven to one, repeated the process on one Sam McAmy.[17] About two months later, McCawley and his friend Ferguson teamed up again for a violent assault on a slave named Bob, who was owned by Isaac Bullard, the ferryman at Smithland.[18] McCawley and Ferguson injured Bob so badly that Bullard sued, charging them as follows:

On the night of the day of August 15, 1809 . . . with force and arms to wit: with hands, fists, feet, sticks, and clubs in and upon the body of one negroe man slave called Bob, the property of said plaintiff, an assault did make on him said negroe man Bob. They did then and there, beat, wound, and ill treat and with a rope they then and there hung said negroe man Bob up by the neck till he was nearly dead, and other outragious violences did to said negroe named Bob. . . . By which said abuse of said negroe man Bob said plaintiff in fact averrs that said negroe is nearly finished in value, health, and strength and that he hath wholly lost the service and labor of said negroe man for the span of two whole months.[19]

139

Bullard sued McCawley and Ferguson for $500. James Mc-Cawley had been, and would again be, in court for other offenses: four times for assault, once for perjury, and again for contempt of court. In spite of these activities, he was a person of some political influence in Smithland. During this period he was a trustee of the town and later a magistrate.

McCawley and Ferguson were two of a kind. The earliest record of Ferguson's presence in Livingston County is found in an indictment of "Richard Ferguson, farmer, for committing a riot on the 11th day of January 1801 at the mouth of the Cumberland River in the county aforesaid by abusing and tarring the clothes and cutting the same and confining James Axley . . . and other enormities then and there."[20]

Thus, fittingly, was Ferguson first introduced into official record. The exact nature of Ferguson's business is unknown, but some aspects of it concerned river transportation. Although listed as a farmer in 1801, by 1806 he had been in a court controversy with Isaac Bullard over the ferry rights to Croghan's Island at the mouth of the Cumberland, and two years later Ferguson was in a dispute with Joseph Woods regarding the rental of a keelboat. Whatever the sources of his income, Ferguson appears to have been solvent. For several years in succession he signed James McCawley's £100 tavern bond as security, and performed similar services for other people. As early as 1803 Ferguson was a captain in the militia and, by the time the Lewises came to Livingston in 1808, he had risen to the rank of major. The next year Ferguson became the justice of the peace and consequently the representative on the county court from the Smithland neighborhood.[21]

The office of justice of the peace was vested with far greater power and influence in the early 1800s than it has today. The county court, which was made up of the several justices of the peace, had powers that were judicial, legislative, and executive and, through this combination of authority, the county court influenced all the affairs, levels, and individuals of society.[22] One of the many powers Ferguson could exercise as a justice of the peace was that of legally judging and sentencing slaves, and it was that power that Ferguson and McCawley used to justify the nearly fatal beating they gave to Bullard's slave, Bob. It appears that Bob had broken one of the oldest of Kentucky statutes, which read as follows: "No slave shall go from the tenements of his master or other person with whom he lives, without a pass, or some letter or token, whereby it may appear that he is proceeding by authority, from his master, employer, or overseer; if he does, it shall be lawful for any person to apprehend and carry him before a justice of the peace, to be by his order punished with stripes, or not, in his discretion."[23]

Bob's offense was considered a misdemeanor, not a felony, and so Ferguson was not required to summon a jury to try him. Ferguson was within the law when he acted as judge, jury, and near executioner. The statutes did limit the extent, if not the ferocity, of Bob's punishment. They specified that such offenders could be sentenced "to receive, on his or her bare back, at the public whipping post, any number of lashes not exceeding thirty nine." Although the law did not specify how Bob was to be fastened to the public whipping post for his punishment, hanging him there by the neck was not called for by law, nor was the use of "hands, fists, feet, sticks, and clubs," which the suit had charged against McCawley and Ferguson.[24]

Bullard's damage suit charged them with assault and was tried before a jury that disregarded the issue of assault and considered the question, not whether Ferguson and McCawley had the right to tie up Bob by the neck and lash him, but rather, had they damaged Bob unreasonably? Their lawyer, Fidelio C. Sharp,[25] presented their defense: "The defendents for the plea in this behalf sayeth that the slave of the plaintiff . . . came on the premises of the defendent without any uttered leave of the same, or uttered leave of said plaintiffs, or any lawfull business of the said plaintiffs, and that the said whipping was by virtue of an act of assembly in such cases made and proved."[26]

Instead of the $500 that Bullard had asked for, the jury awarded him $7.60 in damages, which was about the average rental fee for a man slave for a two-month period. Evidently the jury felt that McCawley and Ferguson had been overzealous, but beyond the damages of $7.60 there is no record of censure for their deed.

These, then, were the most important of the Lewises' neighbors in and near Smithland when they first came to the county: Amos Persons and Jonah Hibbs, farmers, steady and respectable men; Joseph Woods, trustee of Smithland, sharp trader in the shipping and warehousing business; tavern keeper James McCawley, town trustee of Smithland, a man of physical violence; and Richard Ferguson, major in the militia, justice of the peace of the Smithland neighborhood and, like McCawley, a cruel

141

man. These last two close associates, McCawley and Ferguson, had one more thing in common: they were both friends of Lilburne. Regardless of what the friendship between these two violent men and Lilburne Lewis implies about Lilburne's character, it is a fact that within a year or two after Lilburne's arrival in Livingston County he would regard James McCawley as his closest friend in the Smithland neighborhood, with Ferguson not far behind in his regard. Lilburne had one more friend in Smithland during his first two years in Livingston County: Doctor Arthur Campbell, a well-trained young man whose medical skills were much needed in Smithland. Lilburne would see Dr. Campbell frequently in the future.

· 14 ·

ISSUES IN WEST KENTUCKY,
1808

WHEN THE Lewis family arrived in west Kentucky in 1808 the three interwoven issues that most affected the local citizens were the economic depression, impending war with England, and national politics.[1] Of immediate concern was the severe nation-wide trade crisis.

The preceding few years had been marked by business instability. There were a few brief periods of optimism, but these merely set off an otherwise dismal time for all American commerce. America was not the master of her economy, for her prosperity depended upon foreign trade. Events in Europe, primarily the continuing war between France and England, and their efforts to blockade and cripple each other economically, made tatters of American business.[2] During this period the British seized over five hundred American ships, and the French took nearly four hundred.[3] America was outraged, and Jefferson, overestimating the British and French need for American goods, declared an embargo that forbade almost all American commerce with these foreign nations.[4] The results were disastrous, not to Europe, but to America, whose markets were seriously disrupted. The seaports and maritime industries suffered most, but inland the prices of wheat, tobacco, cotton, and hemp, fell so far that, in some cases, the farmers refused to sell. In general, the embargo reduced legitimate trade to one-fourth of the amount transacted in 1807.[5]

Along the cities of the seaboard, and particularly in the northeast, the reaction to Jefferson's policy was intensely critical. *The Embargo*, a satirical poem written by William Cullen Bryant when he was just thirteen, epitomizes this reaction:

> Th' Embargo rages, like a sweeping wind,
> Fear lowers before, and famine stalks behind.
> What words, oh Muse! can paint the mournful scene,
> The saddening street, the desolated green;
> How hungry labourers leave their toil and sigh,
> And sorrow droops in each desponding eye!

Bryant placed the blame squarely on Jefferson and, with a curse characteristic of Federalist sentiment, he continued:

> Palsied be his hand!
> Like Cromwell damn'd to everlasting fame,
> Let unborn ages execrate his name!

Styling the president as an "imbecile slave," Bryant went on:

> And thou, the scorn of every patriot name,
> Thy country's ruin, and her council's shame!
> Poor servile thing! derision of the brave!
> Who erst from Tarleton fled to Carter's cave; . . .
> Go, wretch, resign the presidential chair.[6]

West of the Allegheny Mountains the mood of the people was quite different. For the most part, westerners supported Jefferson's policies enthusiastically.[7] This support was shown in December 1808, when the Kentucky General Assembly passed the following resolutions:

> That the administration of the general government since Thomas Jefferson has been elected to the office of president, has been wise, dignified, and patriotic, and merits the approbation of the Country. *Resolved,* That the embargo was a measure highly judicious, and was the only honorable expedient to avoid war; whilst its direct tendency . . . was to preserve our seamen and property, exposed to the piratical depredations of Foreign Vessels. *Resolved,* That the general assembly of Kentucky would view with the utmost horror a proposition, in any shape, to submit to the tributary exactions of Great Britain. . . . *Resolved,* That Thomas Jefferson is entitled to the thanks of his country, for the ability, uprightness, and intelligence which he has displayed in the management both of our foreign and domestic concerns.[8]

In the Kentucky house these resolutions passed sixty-four to one, with only Humphrey Marshall, the cantankerous Federalist from Frankfort, opposing the measures. Copies were sent to Jefferson and the Kentucky congressmen in Washington.[9]

There is no doubt that the legislature reflected the sympathies of most of the citizens of Kentucky. Several of the public Fourth of July celebrations in Kentucky were reported in detail in the *Kentucky Gazette.* At these ceremonies numerous toasts were proposed; thirty-three were put forward, and presumably drunk, in Lexington. The toasts receiving the most cheers were those that praised the recently retired Jefferson and his policies.

> Thomas Jefferson—His enemies are the enemies of our republican institutions—6 cheers. . . .
>
> Our late president Jefferson, may his highly merited services be remembered with gratitude, and may those who calumniate him be troubled with a guilty conscience. . . .
>
> Thomas Jefferson, . . . he will live in the hearts of his countrymen whilst gratitude exists or exalted patriotism is admired—6 cheers. . . .
>
> The embargo—Congress were dignified in its adoption, pusillanimous in its repeal. . . .
>
> French decrees and British orders of council—The American who would submit to either, deserves a halter—9 cheers.[10]

Although the merchants of the East Coast did not appreciate losing merchant ships and sailors to the English, it was less objectionable to them than Jefferson's embargo, which had destroyed all chances for profit. In the Ohio Valley the settlers blamed the depression on the British, not on Jefferson. In addition, Kentuckians held the British in Canada responsible for arming the Indians and inciting their marauding forays.[11] Not only would Kentuckians have liked to take control of the British fur trade, but they would also have been happy to assuage their injured pride by beating the British to a pulp in Canada.[12]

As early as October 1807, some of Jefferson's political friends and advisors in the west were recommending an invasion of Canada, and even discussing who should lead the expedition. The irascible but influential Col. Arthur Campbell of Tennessee and Kentucky passed on to the president the widely held opinion, which he had "collected by some traveling and a more extensive correspondence," that the wrongs committed by the British could be put to right by "a battle fought on the Plains of Abraham."[13]

Four months later, at the time the Lewis family was arriving in Livingston County, their congressman and nearby neighbor from Eddyville, Matthew Lyon, wrote a similar letter to Jefferson:

> Washington Feby 9th, 1808
>
> Sir
>
> . . . My letters from the Westward express a great anxiety least the Savages be let loose upon the people unawares & before they are alarmed & prepared. I meant also to remind you that the time for preparing to take Montreal for this year . . . is fast slipping away. That place is defenceless & approachable on the River side

145

during the Ice which lasts nearly through the Month of March. . . .
8.000 Men at the season of the year I speak of would be as sure to
effect the object as 20,000 when the St. Lawrence is open. . . .

I am confident that the Legislature are disposed to provide for
and Sanction such a step without a declaration of war. . . .

Your Obedt. Servt.

M. Lyon[14]

There is no doubt that Lyon's views represented the feelings
of his constituents in west Kentucky, and especially Livingston
County where, during that year, forty-five of the Livingston militia men were called to active duty for about a month to serve as
rangers "to guard the frontiers of the county of Livingston
against the invasion and depredations of the Indians."[15] The
privates were paid six dollars a month. At this time no other militia men in the state were on active duty against the Indians, for
Livingston was the only county whose border adjoined the
Chickasaw hunting grounds. It is not known whether the threat
from the Chickasaws was exaggerated in 1808, but the war-like
spirits in the county were high when the Lewises arrived.

It appears that the Chickasaw tribe had more to fear from the
citizens of Livingston County than vice versa. Early in 1809, at
the urging of the west Kentucky legislators, the Kentucky
legislature requested the president of the United States to
strengthen the garrisons at the mouth of the Ohio, and at St.
Louis and Michilimackinac as well.[16] A month later the state
legislature passed the first of many resolutions requesting that
the Indian claim to lands west of the Tennessee River in
Kentucky be extinguished and the use of the land be annexed to
Kentucky.[17] Prior to this time a treaty with the Chickasaw Indians had guaranteed them exclusive possession of their own
huge area for hunting west of the Tennessee River. Nevertheless, the rights of the Chickasaws were frequently violated, and
trespass by the whites was common. The state legislature even
proposed that a highway be built to New Orleans through the
Chickasaw hunting grounds.[18] At this time, while friction was
building with the Chickasaw tribe, far away to the south the
magnificent Shawnee chief, Tecumseh, was trying to forge a
grand confederation of northern and southern tribes. Kentuckians were apprehensive. Although there was great excitement over the Indians in Livingston County during that spring,
it is not likely that Randolph or Lilburne Lewis were immediately involved. They would not have been liable for militia

146

duty until they had lived in Kentucky for three months, and then the regiment to which they belonged, the 24th, did not furnish any men for patrol duty at that time.[19]

In 1808, America was a collection of divided and squabbling people. The antipathy between the western frontier farm pioneers and the residents of the eastern seaboard cities was intense. Their quarrels found the most convenient arena in politics, where Jefferson's Republican party opposed the Federalists, who were personified by Alexander Hamilton. This Federalist-Republican political confrontation sheltered under its umbrella many conflicting attitudes that were not at all political in nature, but which, by chance, were implicit in the people who were politically opposed; thus Federalists, for the most part, tended to differ from Republicans not only in politics, but also in religion, occupation, speech patterns, education, and, in fact, most other aspects of personal beliefs about life and its values.

General statements always have exceptions, as do broad comparisons; nevertheless, the Federalists and Jeffersonians tended to be dissimilar in these ways:

The Jeffersonian Republicans	*The Federalists*
lived in the south and west	lived in the north and east
had an agrarian economy	had a mercantile economy
wanted territorial expansion	wanted development of commerce
favored strong state government	favored strong federal government
were anti-national debt	were pro-national debt
did not trust banks	controlled American banking
opposed excise tax	favored excise tax[20]
were anti-British	were anti-French
favored invasion of Canada	favored trade with Canada[21]
favored protection by state militia	favored protection by a standing national army
were perfunctory about education	emphasized education[22]
were tolerant of slavery	were critical of slavery
were emotionally outgoing in religious practice	were formal and traditional in religious practice

There were few influential Federalists in Kentucky at this time. Joseph H. Daviess, the United States Attorney for Kentucky, who lived in Owensboro, was one. Another, Humphrey Marshall, the brilliant, corrupt, and eccentric historian and politician, lived in Frankfort, as did John Wood and Joseph M. Street, who had moved there to edit *The Western World,* a Federalist newspaper that caused some dismay in the ranks of the Kentucky Republicans.[23]

The United States Marshall of Kentucky, Col. Joseph Crockett, who had been appointed to that office by Jefferson, was a loyal Republican, and he kept Jefferson informed about political events in Kentucky. Crockett was an old acquaintance of Col. Charles L. Lewis. Crockett, like Lewis, was a native of Albemarle County, Virginia, and, moreover, the two men were related by marriage. Crockett had distinguished himself in the Revolution, and afterwards in Kentucky, where he was one of the earliest settlers and most prominent developers of the state.[24]

Colonel Crockett was apprehensive about the effects of *The Western World* on political affairs in Kentucky. Early in 1807 he wrote Jefferson that the newspaper had been set up "for the express purpose of changing the politics of the state from warm republicans to Federalists." He advised Jefferson that even though Kentuckians were alarmed by Aaron Burr's mysterious western journeys, and were propagandized by *The Western World,* nevertheless, he said, "The people in the Country are true friends to the union. I believe I can venture to say there is not one man in twenty dis-affected to the Federal Government."[25]

These, then, were the current problems in west Kentucky when the Lewises arrived in 1808. There was a severe depression, a chronic shortage of specie, and gathering war clouds increased the fear of Indian attacks. It was not the best time to move, but there was no choice for the Lewises. Because of their close relationship to Jefferson, who was tremendously popular in Kentucky, the arrival of the Lewises in Livingston County must have generated uncommon local interest.

Early in that first year in Kentucky, Lucy received a reply to the letter of farewell she had written to her brother the previous fall:

Washington, Apr. 19, 1808.

My dear Sister:
Your letter from Monteagle, written the day before you left it was the first intimation I received of your having ever had a thought of leaving our part of the country. I felt it with deep sensibility. The times in which I have happened to live, and a zeal not to be wanting

to them, have kept me through life in a state of separation from my dearest connections, and now that the prospect of returning to domestic enjoyment presents itself as near at hand, I shall find that time and chance have removed most of them beyond my reach. In point of happiness nothing can fill the place of our natural affections. I do not wonder that you are determined to go with your children. Tho' late the time of life, and long the journey for you, I feel too powerfully myself the force of parental love to consider any pain so great as that of a separation from our children. I learn from you with great pleasure that your situation will be comfortable, and that you carry with you the means of deriving advantages from the rich lands of Cumberland. I do not set it down as impossible that I should see you there. I have never ceased to wish to descend the Ohio & Mississippi to New Orleans, and when I shall have put my home in order, I shall have leisure, and so far I have health also, to amuse myself in seeing what I have not yet seen. But be this as it may, in all situations of life, my dear sister, I shall retain for you the liveliest feelings of affection, feelings of which absence & incessant occupations have too much suppressed the expression, but which have never ceased to warm my heart & will still be cherished to its latest hour by the recollections of our early life. Present me affectionately to Colo. Lewis and all your children, and accept for yourself, my dear sister, assurances of the constant & tender attachment of

Your affectionate brother
Th: Jefferson[26]

Mrs. Lucy Lewis

This letter was probably carried to Lucy by Isham, her youngest son, who stayed behind in Virginia when most of the family emigrated to Kentucky.[27] Isham was at loose ends, was unemployed at this time, had no property of his own to manage in Virginia, and apparently decided to join his family in Livingston County to see what prospects were available for him there. If this was his plan, and if he did visit his brothers and parents during their first summer in Kentucky, he did not stay more than a few days before moving on.

A cousin of Isham's, Meriwether Lewis, had been appointed governor of the Upper Louisiana Territory the year before. The governor lived in St. Louis, and Isham decided to visit him there, perhaps in the hope that his cousin would give him a job in the new territory. This did not work out, evidently, for within six weeks Isham had returned to Albemarle and had been in conference with Jefferson. This information is contained in a

letter Jefferson wrote to Gov. Meriwether Lewis from Monticello at the end of August. "Isham Lewis arrived here last night
and tells me he was with you at St. Louis about the second week
in July, and . . . that four Iowas had been delivered up to you as
guilty of murder . . . and that you supposed three of them would
be hung. It is this latter matter which induces me to write
again."[28]

In the letter Jefferson urged the governor not to execute
more than one of the four Indians, since only one white man
had been killed. He recommended conformity to Indian customs of man-for-man justice in preference to the American code
that held that all concerned were guilty. Jefferson wanted "to
impress them with a firm persuasion that all our dispositions
towards them are fatherly." At this time Meriwether Lewis was
bogged down in his administration, and was an inexcusably poor
correspondent. Jefferson was distressed when the governor
failed to write even once during a nine-month period.[29]

Isham may have been commissioned by Jefferson to make this
trip as a messenger, but the tone of his letter implies that Isham
was in St. Louis on his own initiative, and that Jefferson did not
know Isham had gone there until he spoke to his uncle after
returning. One of Col. Charles L. Lewis's family, at least, had
rendered a service to Jefferson. Jefferson would repay Isham's
favor amply within a year.

·15·

THE COUNTY COURT

THE LEWISES were not truly first-generation pioneers. They came to west Kentucky twenty years too late for that.

In many places the forest was giving way to cleared fields. Food and clothing, which had earlier been supplied by the hunter's gun, were now obtained with a plow. Commerce was established and the flow of goods from farms and forests moved to distant markets over the miserable roads and mighty rivers. The finished goods returned carried in the backpacks of shrewd Yankee peddlers or in boats turned into floating stores; or they were distributed by the local banker-barter storekeepers. By 1808 the law was established throughout the state, with constitution, legislature, and courts having jurisdiction in every part of the commonwealth, operating as effectively as the citizens would permit, and as honestly as the officials were inclined.

In the early 1800s the most important governmental structure in the state was the county court system. It was the task of the county court and the justices of the peace, who composed the court, to manage and regulate most of the public affairs and business that took place in each county. The responsibilities and powers of the county court were impressive in scope. Estates and wills, guardianship and care of orphans, cases of poverty and bastardy, the appointment of local officials, franchising and setting rates for ferries and taverns, establishing roads and drafting labor for their maintenance, assessing and collecting taxes, overseeing apprentices, administering the slave patrol system, and sitting in judgment over minor crimes of whites and all crimes by negroes; all these were in the court's jurisdiction. Even clerical affairs were touched by the county courts, for ministers were required to register with the court.[1]

These powers and duties of the court, and many others not mentioned here, were so extensive that they included legislative and judicial functions as well as executive responsibilities, making the separation of powers practically nonexistent in Kentucky county government of that time. That, however, was not as notable as the fact that the county court, which wielded most of the

151

local power, was made up of men who were appointed for life and who also appointed their own successors. They were never subject to public election.[2] In addition to choosing their own successors, they appointed the county coroner, jailer, court clerk, attorney, constables, and other officials, as well as the most important political figure in the county, the sheriff, who was the chief executive officer of the county, of the circuit or judicial courts, and was, in addition, the highest acting election official. The only officials on a state or county level for whom the citizens could vote were their state senators and representatives, and the governor and lieutenant governor of Kentucky. The fact that the voting was done vocally and in public gave the sheriff great political influence over the few elective offices in the state because he, the chief election authority, could pressure the voters with his power to issue summonses and unexecuted judgments.[3]

Selecting the people who were to serve on juries was also a duty, or privilege, of the sheriff. There were no restrictions on how he made the choices, other than that the jurors be qualified as far as property ownership, place of residence, and a few other criteria. Whereas today juries are chosen by a random drawing of names, in the early 1800s Kentucky sheriffs were free to select whomever they wanted for jury duty. Holding this authority, the sheriff had a wide open, legal opportunity to influence indictments and jury decisions by picking jurors he could coerce, or who were biased in regard to cases that were pending or on the docket.[4] The sheriff's authority in this matter was absolute, and if the court clerk presumed to erase a juror's name from the sheriff's list, the clerk was removed from office.[5] For forty-four years after the founding of the commonwealth, justice held her breath in the circuit courts of Kentucky. Finally, in 1836, the legislature remedied this situation with an act that began with the following preamble: "Whereas, the present mode of summoning jurors is not calculated to promote the ends of justice, or to secure the correct administration of the laws, and operates unequally and oppressively upon the citizens of this commonwealth. . . ."[6]

Of all the official county positions, then, the job of sheriff was most coveted for its power as well as for the income from the fees and charges that were collected by this office. Sheriffs' fees were set by the legislature and, although the fees appear insignificant today, their value then had many times the present buying power.[7] The sheriff's office was a profitable one. The state constitution provided that a sheriff's term was to last two years, after which another sheriff was chosen from the membership of the county court, usually the oldest one, in order to "pay a just regard to seniority in office," as the constitution suggested.[8]

There was considerable prestige in the office of justice of the peace, even though there were no fees or salaries connected with the position. A justice of the peace had only to be patient for a few years, eight or ten on the average, and he would almost automatically step into the best-paying and most powerful official job in the county.[9]

By the time he became sheriff, the senior justice of the peace was often too old to perform the rigorous duties entailed; the majority of new sheriffs, old or young, sick or well, sold their offices for a lump sum or rented them out to other men. This practice was common throughout Kentucky. In a typical west Kentucky county, it was an extremely rare man who, when legally appointed sheriff, was willing to perform the duties of office himself in preference to selling them.[10] It is estimated that in an average Kentucky county, the sheriff's office could be bought for between $500 and $800, or rented or "farmed" out, in all or in part, for a percentage of the fees. The deputy sheriffs normally also bought their jobs, in this case from the sheriff; in addition, they usually bought or rented part of the profits of the sheriff's office. The positions of county court clerk and constable were also sold in Kentucky, though not as routinely as that of sheriff.[11]

The sale of public office had been illegal in Kentucky since 1801, but in the next four decades most of the successive governors, the general assembly, the court of appeals, and the many prosecutors either ignored or conspired to evade this law. The result of this statewide venality was an increasing decline in the quality of office holders and, consequently, a growing inefficiency in county government in Kentucky.[12] There can be no doubt that in Livingston County the sheriff's office was sold as frequently as in any other county in the state. Bearing in mind that the sheriff's term lasted for two years, one can see that during the seven-year period from 1807 to 1813, if the legally appointed sheriff did not sell his position, nor die while in office, there should not have been more than four different sheriffs. In actual fact there were eight.[13] If one can judge from the record of Livingston County sheriffs in returning tax revenues to the commonwealth, during the four years following 1806, Livingston was, for its size and wealth, one of the worst-run counties in the state.[14]

The sale of public office in America reached its culmination in Kentucky. It is not difficult to trace this pattern of venality back to Virginia, the parent state from which Kentucky and her constitution were formed. Indeed, the sale of public office became legal in Virginia in 1829, and had been common there, and in England as well, long before the American Revolution.[15]

The county government was far more important to most Kentuckians than were the state or national governments, which had comparatively little direct influence on the daily lives of the citizens.[16] In spite of this, the county court was practically a closed club. Except for those few men who were justices of the peace, or persons who had influence on them, or who could buy an office, the common citizen had almost no control over the way the local government was run. Secular life on the frontier, in Kentucky at least, has sometimes been pictured as democratic in pattern. In fact, it never was democratic, but operated as a more or less aristocratic oligarchy over which the majority of the citizens had little or no influence or control. Every county office was filled by appointment, not election, and the men who made the appointments, the justices of the peace, appointed their own successors.[17] These men, operating together as the county court, were in continuous but legal disregard of the principle of separation of the powers of the legislative, judicial, and administrative branches of government. In addition, many of the men whom they appointed to office routinely sold their positions, sometimes even at auction.[18]

Thomas Jefferson detested the county court system. He described the all-encompassing powers and the self-perpetuating character of the county courts as "vicious," and felt that the common citizens should have more of a voice in their own local governments.[19]

The ordinary citizens of Livingston had very few ways to influence the county court or its officials. Petition was one means, but obviously it was not always effective. A more drastic means of getting the attention of local officials was to institute impeachment proceedings against them in the state legislature. Two such attempts were made in Livingston County in 1809, one against a justice of the peace, and the other against the county surveyor.[20]

Another way of showing resentment to officials was to indict them for various petty crimes and bring them before the circuit court, the primary judicial body in the state. One Kentucky historian described a typical grand jury session that convened in a neighboring county:

> The April, 1806, Circuit Court came on, and with it that pest of all pests, the grand jury. Judge Knox, one of the Associate Justices, was once again made a victim on account of his passionate indiscretions, and with his usual adamantine face and limitless cheek, confessed the corn and paid his fine. . . . The grand jury was no respector of persons, on the contrary, they rather took a delight in making examples of the leading men whenever the opportunity presented itself. Henry P. Broadnax, Judge of the Circuit Court, and William Featherston, Commonwealth's Attorney . . . were each indicted at this term for profane swearing and fined the round sum of five shillings each, which they paid without a word.[21]

The grand juries of Livingston were equally "pestiferous" to their civil officials. The Honorable David Caldwell, assistant circuit judge of Livingston County, was presented to the jury five times for drunkenness over a two-year period, and his successor, Honorable Dickson Given, was presented for blasphemy.[22] These two judges appeared to accept their public embarrassment with more equanimity than had their predecessor, Judge William Prince. Prince, who had been a captain in the Revolution, was a dominant, aggressive man. It was he who founded the town of Princeton, Kentucky. His son, Enoch Prince, was the first clerk of the circuit court and served for many years in that capacity. In 1808, when Judge Prince was presented to the grand jury for retailing whiskey without a license, his anger at this humiliation was aroused. He paid the fine of ten dollars, and on the following day resigned from the court.[23]

Further down the judicial hierarchy, John Gray, the commonwealth's attorney, received his share of attention when the grand jury indicted him in 1810 "for saying 'God damn your fool soul' to his bay at Harkin's stable." Undismayed by this attention, Gray repeated the same stunt at the same place three months later, when he was "profanely cursing and saying 'I will be God damned' and cursed and swore the said oath at and on the platform of Samuel Harkins . . . against the peace and dignity of the commonwealth."[24]

Next in line for recognition was David Kline, the jailer, indicted "for receiving of Nicholas Tramwell of said county, yeoman, $1.12½ for favor and ease while confined in the jail." The petit jury found Kline guilty of "demanding and receiving the sum of 37½¢ for ease and comfort," from Nicholas Tramwell. Jailer Kline was fined 37½¢. Evidently Kline extorted 37½¢ from Tramwell for a favor, and the remaining 75 was a willing and not unusual prisoner's purchase of some goods from behind bars, with the jailer acting as errand boy. Seventy-five cents was enough to buy three pints of whiskey.[25]

The indictments of Livingston officials were sometimes pranks of gleeful harassment; in other cases, such as Jailer Kline's, they appear to have been justly deserved; and finally, some of them appear to have been prompted by vindictiveness. Robert Kirk is an interesting example of an official who may have been the victim of all three of these motivations. In 1808, when Kirk was a justice of the peace, a certain Joseph Wiley presented Kirk to the grand jury because he "did profanely swear 'by God' fifteen times at his house."[26] Four years later, after Kirk had become sheriff, and while he was in attendance at a sensational court session, he swore twice and was indicted for it. He "acknowledged the truth of the presentment" and paid his five-shilling fine to the court clerk.

Of more serious nature was the effort of one George V. Lusk to have Robert Kirk impeached by the legislature of the state, the only authority that could remove county officials from office. This attempt was made near the close of 1809, when Kirk was still a justice of the peace. Very little information about Lusk or his motives is available.[27] The House Journal record of the proceedings reads as follows:

> The committee . . . beg leave to report, that the only charge exhibited against the said Kirk, which has the authority of any evidence in its support, is that of *intoxication*. It appears from the deposition of Edward Lacey, that the said Kirk did act in his official

156

character when intoxicated; and although this evidence might seem conclusive in establishing the said charge, yet the variety of conflicting testimony, together with the statements made by the member of the house [John Mercer], from Livingston, render it extremely doubtful on the mind of the committee, whether the said Lacey was not mistaken.

Your committee take the liberty of stating, that from the evidence before them, few men could have sustained a more amiable character, both *official* and *private,* than Mr. Kirk. The member from Livingston states, that he has acted with him, as a member of the County court, for eight years; and that he has uniformly esteemed him an independent and intelligent officer—and although he has known him at several times, to drink too much spirits, yet he does not conceive that his usefulness as an officer, is at all impaired thereby; nor does he conceive that he is more liable to become intoxicated *now,* than when he accepted the appointment. . . .

Resolved,

That the charges against Robert Kirk, a justice of the peace for the county of Livingston, are unsupported by evidence; and ought to be dismissed, at the cost of George V. Lusk, the *prosecutor.*

Which being twice read, was concurred in.[28]

The general assembly of that year had received an unusually large number of impeachment petitions. One impeachment and trial removed a justice of the peace from Bracken County who was, at the same time, also a member of the legislature. This man had defrauded and threatened a widow, and in the ensuing investigation had lied, embezzled, and stolen mail. The vote to remove him from office was unanimous.[29] Another impeachment petition was filed in the legislature against a squire from Pendleton County who, it was proved, had sold spiritous liquors without a license. The house committee, being composed of practical men, questioned in their report, "whether an offense of so slight a nature . . . requires the constitutional interposition of the legislature." The house committee added that selling liquor without a license "has no immediate relation to the official duties of the office of the justice of the peace," and that the usual fine for the offense could be levied against the offender. These legislators were tolerant and expected a certain amount of greed, coarseness, and exuberance in the public servants, men being what they are. The committee report went on to express the irritation of the legislature at being flooded with such trivia which, if taken seriously, would be a "great obstruction to other important business." [30]

Squire William Rice, justice of the peace of Livingston County, like the justice of peace from Pendleton County, was indicted for tippling. Rice was charged with "suffering and permitting his man slave, Sam, to sell one quart of cider to James Gordon and to receive of said Gordon the sum of 12½ cents." The cider was sold "without license to be drank about his wagon in Salem." James Gordon, who had "drank" the cider himself, then proceeded to inform the grand jury of Rice's offense. [31] Gordon may not have liked the cider, or he may not have liked Squire Rice, who no doubt was inconvenienced, but at least Rice was exonerated in subsequent court proceedings. [32]

Another local official whose conduct was questioned was William C. Rodgers, the county surveyor. Rodgers had been a member of the local elite since the formation of Livingston County in 1799. He was one of the seven original justices of the peace, a position that no doubt eased his way into the lucrative job of county surveyor. [33] By 1806 Rodgers was a captain in the county militia, and a few years later became a county tax commissioner as well. [34] His impeachment in 1808 and trial in December 1809 by the state legislature must have created a sensation, for, unlike the impeachment petition filed against Squire Robert Kirk earlier that year, the complaint against Rodgers was a serious one. It charged that, while acting as county surveyor, Rodgers had altered the corners and boundaries of a certain military grant survey in Livingston County, and then had surveyed some of the grant in his own name, further claiming ownership by forging certain papers. [35] James Logan, the owner of the land in question, had filed the impeachment petition against Rodgers, and seven men from the county were called as witnesses and made the long cold trip to Frankfort in December. [36] Rodgers claimed complete innocence for himself, and accused Logan of breaking a partnership agreement to buy the land in question.

The procedure for impeachment of county officials described in the state constitution specified that the house had the power of impeachment, and the senate was to try such cases, a two-thirds vote being required for conviction. [37] The special house committee appointed to consider Rodgers's impeachment was composed of four men, two of whom were arch political enemies, Republican Henry Clay and Federalist Humphrey Marshall. Their personal animosity was so intense at this time that within a month Clay and Marshall would try to kill each other with dueling pistols.[38] On this occasion, however, they both agreed that William C. Rodgers deserved to be impeached, and the house followed their recommendation. Rodgers's trial, which was conducted by the senate, lasted for three days just before Christmas of 1809. Again Clay and Marshall were members of a special house committee whose task it was to prosecute Rodgers before the senate. At the end of the trial Rodgers was acquitted, ten votes for guilty against fourteen not guilty. Daniel Ashby, the senator from Livingston, abstained.[39]

William C. Rodgers's troubles with the legislature began in December 1808, and ended just a year later. During this same period Rodgers was involved in another political and real estate maneuver that would make substantial changes in Livingston County (see Map 4). After his plan had been carried out, Livingston County was reduced to one-half its former size, and Caldwell County was formed out of what had been the southern half of Livingston. Another result was that the Livingston county seat was moved away from Centerville to a new and more central location, which just happened to be on some land owned by William C. Rodgers himself. Invariably, towns grew up around county seats, and whoever owned the property adjoining that on which town lots were laid out could sell out later at a profit if the town grew, which it usually did.[40]

Near the end of December 1808, a petition to strike off the new county from Livingston was received by the Kentucky house. Five days after that, there was a laconic entry in the *House Journal* recording that they had received a "petition from sundry inhabitants of Livingston County counter to the petition formerly preferred for division of said county." The names of those who petitioned against the formation of Caldwell County are not recorded, but one can guess that people who had business interests in Centerville would be opposed to losing the county seat.[41]

Those who opposed the formation of Caldwell County lost out. The enabling act was approved by the legislature at the end of January 1809, to take effect on April 17 of that year. A few months later the public buildings at Centerville were put up for

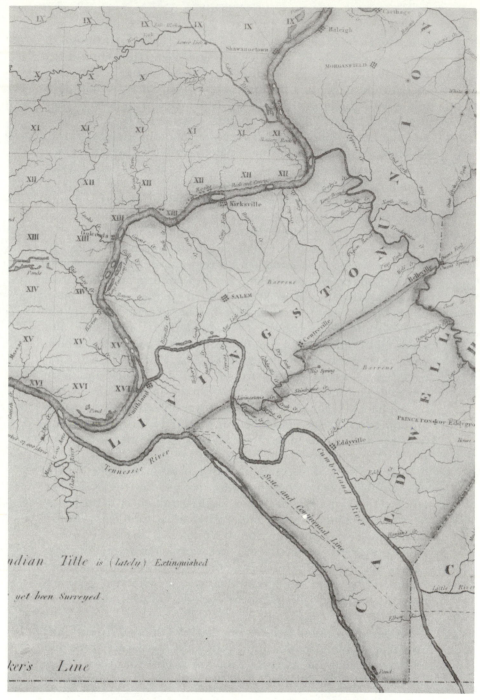

Map 4. Livingston County, circa 1818.
This fragment was taken from Luke Munsell's map of Kentucky.
(Courtesy of the Kentucky Historical Society, Frankfort).

sale.[42] Centerville had not lasted long, having been the county seat for only five years, beginning in April 1804. Earlier the county seat had been Eddyville, established as such on March 25, 1800.[43] In 1804, under much protest from Eddyville residents, the county seat had been moved to a more central location, the ford of Livingston Creek, where Centerville had come into being.

Rodgers made some concessions in order to have the new county seat on his property. He promised to donate two acres for the county square, a stray pen, a well, 180 acres of timber, and to erect "a hewed log courthouse 24 feet square in the clear with a shingle roof with one-half of the house a plank floor with necessary doors, windows, &c. with glass in the windows, three jury rooms, to be finished off in the inside in a workman like manner with necessary bench bar &c. and also a square log jail 12 feet in the clear with cabbin roof and strong lock to the door, and floor and loft of the same kind of timber with the body."[44]

While Rodgers was in the process of putting up these buildings, the county and circuit courts met in the nearby home of Sam C. Harkins or at Rodgers's house.[45] This new location of the county seat was actually a road junction where the road from Eddyville and Centerville split, one branch going north to the ferry over the Ohio at Cave in Rock, and the other going more or less west to the Ohio ferry at Golconda. The crossroads was in a fertile valley, and several families had already settled in the neighborhood. Rodgers finished the jail, and it was accepted by the county court in May, whereupon both Sheriff James Johnson and Jailer David Kline immediately and formally "objected to the sufficiency of the jail."[46] This protest probably had very little to do with the actual condition of the jail; it was a standard complaint in Kentucky at the time that was intended to lessen the personal liability of the sheriff and jailer when prisoners escaped, which they often did. A month later the circuit court met for the first time in the "new house prepared for that purpose on the lands of William C. Rodgers." Both Randolph and Lilburne Lewis were members of the grand jury.[47]

Although Rodgers had not yet fully completed the court house and had not deeded over the county square and stray pen, by October he was ready to cash in on the real estate he owned adjacent to the county seat. Rodgers made a motion to the county court that a town be established on his land. The motion

161

was postponed by the court for the next three months. Rodgers finally got the message and in January deeded the county square, or "jail yard," to the court. In the next session, in February, Rodgers's motion was finally enacted, and the town of Salem was established. Thirty acres were set aside and laid off in lots to be sold by trustees who were duly appointed from the neighborhood.[48]

By the time it was named and legally established, Salem had become an active little settlement. Sam Harkins ran a stable there and would soon open a tavern. Nearby was a blacksmith shop, and the firm of Bradley, King, and Vance operated a stable and general store.[49] This store had been broken into and robbed by two men a few months before. The thieves, who fled the county and were never caught, stole saddles, boots, bundles of stockings, and many bolts of fine cloth.[50] Rodgers's infant town was maturing rapidly. His other opportunities for wealth grew as well. He was county surveyor, county tax commissioner, militia officer, farmer, brawler, real estate promoter, and speculator; a man of several talents, perhaps, but certainly one with many connections to the local source of power, the county court.

·16·

THE YEAR OF TROUBLE,
1809

THE THREE Lewis families spent the year of 1808 establishing themselves in Livingston County. They had to "open" their farms and build their homes, which would not have left them much time for involvement in community affairs. There is almost no mention of the Lewises in any of the 1808 county or state records, but some of the events of their lives during the next year can be reconstructed. The year 1809 was one of trouble and sadness for them all, especially for Lilburne.

That spring, in April, in the most beautiful time of the year, Lilburne's beloved wife, Elizabeth, died. Elizabeth was just twenty-seven years old and had borne five children during the twelve years she and Lilburne had been married. The children had been born approximately two years apart, and from this pattern it appears that Elizabeth may have died as a result of childbirth. Her youngest baby, Robert, was just past two years of age. Her oldest child, Jane, was eleven, and Lilburne, her husband, was about thirty-two. A spot for a graveyard was chosen about three hundred yards back from the south crest of Rocky Hill, and Elizabeth was buried there with a simple fieldstone marker at her head and a smaller one at her feet. She was the first of three who would lie in that spot. Lilburne recorded her death, not in his Bible, but in an 1803 copy of *The Revised Code of the Acts of the General Assembly of Virginia*. Lilburne had owned the book since 1805, when he wrote on the first flyleaf, "L. L. Richmond, May 7, 1805." On the next blank page he inscribed the date of his marriage to Elizabeth, the birthdays of their five children, and then her death, "Betsey Lewis wife of Lilburne Lewis died April 25, 1809, Livingston County, Kentucky."[1]

Lilburne gave no information there about the cause of her death. One would guess childbirth complications, but it is equally possible that she was a victim of illness or disease. The medical record of Lilburne's family for the year shows an extended siege of sickness that lasted all that year and was particularly severe in August and September. Unfortunately,

163

the record did not begin until a month after Elizabeth had died, and contains no mention of her. Subsequent writings of Lilburne's leave no doubt that he loved Betsey deeply. He was burdened not only by his grief, but also by the need to arrange for managing his home, his servants, and caring for his children— tasks his wife had previously directed. Lilburne must have been distraught through that difficult time.

A young doctor, Arthur Campbell, of Smithland, kept a record of the health of Lilburne's family during 1809, in the form of a bill or running account in which the doctor kept the record of his services to Lilburne.[2] It is apparent that Dr. Campbell had received medical training, at least in the use of medicines and rudimentary surgery. He was certainly not a quack and may have been well trained for the times; he used Latin and medical abbreviations extensively. From the treatments he prescribed, the nature of the illnesses that plagued the Lewises can be identified.

First in seriousness was malaria, caused by tiny parasites that were carried and spread by the anopheles mosquito. Although that fact was unknown in 1809, a treatment was available in which a crude form of quinine, pulverized chinchona bark from Peru, was used to control the terrible chill paroxysms during which the victim shook uncontrollably, his teeth chattered, and the skin turned cold and blue. This stage of the disease was called ague or "buck ager," and was followed by a stage of high fever and sweating. Muscle soreness accompanied these attacks, which recurred every three or four days. In severe or long-term cases, damage to vital tissues could result in death.

During the six weeks following the end of June, Lilburne bought chinchona bark at least eleven times, usually sending his teen-age slave boy, George, on the trip to Smithland, four miles away. The short notes that Lilburne sent to Dr. Campbell calling for help or medicine are still in existence.

Aug. 21, 1809

Dr. Campbell; My oldest son is extremely ill. Early this morning he had a chill and fever followed and although his fever appears not very high, yet he is out of his head at times. Pray do me the favor to ride up as soon as you can.
Yours etc. L. Lewis

Aug. 29, 1809

Dear Doctor, Lucy my second daughter has a slight fever. I suppose it is the effects of an overcharge of bile. Little Robert is still sick. The rest of the sick are better. When convenient ride up to see us. Yours sincerely, L. Lewis

N. B. more bark

Sept. 8 - 1809

D. Doctor, The family is mending but had we not better continue the bark for a few days. Dispatch George with an ounce and oblige.

L. Lewis

Sept. 18 - 1809

D. Doctor. Lilburne [the seven year old son] has the Ague & Fever again, he has his Ague at this time. I am within a squirrel's jump of one today for I feel very unwell, let us have a dose of Calomel and Gallap [Jalap] apiece. Your friend.

L. Lewis

Dr. Campbell we are out of bark again.

signed L. Lewis [no date][3]

Following malaria in frequency of treatment was the astonishing amount of tampering with the functioning of the alimentary canal. Laxatives were taken at the slightest excuse, and even, at certain times of year, for no reason at all. The medicines used ranged from senna, castor oil, and tincture of aloes, through the more drastic jalap, to rhamnus or buckthorn, a violent cathartic, and calomel or chloride of mercury, which was a poison irritant. At the other end of the digestive system, vomiting was induced by senna or antimony, and if the patient's insides needed to be pacified rather than emptied, there was available opium or paregoric, lac paturne made from lettuce juice, and spirit of nitrous ether.[4]

During August and September, Dr. Campbell made over a dozen house calls for the Lewises, charging two dollars for the eight-mile round trip during the day, and three dollars for a night call. He bled them. He treated them for pain, cramps, insomnia, and other ailments, including the common frontier complaint of body lice.[5] A typical situation occurred on August 5, when Lilburne wrote to Dr. Campbell: "Dear Doctor, My sister's face is a good deal sweeled, what can be the matter with it, I know not; do me the favor to ride up and see her. Believe me yours etc. Lilburne Lewis."

Dr. Campbell went that night to treat Nancy's swollen face. He bled her and gave her a laxative, charging fifty cents for each of these remedies, plus three dollars for the trip.[6] It appears that Nancy was a part of Lilburne's household, perhaps helping to care for the children after Elizabeth had died. At this same time, at least one of Lilburne's daughters was living at Randolph's home and fell ill while there. In addition to this daughter and his sister Nancy, Lilburne himself, both of his sons, and at least six of his slaves were sick that summer. Isham, Lilburne's younger brother, apparently had come from Virginia and stopped by Rocky Hill for a visit in August. His presence and illness are recorded in the medical bill, "Ague pill for Isham Lewis, August 26."

The total amount of money that Lilburne owed to Dr. Campbell for medicines and services for that year was about sixty-five dollars. Slightly more than ten dollars of that total had been spent on Lilburne's slaves, a ratio of about one to five, even though there were as many slaves under his wing as there were whites. The treatments given to the slaves were similar to those received by the Lewises: castor oil and other laxatives, bleeding, a liver pill, bark for malaria, and in the case of "Ursely [Ursula], opening a breast," which could have been either lancing a boil or removing a tumor.

"Ursely," like two or three others of Lilburne's slaves, had been rented out to other people. Ursula had been rented to Robert T. Erwin of Smithland on a long-term lease agreement with Lilburne, and the same sort of arrangement had been made with James McCawley for the services of Patty.[7] Another slave was let out for a shorter time, probably a year, to John Daniel, who owned land, kept a tavern, and ran a ferry at the Point, at the mouth of the Cumberland. Ursula's value at that time was $325, and Patty's worth was appraised at about $285. In Livingston, adult women slaves rented annually for about ten percent of their value and men slaves for about fifteen percent.[8] The rent received for Ursula and Patty, if received in cash, would have roughly equaled Lilburne's medical expenses for the year. There was not much cash in circulation, however, for, as Governor Scott had advised the legislature at that time, "the scarcity of specie has become proverbial."[9] This may have been one of the reasons Lilburne was to have difficulty in paying Dr. Campbell's bill.

In the short letters that Lilburne wrote to Campbell in August and September of 1809, relations between the two men seemed amicable. Lilburne referred to Campbell as his friend in one note, and in another asked the doctor to pass on a personal message to a young lady whom they both knew. "P.S. Tell Miss Price I had a beatific dream last night in beating her at backgammon. Don't forget." When he wrote this, Lilburne had been a widower for five months, and evidently was taking some interest in feminine companionship again.

Three days after the "beatific" dream about Miss Price, Lilburne wrote Dr. Campbell that he felt very unwell, was on the verge of a malarial ague, and added, "Tell the ladies God help our Lexington expedition." Lilburne and the doctor had evidently planned a trip together to the Bluegrass with Dr. Campbell's new bride and, perhaps, one or more other ladies.[10] Campbell's bride may have been homesick for her family in Lexington. The trip was postponed for a short while and then, in October, Campbell and Lilburne made the journey. At one point in the trip the party passed through Danville, where Lilburne paid Campbell part of his bill. "Danville, October 21, 1809, rec. of L. Lewis $23.00 it being part of his account with me. signed A. Campbell." It may have been that Lilburne had collected some money in Danville, either from a loan or business deal, and that was one of his reasons for making the trip. Another reason Lilburne made the journey was that he wanted the job of taking the ten-year federal census in Livingston County, which was due the next year. The county census takers were appointed by United States Marshal of Kentucky, Col. Joseph Crockett, a friend of Jefferson's, and an in-law of Lilburne's. Crockett was a resident of Nicholasville, a few miles south of Lexington. He gave Lilburne the job.[11]

Another, and perhaps the main, reason for the trip was to place Lilburne's two oldest daughters, Lucy and Jane, in a boarding house in the Bluegrass, a region that not only had better schools than were available in Livingston, but also was comparatively free of malaria because of the excellent drainage of the limestone-based soil. It must have been in Lilburne's mind that he, a widower, was not able to provide the feminine attention that girls of nine and eleven years required. In mid-December in Mercer County, probably in or near Harrodsburg, Lilburne made an agreement with one William C. Bradburn to

167

board, lodge, and wash for the two girls at the cost of $100 per year "to be paid annually or at the end of their boarding." Lilburne agreed to pay Bradburn extra to have clothes made for the girls. Bradburn also, "at the special insistance and request of him the said Lilburne," sent the two girls to a dancing school for three months. Lilburne left his daughters with Bradburn, where they remained for a year and a half.[12] Lilburne returned to Livingston at the end of December.

There is no indication that Dr. Campbell and Lilburne were on unfriendly terms before this time, but without doubt Dr. Campbell was a man who liked to collect his bills. Early in January, shortly after Lilburne returned to Livingston from the Bluegrass trip, Dr. Campbell asked Lilburne to pay his debt, which Lilburne promised to do. Probably Lilburne did not have the money, but in any event, he did not pay Campbell. The doctor filed a suit and never treated the Lewises again. Their friendship had ended. At the same time, Campbell filed a suit to collect money from another patient. It appears that Dr. Campbell was preparing to move out of Livingston for good, and he wanted to straighten out his accounts before leaving. The county census of 1810 does not contain his name. Campbell's lawyer, John Gray, continued to press the doctor's case against Lilburne in court, but it was not settled until four years later.[13]

Other money troubles were piling up for Lilburne in 1809. Lilburne could not pay his doctor's bill, he had contracted to spend over $100 a year for his daughters' room and board, and then, in mid-year, it became clear that he would have to pay an old debt claim, plus damages, amounting to more than $300. This debt had been incurred over three years before, when Lilburne had come to Livingston County for his first visit in 1806. The chaotic practices of financing and banking in Kentucky at that time need some explanation before one can appreciate the complex nature of this debt of Lilburne's.

There were no true banks in Kentucky in early 1806. Prior to that time the Kentucky Insurance Company had issued bank notes, but they were of dubious reliability, and the First, or Old, Bank of Kentucky did not receive its charter until the end of 1806. Furthermore, Kentuckians still retained their prejudice against paper money, a distrust that had been engendered by the unpaid issues of the Revolutionary War.[14] Since loans from banks were not available, most loans and credit were arranged between individuals. Personal drafts and notes passed from person to person, gathering endorsements as they went along, all without the owner's knowledge. Because cash was scarce, these personal documents were generallly regarded as negotiable, and they circulated as cash does today, but without a fraction of the security inherent in sound money. Because of slow and haphazard communications, a person's solvency, or lack of it, was difficult to ascertain at short notice. If a note or draft was worthless when written, or the writer would or could not honor it later, then every subsequent transaction in which that note had been instrumental became invalid, and each person through whose hands the note had passed had to go back to the previous endorser for restitution. Sometimes these chains of liability involved more than a dozen individuals and two or three years of time.

John Gray, Dr. Campbell's lawyer and the commonwealth's attorney of Livingston County, was involved in the embarrassment of having his name advertised in connection with a note of this sort. *The Farmer's Friend,* which was published in Russellville, Kentucky, was the only newspaper in far west Kentucky, and was widely read in Livingston County. It carried local and general news, advertisements, and legal notices of the neighboring counties, such as the posting of an outlaw, sales of property at the courthouse door to settle estates, and the letting out of orphans to guardians. John Gray could not have been pleased when he read this advertisement in *The Farmer's Friend:* "This is to forewarn all persons from taking an assignment on a note of 50 dollars payable at sight, about the last of March, given by me to John Gray, Esq. Livingston County & State of Kentucky, as the same note was given for no value received I am determined not to pay it unless compelled by law. WILLIAM CROSS."[15]

William Cross had evidently paid Gray with a note for services that Gray had rendered or was to perform for Cross. Cross became disgruntled with Gray's performance, or lack of it, and in an effort to keep Gray from realizing any benefit from their agreement, stated in a public announcement that he, William Cross, was determined not to redeem the note. In effect he was not only stopping the payment of a check, but, at the same time, he struck a resentful blow at Gray's reputation. Advertisements similar to the one placed by William Cross were not uncommon in the newspapers of that time.

The complexity of handling loans and credits without the benefit of banks, communications, or stable currency, is better illustrated by the intricate transaction in which Lilburne was the key figure. Before it was straightened out, five years had gone by and the draft, whose payment was in question, had passed from George Pickett, who wrote it in Virginia, through the possession of three other men. Furthermore, it had been in court twice and personally involved at least five additional men who played such varied roles as financial agent, debtor, courier, witness, and lawyer.

These were not ordinary men. In later years one of them became a state representative, three would be state senators, and one had been Kentucky's first convict. The people involved in this financial mess were residents of the following widely dispersed places: Richmond, Virginia; Richmond, Kentucky; and the Kentucky counties of Livingston, Fayette, and Warren. The paragraphs below give an account of the transaction. Even though it is difficult to follow, it furnishes one example of the complexity of frontier finance and Lilburne's troubles.

On January 23, 1806, when Lilburne was in Livingston County to look over the land that he and Randolph considered buying from George Pickett, Lilburne, evidently short on cash, stopped at Boaz Station in Livingston County and borrowed $275 from a man named Lynch Brooks.[16] As security for the loan Lilburne himself copied by hand a draft for about £400 that George Pickett had made out to Lilburne. In this draft Pickett had instructed Sen. Peyton Short of Lexington, Kentucky, to give Lilburne £400, which Lilburne would then turn over to Pickett when he returned to Virginia. Short had owed Pickett this money for some time.

Peyton Short, born a Virginian, had been educated at William and Mary and moved to Kentucky with his wife in 1790.[17] He was elected state senator shortly afterward. In his younger days Peyton Short was very well acquainted with the "pure and virtuous" Rachel Donelson who later became the wife of Andrew Jackson. In fact, Rachel's first husband, the scurvy Lewis Robards, accused Peyton Short of causing the breakup of their marriage.[18] Another, though less exciting, connection of Peyton Short's was his short-lived and unprofitable partnership in a store in Frankfort with the well-known scoundrel, Gen. James Wilkinson. In 1790, Short advertised that the store was willing to barter merchandise, dry goods, hardware, and groceries in exchange for "tobacco, corn, wheat, rye, pork, beef, bacon, hemp, flour, furs of every kind, tar, pitch, and turpentine, &c.&c.&c."[19] Short was also a speculator who, "influenced by the mania for land speculation which was prevalent at that time . . . became the owner of thousands of acres of pioneer lands in Kentucky and Ohio." Short sustained large financial losses, primarily from his land speculation, and in 1809 he went to the Mississippi Territory in an attempt to recover his fortune.[20] Short's brother, William, was the secretary and confidant whom President Jefferson entrusted with the European negotiations to open the Mississippi River to western trade.

Peyton Short's debt of £400 to George Pickett was secured by two notes that were being held by Pickett's financial agent in Kentucky, George Trotter, who kept a store in Lexington on the corner of Main and Mill Streets. When Henry Clay was elected United States Senator in 1809, George Trotter was chosen to fill Clay's vacant place in the Kentucky legislature.[21]

After copying Pickett's draft, Lilburne then wrote instructions on this copy asking Short to pay Lynch Brooks the $275 and to deduct $275 from the £400 which Lilburne was to collect from Short at a later time. Lilburne evidently kept the original draft so that he could collect the remainder of the £400 from Short. It is presumed that Lilburne would have made up this $275 to Pickett when he returned to Virginia.

At this point Lilburne gave the copy of the draft to Lynch Brooks. Lilburne's instructions to Short written on this copy read as follows:

Beau Station 23 Jan. 1806

Sirs:
Within you will receive the copy of a draft from George Pickett, Esq. of Richmond in my favor. Be pleased to pay Mr. Lynch Brooks $275 and his receipt shall be good against the within claim to that amount.

Your obdt. Svt.
Lilburne Lewis

Mr. Peyton Short
   Kentucky
Test
   James Kennedy
   Henry Brooks[22]

171

Neither Lilburne nor Brooks had reason to doubt that Lilburne's instructions would be carried out by Short, and that the matter would be settled as soon as Brooks presented the paper to Short. Lilburne and Brooks then went their own ways. In time, Lilburne returned to Virginia. But for some reason he had failed to collect and take. back to Pickett the remainder of the £400 that Short owed to Pickett. Perhaps Short was feeling the pinch of his unsuccessful speculations.

Apparently Brooks was not pressed for money, because he held this paper for a year and a half before presenting it to Short for payment. In June of 1807, Brooks confronted Short with the paper and Short said to Brooks in effect: "I won't pay you the $275 until I get the approval of the transaction from Mr. Pickett's agent, Mr. Trotter, and he agrees to credit this amount to the £400 debt I owe Mr. Pickett." Short's actual statement, which he wrote on the draft under Lilburne's request, reads, "I can agree to accept this order on no other condition than that Mr. George Trotter, who holds my obligations within referred to in his hands, shall credit me by the amount so soon as accepted or paid. signed Peyton Short." Lynch Brooks did not get his $275 from Short at that time.

At the end of seven more months, Lynch Brooks gave up trying to collect the $275 from Short and he passed the confused and controversial claim on to Cornelius Turner of Kentucky, in payment for "value" that Brooks had received from Turner. This "value" could have been cash, services, or goods. Cornelius Turner was, or would become, a resident of Warren County, Kentucky. From 1816 to 1819 he was the state representative from that county and in 1820 became state senator.

The transfer of this claim is recorded along the side of the document, which by this time was becoming somewhat crowded with written statements. "January the 19th 1808. I do assign the within claim to Cornelius Turner for value received of him; as witness I have hear unto set my hand this day and date above mentioned. signed Lynch Brooks. Attest: Lynch Brooks; John Turner."[23]

Very shortly after this time the Lewis families arrived in Livingston County to live. Lilburne was met there by the controversy over the note he had written two years before.

The Lynch Brooks who signed this last endorsement as a witness must have been the son or father of the Lynch Brooks who was the signatory. The scripts of the signatures are quite dissimilar. The other witness, John Turner, may have been a kinsman of the distinguished Cornelius Turner, but, whatever the relationship, he enjoyed fame of a different sort. When the penitentiary in Kentucky was completed in 1800, John Turner, from Madison County, was the first convict confined to it. He was sentenced to serve two years for horse stealing, but was "recommended to mercy because his first offense."[24] John Turner was fortunate in his timing. Just a year before, under the leadership of John Breckenridge, the legislature of Kentucky had revised the cruel penal code of the state and eliminated the death penalty for whites except in cases of first degree murder. Two years earlier Turner could have been hung.[25]

Cornelius Turner held this financial claim for over a year and on May 2, 1809, tried to collect it. On that day Peyton Short was in Livingston County, evidently on his way to Mississippi, and the much-traveled claim was again presented to him, this time by Cornelius Turner through his lawyer. Again Short refused to pay, and in the last open space on the document wrote the following statement: "Having since writing the above received a positive injunction from Pickett's agent [George Trotter] not to pay the amount of the above draft on his, said Pickett's account, I do therefore by these presents refuse to accept the payment there of given under my hand the 2nd of May 1809. Peyton Short."[26]

At this point the travels of the draft ended, and its career in court began. Trotter, evidently acting on instructions from George Pickett, his employer, had stated that Lilburne's original $275 pay order to Lynch Brooks was no longer valid and would not be honored. As a result of this statement Lynch Brooks would have to find some way to get his money directly from Lilburne, and in turn Cornelius Turner would have to go back to Lynch Brooks for the recovery of his $275.

At the end of May, just a month after Elizabeth had died, Enoch Prince, the clerk of the circuit court, issued a summons ordering Lilburne to be in court in Salem on the first day of the June term to answer Lynch Brooks's legal plea for his money, plus damages, amounting to a total of $500. James Johnson, the sheriff of the county, was unable to locate Lilburne and wrote on the back of the summons: "the Defendent not found within my bailiwick but a copy of the within left at his usual place of residence." If Lilburne received the summons, apparently he neglected it, for in mid-August of 1809, when sickness was rampant at Rocky Hill, Lilburne was served personally with another summons by Sheriff Johnson, ordering him to appear at court in September. Having received this court order, Lilburne became liable to pay Brooks the money.

This case was not settled and was continued for a year, when finally Attorney John Gray, acting for Lynch Brooks, filed a suit in September 1810. Gray summarized Lilburne's conduct in the affair with the following statement: "Lewis thus and then had due notice by virtue of which premise the said Lewis became liable to pay said Plaintiff [Brooks] said sum of money, nevertheless said Lewis although often thereto requested hath not yet paid said plaintiff the same or any part thereof but the same to him to pay the said defendant [Lewis], hath hereto wholly refused and still doth refuse to the plaintiff. Damages $500.00 and therefore he sues. Gray."[27]

The case was finally settled in March of 1811, five years after Lilburne borrowed the money.

The year of 1809 had been a dismal one for Lilburne and his family. His wife died early in the year. In midsummer the whole family fell ill with malaria and a variety of other ailments, and continued so for several months. At the same time that he was being sued for a debt by Lynch Brooks, Lilburne was being dunned by Dr. Arthur Campbell for medical bills; and finally, at the end of the year, he felt it necessary to send two of his little girls away to board, an expense he probably knew he could not afford. As the winter progressed it appeared that the family would suffer another grievous loss, for Lucy, Lilburne's mother, was losing weight and strength from a serious if not fatal illness.[28]

·17·

LILBURNE ENTERS
PUBLIC LIFE

EVEN THOUGH several aspects of the Lewises' private lives were going badly, Randolph and Lilburne, in the Virginia tradition, began to take part in community affairs. At the beginning of the year Livingston had been divided to form Caldwell County, and the county seat of Livingston was removed from Centerville. At the end of June the circuit court was convened in "a new house prepared for that purpose on the lands of William C. Rodgers."[1] This was the first time the court had met at Salem, a location more than ten miles closer to Smithland and Rocky Hill than Centerville had been. Among those serving on the grand jury at that June term of court were both Randolph and Lilburne Lewis. The foreman of that grand jury was Col. Jonathan Ramsey, one of Livingston's most important citizens. Ramsey was an early resident of the area, having been one of the original county magistrates. A surveyor, it was he who made the first plat of Smithland.[2] He was also a lawyer, a member of the state legislature, and a colonel in the state militia. If wealth can be indicated by ownership of slaves, Ramsey, who owned fifteen, was comparatively well off.[3] Three other members of that grand jury were magistrates: Obediah Roberts, Edward Lacey, and Moses Shelby, Revolutionary War hero and brother of Isaac Shelby, Kentucky's first governor.[4] Also on the grand jury were William Pippin and Thomas Hodge, two men whom Lilburne would meet on another grand jury a few years later. Thomas Champion, also on the jury, had just begun his climb in the official county hierarchy as constable. A resident of Salem, Champion would hold several county jobs in the next few years: keeper of the stray pen, tax collector, "padroller," deputy sheriff, trustee of Salem, and jailer.[5] If Lilburne had not met these men before, he would learn to know them well enough in the future, as he would the circuit court judges and John Gray, the commonwealth's attorney.

In Kentucky a circuit judge was assigned to each of the ten ju-

175

dicial districts or circuits. The districts contained an average of about five counties each at that time.[6] The circuit judge traveled to each of the counties three times a year, holding court for a week or two in each county. In the counties two local residents served as assistant circuit court judges. The circuit judge alone, or the two assistant judges, or the circuit judge and one assistant were sufficient to constitute a court.[7] In general, the circuit judges were well trained in the law and made competent judges, whereas the assistant judges were not usually as well qualified.[8] David Caldwell and Jesse Ford were the assistant judges at that June term of court, and the Honorable Henry P. Broadnax was the circuit judge.

Livingston was in the Seventh District, which included the entire southwest part of Kentucky, a circuit that stretched 160 miles from one end to the other. Judge William Wallace was regularly assigned to this district, but for some reason he was not present for this term of court and his place was filled by Broadnax, whose circuit, the Sixth District, lay north of Wallace's. Exchanging their circuits and substituting for each other when they thought necessary was provided for by law.[9] A closer look at these two men, who were both residents of Russellville, gives an idea of the character and individuality of the frontier judges. The record is sparse regarding Wallace, but "tradition describes him as a tall, fair haired man, of few words and much learning, who often passed on foot from one court to another, with his rifle on his shoulder, and that he was an unerring shot." Wallace was appointed a circuit judge in early 1807 when Ninian Edwards, having been promoted to the court of appeals, left a vacancy on the bench. As might be expected, Wallace was a Jeffersonian Republican. In 1808, when Wallace was a presidential elector, he publicly declared his intention to vote for James Madison.[10]

Henry Broadnax was apparently more colorful than Wallace. Several reminiscences of him are available. Broadnax had emigrated to Kentucky from Dinwiddie County, Virginia, before 1800. Unlike Judge Wallace, Broadnax was a bachelor. An old letter describes his broken romance: "Mary Bibb, a sister of George M. Bibb, jilted Judge Henry Broadnax and married another man. Judge Broadnax remained a bachelor for her sake."[11]

Other reports are less fragmentary.

He was a stately, high-toned Virginia gentleman, who dressed in shorts, silk stockings, and top-boots; he had an exalted sense of the dignity of the court, and a great contempt for meanness, rascality, and all low rowdyism. Mr. Crittenden used to describe, in his most inimitable manner, a scene which took place in the courtroom, in Logan, where Judge Broadnax presided. A man had been indicted for biting off another man's ear, in a street brawl. This was a penitentiary offense, and Mr. Crittenden was engaged to defend the prisoner.

Judge Broadnax was a warm friend and admirer of Mr. Crittenden, but he railed at him fiercely for taking fees of such *low rascals*. The judge was, at heart, an aristocrat.

In this case, after great difficulty and delay, eleven jurymen had been obtained. Many respectable-looking men had been summoned, and rejected by the counsel for the prisoner, and both the judge and sheriff were much exasperated. At last an ill-looking fellow, with a tattered straw hat on his head, half the brim being torn off, a piece of his nose gone, and his face bearing many other evidences of drunken brawls, was brought in. After looking at him a moment and asking him a few questions, Mr. Crittenden said, "Well, judge, rather than be the cause of any *more delay,* I'll take this man."

The judge, who had been looking on angrily, could no longer control himself. He sprang to his feet, exclaiming, "I knew it; yes, I knew it!—the moment I laid my eyes on the fellow I knew you would accept him." Then, taking a contemptuous survey of the jury, he exclaimed, aloud, "Did any living man ever see such a jury before?"

Mr. Crittenden quietly replied, "Why, your Honor, I pronounce this a most respectable jury."

After that speech of the judge, Mr. Crittenden said his mind was at ease about his client; he knew he would be acquitted, and he was.[12]

That incident took place in Russellville, but wherever he was, Broadnax displayed the same remarkable personality. Eighty miles from Russellville, in Henderson, where a few years before he had been fined for profanity, another courtroom drama took place:

At the July term of the Circuit Court Judge Broadnax had his temper and judicial courage thoroughly tested by Edward Cheatham, one of the veniremen, who was a man of some importance at that time.

Mr. Cheatham engaged in conversation, and being rather strong of lung, interrupted the business of the court. He was admonished by the Judge and yet persisted. He was fined six dollars, and this seemed to incense him; he was fined ten dollars once, twice, and yet he refused to be quiet; he was fined thirty dollars, once, twice, and three times, and still he defied his Honor, the Judge. Finally he was ordered to prison in the custody of the jailer, there to remain until his several fines, aggregating one hundred and sixteen dollars, were paid, or secured to the Commonwealth. He ranted and raved, as he journeyed on to the house of correction, and not until having slept one night a prisoner, and calculating the cost, did he come to a proper understanding of how foolishly he had acted, and the extent of his beligerency. He succumbed to the majesty of the law, and prayed pardon, which was granted next day. This determined course of Judge Broadnax ever afterwards secured him the respect due his position, and no more self-important men tempted his authority.[13]

Judge Broadnax found that the citizens of Ohio County were somewhat harder to control than those of Henderson. On one occasion Judge Broadnax was presented to the grand jury of Ohio County for shooting caterpillars on Sunday. Another anecdote concerning his difficulties in the Ohio County courthouse illustrates the temper of the times.

In 1800 the courthouse was built. This house was a novelty in architecture. It was a log structure built on top of the jail, which was also of logs. The walls of the court room projected all around to enlarge its dimensions, and much resembled a huge bale-box set on a smaller one. The jail was entered through a trap door in the floor of the court room.

An incident is related of the conduct of the prisoners there in the early days. During the session of the circuit court Judge Henry P. Broadnax—alike remarkable for his love of law and order, and his petulant, imperious temper—was presiding. He had just closed his charge to the grand jury and commenced the call of his docket when a most furious uproar was heard in the jail below. The sounds seemed to reverberate with increased force in the court room. "Silence!" called the judge. "Sheriff, keep silence!" The sheriff, in a loud, commanding tone, called to the prisoner below to be still, and the judge renewed the call of the docket, when again disturbing sounds arose. Loud shouts, songs, and hallelujahs came up from the prisoner's cell.

Then the judge sprang from his seat, took several strides across the floor, and commanded the sheriff to being the noisy prisoner into court. The sheriff obeyed, and the prisoner greeted the judge with a most profound bow, saying in a submissive manner: "May it please your Honor, I did not think you would call my case so soon. I thought the grand jury had to find a true bill before a prisoner could be brought to trial."

"Scoundrel!" shouted the judge, "I did not have you brought up for trial, but to make you stop that infernal noise."

"Noise! Oh, I ask your Honor's pardon. Excuse me, and I will explain. You know there is a great religious excitement now prevailing in the country, and, like yourself, Judge, I am a very excitable man and I was at the time laboring under religious excitement."

"Scoundrel! Do not mock religion in my presence; I'll fine you!"

"Fine me, your Honor, but how will you collect it?"

"I will send you to prison," responded the furious judge.

"Prison, your Honor? Ain't I already in prison?"

The judge, now almost demented with rage, hesitated a moment, then, as if not knowing anything else to do, asked the sheriff to remove the "scoundrel" from the court back to prison. Before leaving the prisoner remarked: "Judge, that jail is a very dry place. You know we all have our weak points, and mine is to become excited and noisy when dry."

The Judge looked daggers, and would no doubt have adjourned court until the next term rather than comply with the hint. A friend in court—*amicus curia*, as the lawyers term it—left hastily, and returned soon, and with the sheriff descended into the prisoner's cell. Tradition says that the peace of the court was purchased at the rate of a tickler of whiskey per day.[14]

Broadnax owned a plantation and house at Russellville. It was remembered there that when the judge was not on the circuit he would climb onto the platform of a small wooden tower he had had built near his house, and from this vantage point watch his slaves at work on the plantation. It is said that the tower stood until after 1900.[15]

This, then, was the stern and eccentric man who presided over the circuit court in Livingston County when Lilburne and Randolph were on the grand jury. The grand jury met for four days and then returned a few minor indictments for swearing, drunkenness, assault and battery, building a fence across a public road, and so forth. It was a routine batch of indictments, most of which were dismissed at the next term of court.[16]

Of slightly more significance than jury duty was the appointment of Lilburne as a special arbitrator in a legal dispute between Col. Jonathan Ramsey and Micajah Phelps. The two

179

litigants had agreed to submit their differences to the five arbitrators "or any of them, and that their award when made and returned should be made the judgement of the court." Of the five men, three were magistrates, one was the sheriff, and Lilburne was the fifth, not yet an office holder, but evidently considered to be a reliable and intelligent citizen by Judge Broadnax. Lilburne and the other arbitrators decided in favor of Colonel Ramsey, their own commanding officer, and the case was closed with the customary quaint phrase, "All suits, disputes, controversies and differences either in law or in equity heretofore shall cease and be dropped and be buried in oblivion."[17]

In addition to serving the judicial system as jurors, Lilburne and Randolph were required to render duty as part-time soldiers in the militia. Only a few men in special categories were exempt from this duty, and all other free males between eighteen and forty-five years of age were obliged to serve after they had been a resident of the state for three months.[18] A person was not eligible to be an officer until he had been a Kentucky resident for one year. Randolph and Lilburne were serving in the militia by the summer of 1808, and were eligible for officers' commissions by late spring of 1809. Militia records are very scattered and there is no information available about Randolph's service. Lilburne, however, would eventually become a captain, and it appears that by 1809 he may have been nominated as an ensign or lieutenant. When a vacancy occurred among the officers the regimental officers held an election and nominated someone to fill the empty spot. A majority was required, and the nomination was then set to the governor, who made the appointment with the advice and consent of the Senate.[19]

At that time, and until several years after the war of 1812, militia service was a serious affair, given purpose by Indian raids at home and war clouds abroad.[20] A company of the Livingston militia had been called out to "guard the frontiers of the county of Livingston against the invasion and depredations of the Indians in the year of 1808."[21] Officers were not nominated casually at that time. The fact that Lilburne was chosen to be commissioned indicates that the other officers of the Livingston militia (who, for the most part, were the leaders of the community) respected Lilburne's intelligence and leadership qualities.

Although the militia uniforms on the frontier were apt to be idiosyncratic, the law specified a certain colorful outfit as regulation for officers of Lilburne's rank. "Captains, subalterns and regimental staff officers . . . shall appear in uniform and side arms, viz. with a coat of blue, lappells of red, epaulets of silver, and white underclothes, a round black hat, cockade, plume and sword or hanger."[22]

Except in wartime, the militia had very few duties. They occasionally posted extra guards for important inmates of the flimsy jails, or assisted the country patrol, whose function was to regulate slaves.[23] Far more interesting than these duties were the regularly scheduled musters held four times each year. From year to year the legislature varied the schedule of these musters, but the following was typical: the first two reviews of the year were the company musters held in June and July; in August the battalion mustered; and in September came "the big muster," a two-day affair at which the entire regiment was present to exercise, drill, be counted, and reviewed.[24] Once a year in the fall, almost every able-bodied man in the county who was not approaching middle age gathered in Salem. The "big musters" were remarkable affairs. Such a concentration of voters in one place provided an irresistible temptation for political candidates, who openly solicited votes and were not at all reluctant to "treat" with whiskey anyone who looked thirsty.

A typical instance of this in 1809 involved Senator Jereboam Beauchamp of Washington County. Beauchamp's election was contested because he had "unlawfully treated with spirituous liquors" at a battalion militia muster just three days before election. In the senator's trial, evidence was introduced that it was customary to treat at musters, that the officers frequently treated their men for no particular reason, and that treats by politicians were routine on circuit court days as well. Beauchamp was not convicted that time, and took his seat in the senate.[25]

In later years the musters became rollicking social festivals, and the military aspects became a pure farce. Horses were raced, shod, and swapped. Huge picnic feasts were washed down in floods of whiskey, fights were routine, friendships were renewed, and the unsteady militiamen ambled through their parade exercises with aimless and haphazard abandon. Most of the crowd had a lovely time.[26] There was, no doubt, some socializing when Lilburne's company met for muster, but the impending war with England must have cast an air of seriousness over the training exercises. The enlistment figures and the combat record of Kentucky soldiers in the War of 1812 leave no doubt that most Kentuckians were eager and able to fight. Lilburne was in the First Battalion of the Twenty-fourth Regiment. His superior officers were Maj. James Elder and Col. Jonathan Ramsey. The Second Battalion of the Twenty-fourth was under the command of Maj. Jonah Hibbs, Lilburne's neighbor, whose farm lay next to Rocky Hill.[27]

While Randolph and Lilburne were taking their place in the community they were also working to complete the final details of their Kentucky land purchases from George Pickett. It appears that their younger brother, Isham, was some help to them as a courier in this matter. The Lewis brothers wanted to have their purchases recorded in Richmond, Virginia, so that Randolph could sell part of his large holdings, and so he and Lilburne could divide another section between them. Apparently they sent the deeds back to Virginia by Isham when he returned there from St. Louis in August of 1808. The deeds were recorded that fall in Richmond.[28]

At this time Isham was very much at loose ends. There are few traces of what he did during the months following his return to Virginia from St. Louis. It seems probable that he lived at least some of the time with his uncle, Randolph Jefferson, at Snowden. Randolph Jefferson had inherited this 1,300-acre estate, with slaves and other properties, from his father, Peter Jefferson. It was only twenty miles from Monticello to Snowden. The plantation house was on a high bluff over the great bend in the James River at Scottsville. Eight months after coming back to Virginia, Isham wrote to Thomas Jefferson from Snowden; Jefferson had retired from the presidency barely two months before.

Dear Sir.   Snowden. 27th April 1809
    The great desire which I feel to be placed in some employ whereby I may secure to myself the happiness derivable from the idea of enjoying the fruits of well spent industry and the difficulty I find in attaining this object unassisted by any influential friend has induced me to beg the favor of your endeavors in my behalf. I am in hopes you will be less disposed to think hard of this request when I assure you it is produced from necessity, brought on not from my own imprudences but those of an unfortunate father whose

promises of wealth and neglect to bring me up in any useful pursuit has brought on me the want of the former and occasions me to deplore his inattention to the latter. It is too commonly the case that after we are sensible of having erred to excuse ourselves we endeavor to throw the blame on the innocent. Whether or not this is the case with me you and all those who are acquainted with the cause of my situation are left to determin. I can only say that if I am chargable in this respect it proceeds from an error in judgment, and not from a wish to charge a father wrongfully whose foibles I would with the greatest freedom alleviate, was it in my power. But I fear I am dwelling too long on a subject which however it effects me, may appear to you unimportant, and I shall therefore conclude with the firmest belief of your readiness to do the best for me in your power.

I am with affectionate respect yrs etc.
Ihm Lewis

N. B. I will thank you to inform me whether you suppose the Louisiana country will be laid off into Townships etc. within any short time, and provided it should be, whether you suppose it will be in my power to get a part of the undertaking.

I. L.[29]

Three days later Jefferson replied to Isham's request:

May 1, 1809   Monticello

Dear Sir, It is with real concern that I learn the disagreeable situation in which you are for want of employment, and the more so as I do not see any way in which I can propose to you any certain relief. As to offices under the government, they are few, are always full, and twenty applicants for one vacancy when it happens. They are miserable also, giving a bare subsistence without the least chance of doing anything for the future. The army is full and, in consequence of the late pacification, will probably be reduced, so that from the government nothing seems attainable and besides in that way I could not be useful to you, as I stand solemnly engaged never to solicit it for any person. The public lands in the Orleans and Mississippi territories are now under a course of survey, and offer, I think the best chance of employment. I am acquainted with the surveyor general, Mr. Pease, and could give you a letter to him which might probably induce him to employ you as a surveyor, if there be any room: and this would give chances of doing something for yourself. Mr. Gideon Fitch, whom you know, is in that department. If you have never learnt to survey, and will come and stay here some time, I will teach it to you. It is not the affair of more

183

than a week or a fortnight, if you already understand common arithmetic, say multiplication and division. If you will do us the favor to come and see us, perhaps in this or some other way, something may, on consultation, be thought of.

I salute you with affectionate esteem,

Th:Jefferson[30]

· This letter has been published in recent years as an example of Jefferson's distaste for nepotism. Jefferson had enunciated this same principle even more emphatically eight years before. "The public will never be made to believe that an appointment of a relative is made on the ground of merit alone, uninfluenced by family views; nor can they ever see with approbation offices, the disposal of which they entrust to their Presidents for public purposes, divided out as family property. Mr. Adams degraded himself infinitely by his conduct on this subject, as General Washington had done himself the greatest honor. With two such examples to proceed by, I should be doubly inexcusable to err."[31] A year later Jefferson would repeat the principle, "I therefore laid it down as a law of conduct for myself, never to give an appointment to a relation."[32]

Jefferson did not patently compromise himself in this offer to help Isham, his nephew. Although he used his influence in 1806 to obtain an army officer's commission for Isham's brother Charles, and again in 1809 to find Isham employment in a government agency, nevertheless Jefferson did not himself appoint them to an office.

It is evident in the tone of the letter that Jefferson was sympathetic to Isham. He invited Isham to stay with him at Monticello for a week or two, during which interval Jefferson gave his time teaching Isham to survey. At the end of Isham's instruction, Jefferson wrote two letters of introduction, which praised Isham's character and were explicit about Jefferson's concern for his nephew. One letter was addressed to Gideon Fitch in the United States Surveyor General's office in Washington, Mississippi, the small capitol town ten miles from Natchez:

Dear Sir   Monticello May 23,09.
The bearer hereof is Mr. Isham Lewis, son of Colo. Charles L. Lewis of Buckisland, whom you must have known while you resided in this part of the country. He is my nephew, & a young man of excellent dispositions, correct conduct, & good understand-

184

ing, little aided by education. The shipwreck of the fortunes of his family leaves him without resource but in his own industry, & the defects in his education narrow his means of exertion. He has learned the common principles of surveying & therefore proposes to try himself in that line, and carries from me a letter to Mr. Pease, recommending him to his patronage. His capacity will enable him, with time, opportunity & practice, to attain any eminence in the higher branches of surveying which may be useful. Arriving among you a stranger, I recommend him to your attentions & pray you to take him by the hand & befriend him in the getting into emploiment. His entire want of resources will render early emploiment very important to him. Any insight too which you can give him into the functions of his new vocation will be worthily bestowed on him. Having his success & welfare much at heart, any service in his promotion which you can render him will be considered an obligation to Dear Sir

Mr. Gideon Fitch

Your friend &—
Th:Jefferson[33]

The second letter was addressed to Seth Pease, the surveyor general in Mississippi. It was similar to the first letter, but contained a few additional words of praise for Isham. Jefferson said he would not recommend Isham "were he not worthy of . . . entire confidence, and possessing qualities which might render him useful and of value. . . . He has the capacity and the desire of advancing himself in it's [surveying's] higher branches, and if favored by proper opportunities, will make himself eminent."[34]

This series of letters helps to clarify the relationship between Jefferson, Isham, and Colonel Lewis. Isham's request for help is surprising in its revelation of Isham's outspoken resentment against his father, and Isham's conviction that he himself had no responsibility in the matter of his own unhappy situation. Evidently Colonel Lewis had promised Isham that he would make him wealthy, and so had not taught him any way of making a living for himself. More intriguing is Isham's cryptic mention of his father's "foibles." If the colonel did have some frailty of character, we can only guess at its nature. It could have been gambling, laziness, drunkenness, bad judgment, or one of many other faults. We do not know which ones. As for Isham, he himself was not perfect. Isham was willing to work, but expected his influential uncle, Jefferson, to place him in a job, as though it were an obligation.

In his reply to Isham, Jefferson neither mentioned Colonel

185

Lewis nor commented on the causes of Isham's situation, but instead, turned to the problem and offered Isham his home, his time, and his "affectionate esteem." Three weeks later, with Isham's visit and training completed, Jefferson was effusive in Isham's praise, saying nothing derogatory about his nephew except that his education was limited. Isham's character was splendid, he said, "of excellent dispositions, correct in his conduct, and of a sound understanding." For Jefferson to speak so favorably of Isham after having lived and worked with him for two weeks, indicates that Jefferson was rather well pleased with him. So it appears on the surface. It is possible, however, that Jefferson felt quite differently about Isham, and was, in fact, anxious to be rid of him. On the same day he wrote the letters for Isham, Jefferson made an entry in his account book noting that he had given Isham an order on a Mr. D. Higgenbotham for fifty shillings "as a gift to bear his expenses back to Tennessee."[35] Jefferson could ill afford that generosity, even though it was a modest amount. Had Jefferson found Isham offensive, the fifty-shilling gift might not have been forthcoming. Jefferson's mention of Tennessee indicates that Isham was going via the Tennessee Fork of the Wilderness Road, thence down the Cumberland River to Smithland to visit with his family, and then continue on downstream to Mississippi and his job as surveyor. By August Isham was at Rocky Hill.

It seems likely that Isham left Albemarle in May, and within a month or two reached Livingston County, bringing with him the deeds from George Pickett that had been recorded in Richmond. With the recording out of the way, Randolph was clear to sell and give a good title to any of his land in Kentucky; or at least he was free to try. He placed the following advertisement in the Russellville weekly paper, *The Farmer's Friend,* and ran it continuously from the end of June until the end of the year.

ADVERTISEMENT

The subscriber offers for sale a MILITARY TRACT OF LAND, of the first rate, containing one thousand, three hundred, thirty three and one third acres by survey bearing date the eleventh of May, one thousand seven hundred and eighty five, lying and being on the waters of the North Fork of Trade Water River, which tract or parcel of land was granted by James Garrard esq. governor of the commonwealth of Kentucky unto Robert Pollard. If necessary the subscriber will divide the said tract of land so as to accomodate purchasers, the terms of sale will be for cash or Negroes, and a general warantee deed given to the purchaser. Further particulars will be made known by application to

Randolph Lewis[36]

Livingston County

This was one of the three tracts that were forty or fifty miles distant from Randolph's home. They were too far away for Randolph to farm under one management, even if he had enough slaves. He had about $7,400 tied up in these tracts, money he could have used. Randolph was unable to sell this 1,333-acre tract even though he advertised it for over six months. Why Randolph did not offer the other two far-distant tracts for sale at the same time is not known. Perhaps he wanted to hold them for his sons, as his father had done for him and Lilburne, in the tradition of Virginia gentry.

There was one other procedure that Randolph and Lilburne had to complete before their land holdings were in legal order. The 1,000-acre farm on the Ohio that the two brothers had bought together was half of an undivided 2,000-acre tract Pickett had owned. They needed to have Pickett's land divided in half, and then repeat the process on their 1000 acres so that they each had 500 acres legally described and surveyed. In order for this to be done properly, first the deed had to be recorded at the state capitol in Frankfort, and then the county court had to appoint commissioners to see that the division was fairly done. The deed was recorded in Frankfort on August 22, and six days later Randolph appeared before the county court with his request.[37] The court appointed Jesse Ford, William Rice, and Joseph Ray to act as commissioners to divide the land.[38] Jesse Ford was the new assistant judge of the circuit court, a position he could use a few years later, if he were willing, to make a tremendously important decision for Lilburne. Ford was a Revolutionary War veteran and one of the first four trustees of Smithland in 1805. He was elected to the Kentucky legislature in 1806, and was a magistrate of Livingston County in 1808.[39] Joseph Ray, a farmer in the Smithland neighborhood, was not in local politics but did serve from time to time on juries and commissions. In about a year Ray and Lilburne would become brothers-in-law. William Rice, the last of the three commissioners, would also become closely associated with the Lewises before too long. Rice was the justice of the peace who had been falsely accused and then exonerated on a charge of tippling. Rice and his three brothers, Patrick, James, and David, were sons of the famous "Father" David Rice, the first Presbyterian minister in Kentucky, a fervent abolitionist, and a man of outstanding character and education.

Commissioners Rice, Ray, and Ford made their division of the Lewis land with the aid of County Surveyor William C. Rodgers, who actually did most of the work. In mid-October the job was completed.[40] It was only one of many events that drew the Lewises into community affairs and introduced them to the more influential citizens of the county. They were becoming well known.

·18·

THE CHURCH IN
WEST KENTUCKY

BEGINNING IN 1797, there was a period of religious fervor and
upheaval in Kentucky and neighboring southern states that
lasted for more than a decade. Out of this Great Revival came
the camp meeting, three new protestant denominations, and a
tremendous surge of religious fundamentalism with all its suspicion of the human intellect, of the arts, and of education. In addition to leaving its mark on the Lewis family, the revival had
far-reaching, long-lasting, and most unfortunate effects on the
development of the South. At least one scholar believes that the
impact of the revival on the character and growth of the South
was more important than any other event in American history
except for the Civil War.[1]

Strangely enough, this spectacular religious event began in a
place where there was probably the greatest concentration of
criminals on the frontier, Logan County, in west Kentucky—or,
as one resident called it, "Rogues' Harbor."

Logan County, when my father moved to it, was called "Rogues'
Harbor." Here many refugees, from almost all parts of the Union,
fled to escape justice or punishment; for although there was law,
yet it could not be executed, and it was a desperate state of society.
Murderers, horse thieves, highway robbers, and counterfeiters fled
here until they combined and actually formed a majority. The
honest and civil part of the citizens would prosecute these wretched
bandetti, but they would swear each other clear; and they really put
all law at defiance, and carried on such desperate violance and outrage that the honest part of the citizens seemed to be driven to the
necessity of uniting and combining together, and taking the law
into their own hands, under the name of Regulators. This was a
very desperate state of things.

Shortly after the Regulators had formed themselves into a society, and established their code of by-laws, on a court day at
Russellville, the two bands met in town. Soon a quarrel commenced, and a general battle ensued between the rogues and
Regulators, and they fought with guns, pistols, dirks, knives, and
clubs. Some were actually killed, many wounded; the rogues

189

proved victors, kept the ground, and drove the Regulators out of town. The Regulators rallied again, hunted, killed, and lynched many of the rogues, until several of them fled, and left for parts unknown. Many lives were lost on both sides, to the great scandal of civilized people.[2]

This area, which was also known as "Satan's Stronghold," in 1800 underwent a moral awakening such as the continent had never before seen.

Credit for lighting the fuse of this ecclesiastical explosion belongs to the Reverend James McGready, a Presbyterian minister who served three churches in Logan County. Mc-Gready was not a typical Presbyterian preacher. His meetings were known for their unusual noise, excitement, and emotionalism.[3] Many Presbyterian ministers in Kentucky came from Virginia, where they had been trained or influenced by Hampden-Sidney and Liberty Hall, schools that condemned enthusiastic emotionalism such as the Reverend James McGready displayed.[4] The divinity graduates of Princeton College also tended to be more scholarly than evangelistic.

McGready was tall, with brilliant blue, bulging eyes and a huge beak of a nose, not a handsome man, but a persuasive one, if his daughter is to be believed.

> His voice was most charming. In describing the beauties of Heaven, his voice was soft, full of love for that state, thrilling, gently longing and joyful. His audience could be listening intently on the edge of the seats. Then in describing the horrors of Hell, his voice would grow harsh, filled with anguish and despair, and groaning and pity. Then an angry shout at the unrepentant sinner caused many listeners to fall off the seats. The men would get back with startled faces. The women often remained on the floor weeping. Then his voice would grow soft and comforting and his prayers to end were always beautiful.[5]

For at least three years before 1800, there had been small short-lived revivals here and there across the South, and Mc-Gready himself had led more than a few sinners to salvation. He and other ministers predicted that there would soon be an extraordinary outpouring of the Spirit. Thus primed, his three congregations, four or five hundred people altogether, met for a joint communion service presided over by McGready and four of his associates.[6] It was at this Red River Meeting House that the revival began. While the preachers went through the house "shouting and exhorting with all possible ecstasy and energy," the sinners fell down in trances of miraculous deliverance from Satan, and the floor was covered with the religiously "slain."

The meeting was such a success that another was soon planned for the Gaspar River Church, a meeting which, because of the sensational nature of the previous one, attracted people who came from hundreds of miles away to stay for a day or two, bringing their wagons, beds, and food. The crowd numbered "many thousands." This three-day affair was the first large camp meeting. Ecumenism was the order of the day, and several denominations, Methodist, Baptist, and Presbyterian, were represented among both the worshipers and the preachers. The worshipers, as at Red River, were prostrated by the divine flame that spread through the multitude and left them crying and shouting for God's mercy. This Gaspar River meeting was the departure point for the Great Revival itself, which spread in a chain reaction across the South.[7]

Throughout the South, crops and homes were untended for weeks and settlements were deserted. The meetings sometimes lasted for seven days and even at night, when, as McMaster recorded,

> nothing was then wanting that could strike terror into minds weak, timid, and harassed. The red glare of the camp-fires reflected from hundreds of tents and wagons; the dense blackness of the flickering shadows, the darkness of the surrounding forest, made still more terrible by the groans and screams of the "spiritually wounded," . . . were too much. . . . The heart swelled, the nerves gave way, the hands and feet grew cold and, motionless and speechless, they fell headlong to the ground. In a moment crowds gathered about them to pray and shout. Some lay still as death. Some passed through frightful twitchings of face and limb. At Cabin Creek so many fell that, lest the multitude should tread on them, they were carried to the meeting-house and laid in rows on the floor. . . .
>
> As the meetings grew more and more frequent, this nervous excitement assumed new and more terrible forms. One was known as jerking; another, as the barking exercise; a third, as the Holy Laugh. "The jerks" began in the head and spread rapidly to the feet. The head would be thrown from side to side so swiftly that the features would be blotted out and the hair made to snap. When the body was affected, the sufferer was hurled over hindrances that came in his way, and finally dashed on the ground to bounce about

191

like a ball. At camp meetings in the far South, saplings were cut off breast-high and left "for the people to jerk by." One who visited such a camp-ground declares that about the roots of from fifty to one hundred saplings the earth was kicked up "as by a horse stamping flies."[8]

The great revival increased in intensity until an amazing climax was reached at Cane Ridge, near Paris, in the Bluegrass region. Although this was in the more highly populated area of the state, it was still uncrowded farm country. The meeting was widely publicized in advance, and early in August of 1801 an incredible crowd for the time, estimated variously from twenty to thirty thousand people, assembled at the small log Cane Ridge Meeting House, having traveled there by foot, on horse and, it is recorded, with the help of 1,145 wagons and sleds. Eighteen Presbyterian preachers and at least that many more Baptist and Methodist ministers exhorted the multitude from stands, stumps, wagons, and tree limbs. Except for its scale and intensity, the Cane Ridge Meeting was similar in procedure to the ones that led up to it.[9]

The southern evangelizing preachers of the times were not socially oriented in their profession, and were far less interested in bettering the community at large than they were in converting the individual sinner. Hell was real, the Devil was terrifying, and punishment could be avoided only by "accepting Jesus Christ" and by renouncing future sins and repenting old ones. If accompanied by enough sincere purpose, this conversion would admit the ex-sinner, upon his demise, to Everlasting Glory. Hell and Heaven were actual realities to most of the revivalists, and for them a conversion truly replaced fear with confidence in the fate of their souls. In the hypnotic atmosphere of the revival, the emotion generated by the switch from sin to salvation was sometimes expressed by one of the "exercises" described as falling or fainting, rolling, the jerks, barking, dancing, laughing, and singing, but in many conversions these exercises did not appear.[10]

One of the more interesting aspects of the Great Revival as it spread across the south from 1801 to 1803 was the close cooperation between the Methodist, Baptist, and the Presbyterian preachers. More often than not preachers from all three denominations cooperated actively at revivals and camp meetings. By the end of the revival in 1805, however, this was no longer the case, for thereafter denominational differences in attitude and practice separated the churches. During the early part of the Great Revival, even the most conventional Presbyterians thought that the camp meeting revival exercises were the special will of God. But, as the conduct of the meetings became more bizarre, most Presbyterians withdrew from participation in camp meetings, as did the Baptists to a lesser degree. Thus, by 1804 the camp meeting had become pretty much a Methodist institution, presided over by such zealous circuit riders as Peter Cartwright, an early resident of Livingston County.[11]

Another preacher of this type was Rev. William Barnett of Livingston and Caldwell counties, one of the "fathers" of the Cumberland Presbyterian church, and one of its earliest and most influential ministers. Mr. Barnett was a remarkable man who, in addition to his wonderful pulpit and revival powers, possessed a voice "absolutely surpassing belief." "Because of his great zeal and his tremendous voice . . . it is said that, when preaching on a clear day, he could be heard three miles away. . . . He was called 'Boanerges,' Son of Thunder."[12]

Even though most of the camp meeting conversions had been lacking in formal ritual, there were, nevertheless, a tremendous number of them, and these sincere new-found Christians created a pressing demand for more ministers. The Presbyterian church was particularly distressed in trying to fill this need for more preachers because of a traditional and firm insistence that their ministers be broadly and thoroughly educated before they were ordained. At that time there were only one or two theological schools west of the mountains, and the expense of eastern colleges was not easily met by the rare frontiersman interested in eastern college education.[13]

Although the evangelist preachers seldom stood by silently when blatant injustice took place in their communities, their first goal was the improvement of personal morality as a means of saving souls from Hell, not the education of minds. This was also the order of priorities among the Baptist and Methodist preachers. But the established Presbyterians believed that social institutions, if properly directed, could be a vital influence in elevating the spiritual quality of people's lives. They felt it was a moral duty to improve their communities and prepare their children for responsibility. Education was one of the traditional Presbyterian imperatives.

A Kentucky scholar has described the different approaches

used by the denominations in their search for more preachers:

> Unlike the Presbyterians, the Baptists and Methodists did not
> want a learned clergy. The Baptists drew their leaders from the
> gifted among their members, while the Methodists employed cir-
> cuit riders distinguished by zeal and devotion. The Baptists, be-
> cause of their experience in Virginia, were strong advocates of the
> separation of church and state. The Methodists were devoted to
> the spiritual needs of their people. Neither sect was intent upon the
> control of education. The Presbyterians, on the other hand, were
> anxious to educate their laity to become Christian politicians; but
> their church was not interested in carrying its religious mores to
> the lowly. The Presbyterians were ambitious to educate political
> and commercial leaders who would dominate the government
> policy and social life of the state.[14]

In short, the Presbyterians, who were largely of the leadership
class, sought to control education of the young and direct it
along Calvinistic lines, thus establishing the moral tone of the
country.[15] The Baptists and especially the Methodists, believing
that the salvation of the largest possible number of individual
souls in the country was the answer to evil in the world,
concentrated on the average and lower class of citizens, many of
whom, being uneducated themselves, resented any signs of
learning in their preachers. Anti-intellectualism was given
tremendous energy by the Great Revival, and has since then
been a force of considerable influence in the South.

A tally of the "Christian population" of Kentucky taken in
1820 gives an idea of the relative numbers of members of these
three sects. There were just over twenty-one thousand Baptists,
and the Methodists counted a following of approximately the
same number. The Presbyterian church, however, had only
twenty-seven hundred members in Kentucky, less than one-
seventh of either of the other two sects. It is plain to see that if
the Presbyterians were to be influential in Kentucky, it would
have to be by having members in positions of leadership in
social, economic, and political institutions rather than by merely
outnumbering the other denominations.[16]

Feelings of resentment between the sects became apparent
after the Great Revival, and soon several of the churches
themselves became divided. The personalities and issues involved in the conflict within the Presbyterian church in west
Kentucky and Tennessee were complicated. On the surface, the

basic problem was whether or not the church should license young preachers who had not completed the usual classical education. Behind this issue was the equally controversial argument over the emotional, salvation style of preaching used by some of the Presbyterian preachers. This technique offended the traditional and established authorities of the church, who disliked the unsophisticated tumult, noise, and emotionalism of preachers like James McGready. There was also serious dispute over the doctrine of election and the interpretation of the confession of faith. These differences, which sprang up early in the Great Revival led, in 1810, to the splitting off of the revivalist faction of the Cumberland Presbytery from the authority of the parent church. The territory involved at first was the Green River country, or southwestern Kentucky, which included Livingston County. This faction grew into the Cumberland Presbyterian church which, because of its revivalistic character, thrived in west Kentucky. The traditional Presbyterians still held forth there, but in diminished numbers.[17] A letter written in late 1809 by one of the three ministers who organized the Cumberland Presbyterian church states clearly that revivalism had many followers in Livingston County: "I will inform you that I have just visited Livingston County and the brethren there seem bound to our committee by stronger cords if possible, than ever before."[18]

The effect of this religious upheaval on the Lewis family is unknown, but it is certain that when their church was split apart by the Cumberland Presbyterians, the Lewis family remained with the older, more dignified, parent church—at least Randolph's family and his sisters did. Lilburne's affiliation was probably the same as theirs.[19]

The second church that was born during the Great Revival was the Christian (Disciples of Christ) Church. It began as a collection of splinter groups that had broken away from various Protestant denominations, primarily the Presbyterian. Methodist Peter Cartwright's description of the origin of this denomination is shorter than most. Cartwright was not in a Christian mood of brotherly love when he wrote it.

These ministers then rose up and unitedly renounced the jurisdiction of the Presbyterian Church, organized a Church of their own, and dubbed it with the name of *Christian*. Here was the origin of what was called the *New Lights*. They renounced the Westminster

195

Confession of Faith, and all Church discipline, and professed to take the New Testament for their Church discipline. They established no standard of doctrine; every one was to take the New Testament, read it, and abide his own construction of it. Marhsall, M'Namar, Dunlevy, Stone, Huston, and others, were the chief leaders in this *trash trap*. Soon a diversity of opinion sprang up, and they got into a Babel confusion . . . so that in a few years you could not tell what was *harped* or what was *danced*. They adopted the mode of immersion, the water-god of all exclusive errorists; and directly there was a mighty controversy about the way to heaven, whether it was by water or by dry land.[20]

Cartwright's version goes on in the same vein. The Disciples seemed to thrive on Cartwright's ill will, and are flourishing today, although the camp meeting has been abandoned.

Another sect that achieved prominence in Kentucky as a result of the Great Revival was the Shakers. Unlike the Disciples of Christ, the Shakers are not flourishing today. During the enthusiasm of the revival they recruited a sizable membership, but because of their strict doctrine of chastity for all members they did not replace themselves, and have long since dwindled away. Theirs was a gentle society of industrious people.

The early 1800s was a time when people took their theology seriously. Debates between preachers of conflicting doctrines used to take pace publicly, sometimes lasted two or three days, and were well attended. "Dr. Robert J. Breckinridge brawled with the Campbellites, the Methodists, the New School, the Catholics, anybody who dared have a different opinion. . . . Breckinridge and the Catholic Archbishop John Hughes had a debate through two religious papers, later published in a 467-page volume, studded with horrified *italics* and vociferous SMALL CAPS, which represented the shouting they would have done had the debate been oral."[21] Often the differences that separated denominations were merely matters of form, such as whether in baptism the neophyte should be sprinkled with water or immersed in it. For example, the father of Methodist Reverend James Finlay once stated, "I will not say that any man who baptizes by immersion is an indecent man, but I will say he has been guilty of an indecent act."[22] If such fine points caused arguments between friends and kept congregations apart, it must be clear that the very significant ways in which the Presbyterian church differed from the other frontier denominations set that church and her members apart from the majority of western

Kentucky settlers. Since the Lewises were Presbyterians, it may be interesting to examine further the characteristics of their church that made its members different from most of the other people in Livingston County.

First, the Presbyterian church in Kentucky in 1809 was not what could be called "liberal." It was dedicated to the destruction of the least trace of independent theological thought that might arise among the clergy or the members at large. It adhered rigidly to the tenets of Calvin, and regarded all other persuasions as heretical. The other major Protestant sects, the Baptist and Methodist, were far more tolerant and democratic and, remembering the years of suffering in England the the freedoms so recently won in war, insisted on religious freedom.[23]

While the other Protestant denominations, and especially the Baptists, insisted on the separation of church and state, the Presbyterians on the frontier made little distinction between religious and secular life, maintained an interest in all facets of community affairs, and tried to change them for the better.[24] The Presbyterians were widely accused of trying to become the official church of the state, as the Church of England had been in colonial Virginia.[25] The Baptists and Methodists, stressing the fundamental importance of the experience of conversion, thought that faith was the only proper realm of the church, not the leadership and moral improvement of secular and community affairs that the Presbyterians and Quakers considered to be a religious obligation. The controversy took strange forms. For example, in December 1810, when the Kentucky Senate resolved that a chaplain was needed for the general assembly, the lower house voted thirty-nine to twenty-two to reject the proposal, and to keep affairs of church and state separate. While the state legislature did observe Sunday, as late as 1805 sessions were held on Christmas day.[26]

It was this basic contrast of opinion about the proper role of the church that led to one remarkable difference in these churches—the anti-intellectualism of the Baptists and Methodists, as opposed to the efforts of the Presbyterians to promote education and improve secular society.[27] The Presbyterian church regarded the education of children as an unavoidable responsibility. Most western Presbyterian ministers were teachers. Of the fourteen colleges and universities founded west of the Appalachians prior to 1829, Presbyterians helped organize twelve of them, and dominated nearly every one. The

197

educational standards set for the ministers were extremely high, and Princeton and Yale graduated a large number of them. The classics and dead languages were among the requirements. The lengthy time required to train a qualified Presbyterian preacher was partly responsible for the slow spread of the sect on the frontier, and the dry, stiff, technical theology and the formality of the worship services conducted by these ministers did not appeal to most frontiersmen as much as did the enthusiasm found in the revivalist church meetings.[28]

Unlike the Presbyterians, the Baptists and Methodists were consistently hostile to education and learning, to certain forms of recreation, and to fine arts as well. The frontier Baptists feared a professional priesthood, and insisted that conversion was the only way to be "saved." Thus they opposed any theological training for their preachers. Their illiteracy and ignorance were shocking to Baptist ministers who came from the east. By 1823 only about 100 out of 2,000 Baptist ministers had been "liberally educated," and almost none of the 100 were in the west. Baptists who moved from Kentucky across the Ohio River to the old northwest spread this suspicion and prejudice against learning.[29]

The Methodist attitude was similar to that held by the Baptists. Bishop Asbury preferred his itinerant preachers to be unlettered, and said that a simple man was adequate to speak for simple, plain people. Asbury preferred preachers who had received the "true call" over those ministers who were "man made." Although the Methodists did have a religious book publishing concern, and the schools founded by Asbury became successful at a later time, nevertheless, prior to 1816 American Methodists failed resoundingly in efforts to found schools and colleges for the children of their people. The Kentucky Methodists and other evangelistic churches also opposed all secular and formal church music. Peter Cartwright angrily denounced the use of organs, instruments, or choirs, and the church also opposed dancing, drama, and fiction.[30]

Like the Methodists, the poorer Baptists who came from Virginia to Kentucky to settle brought with them not only a sectarian hostility to scholarly and artistic activities, but also a strong antagonism to the plantation aristocrats and to the class conscious old families of Virginia society. The members of the upper class, which included the Lewises, were scarcely touched

by the revival, with the result that the Baptist and Methodist revivalists tended to look on the unconverted upper classes as "bad
folk." The membership of the Presbyterian church on the frontier was in striking contrast to the revivalists. While the Methodists and Baptists directed their message at the poor and un-
cultivated majority, the Presbyterians were disinclined to reach
down and proselytize the ignorant and uneducated lower
classes.[31] The result was that while Presbyterians in Kentucky
were definitely in the minority, they were just as clearly an upper-class, if not aristocratic, denomination. It is very doubtful
that the majority of the settlers were, as Frederick Turner pictured them, creative in matters of religion, education, literature,
and government. Arthur Moore probably came much closer to
the truth when he portrayed them as barbarians in the Garden
of Eden, a brutalized class of people who were anti-intellectual,
materialistic, prejudiced, and narrowly sectarian.[32] Agreeing
with Moore, Richard Hofstadter described the revivalistic congregations as "anti-authority, anti-aristocracy, anti-eastern, and
anti-learning."[33]

In the matter of slavery and racial prejudice, the Presbyterians
again differed from the other denominations, although less
sharply than in some issues. "Father" David Rice, the most
influential of the pioneer Presbyterian ministers in Kentucky,
actively opposed slavery in the state. He addressed the first
constitutional convention in an unsuccessful attempt to make
slavery unconstitutional in Kentucky. Other Presbyterians were
active in anti-slavery organizations in Kentucky and the other
border states, but these efforts were not uniformly supported
throughout the denomination. Many Presbyterians were openly
antagonistic toward negroes as individuals and as a race, and
many of the rest were too indifferent to oppose the deliberate
and callous brutality with which the negroes were treated. Only
the Quakers and Shakers fought against slavery consistently and
directly on religious grounds.[34]

The Baptists did not make opposition to slavery a broad denominational policy. Quite the contrary, in 1806 a Baptist
minister, David Barrow, was expelled from his association for
"preaching the doctrines of emancipation to the hurt and injury
of the brotherhood." The Baptists treated slavery as a secular
issue and, in keeping with their policy of separation of church
and state, denied that the slavery question was a proper religious

199

issue. While there was some early abolitionist activity among the Baptists, it faded out as an increasing number of Baptists became slave owners.[35]

Like the Baptists, the Methodists in general held that religion had nothing to do with racism or slavery, and while many western Methodists vigorously opposed the institution, they were at the same time highly prejudiced against negroes. Peter Cartwright customarily referred to negroes in language that today would be thought outrageous and shocking. More than any other major denomination in Kentucky the Methodists were active in Christianizing the slaves, but a selfish motive has been detected in some of this work. It was noted that when a slave was converted he usually became more tractable and contented, more honest, sober, industrious and, above all, profitable. After converting the slaves of two Methodist planters, Peter Cartwright reported that the grateful owners claimed he "had . . . bettered or enhanced the value of their servants more than a thousand dollars; they ceased getting drunk, stealing, and breaking the sabboth."[36]

In general, racism and prejudice were not only openly accepted on the frontier, they were respectable and unconcealed in most religious denominations. The Presbyterian church, alone among the larger denominations, had a policy of abolition, even though it was indifferently and unevenly proclaimed. As for the effect of this church policy on the Lewises in Livingston, it is not likely that it set them apart from the community at large. Neither their family traditions nor the number of slaves they owned indicated that they held abolitionist sentiments.

There is one other aspect of Kentucky Presbyterianism that may help to clarify the relationship of the Lewises to their neighbors. That is the attitude of the Presbyterian leadership toward the policies of Thomas Jefferson. Jeffersonian Republicanism was overwhelmingly supported by the Baptist and Methodist church members in Kentucky. Perhaps the most important area in which Jefferson's ideas differed from those of the revivalist frontiersmen was that of intellectual achievement. While these two churches opposed education, Jefferson steadfastly maintained that no nation can be ignorant, free, and civilized at the same time.[37] It is ironic that the two denominations whose membership gave Jefferson his most unqualified political support, the Baptists and Methodists, were the same ones that, in the early 1800s, condemned and obstructed the one thing, education, that Jefferson felt was essential to the realization of American potential. This issue, and perhaps a difference in approach to the issue of slavery, would have been the main sources of disagreement between the revivalistic frontiersmen and Jefferson. However, these issues were not considered critical at that time in Kentucky, and they did not diminish Jefferson's overwhelming popularity.

While Federalists were scarce and unpopular in Kentucky, a good many of that political party were also members of the Presbyterian church. Neither the Federalist party nor the Presbyterians were particularly disturbed by the idea of having a close alliance between church and state, even to the extent of having the state subsidize religion.[38] This was a reversal in attitude from the Presbyterian Reverend David Rice's earlier agitation in Virginia for dissenter's toleration and for separation of church and state, but nonetheless it was a trend in the Presbyterian church, one that displeased most Kentuckians and drove Jefferson to clear expressions of his anger against the Presbyterian clergy.[39]

The close family connection of the Lewises to Jefferson, while they were at the same time Presbyterians, might have evoked conflicting feelings in the average citizens of Livingston County. They would have been intrigued, and perhaps awed, by the Lewis kinship to Jefferson, but the Lewises' affiliation with the Presbyterian church would have alienated these relatives of Jefferson from some of the staunch Baptists and Methodists in the community.

Summarizing the general characteristics of Presbyterians in Kentucky after the time of the revival may indicate something about the relationship between the Lewis family and the average citizens of Livingston County. A substantial number of the Kentucky Presbyterians were members of the upper classes, a social group that was disliked, envied, and resented by the average uneducated settler.[40] After the first frenzy of the revival, the Presbyterians remained aloof from camp meetings and hysterical religious conversion. This restraint was interpreted by the revivalistic church members to mean that Presbyterians were far less adamant about the separation of church and state in Kentucky than were the Baptists and Methodists, who consequently suspected that the Presbyterians were trying to maneuver them out of their cherished freedom of religion. Even though they were outnumbered sixteen to one by the Baptists and Methodists, the Presbyterians, because of their education and social position, controlled a disproportionate number of the positions of leadership in both business and politics. The impoverished frontiersman, with his ingrained suspicion and dislike for authority, would have thoroughly resented such people. The Presbyterian respect for literature, education, and other cultural achievements would have been considered by the average frontiersman to be effete, snobbish, and a waste of time; and he would have thought that the formal and reserved worship services of the Presbyterian church indicated that the members of that church were cool, standoffish, and unfriendly.

Clearly, it would be foolish to state that because the above generalizations applied to Kentucky Presbyterians as a whole in 1809, that it gives an accurate picture of the Lewises. There is, however, some other evidence, unfortunately slim and of a legendary nature, but which is interesting because it reinforces a few of the above speculations at least as far as the father, Col. Charles L. Lewis, is concerned. One romanticized and partly fictitious newspaper article written in 1894 stated that Colonel Lewis was "taciturn, moody, abstracted, and queer."[41] Colonel Lewis may, indeed, have been an eccentric, or he may simply have been affecting the pride that was common among Virginia plantation owners, the "lords of little domains," whose easy dignity sometimes "degenerated into starchy hauteur."[42] Another fanciful story has one character say that Colonel Lewis was "to say the least, a very, very strange man."

In another chapter of this same account, a hunter who lived in Livingston County reported with amazement that one night while hunting he had found Isham near home but completely lost in the woods and driven up a tree by wolves. How anyone could be so incompetent in woodsmanship was beyond the frontiersman's understanding. He guided Isham the short distance to Rocky Hill and was offered handsome pay for the service, which was also thought to be strange behavior on Isham's part, considering the time and place.[43]

These legends may or may not be true, but there is ample proof that the Lewises, when compared to the average Livingston County family, were aristocratic, well educated, wealthy, highly connected in business and political affairs, sophisticated, and rising into positions of local leadership. It seems inevitable that some of their fellow citizens would have envied and resented them.

·19·

THE PRESBYTERIAN
LEWISES

THE REVEREND David Rice, widely known as "Father Rice," was
one of the most important figures in the early years of the
Presbyterian church in Kentucky. Born in Hanover County, Virginia, Rice, was encouraged in his early manhood by the
Reverend Samuel Davies to obtain a sound education, and when
Davies became president of the College of New Jersey (later
Princeton), Rice matriculated there and graduated in 1761. A
year later he became a minister, and for thirteen years cared for
a parish in Bedford County, Virginia. During this period he was
instrumental in founding the college that would become Hampden-Sidney.[1] In 1783, when Rice was fifty, he moved with his
large family to Danville in the district of Kentucky where three
hundred residents had petitioned him to establish a church. Immediately after his arrival, he became involved in founding
Transylvania Seminary. He was chosen to be chairman of the
board, and the first classes were held in his cabin home. Among
others serving on the board were George Rogers Clark, John
Crittenden, and two future Kentucky governors, Isaac Shelby
and Christopher Greenup.[2]

Throughout his long ministry Rice was opposed to slavery,
and even though he failed in his effort to have Kentucky admitted as a free state, his memorable pamphlet, *Slavery Inconsistent
with Justice and Good Policy,* became an anti-slavery classic.[3] He
was equally adamant in opposition to any use of alcoholic
beverages, which he condemned in the strongest terms. Although Father Rice believed in revivals, he nevertheless criticized the extreme emotionalism that came to be associated with
them. One Methodist minister, recalling Father Rice, said that at
revivals when the "Methodism and enthusiasm . . . would get
very high—which they often did after sermon—he would rise to
his feet, look over the assembly with great solemnity, and ex-
claim, 'High sail and little ballast!' then gather up his hat and
cane, and take his departure."[4] Father Rice was a force for unity
in his denomination, but worked in vain to moderate the sharp
controversies that divided and weakened it.[5]

Although Father Rice may have preached occasionally in far west Kentucky, he did not reside or have a church there. Nevertheless, his influence was felt in Livingston County in other ways. He had a large family, six sons and five daughters, and of the eleven children, three grown sons were residents of Livingston County when the Lewises lived there.[6] These three men and their families were prominent in the area, and became very closely connected to the Lewises.

Father Rice's influence in Livingston was also felt through the presence of his protégé, Reverend Terah Templin. Templin had studied first under Father Rice and then at Liberty Hall in Virginia, after which Rice guided him into the ministry. Templin then removed to Washington County, Kentucky, where he organized several churches and served them for about fifteen years. Although Templin was younger than his mentor, he preceded Father Rice to Kentucky. In 1781 Templin preached the first sermon ever delivered in the state by a Presbyterian minister.[7] He was unmarried and made his home with General John Caldwell, an elder in Templin's church. In 1796, Templin and General Caldwell moved to Livingston County with the majority of Templin's former parishioners. They settled in Centerville and founded the Livingston church. It was the first church of any denomination west of the Green River in Kentucky.[8] The presence of this congregation is said to have greatly improved the character of the Centerville neighborhood. In 1804, Caldwell was elected lieutenant governor of the state, but died shortly thereafter. Templin remained in western Kentucky until 1816 when, at the age of seventy-four, he returned to Washington County. Templin's personality has been described by one who knew him well, James H. Rice, one of Father Rice's sons who lived in west Kentucky.

> He never married, and although he laboured in the gospel ministry for upwards of 40 years, he received little or no support of any pecuniary nature. He was not possessed of the first order of talents, but his performances were respectable, and his subjects always well digested. His sentiments were orthodox—his manner tender and solemn so that he rarely failed to solemnize his audience. He was a plain practical preacher, and was much esteemed by his brethren for his modesty and unaffected integrety.[9]

Templin's first church, the Livingston church near Centerville, was built of logs and had a dirt floor. There was no chimney, and the smoke escaped through a large hole in the center of the roof. A chimney was added later. When it became necessary to make an addition to the building, it was located on the end where the chimney stood and another fireplace was added to the back side of the chimney, so that there were two fireplaces, back to back, in the center of the remodeled structure. Since the wilderness did not then permit the use of wagons, people walked or rode horseback from as far as thirty miles away to attend services.[10] While Templin lived in Livingston County he formed three other Presbyterian churches.[11]

The Lewises were not members of the Livingston church, located far from Rocky Hill. Their minister was another Presbyterian preacher, Reverend William Dickey, a close friend of Terah Templin's (see Figure 2). When Dickey was ordained in 1805 at the Bethany meeting house at Crooked Creek, Templin presided at the service and gave the charge.[12]

Dickey had been born in South Carolina, but grew to manhood in Logan County, Kentucky, where, it is reported, "he was convicted of sin at an evening meeting to which he had gone, according to his own statement, very careless in religious matters. Mr. McGready was the preacher on that occasion. . . . His convictions were exceedingly deep and pungent, and when at last he found peace in believing, he at once turned his attention to the ministry."[13]

Dickey had married Rebecca Ross in 1799 and ten children were eventually born to them. He customarily wore homespun clothes, as did most west Kentuckians, and it is said that his "exterior was rough."[14] This description is borne out by a portrait that survives from his later life. It gives the impression of a man of great determination. His face was broad through the forehead and cheekbones, the chin firm, and his cheeks and brow were wrinkled with deep lines. His nose was wider at the base than usual, and his mouth somewhat more full on the left side. He wore his hair rather long, combed straight back on his head. In the portrait the Reverend Mr. Dickey appears to have been a man of severity and strength.[15]

Rev. William Dickey's appearance, that of an unpolished frontiersman, covered a gentle but outgoing personality: "his kindness of spirit, refinement of feeling, and unusual conversational powers rendered him very agreeable company." He had a

Figure 2. William Dickey.
(Courtesy of The Presbyterian *Historical Society, Philadelphia.)*

sensitive nature, and was especially interested in working with children.[16]

Dickey's attitude toward the role of the church and the conduct of its members was quite strict but, in general, was the same as that of Terah Templin and Father Rice. He was opposed to slavery and also to sabbath breaking, dancing, "and such amusements." In a memoir Dickey recalled the time that he had "received a line from a young lawyer, stating to me the distress of his lady's mind, and pressing my attention. I found her in tears and left her in tears. Yes, she that had found time to dance had found a time to weep." (One does not need to wonder what Dickey would have thought about Lilburne's "special insistence and request" that his two daughters in Mercer County be sent to dancing school.) Dickey also reported that he had a wounded conscience because as a youth he had yielded to the sinful practice of "drawing cuts, or throwing up wet or dry." This was the frontier equivalent of tossing a coin, heads or tails, to choose up sides for a game. They would spit on one side of a paddle or chip, toss it up, and cry "wet or dry."[17] It seems likely that Dickey also opposed the use of alcohol.

Dickey's preaching technique was somewhat more heated than that of the orthodox Terah Templin, who "rarely failed to solemnize his audience." It was reported that in the pulpit Dickey's "lips seemed to have been touched with a live coal from the altar." He frequently aroused the emotions of his congregations, putting them in a condition that Dickey referred to as "glow," or "pleasing appearance." His flocks were often moved to tears, or were very "tenderly affected." In his later life he lamented that "people do not weep under preaching now as they did then." Evidently Dickey was far more willing to use revivalist techniques than Father Rice or Terah Templin. Dickey remembered one fervid church meeting without any apparent dismay. "This afternoon I administered the Lord's Supper to a congregation variously exercised—some jerked, some shouted, but many wept."[18] In the opinion of Father David Rice, the proper manner of preaching lay somewhere between the solemnity of Templin and the glow of Dickey. Rice warned of the dangers of both styles. "There is great mischief done, and sin committed in the pulpit, by warm, lively preaching, as well as by cold, lifeless preaching. The one inspires men with false hopes and joys, the other sinks them into a profound sleep."[19]

Even though William Dickey was not averse to gaining converts by the moderate use of revival techniques, he, Terah Templin, and David Rice did oppose the tumult and extreme emotional displays of the revivalist sects.[20] William Dickey was the pastor of the Lewis family, and it is fairly certain that they were not the camp-meeting variety of worshipers.

Dickey preached at Randolph's home on several occasions. In a letter to his brother, Dickey described how he converted one of Randolph's slaves. This long letter indicates Dickey's concern for the spiritual life of the negroes, and also reveals that Randolph and Mary were kindly owners who cared for their servants. The aged slave recounted that his "pious Massa and Misis" customarily urged the negroes to attend worship with the family to hear the scriptures read.[21] The slave was old Frank who, with his wife Sarah and their four children, had been given to Randolph by Colonel Lewis nineteen years before.[22]

> Dear Brother. . . . Having preached, some months ago in a privet house, & taken my leave of the white part of the family, I had my foot in the stirrup remembering that I must preach the same evening six miles off: When I found myself surrounded with the servants, among whom was a venerable old man, to whom I said . . . Well Daddy, what do you think of these things? I don't know, Sir, said he, I don't know, I have my doubts—What, said I, doubt the truth of the gospel? I don't know, said he again, but I doubt that is but a contrivance of men—My appointment for the evening would not allow me time to enter the lists with an Infidel—I bade him farewell, promising him a visit the next time I might come that way—It was a month, or six weeks after, I had an invitation to preach at the same house. . . . After Sermon I remembered my promise & went to his [Frank's] house—I found him there alone —He received me with apparent respect, set me a stool & gave me a twist of tobacco, which I received as an expression of his regard—I asked him of his age—He said I doknow but old Massa [Colonel Lewis] say I ninty yarse odd. He told me that he had served four generations. I asked have you been healthy & prosperous? He said, yes Massa berry hathy, almost neber sick in my life—I enquired if this goodness of God did not lay him under obligations to love & serve Him? To this he yiealded a ready affirmative—I asked if he could read? He answered as I expected him to do. . . . I enquired if he had ever in his life attempted to pray? He said never, . . . tilt a few weeks past—I go often in de wishes [bushes], where nobody see me. I asked if he thought it right to pray in his house too? He said, O yes I prays in my house ebry night

& morning & it make my wife bery glad — (She is a Baptist) I asked
if he thought he was gitting better than he was when I saw him
before? He said, better! no, but I am wus & wus, ebery day — dat I
is Massa — I see better than I did, I see I am a sinner, & I see that
Jesus is a Saviour, but I am no better yet — I enquired if he was willing to give himself away to this Savior? He said I have lived so long
in sin, I have been neglecting God & pleasing myself so long Massa!
Till I has wored out (holding up his old trembling arms & looking
at them) til I has wored out dis old body & now Massa will de Lord,
will de Lord have it? He might justly refuse.

I assure you Brother that this was one of the most interesting
conversations I ever had. The features of the New man appeared
in the face of the Old Negro!!!

Let Angels Shout, an Infidel reclaim'd, His life is that of an humble penitant.[23]

This letter does not mention anyone from Lilburne's
household. It is not known whether Dickey ever preached at
Rocky Hill, or if Lilburne was as devout as Randolph. Both Randolph and Mary were "pious." They read scripture in regular
family services, and they urged their slaves to attend but were
understanding enough not to force them. Randolph's and Lilburne's sisters were, as Dickey put it, "worthy members of the
church of which I was pastor."[24] It is probable that all the
Lewises at one time or another received some spiritual guidance
from William Dickey, either at their homes or at his Salem
church.

Another prominent family that surely was represented in
William Dickey's Salem church was the Rices, William and
Patrick H., two of Father David's grown sons. From all indications, William had come to the county about the same time as the
Lewises, or perhaps earlier. By 1810 he, his wife Ally, and their
three small daughters were well established in the community.
In 1809, William had been appointed justice of the peace and
served as magistrate for several years thereafter. He lived on the
road from Salem to the Point at Smithland. In addition to his
official duties he operated a horse-driven grist mill. As a
member of the power structure of the county, he was appointed
to various community tasks, one of which was serving as a commissioner to let out the contract for building the new jail at
Salem. He served on occasion as an estate administrator, and
was one of the commissioners who had been appointed to divide
the tract of land Randolph and Lilburne had bought together

from George Pickett. He was the same William Rice who was presented to the grand jury for retailing spirits, a situation that would have upset his reverend father, even though the charge was dismissed. William Rice owned five slaves, a fact that his abolitionist father must have known to his dismay.

William's brother, Patrick H. Rice, moved to Livingston shortly after the census of 1810 was taken. He settled in the Salem neighborhood and, like his brother, soon had a position of influence. Within a year he, too, was a justice of the peace, and thereafter served on various local commissions. Patrick married Sally Rutter, one of the five daughters of James Rutter, Sr., who was a well-to-do, respected, and influential man of German extraction. The Rutter family, like the Rices, were among the leaders in the county, and of the upper class without any doubt.

Another son of Father Rice was Dr. James H. Rice who, at a later time, moved to Hopkinsville in west Kentucky, about fifty miles southeast of Salem. He was a community leader in the best Presbyterian tradition, for, in addition to practicing medicine, James taught school.[25] Dr. James Rice was also a writer of some skill whose sketches of his father and of Terah Templin are included in Bishop's *History of the Church in Kentucky*.

The connections between these three Rice men and the Lewis families are interesting, for within the four or five years following 1809 they would become very closely intertwined through marriage, social position, religious associations, and even by orders given by the county court.

At the end of 1809, the year that had brought such heartbreak to the Lewises, a foreboding event occurred on the western frontier, involving a distant relation of the Lewis family. At that time the family was being split up; Elizabeth had died, Lucy was gravely ill, and two of Lilburne's daughters had been sent to the Bluegrass to live and attend school. The family's health had been weakened by severe illness during the summer and fall and, at the same time, it had become public knowledge that Lilburne was in debt for sizable sums to Dr. Arthur Campbell and Lynch Brooks. On top of these disasters came the news in October of 1809 that their cousin, the famous Meriwether Lewis, had committed suicide in western Tennessee. The news was published at Russellville, Kentucky, in *The Farmer's Friend;* the date line was Nashville, October 20, 1809.

It is with extreme regret we have to record the melancholy death of his excellency MERRIWETHER LEWIS, Governor of Upper

Louisiana, on his way to the city of Washington. The following particulars, are given us by a gentleman who travelled with him from the Chickasaw Bluffs:

The governor had been in a bad state of health, but having recovered in some degree, set out from the Chickasaw Bluffs and in travelling from that to the Chickasaw nation, our informant says, he discovered that the governor appeared at times considerably deranged, and on their arrival in the nation, having lost two horses, the governor proceeded on, and the gentleman detained with a view of hunting the horses. The governor went on to a Mr. Grinder's on the road, found no person at home but a woman: she observing something wild in his appearance, became frightened and left the house to sleep in another near it, and the two servants that was with him went to sleep in the stable. About three o'clock the woman says she heard the report of two pistols in the room where he lay, and immediately awaked the servants, who rushed into the house, but too late he had shot himself in the head and just below the breast, and was in the act of cutting himself with a knife. The only words he uttered was "It is done, my good servant give me some water," and expired in a few moments after.

It is impossible to form any correct conjecture what ever could have produced so horrid a determination in the mind of a man, whose respectability and talents were as preeminent as those of the deceased, his mind had been accustomed to the greatest industry and enterprize, his expedition up the Missouri, and travels to the Pacific Ocean, will be productive of the most beneficial results to our country, and will at once show the greatness of the man. Our informant has taken charge of his two trunks of papers which is supposed to contain the manuscripts of his travels to the Pacific Ocean. He gave directions some days previous to his committing the act, that if any accident should happen to him, his trunks should be sent on to the President of the United States; from which circumstance, we concluded that from some unknown cause, he had been induced to commit the rash deed. He had been often heard to speak of drafts which had been protested by the Secretary of War, and it is supposed this circumstance may have occasioned his uneasiness of mind.

He was as decently interred as the place would admit.[26]

The degree of kinship between Meriwether Lewis and the Lewises in Livingston was rather distant. Meriwether's grandfather, Col. Robert Lewis of Belvoir, was the brother of Col. Charles L. Lewis's grandfather, Charles Lewis of The Byrd and Goochland. Such a remote connection today would be considered of little significance, but among Virginians at that time kinship was a matter of importance. Brothers-in-law and sisters-in-law were usually spoken of simply as brother or sister, and cousins, however distant, were regarded almost as family members. It is not known whether the Lewises took their kinship to Meriwether very seriously or not. They had spent little or no time with him—except for Isham, who had visited with Governor Lewis in St. Louis in the summer of 1808.

In addition to their blood ties to Meriwether, the Lewises of Livingston were connected to him by their common background and friends in Albemarle County, and by association with Jefferson. Meriwether Lewis had been Jefferson's personal secretary for three years prior to his leading the Lewis and Clark expedition to the Pacific coast. Jefferson had no sons of his own and had an almost paternal regard for this keen young man.[27] Jefferson named one of his grandchildren after Meriwether Lewis. Three months after Meriwether returned from his expedition, Jefferson appointed him governor of the Territory of Upper Louisiana.[28] In the biography Jefferson wrote a few years later, he described Meriwether's good qualities: "of courage undaunted; possessing a firmness and perseverance of purpose which nothing but impossibilities could divert from its direction; careful as a father of those committed to his charge, . . . honest, disinterested, liberal, of sound understanding, and a fidelity to truth."[29]

The death of Meriwether Lewis was a shock to Americans, and especially to the westerners who, like Jefferson, held him in high regard. The fact that Meriwether was so depressed that he committed suicide must have caused widespread speculation. Actually, he was being unmercifully hounded by officials in Washington who would not honor the drafts he issued as governor of Louisiana, and his subordinates in the territory obstructed him at every turn. This was not widely known, but the governor's unbalanced condition at the time of his death did become public knowledge. The news account mentioned his "uneasiness of mind," that he appeared at times "considerably deranged," and that Mrs. Grinder "observing something wild in his appearance, left the house." One would naturally wonder whether this mental instability was only temporary and was occasioned by the pressure of his situation, or whether it was a personality flaw of more permanent nature. Jefferson thought he knew the answer. A few years after the suicide he wrote a short and highly laudatory biography of Meriwether, which contains Jefferson's thoughts about the cause of the suicide.

Captain Lewis was soon after appointed Governor of Louisiana. . . . A considerable time intervened before the Governor's arrival at St. Louis. He found the territory distracted by feuds and contentions among the officers of the Government, and the people themselves divided by these into factions and parties. He determined at once to take no sides with either, but to use every endeavor to conciliate and harmonize them.

Governor Lewis had been from early life subject to hypochondriacal affections. It was a constitutional disposition in all the nearer branches of the family of his name and was more immediately inherited by him from his father. They had not, however, been so strong as to give uneasiness to his family while he lived with me in Washington. I observed at times sensible depressions of mind, but knowing their constitutional source I estimated their course by what I had seen in the family. During his Western expedition the constant exertion which that required of all the faculties of body and mind, suspended these distressing affections, but after his establishment at St. Louis in sedentary occupations they returned upon him with redoubled vigor, and began seriously to alarm his friends. He was in a paroxysm of one of these when his affairs rendered it necessary for him to go to Washington. He proceeded to the Chickasaw Bluffs, where he arrived on the 16th of September, 1809, with a view of continuing his journey thence by water. Mr. Neely, agent of the United States with the Chickasaw Indians, arriving there two days after, found him extremely indisposed and betraying at times some symptoms of a derangement of mind. . . . He stopped at the house of a Mr. Grinder, who not being at home, his wife, alarmed at the symptoms of derangement she discovered, gave him up the house and retired to rest herself in an out-house, the Governor's and Neely's servants lodging in another. About three o'clock in the night he killed himself, which plunged his friends into affliction and deprived his country of one of her most valued citizens, whose valor and intelligence would have been now employed in avenging the wrongs of his country and in emulating by land the splendid deeds which have honored her arms on the ocean. . . . To this melancholy close of the life of one, whom posterity will declare not to have lived in vain, I have only to add, that all the facts I have stated are either known to myself or communicated by his family or others for whose truth I have no hesitation to make myself responsible, and I conclude with tendering you the assurances of my respect and consideration.

Thomas Jefferson[30]

Charlottesville, Va., 1813.

Jefferson stated that melancholia or depression was a "constitutional disposition" in *all* the "nearer branches" of the Lewis

family. He published this as a fact, and made himself responsible
for its truth. It is problematical whether Jefferson considered
that Col. Charles L. Lewis, his children, his father, and grandfather composed one of these "nearer branches," or whether,
in fact, any of them shared the symptoms of Meriwether's
"constitutional disposition." Again, the relationship between the
two family lines was this: Meriwether's grandfather and Col.
Charles L. Lewis's grandfather were brothers.

Two legends, which admittedly are inaccurate in many of
their details, mention first that Colonel Lewis was "taciturn,
moody, abstracted, and queer," and again, that he was, "to say
the least, a very strange man."[31] The fact that Col. Charles L.
Lewis, who once was one of the richest men in Albemarle
County, had lost his fortune and was finally destitute and dependent on his children, would naturally depress him and make him
moody and taciturn. It would most men. But it is also natural to
wonder whether Colonel Lewis and his sons suffered the same
"constitutional hypochondria" that afflicted Meriwether. The
citizens of Livingston County who knew of the family connections no doubt wondered, too.

·20·

INSECURITY

To many of the people in Livingston County, it must have appeared that the Lewises were well-to-do people. They had family connections with people in high positions and were themselves becoming influential on a local level. Lilburne, having lived in the county for only two years, was already an officer in the militia. He had served on several juries, once as foreman, and as a special court-appointed arbitrator. He was a county road supervisor and in January, when Randolph was nominated to be justice of the peace for the "Bio" Creek Neighborhood, Lilburne was named as alternate choice for the position.[1] Owning extensive tracts of land, a comparatively large number of slaves, new homes, and, as Lucy said, "everything to make us comfortable," the Lewises had all the appearances of wealth.

Unfortunately for the Lewises, their actual financial condition was not secure. Lilburne was being sued simultaneously by Lynch Brooks and Dr. Campbell for a total of more than eight hundred dollars, and the expense of school, board, and dancing lessons for his two oldest daughters cost him over one hundred dollars a year. These obligations could be paid off in time, provided Lilburne had enough income from his farm and slaves, or that he could sell some of his land or negroes. Two miles up the river from Rocky Hill lay the 500-acre tract of land that Lilburne owned. He had paid over $1,650 for this piece of property, which was worthless to him unless he could sell it. He needed the money, but for some reason he did not try, or was not able, to find a buyer for this tract.

As for Lilburne's slaves, the tax records for 1810 show that Lilburne owned a total of fourteen negroes, and the census figures for the same year indicate that only seven of these slaves were living at Rocky Hill. Evidently half of Lilburne's slaves were rented out to other people. It is known that Ursula was rented to John Daniel, the ferryman at the mouth of the Cumberland, and that Patsy was rented to James McCawley in Smithland.[2] The location of the other five slaves who did not live at Rocky Hill in 1810 is not known, but if all seven were rented out they would

215

not have earned Lilburne much more than $250 a year.[3] Of the seven slaves who lived at Rocky Hill, three, Mary, Celia, and William, were under sixteen and evidently not very valuable. Two years later Mary and Celia were rented out for a total of three dollars, and William "fed and cloathed . . . for what he will do."[4] The remaining four slaves, one or two of them no doubt being house servants, could not have raised enough crops on Lilburne's farm to bring in more than a very modest income. This situation, for a man whose occupation in Livingston was listed as "farmer," could not have been encouraging.

Thus limited in the amount of income he could derive from his land and negroes, Lilburne branched out into real estate, and attempted to establish a new town by the name of Westwood, to be located on twenty-five acres at the point of land across the Cumberland River from Smithland. This town site stood at a lower elevation than Smithland and was more subject to flooding, but, considering the large amount of river traffic passing through the place, it was a justifiable location for a town. Furthermore, the ferry across the Cumberland, operated by Justice of the Peace John Daniel, had its north landing where Westwood was to be laid out. Lilburne was one of five trustees who were to manage the scheme. Lilburne may not have been the prime organizer of the project, but he would have known very well how to go about it, since his father, Col. Charles L. Lewis, had done the same thing rather successfully twenty-two years before in founding the town of Milton on the Rivanna River. Like Milton, the town of Westwood is no longer in existence. As late as 1950, however, there remained traces of the old road to the Point, and on each side of it stood several old buildings, the relics of a small village.

The county court authorized the establishment of Westwood midyear in 1811, and the tax rolls note that thereafter Lilburne became the owner of town lots valued at $450. There is no official record that Lilburne ever sold them. The court record is all that survives of Westwood.[5]

Another enterprise that occupied Lilburne during much of 1810 was taking the federal census of Livingston County. The pay was two and a half cents for each person listed, a fee system that yielded rather little in such sparsely settled counties as Livingston. Even at that time it was one of the better jobs in the county, and Lilburne, needing the money, was lucky that his family connections enabled him to get the position.

The man who appointed him was Col. Joseph Crockett, the federal marshal of the state of Kentucky, and one of the more outstanding and capable men in the early history of the state.[6] Crockett established a record of distinction in many fields: in the army during the Revolution, and afterward in education, politics, and the development of towns and transportation. He was a crucial figure in the establishment of Kentucky as a state, and a personal friend of George Washington, Lafayette, and Thomas Jefferson. Colonel Crockett had been a resident of Albemarle County when the Lewises lived there, and had married Elizabeth Moore, a sister-in-law of Col. Charles L. Lewis. One of Crockett's daughters, Polly, had married Bennett Henderson, a cousin of Lilburne.[7] These family alliances and the fact that Lilburne's uncle, Thomas Jefferson, had appointed Colonel Crockett to the position of marshal of Kentucky, surely were helpful in getting Lilburne the job of taking the census.

The form of the census report was practically the same as that which had been used for several generations in Virginia to record the tax rolls. The only persons listed by name were the heads of each household. Next were listed, by number only, the members of the household, beginning with "free white males" in five different age brackets. The next category was "free white females," who were listed in the same age groups. In the third general grouping were "all other free persons, except Indians not taxed," and in the final column the slaves were enumerated.

The Livingston County report was written into a large notebook in Lilburne's own handwriting, which was easily readable, clear, fluid, and a bit ornate in style. The report was submitted in the fall. The total population of the county was listed as 3,674 inhabitants, broken down as follows: 2,932 whites, 718 slaves, and 24 free negroes.[8] Evidently Lilburne wanted his pay promptly, for directly beside the final summary of figures he noted that at the rate of two and a half cents per head, plus $4.00 for two copy books, $95.85 was due him for taking the census.[9] There is no notation on the report that Lilburne had others to help him with the job. If he hired workers, their pay would have reduced the $91.85 he received for the task. If he did the work alone, then it is certain that in interviewing the adults he became one of the more widely known persons in that county.

Lilburne must have had some sources of income in addition to his farm, slaves, and job as census taker. Information is disappointingly scarce, and although it is possible, there is no indica-

217

tion that Lilburne himself ever operated any regular type of business or worked as an agent for any firms in Virginia or Kentucky. It appears from scanty sources that, for the year of 1810, Lilburne's income was somewhat less than $350.

This situation was one that might change for the better if fortune were kind, but early in 1810 the Lewises suffered an irrevocable loss in the death of Lucy. A few months later Lucy's three daughters wrote to their uncle, Thomas Jefferson, and in a few words told him the news:

> 17 Sept 1810 Livingston County Kent [a]
>
> Dear Uncle
> No doubt you have before this, heard of the iraparable loss we have experienced, in the death of the best of mothers, and sister, which event took place on the twenty sixth day, of last may. She gragulery waisted away with little or no pain, for eighteen months enturely sensable to her last moments, quite resind to meat the aughfull fate. Her remains was entered the twenty eighth on a high emmenence, in view of that majestic river the Ohio.[10]

Lucy was fifty-seven when she died. Her grave was marked by a flat untrimmed piece of fieldstone, two or three feet high, set upright in the ground. Her name was not carved in the stone, or, if it was, it was so shallowly inscribed that it has worn away. Stones of this sort may still be seen in Livingston in several of the small family cemeteries that predate 1820.

The legends claim that Lucy was buried on Lilburne's plantation. All the graves in the cemetery on Rocky Hill can be accounted for, and Lucy's is not one of these. It is most probable that she lies in the upper corner of the cemetery, at the top of the high ground overlooking the river on Randolph's farm, near where she lived for so few months after she moved to Kentucky.

In spite of his mother's death early in the year, and his own continuing financial troubles, there was one note of happiness in Lilburne's family life. He had been a widower since the previous April, a year and a half. During those months he had begun to court a young lady, Letitia G. Rutter, who was reportedly the "belle of the county." According to the only surviving accounts of her, she was "accomplished and beautiful . . . a bright eyed, pulsing, Kentucky beauty."[11] In November, Lilburne, with Randolph as his security, posted his marriage bond in the sum of fifty pounds. The marriage bond was required by state law as a measure to prevent illegal marriages. If a marriage were discovered to be bigamous, or if either partner were too young, or the couple were too closely related to each other, then the fifty-pound bond was forfeited to the state.[12]

Three days after the bond was posted, the marriage took place, and Lilburne recorded it in the book where he kept his family records, the 1803 copy of *The Acts of the General Assembly of Virginia.* He wrote that "Lilburne Lewis and Letitia Griffin Rutter was married November 22nd, 1810, at her father's, James Rutter, Senr., Livingston County, Kentucky."[13]

The Rutter family was one of the largest and most prominent in the county. There were four sons and five daughters, all of them grown. Two of the sons, James Rutter, Jr., and William, resided in Livingston County in the Salem neighborhood. All of the daughters lived in the county and, of the five of them, Letitia was the last to marry. Peggy had married Joseph Ray, who lived in the Smithland area. Sally had married Patrick H. Rice, the son of Father David Rice, and lived in the Salem neighborhood. Polly was the wife of Mark Phillips, and Elizabeth had married William C. Rodgers, the founder of Salem, and the controversial county surveyor who had been impeached in December of 1809 for falsifying boundaries in order to steal land. Rodgers was exonerated by the senate in a close vote, continued as county surveyor, and at the same time held the position of tax commissioner.[14] Shortly after Lilburne's marriage, Rodgers turned over the county surveyor's job to his brother-in-law, James Rutter, Jr.[15] Elizabeth's marriage to William C. Rodgers had not turned out very well. They had been married for eight or ten years, had five children, and then separated. Divorces were frowned upon and were difficult to obtain, since each divorce required a separate act of legislature. In 1809 the authority to grant divorce was given to the circuit courts, and shortly thereafter Elizabeth and William C. Rodgers divided their property, "agreeable to both," and obtained a "friendly" divorce.[16]

The men in the Rutter family were members of the power elite of the county. Even though they were not justices of the peace, the presence of brothers-in-law and friends who were justices on the county court gave the Rutters substantial influence in Livingston. In 1809, when James Rutter was appointed coroner, his in-law, William Rice, was on the court, and the next year, when William C. Rodgers resigned as county surveyor, Randolph Lewis and William Rice were members of the court that appointed their brother-in-law, James Rutter, to the county surveyor's job, thus keeping it in the family. Rodgers and Mark Phillips signed James's $3,000 bond as securities.[17] In early 1810, when Salem was "laid out" on the land of William C. Rodgers, William Rutter was appointed one of the five original trustees. The town of Salem was more or less a Rutter family enterprise.

With the possible exception of Patrick H. Rice, all of the Rutter family and their in-laws were slave owners.[18] William Rutter owned two slaves, and James Rutter, Jr. had three, as did Joseph Ray and Mark Phillips. Apparently in these households the slaves were kept for domestic service, not profit. James Rutter, Sr. and Rodgers each owned seven negroes, and Lilburne owned fourteen. Only seven men in the country owned more slaves than Lilburne. It appears that James Rutter, Sr. was a grateful and kindly master to his negroes. He wrote in his will that he wished his negro woman, Rachel, and her children not to be sold out of the family. He requested one of his daughters to buy Rachel so that "she may be treated with tenderness and humanity for the many services she has rendered to myself and family."[19]

The Rutter family reputation was remembered with justifiable pride by a direct descendant who, until recently, lived in Salem.[20] He recalled in an interview that the family had always been decent folks and, even as far back as the earliest days, had never been in any trouble because of bad behavior. The court records bear out his statement. The will of James Rutter, Sr. indicates that, in addition to being kindly, the Rutters were religious people. Even though it was customary to begin a will by commending one's soul to God, Rutter's dedication was more eloquent than usual: "First I commend my soul to God who gave it and I hope through his mercy and the merit of Jesus Christ to obtain salvation." He continued with the request to be "decently buried in a Christian like manner," and then proceeded to dispose his property which it had "pleased God to bless my industry with."[21]

If any families in the county could be called "pillars of society," the Rutters and the Rices deserved the title. With the marriage of Lilburne and Letitia, the Lewises were joined to them as in-laws.

Connections such as these were valuable, especially in county politics where the justices of the peace, who made up the county court, appointed their own successors. In 1810 there were seven vacancies on the court, and early in the year Randolph, with Lilburne as alternate choice, was nominated to fill the position for the Bayou Creek neighborhood.

The law specified that two nominations be forwarded to the governor, who would then commission one of them. Normally the governor commissioned the first person listed; hence, to be the first nominee of the court was usually tantamount to receiving the position.[22] Randolph took the oath of office in Salem at the beginning of August, four weeks after his baby son, Warner, had been born.[23] The justices of the peace were required to assemble each month and then, sitting in session as the county court, direct the affairs of the county. As a rule, however, attendance by the justices at the court sessions was poor, and Randolph's record was as bad as any, for, while he no doubt performed the magisterial functions in his neighborhood, he did not attend any sessions of the court after his commissioning. The reason for this absenteeism is not positively known. Also unknown is the reason why Randolph was nominated first over Lilburne. Randolph was the older, and Lilburne had been out of the county on an extended trip to the Bluegrass just before the nominations were made. Perhaps the court members thought Lilburne would be away too often to do the job as well as Randolph, or perhaps the fact that Randolph's home was two miles closer to the center of Bayou Creek Neighborhood made the difference. It may have been that the two brothers differed substantially in character and personality, with Randolph appearing the more dependable, or perhaps Lilburne's unsettled suits for debt inclined the court to pick Randolph over Lilburne.

If Lilburne's debts were the reason for choosing Randolph, it was a questionable choice, for Randolph's financial situation was not much better than Lilburne's. With an impressive net worth, mostly in land, Randolph, nevertheless had very little income. Most of his money was tied up in raw land, which is among the least liquid of financial assets, especially in a time of economic recession, as was the year of 1810. Randolph's financial situation is a good illustration of being "land poor."

Although Randolph owned seven slaves valued at $2,220, only two of them were grown men. Of these seven slaves, two were apparently rented out, and did not live on Randolph's farm.[24]

Of the five slaves who did live with Randolph, Sarah and Frank were in advanced old age, and "yellow" Matilda was only ten years old. The remaining two slaves, however strong and industrious they might have been, could not have earned much income for Randolph by farming.

In regard to producing income, Randolph's land was in the same general category as his slaves. Randolph had paid nearly $9,100 for the land he bought in Kentucky, slightly more than 3,800 acres.[25] He did not intend to sell the 500-acre tract where he lived, but he was trying without success to sell part of the other land. Randolph was in immediate need of income. He was so short of cash that he could not pay the modest debt of $18.25 he owed to a merchandising firm in Salem.

This firm, Bradley, King, and Vance, was one of the more enterprising businesses on the frontier, operating branches in Palmyra, Tennessee, and Eddyville, Kentucky, both towns located on the Cumberland River, and a store, stable, and warehouse in Salem. One of the three partners had died and, in the fall of 1810, the firm published notice that it was going to dissolve.[26] As part of the procedure, suits were filed for outstanding debts, one of which was Randolph's. Randolph was summoned to appear before the circuit court at the September session. A few days later Colonel Lewis came into court and signed his son's bail. In the next meeting of the circuit court the clerk noted in the order book that Randolph had not obeyed the summons, and that judgment was subsequently passed upon him. "26 September 1810 . . . the defendant being arrested was solemnly called and came not. Its therefore considered by the court that the plaintiffs recover against the defendant eighteen Dollars Twenty five cents, the debt in the declaration mentioned, with interest thereon . . . six percentum per annum from the 7th Day of August 1810 untill paid . . . and the defendant in mercy be."[27]

If anyone ever needed mercy, it was Randolph at this time, for it appears that his health was failing, and that this was the reason for his absence at the meetings of the county court and at the trial of his suit for debt. About three months later, in mid-January, Randolph wrote his will, an action rarely taken except in cases of anticipated death or extreme danger. On Christmas eve, the deeds to all the land the Lewis brothers had bought in Kentucky were recorded in the courthouse at Salem.[28] They had been recorded previously in Frankfort, Kentucky, and in Richmond, Virginia. There was no reason to record them at that time in Livingston unless Randolph's death appeared imminent.

Far to the south, in Natchez, Mississippi, the youngest son of the family, Isham, was also in need of money. He had left Albemarle in the late spring of 1809, having been trained in the rudiments of surveying by his uncle, Thomas Jefferson. Jefferson had given Isham letters recommending his employment in Mississippi and had sent him off with a gift of fifty shillings "to bear his expenses." By mid-summer Isham arrived at Rocky Hill, where he became sick for a while with malaria. The bill for his treatment by Dr. Campbell was put on Lilburne's account. After recovering from his illness, Isham continued on to Natchez, arriving sometime before April 1810. Whether or not Isham was able to find a job surveying is unknown, but it is certain he needed money, for on April third he borrowed $235 from a man who died not too long afterward.[29]

Like all of his sons at this time, Colonel Lewis was also in deep trouble. When he rented his four slaves and the furniture from Craven Peyton, he had pledged to pay Peyton $140 annual rent. He had not honored this agreement with his son-in-law, nor did he have any prospects for paying him in the future. He became fearful, now that Lucy was dead, that Peyton would repossess his slaves. The old widower wrote a letter to Peyton, and another to Jefferson, asking him to intercede in the matter in the colonel's behalf. It appears that Colonel Lewis had little confidence in the strength of his relationship with Peyton, or with Jefferson either, for that matter—for instead of signing this letter himself, Colonel Lewis composed it as though his three daughters had written it, and then had them sign it. This play for Jefferson's sympathy was obvious, for the letter is unmistakably the old man's handwriting and style. At least one of the girls could have written the letter herself, if her father had permitted, for Martha's script and spelling both were better than her father's.[30]

17 Sept 1810 Livingston County Kent[a]

Dear Uncle

. . . . Permit us now Sir. to give a detail of our present, & future prospects. When my father and fameliy removed to the western countra, it was truly under imberast circomstances, we could bring no property that we could call our own. Three or four old domisticks, were convaid with three beds and ferniture &c by Mr. Peyton on hier, to be paid annually, subject to his order when called for, both the annual heir and the negroes, and ferniture. A call has not as yet been for either. We apprehend the death of our dear Mother may bring about some change, that the above mentioned property may be called for. In the event of a call being made, we should be in a very distrest situation, no seport left, except what our brothers could do for us, even tolerable. The loss of our old domestics, would be almost equal to the loss of our own dear Mother, having been allways with them from children. My father has rote to Mr. Peyton, on the subject. What finely will be done is all conjectural. We beg my dear Uncle for the intercession of yourself, Uncle Randolph, Mr. Randolph, Mr. P. Carr, & D. Carr, and all our dear connections, to use what influanc they can by indeavering with Mr. Peyton, not to distres us. Any assistance that our dear relations can be of in any shape will be very exceptable. In our distrest situation, should we not succeed in our wish, we shall have to pine out our days, be them few or many, with the mallencolley reflection, that to be once in affluence, is truly a mis fortune when reverst, and these pore hands of ours been from our infancey acustomed to drudgery. Our feelings dear Uncle is much injured at the thought of injuring yours, and our dear relations. Necessity alone is, we hope, a suffitiant apolege for any uneasy sincations, this relation of our situation may have, or give, to any of our friend. Be so good, sir, to give us an answer. Present our most respectful love to aunt Carr, Mrs. Randolph, cousin polle Carr, and for you will pleas to except our Best wises, adieu.

Martha C. Lewis
Lucy B. Lewis
Ann M. Lewis[31]

Jefferson received this letter a month later, waited several weeks, and then wrote to Peyton, again coming to the rescue of his sister's family.

Monticello Dec. 6.10.

Dear Sir

I have received a letter from Colo. Lewis now of Kentucky expressing apprehensions that 3-or-4 domestics which he holds from you on hire, and who have been with his children from their infancy may be called for by you, in which case the family would be in infinite distress and without any aid or means of subsistence, and requesting me to speak with you on the subject. Being an entire stranger to the whole matter, I can do no more than mention it to you, and ask the favor of you to enable me to explain to him your intentions, which I have no doubt are as favorable towards them as their distressed circumstances seem to plead for. I had intended to court on Monday in the hope of meeting you there, and of mentioning this subject to you, but the day was such that I could not go out. Accept the assurances of my great esteem & respect.

Th. Jefferson[32]

As might have been expected, Craven Peyton reacted with charity toward the Lewises, for his slaves were still in Kentucky two years later. There is, however, one curious element in the incident of the colonel's hired domestics. The federal census report, as well as the county tax records, both clearly list Colonel Lewis as having only two slaves in his possession. Two slaves out of the four who had left Albemarle with Lucy and her husband were missing. They may have died, or they may have been sub-rented, or perhaps even sold, by Colonel Lewis. When Lewis wrote to Jefferson, he was indefinite, or else lied, about the number, and Jefferson assumed Colonel Lewis still had possession of these three or four domestics. If the colonel had only two left of the original four slaves, he did not want Peyton to know it, and deceived him in this fact, as he had in others.

If, on the other hand, Colonel Lewis still had possession of the four slaves at his home, he had turned in a fraudulent tax list, and, in addition, Lilburne had deliberately falsified his census report. Something in this affair attracted the suspicions of the county officials, and, in the fall of 1811, Colonel Lewis was summoned to appear in county court "to show cause if he can why he shall not be fined and treble taxed for giving in fraudulent lists of taxable property." The tax commissioner for the district was Mark Phillips who had married Polly Rutter, Letitia's sister. Thus, through Lilburne's marriage, the colonel and the tax collector had become in-laws. There may have been a conspiracy in the colonel's behalf, for Mark Phillips was also summoned to appear in court. The outcome of the matter is unknown, but apparently it was somehow straightened out, for the tax rolls of the following few years show that Colonel Lewis had possession of only two slaves.[33]

Life on the west Kentucky frontier in those early years was hard for all, but for the Lewises the difficulties were appalling. Nothing stood between Colonel Lewis's household and "infinite distress," but two (or three or four) "old domestics." If they lost the slaves they would have been "without any aid or means of subsistence." At Christmas time it appeared that Randolph was mortally ill, and Lilburne, like the rest of them, had more debts than cash, and everyone in the county knew it. The Christmas of 1810 was a time of mounting dismay for the whole family.

·21·

COMMUNITY AFFAIRS,

1810

IN 1810, Kentuckians were becoming increasingly angry at the British for strengthening their frontier posts and inciting the Indians in the northwest against the Americans. The citizens elected war hawks Henry Clay and Richard M. Johnson to congress, and prepared to fight to defend their state. Service in the militia became a very serious matter as the possibility of armed conflict became more certain. Unfortunately, the state militia was poorly organized and armed. During the previous Winter Governor Scott had warned the legislators that half of the militia companies in Kentucky had not turned in their muster rolls to headquarters and that, of the half that were accounted for, not one-fifth were armed or prepared for service. During this time Lilburne became a captain, and was given command of a company of his neighbors.[1]

In Livingston there was no love lost toward the Indians, especially the nearby Chickasaws, who had been so hostile in recent years that the militia had been called out to guard the county borders. Across the Ohio River in the Northwest Territory, settlers were being murdered, and there were bitter memories of past killings in Livingston County. In 1793, Moses Shelby, the brother of Governor Isaac Shelby, was hunting in southwest Kentucky on Little Creek with his brother, Evan, and two other companions. Evan and the two friends were ambushed and killed by Indians, but Moses was able to escape unhurt.[2] Reacting to such incidents, and aggravated further by greed for the land occupied by the Chickasaws, many of the settlers regarded the Indians as little better than animals, and treated them accordingly.

An extreme example of this attitude occurred in an encounter that took place in Eddyville in 1803. At that time James Ivy had not yet moved his tavern to Centerville, but was running a comparable dramshop in Matthew Lyon's new town on the Cumberland River. One night in early March, shortly before ten o'clock, a group of about twenty men were drinking in Ivy's barroom. Among the crowd were three Chickasaw Indians, one of whom, named Jimmy, had been given liquor by the crowd until he was in a drunken stupor. One man in the crowd, sensing a surly mood in the room, and observing that Jimmy was "of a very peaceable demeanor giving offence to no person," dragged Jimmy into the corner of the room and left him there "that he should be out of harm's way." At that point the other two Indians, one of whom was drunk but still able to walk, left the tavern and went outside. They were followed immediately by two men, Matthias Cook and Isaac Ferguson, who were carrying clubs, "one a beech about 3 feet long, 1½ inch through, with a sort of snag on the bottom; the other a sugar tree limb two feet long and an inch or more through." As they walked after the Chickasaws, Cook and Ferguson were overheard planning to kill the Indians. Help was summoned quickly for the Chickasaws, and the double murder was prevented. One of the Indians was found "bleeding fast from a wound he had received in the forehead."

While this was going on outside, back in Ivy's tavern a man named Reuben Cook dragged the comatose Jimmy out of the corner and threw him face down in front of the fireplace. Cook then proceeded to kick burning coals out of the fire "onto Jimmy which flew onto his naked body and burned him badly, without any provocation." No one in the tavern interfered, and Jimmy was allowed to crawl outside where he was heard to "moan badly" as Ferguson and the two Cooks kicked him in the face and beat him with the clubs. One witness, intending to help Jimmy, was intercepted by the three thugs, who "threatened beating him for taking the part of the Indian." Somewhat later a search was made and Jimmy was found barely breathing, with his head half buried in the mud. His face was mangled and "in one place on his head the skull seemed indented." Jimmy was placed on a sled and taken to Ivy's house, where he "languished" and died two days later.

A coroner's jury was assembled, and Congressman Matthew Lyon was appointed foreman. He took the depositions of three men and wrote down the findings of the inquest. The coroner made his report, and two of the murderers were put in jail. The third, Matthias Cook, had absconded. On May 4, 1803, a jury found the three defendants not guilty.[3]

During the 1809-1810 session of the Kentucky legislature, the matter of abolishing the Chickasaw land claim in west Kentucky was again brought up. In order to negotiate a treaty the governor first had to appoint a commissioner to serve with the federal agent, Return J. Meigs. There was no difficulty in that step, but the governor warned the legislature that while the state should pay the expenses and compensation of its own commissioner, it could not afford to pay the entire cost of extinguishing the Indian title as well as bearing the expenses of the treaty. The federal government would have to do that, and Governor Scott would not proceed without this agreement from the United States government.[4] This was one of the issues which for a decade delayed the acquisition of the land known as the Jackson Purchase.

In one of the following terms of the legislature, Gen. Samuel Hopkins, who was then state senator representing Livingston County, carried to the legislature the sentiments of west Kentuckians on this issue. He read the following resolution:

WHEREAS that desirable and inviting country, lying south of the Tennessee river, and within the chartered limits of the state of Kentucky, is wholly unoccupied, in consequence of the claim held to it by the Chickasaw Indians. And whereas many deserving citizens hold titles to the greater part of the soil, as the reward of their revolutionary labors, without being permitted to look forward to any particular period, for the enjoyment of the fruits of their valour and patriotism. And whereas the Indians have not, for a very long time past, used the land within this boundary, for any of the purposes of cultivation or hunting; and only retain their title to apologize for the many vexatious insults, and marauding incursions with which they are in the constant habit of alarming and injuring our citizens on the frontiers. And whereas the acquisition of this territory, would greatly facilitate our commercial intercourse with the markets on the Mississippi, by opening a direct passage by which we can communicate with them, in a distance greatly short of the present route through the state of Tennessee, and in which our traders would be not only relieved from the hardship of prosecuting a longer journey, but also from many arbitrary impositions and heavy exactions, with which the Indians never fail to oppress them. Wherefore,

Resolved—That our senators in Congress be positively instructed, and our representatives requested, to use all constitutional means to procure from the competent authorities of the general government, the extinguishment of the claim held by the Chickasaw Indians, to the tract of country situated below the Tennessee river, and within the boundary of the state of Kentucky.[5]

In the previous session the Kentucky senate and house had resolved unanimously that the extinguishment of the Indian claims was "imperatively required," and that the Kentucky congressmen and senators in Washington be directed to "effect this desirable and important object."[6]

Another community interest was the growth of Salem and the construction of the county buildings. In January the jail bounds, or public square, was laid out. On this plot would be built the courthouse, stray pen, and the jail and debtors' room. A continuing problem in frontier settlements was building a jail strong enough to prevent jail breaks. Livingston County was no different from the others. In Centerville the jailer, David Kline, had been indicted because he "unlawfully and negligently did permit the said Robert Trimble a murderer to egress out of the said jail and escape at large whether so ever he would." A year or so later one Isaac Hicks, "late of said county," took the initiative and "with force and arms did break the jail in Salem." He escaped. In 1810 one Margaret Smith was "committed to jail for making an attempt to break the jail of Livingston County and to rescue the persons there committed for felony." She spent the next twenty-three days inside with her friends. Sheriff James Johnson complained to the court that no part of the new jail at Salem was strong, not even the room in front of the jail, which was set aside for debtors.[7]

A more routine bit of county business was the appointment of young Henry F. Delany as the county attorney. He was to be the legal advisor and agent in all the county court business, both judicial and executive. Delany was about twenty-five years old and was married, had an infant son, and owned three slaves at that time. His wife, Rhoda, was the daughter of Capt. William Prince, the founder of Princeton, Kentucky.[8] Rhoda's brother was Enoch Prince, the clerk of both the county and circuit courts in Livingston. It was not unusual for one man to hold both these offices, and it did give Delany an influential connection in all the legal affairs of Livingston.

Henry Delany was a handsome and impressive man. A close acquaintance, writing years later, remembered him clearly:

In his physical form he was tall, erect, symmetrical, at once commanding and attractive; complexion dark; projecting brow, almost concealing a dark, gray, bright, keen, intelligent eye. Raven curls fell gracefully around his neck and about a high, broad, smooth, marble-like forehead.

His manner, in all circles of social life smooth, affable, pleasant,

229

dignified, commanding and pleasing. But it was in ... [public speaking] especially where he excelled in ease, gravity, dignity. His voice, a tenor key, soft, musical as a flute, but of great strength. Intonations and pronounciation distinct, euphonious—an eloquent declaimer—every gesture had a voice and language that might have arrested, impressed and interested the mute. Not violent—deliberative, animated, peculiarly engaging and impressive. He, who heard Delany but once, would never forget the man, his manner or matter.

His natural mind was quick, penetrating, searching, and of that resolute, persevering character that mastered and subdued. His education, liberal; intelligence, general and miscellaneous.[9]

Delaney had practiced law in various west Kentucky circuits since his twentieth birthday, and by 1809 he was a resident of the Centerville district where, in addition to his law practice, he served as captain of the patrol. He was the first county court clerk of Caldwell County, helping out in the early sessions held at Eddyville after the county was formed. Early in 1810 Delany was sworn in as the Livingston County attorney, and he moved his family to the Salem area, where be bought thirty acres on Sandy Creek. In October the county court paid him $60 for "services as county attorney for commonwealth up to this time." This was a small amount for nine months' work, but Delany had other clients to provide him with a living. Among these were Lilburne Lewis and the Rutter family.[10]

When Delany defended Lilburne in the suits brought by Dr. Campbell and Lynch Brooks, he was opposed by lawyer John Gray, who was the commonwealth prosecuting attorney for the circuit court in the seventh district. In these two cases Gray was engaging in private practice, but as commonwealth attorney for the circuit court Gray received more salary than Delany did on the county court: $150 per annum for the years 1808 to 1811. Occasionally Delany and Gray exchanged jobs, or rather, if one could not attend his duties temporarily, the other was appointed to fill in.[11]

John Gray had lived in Russellville, in Logan County, where he served as postmaster in 1801, and married a sister of Ninian Edwards.[12] By 1804 Gray had become a lawyer and practiced in the courts of Henderson, Christian, and Livingston counties. He moved to the Centerville area prior to 1807, and was one of the original trustees of that town when it was established. He continued his residence there after it became part of Caldwell

County. Gray was somewhat pretentious, if his writing style is any indication. The indictments and other documents he composed were so prolix and crammed with "saids, aforesaids, and whereases," and other legal flourishes, that their meaning was often obscured.[13]

Although John Gray and Lilburne were very well acquainted, it is doubtful that they were especially friendly. In the two suits that brought Lilburne into the circuit court in 1810, John Gray was legal counsel for Lilburne's opposition. Gray and Lilburne were thrown together in several other matters of court business. In March, Lilburne was made foreman of the grand jury. Judge Broadnax and the assistant judges, David Caldwell and Jesse Ford, were presiding in court, and after three days of deliberation Lilburne and the jury returned a handful of routine indictments and presentments for swearing, drunkenness, and adultery. They also indicted the two men who had broken into Bradley, King, and Vance's store, but the thieves had fled the county and nothing resulted from the indictment except that the absentees were declared "outlaw" in a later term of court.[14] Micajah Phelps, a hatter, was also indicted because he "did feloniously steal, take and carry away one meal bag with two and a half bushels of Indian cornmeal therein of the value of three dollars the proper goods and chattels of a certain James Henderson of the said county, blacksmith." On this occasion Lilburne did not stir up much work for Commonwealth Attorney John Gray.[15]

Of the twenty-one men on Lilburne's grand jury panel, seven of them were, or would soon become, vitally intertwined in his life. Mark Phillips and Joseph Ray would become his brothers-in-law in a few months. Edward Lacey was his superior officer in the Twenty-fourth Militia Regiment. Thomas Terry would be threatened by Lilburne with a suit for trespass, and William Pippin and two other men on this grand jury would, at a later date, sit on a jury that voted a "true bill" indictment against Lilburne in a case prosecuted by John Gray and heard by Assistant Judge Jesse Ford.[16] William Pippin and Mark Phillips would also serve in the future on a coroner's jury with which Lilburne had some connection.

This term of court did not end Lilburne's jury duty for the year. In September he was a venireman on a petty jury that awarded $52.50 to his good friend, the Smithland tavern keeper and justice of the peace, James McCawley.[17] In this same September term, the two suits for debt against Lilburne were post-poned again because of absent witnesses. Considering the amount of time Lilburne spent in circuit court, it seems fitting that he kept his family records on the flyleaf of a book of state laws rather than the Bible.

A few cases that went off the docket in this term of court give some idea of the pastimes of the rougher elements in Livingston County during that year. Various forms of liquor usually laid the groundwork for lower-class entertainment. Cider, whiskey, beer, and brandy were all more or less common items, but among the more exotic libations was a pop-skull blend of cider and brandy called "cider oil," which was made by boiling cider down to half its bulk and adding apple brandy.[18] Cider oil may have been a contributing factor to an indictment that was dismissed because the roughneck, James Stevenson, "late of said county," could not be found. "James Stevenson, yeoman, . . . at the house of William Woods, at the mouth of the Hurricane Creek, did unlawfully make an assault on William Love . . . and without being compelled thereto in self defense, did bite off the right ear of him the said William Love."[19]

A similar case heard in the same term of court was that of Robert Woods, a laborer and agent for the firm of Joseph Woods and Co., the warehousing and mercantile firm at Smith-land. "The grand jury . . . on their oaths present that Robert Woods, laborer, . . . being a wicked and evil disposed person, . . . did make an assult on the body of one Jeremiah Moore, carpenter, of said county and unlawfully bite off the lip of said Jeremiah Moore." Robert Woods had been "required" by the court in the five preceding terms of the circuit court and Woods was finally declared outlawed for not surrendering himself.[20]

Disfigurement commonly resulted from such brawls and "no holds barred" fighting, which, as often as not, was a form of recreation for this class of riff-raff. A missing nose, lip, ear, or an eye, more often identified a ruffian than it did the victim of an accident. In order to preserve a good reputation, the better class of citizens sometimes recorded the fact when they had been accidentally injured. "Be it remembered that this day Christopher Haynes came into court and presented his infant son, William Bryant Haynes, who has by accident been disfigured in the under part of his right ear, which is ordered to be recorded."[21]

There was little thought of rehabilitating criminals on the frontier. One was either a good citizen or "a wicked and evil disposed person." The indictments for brawling and affray usually included the following comment: "to the terror of the good citizens of the commonwealth and to the evil example of all others." An unfortunate childhood was irrelevant, and psychological problems were unheard of; a person was either good or evil, and punishment was the obvious remedy for those in the latter category.

When punishment failed, the primary hope for personal reform lay in religious conversion, in which one repented his past sins and turned over a new leaf. In February of 1810 a strong force for regeneration and decency came into being in west Kentucky. The Cumberland Presbytery broke away from its formalistic parent church and established itself as the Cumberland Presbyterian church.[22] It was revivalistic and fervent in character, found enthusiastic support in Livingston, and enrolled many members there. The founding of this church was one of the more interesting events of the year in Livingston County.

· 22 ·

SLAVERY IN LIVINGSTON

SLAVERY IN the South and in Kentucky has been the subject of so many excellent studies that lengthy discussion is not needed here.[1] A summary of general statements may, however, help to set the background of the institution as it existed in Livingston County at the time the Lewises lived there.

The almost unanimous attitude among the southern whites, carried over from colonial days, was that slavery was a matter of fact. It was not regarded as a crime nor even a matter for apology, but rather a natural and moral necessity.[2] Of those few people in the South who opposed slavery and the slave trade, almost none harbored any suspicion that the negro race was not inherently inferior to the white.[3]

In spite of this, and underlying the whole history of American slavery, there were two repressed but constant fears that gnawed at southern whites. One was the dread of a slave and free negro uprising.[4] The other, having its roots deep in the conviction of white superiority, was the fear that the two races, given the chance, would blend and supposedly corrupt the genetic reservoir of the white race. The only noticeable initiative taken in this direction was by white males themselves—men of all social classes. The carnal use of negro women by white men was not at all rare or isolated.[5] Inconsistently enough, at the same time southern white men had a nearly obsessive concern that a white woman would be forced to have, or might even desire, sexual contact with a negro man. For the negro man in rape cases, death was almost always inflicted without delay.

Another inconsistency was that while the ownership of a sizable number of slaves invariably afforded social prestige to the owner, in many cases chattel slavery in Kentucky was not profitable, because the care of the slaves, including the children and the aged, cost more than their earnings.[6] Slavery, however, was not universally unprofitable. On a few especially well-managed plantations slave labor was found to be more efficient than hired free negro or white southern laborers.[7]

During the frontier and settlement days in Kentucky, before

the intensive cultivation of large plantations in a cash crop system, there were few men who owned large numbers of slaves, and the role of the slaves was different from their later role under the plantation system. For the negro men there were a variety of tasks; clearing ground, erecting buildings, growing diversified foods and fibers, cutting firewood, and so forth, but almost all labor was spent in providing for the needs and comfort of the family, not the raising of crops for cash. For slave women there were the endless tasks about the home, such as spinning, weaving, washing, cooking, and cleaning. As a rule the women were part of the home, and not often used as field hands. This personal interdependence and close contact between the Kentucky masters and slaves in the very early 1800s generally led to better feelings and kinder treatment than was the case in mid-century. Even as the Civil War drew near and the oppressions of southern plantation slavery became more harsh, it was recognized that the system of slavery in Kentucky was milder, and more relaxed and tolerant than in any other state.[8]

At this time the number of slaves in the state had not grown to the extent that slaves could be spared from the labor at hand and sold for profit, as was the case a few decades later. After 1820 the breeding of slaves for sale "down the river" became one of the most profitable aspects of slave labor in Kentucky. In a thirty-year period Kentuckians exported approximately eighty-two thousand slaves to the deep South, a figure that put the state well ahead of most others in this type of commerce.[9] Kentucky would become the slave "breeding pen" of the South.[10] In Livingston County, however, when the Lewises lived there, a cooperative and healthy slave was seldom sold except in cases of pressing financial need. In the settlement period of west Kentucky, for some families the labor done by slaves made the difference between a life of comparative comfort and leisure and an insecure existence of grinding hardship. This was the case with the Lewises.

The constitution and laws of Kentucky that were in effect prior to 1815 regulated the conduct and treatment of slaves in some detail. Article seven of the constitution was rather brief, dealing mostly with the emancipation and sale of slaves, but it also permitted laws to be made obliging owners to treat their slaves "with humanity," to provide food and clothes, and to abstain from injuring them. It guaranteed slaves the privilege of a jury trial in cases of felony but, under its terms, slaves could be prosecuted without indictment by a grand jury.[11]

The acts of legislature contained nearly sixty laws concerning not only slaves and slavery, but also negroes and mulattoes, both slave and free. The sections that pertained to free negroes and mulattoes are contained in chapter 174, which is entitled "Slaves," a curious contradiction. Free negroes and mulattoes were in fact, only partly free. They did not have all the privileges of full citizenship. No free negro or mulatto could be a witness in a trial involving whites, nor could he keep or carry any weapon whatsoever, unless he were a housekeeper or located on a frontier plantation. For carrying a weapon the punishment was thirty-nine lashes. If one lifted his hand "in opposition to" any white, a justice of the peace could order him to receive "30 lashes on his or her bare back, well laid on." While it was a felony for any free negro to conspire to create a rebellion or insurrection, a slave who did the same was executed. A free negro or mulatto convicted of manslaughter suffered death, and if he should "consult or advise the murder of any person whatsoever" he could be punished by as many as one hundred stripes. There was one set of laws for free whites, another for free mulattoes and blacks, and a third for slaves. In Kentucky it was not enough for a citizen to be free; he had to be free and white for full equality before the law.[12]

In nearly all cases, the laws regulating slaves were harsher than those concerning free negroes and mulattoes. No slave could leave his master's property without written permission or pass. For "riots, routs, unlawful assemblies, trespasses and seditious speeches," a slave could be lashed without any limit except the "discretion" of the justice of the peace. For the following crimes slaves were put to death: voluntary manslaughter, murder, arson, rape of a white woman, personal robbery, burglary, and intent to poison. For lesser crimes, slaves were lashed. They were not permitted to receive a penitentiary sentence, as were free negroes.[13]

The financial interest of the slave owner was clearly a factor in the laws regarding the punishment of slaves. The time spent by a slave in prison would be lost to the master; hence the resort to the lash. In cases where a slave was convicted and executed, the state was required to pay the owner the full value of the slave. The status of a slave before the law of Kentucky was bluntly expressed in the statutes. "All negro, mulatto, or Indian slaves, in all courts of judicature and other places within this common-wealth, shall be held, taken, and adjudged to be real estate."[14]

As the decades went by and the negro and slave population in the state increased, the laws governing these people became increasingly severe. For example, the constitution of 1800 re-quired that an owner who emancipated a negro guarantee that the ex-slave would not "become a charge to any county in the commonwealth."[15] When the constitution was revised in 1850 this provision was changed so that emancipation became equivalent to banishment. "The General Assembly shall pass laws providing that any free negro or mulatto hereafter immi-grating to, and any slave hereafter emancipated in, and refusing to leave this State, or having left, shall return and settle within this State, shall be deemed guilty of felony, and punished by confinement in the penitentiary thereof."[16]

The patrol system was the device set up to control the move-ment and gatherings of slaves. The law required each county to establish districts within the county, and, for each district, to ap-point a captain and two or three other men who were to patrol not less than twelve hours a month. Their responsibilities were to punish slaves who were found "strolling about from one plantation to another without a pass," or slaves who were unlaw-fully assembled. Since slaves were not permitted to buy or sell any article of property without written permission, the patrol could also punish slaves who had any object of value without a written permit. The punishment for these offenses was limited to ten lashes administered by the patrol on the spot, or thirty-nine lashes if the miscreant were taken to a justice of the peace. The patrollers were paid a few shillings a month out of the county tax levy, and were exempted from militia duty during the year's service on patrol.[17]

The patrols were usually made at night, a time feared by many of the superstitious blacks. Intimidation was an important aspect of the patrol, and its members were often recruited out of the "poor white trash" class in the community, young men who were brutal and casually cruel in this job.[18] The negroes were terrified of the patrol, a forerunner of the Ku Klux Klan, and the memory of this fear existed well into the present century in the warning to mischievous negro children, "Be good or the paddy roller get you."[19]

237

In Livingston County in 1810, 718 of the 3,674 people in the county were slaves, about 20 percent. Less than half of the white families owned slaves and of those who did, the majority owned 4 or fewer, usually 1 or 2, who were domestic servants. There were 43 men in the county who owned as many as 7 or more slaves. The total number of slaves owned by this group was 430, well over half the slaves in Livingston. The largest slave holder owned 17 negroes, and there were just 15 men who owned over ten blacks. Only five men in the county owned more slaves than Lilburne. He had 14 and Randolph had 7.[20] These figures indicate that in Livingston County the primary use of slaves was for domestic and handyman work. There were very few people who depended on slaves for sizable business or farming enterprises. Slavery in Livingston was mainly a family-oriented system, not a commercial one, and it is likely that the typical slave owner was more like the kindly James Rutter, Sr. than he was like Justice of the Peace Richard Ferguson and tavern keeper James McCawley, who beat the slave, Bob, nearly to death with a whip.

The treatment received by the slaves in Livingston should be considered in the light of two circumstances. First, the law of the state forbade any negro to raise his hand against a white under a thirty-lash penalty; hence the slave was utterly defenseless. Second, brutality was common at that time in Kentucky when the callous and ignorant white trash gouged, bit, and maimed each other purely for entertainment, when no argument was available as an excuse. Under these circumstances it is not surprising that there were some shocking examples of cruelty to slaves. It is related that James Ford, who would later become a criminal mastermind in the area, once bound an offending slave hand and foot and dragged him to death behind a mule through a field of stumps.[21] In another Livingston incident, which took place in 1804, a runaway slave was beaten to death with a club near Eddyville.[22]

In that same year another Livingston coroner's jury reported its findings in the death of "a negro woman named Rachel, the property of Thos. Hawkins." The inquest report noted that Rachel had sustained "an exceeding bad wound behind the right ear, supposed to be struck with a club or some other unlawful weapon. The appearance of the wound had affected the side of the head unto the left nostril and Blood appeared to issue therefrom, together with sundry smaller wounds appeared to be from severe whipping and the appearance of being seeded in a number of places by large blisters."[23] The members of the coroner's jury reported that they did "give it as our opinion" that Hawkins and his wife, at their plantation, had murdered Rachel with "malice aforethought."

These were extreme cases, and there may have been others of the kind. One would rather think, however, that the attitude of Gen. Jonathan Ramsey toward slavery was more typical of Livingstonians. Ramsey represented the county in the state legislature, and in 1811, when a harsh bill was presented to the house providing for the execution of slaves for a number of offenses, General Ramsey voted against it.[24] The bill passed forty to twenty-four, but Ramsey surely expressed the wishes of many of his constituents when he voted "nay." A further indication that the slaves in Livingston County were not rebellious, and that relations between the whites and blacks generally were quiescent at that time, is the following order of the county court: "Oct. 28, 1811—Ordered that all the pad rollers in the county be discharged from any longer serving as pad rollers."[25]

If a slave in Livingston were to break the law, however, tolerance was laid aside, as one slave named Abraham found out. He was owned by John Gray. The county court, which was the final court of appeal for all negroes, met to try Abraham on a charge of burglary. Among the four presiding justices of the peace was William Rice, the son of the abolitionist, Father David Rice. Because of his ownership of Abraham, John Gray did not act as the prosecuting attorney for the county in this case. A jury of twelve men was chosen, the trial was held, and the verdict was recorded. "The jury upon their oaths do say that they find the defendant not guilty of burglary, but guilty of larceny and to receive 39 lashes on the bare back and it is therefore considered and ordered by the court that the sheriff execute the above verdict immediately which was executed accordingly."[26]

The change of the charge against Abraham from burglary to larceny made a difference in the punishment. A slave was executed for burglary and lashed for larceny. It was a Christmas present of sorts to Abraham, for on that very same day in the state capitol, the legislature, which was then in general session, did not meet, observing the fact that it was Christmas day.[27]

239

·23·

TREMORS IN THE

DYNASTY

FOR THE Lewis family the year of 1811 began disastrously. They had come to Kentucky three years before, full of hope, expecting to establish a prosperous life for themselves in the fabled land of milk and honey. Since then Lucy and Elizabeth had died, Randolph and Lilburne were both in debt, and their father and sisters were nearly destitute. They had the basic necessities of life, and a few of the luxuries, but they had suffered ill health and the public mortification of continuing law suits over money matters. Their dreams, which were falling apart, must have been shattered when Randolph died early in the year.

There are some indications that he had been in declining health, and when he wrote his will in mid-January it was probably in anticipation of death in the near future, which did come sometime before the end of the next month. The cause of his death is unknown. One of the legends tells the questionable story that he died from the effects of a snake bite, a possible but unlikely accident in mid-January, when snakes are usually in hibernation.[1]

Randolph's will was dictated to his friend and neighbor, Amos Persons, and then signed by Randolph. The witnesses were Persons, Colonel Lewis, and Randolph's sister, Martha. In the will Randolph left all of his estate to Mary, his wife, for as long as she lived, after which it was to be divided among his eight children. Lilburne, Colonel Lewis, Mary, and Henry Williams, a magistrate who lived in Salem, were named as executors.[2] Lilburne and his father presented the will to the county court and a certificate of probate was granted to them at the end of February. A few days earlier they had posted an eight-thousand-dollar executors' bond, which was signed as securities by Amos Persons and Lilburne's brother-in-law, Mark Phillips.[3]

An appraisal of Randolph's estate was made for the court:

> In obedience to an order of the Worshipful court of Livingston
> County to us directed (being first sworn) we the undersigned have

240

this day proceeded to appraise the goods and Chattels belonging to the Estate of Randolph Lewis Deced. to Wit.

Adam	550
Andrew	500
Aggy	400
Judah [Judy]	400
Sarah [and Frank]	70
Matilda	300
5 head horses	150
6 head cattle	30
31 head hogs	35
23 beds and furnitures	100
4 trunks	9
	2544

1 case bottles	4.00
1 spy glass, 2 candle stands	9
2 guns $33—7 chairs $3½	36.50
Castings	16.50
2 pr. traces, 2 ploughs	6.50
2 axes $4—4 hoes $3	7.00
2 cotton wheels	4.00
1 reel $½—1 loom $9	9.50
2 slays $2—1 pr Stilyards $3½	5.50
1 saddle & bridle	6.50
Fiddle and case $12, Books $85	97.00
	202.00
	2544
Total Amount	2746

Given under our hands this 28th day of February

> A. Persons
> Patrick Calhoun
> David Fort
> Lilburne Lewis
> Chas. L. Lewis[4]

This was not a detailed listing of all of Randolph's possessions, but it does include the most valuable items. Randolph's land, nearly four thousand acres, was not part of this appraisal. It is interesting to note that two of the three female slaves, Aggy and Matilda, were mulattoes, described elsewhere as "yellow."

241

Matilda's father was Randolph's brother, Charles, who died in 1806; Randolph's own niece was thus his slave. Frank, Sarah's husband, the old slave who was led to religion by the Reverend William Dickey, was not named in this list, but it was probably understood that the feeble old man would go with his wife as part of the seventy-dollar value placed on her.

The scarcity of information about Randolph makes it difficult to assess the effect of his death on the family. There was, one supposes, the natural grief and shock, for he was only thirty-eight years old, and left eight children fatherless. His oldest son, Charles, however, was about nineteen, old enough to become the man of the household if he were capable. There were sufficient slaves, tools, livestock, and horses so that the family could produce their food and clothes, and there is no record that Randolph left more debts than the $18.25 he owed Bradley, King, and Vance. Certainly his indebtedness was not as great or pressing as Lilburne's.

It is possible to sketch parts of Randolph's personality. The Reverend William Dickey has described Randolph and Mary as pious and kind. If Dickey called them pious, there can be no doubt that they were, for Dickey himself approached fanaticism in his strictness and dedication to the Christian virtues of the time. Randolph treated his slaves well, and encouraged them to worship with his family. Although Randolph was far less active in community affairs than Lilburne, he was nevertheless intelligent and respected enough to be appointed justice of the peace by the county court. Two items in Randolph's estate indicate that he was a person of some artistic and intellectual refinement: the violin and eighty-five dollars worth of books, a respectable library for the Kentucky frontier. Another incident that illuminates Randolph's character was his sale of Mary, a slave woman, and her children to Jefferson before Randolph left Virginia. Mary's husband belonged to Jefferson, and Randolph did not want to break up this family by taking Mary and her children with him to Kentucky.

Among the scanty records that survive, wherever Randolph's name is mentioned in connection with another person or family, they were solid and respected persons. Lilburne's associates were much more widely scattered in the social spectrum, and included tavern keeper James McCawley, brutal Richard Ferguson, and the intriguing surveyor William C. Rodgers.

The relationship between Randolph and Lilburne seems to have been fairly close. At least it was close enough that they left Virginia together with their families, and intended to spend the rest of their lives as neighbors. To compare the two of them, Randolph appears to have been more steady than the mercurial Lilburne, a personality difference that could lead one to guess that if the brothers depended upon each other emotionally, then Randolph, the older brother, with his self-control, provided Lilburne with a sense of security and confidence. If this is true, then after Randolph's death Lilburne found himself alone at the head of the Lewis families, and in some degree responsible for them all, without Randolph's reassuring presence.

Randolph's death had left vacant the magistrate's position for the neighborhood. On the same day that Lilburne and his father posted their executor's bond, the county court nominated Lilburne "as a fit person" to take over Randolph's job as justice of the peace.[5] It was very rare for the governor not to follow the recommendation of the county courts and commission their first choice of nominees. At this time in Kentucky, before the emergence of a two-party political system, the nominees for the court were supported or opposed on the basis of their personalities, reputations, qualifications, or place of residence rather than their loyalty to a political party.[6] Thus, when, in May, Governor Scott commissioned Amos Persons instead of Lilburne, it would seem that someone had questioned Lilburne's fitness for the job.[7] It is possible that Lilburne changed his mind about wanting the position and withdrew his nomination from the governor, but if he had not, then the choice of Amos Persons over Lilburne would have been a public humiliation for Lilburne. This incident may have reminded Lilburne's father of the time in Albemarle when he himself had been rejected while seeking public office.

Since the appointment to public office was more a personality than a political contest, it appears that someone in the community did not regard Lilburne very highly. Some people may have resented his aristocratic connections, and others such as John Gray, Lynch Brooks, Peyton Short, or Dr. Arthur Campbell, may have had more personal reasons. Another such individual was a lawyer, James H. McLaughlan, a resident of Hopkinsville in Christian County, and the long-time clerk of that circuit court.[8] He had been a lawyer since 1803 and frequently represented clients in the Livingston circuit court where, on a few occasions, he himself had been presented to the grand jury for profanity. In March, about two months before the governor passed over Lilburne for the magistracy, the circuit court was in session in Salem, and Lilburne, as usual, was there to defend himself in the two suits for debt. He was not on the grand jury at that term but he did appear before them, requesting that they indict James McLaughlan for cursing him with these words, "God damn your soul."[9] This curse is the only documented piece of dialogue to be found in the known records of Lilburne's life. There is no way to discover what Lilburne had done to make McLaughlan angry, but Lilburne retaliated to the curse by informing to the grand jury.

The next day in court the Lynch Brooks case was finally settled. During the preceding two years, Lilburne had been summoned four times in connection with this suit, and repeatedly had promised to pay Brooks. At last Lilburne admitted his responsibility to Brooks in court, and the decision of the court was handed down: "This day came the plaintiff by his attorney and the defendant in his proper person and acknowledged that the plaintiff had sustained damages by reason of his non-performance of his promise and assumption in the declaration mentioned to three hundred and sixty dollars and twenty-five cents in manner and form aforesaid confessed and his costs by him about his suit in this behalf expended and the defendant in mercy be."[10]

From the time Lilburne had borrowed the money and given the draft to Brooks, until the time it became clear that Pickett's agent would not honor the draft, more than three years had elapsed. During the first part of this period there was no reason for Lilburne to think that the draft he had given Brooks was valueless, and he was not liable until it became clear that it was. For the first thirty-nine months Brooks was a victim of the risky inconvenience of conducting financial affairs on the frontier. But even if Lilburne were given the benefit of the doubt for the first thirty-nine months, it is clear that for the last twenty-two months of the dispute, Lilburne was at fault. He admitted this in court.

Lilburne may not have had the money to pay this debt at an earlier time, but if he did he was either naturally contentious or a deadbeat. After the court handed down its decision, Lilburne somehow got enough money together to pay off the debt. On the following day Lilburne was made foreman of a petit jury. This was the second time he had served on a petit jury in Salem. Both times Lilburne's friend, James McCawley, was a party in cases that were tried, and both times the jury decided in Mc-Cawley's favor. In this case John Gray charged that McCawley "did falsely, wickedly, willfully, maliciously, and corruptly commit willful and corrupt perjury to the great displeasure of Almighty God in contempt of the laws of the Commonwealth."[11] Gray claimed that the perjury was committed when McCawley testified in the trial of Joseph Woods and another man for removing tobacco from hogsheads stored in Woods's warehouse in Smithland and replacing it with cotton. McCawley was Woods's friend, and when McCawley was indicted for perjury, Woods signed his $1,000 bail bond as security. Lilburne was also Mc-Cawley's friend and, as foreman of the jury, may have influenced the decision of the veniremen when they found Mc-Cawley not guilty.

The personal affairs of the other members of this petit jury were curiously interwoven with those of Lilburne. Mark Phillips, William Rice, and Joseph Ray were his brothers-in-law. Amos Persons had been the close friend and neighbor of Randolph and had appraised his estate. The other two of Randolph's appraisers, Patrick Calhoun and David Fort, were also on this jury.[12] Another juryman, John Daniel, the ferryman at Smithland, had previously rented one of Lilburne's slaves and was also in business with Lilburne in the promotion of the town of Westwood at the mouth of the Cumberland River. It was a cozy little group that found McCawley not guilty.

March 27 was a busy day in court for Lilburne, for, in addition to serving on McCawley's petit jury, he was a principal in the suit by Dr. Arthur Campbell, which was tried that same day. Lilburne's lawyer, probably Henry F. Delany, claimed that Dr. Campbell's charges were false, but the jury thought otherwise and ordered Lilburne to pay the bills, plus court costs and thirty dollars in damages. Lilburne's lawyer then protested that the verdict and evidence were contrary to law and asked for a new trial. This motion was granted three days later, and the suit dragged on. In the June term of court an attachment was issued against Lilburne's three sisters requiring them to be witnesses for Dr. Campbell, but in the September term, when they were to appear, the case was again postponed.[13]

It was in the summer of that year that Lilburne and four other men launched the Westwood town promotion.[14] It is not known how much Lilburne invested in the scheme, but the tax rolls for that year credit him with town lots valued at $450. This, of course, could not be realized until the lots were sold, but at least Lilburne had hopes for the venture. As a trustee of the town, Lilburne had some authority and several responsibilities that were conveyed by law. Among these was the provision passed by the Kentucky legislature just six months before, that if any slave misbehaved in a town, a trustee had all the power to punish the slave as was then vested in a justice of the peace. This punishment was limited to administering up to thirty-nine lashes without a jury trial.[15] Another community task that Lilburne had to complete that month was the annual report, or return, of the militia company of which he was captain. It would include the roster of men, a financial accounting of expenses and fines collected, an inventory of weapons and ammunition available, and other details. It was a routine task, but perhaps a bothersome one for a busy person.[16]

At Rocky Hill there had been some rather important changes in Lilburne's family life during the last half of the year. At the end of June, Jane and Lucy, who were then thirteen and eleven respectively, returned home from Harrodsburg, where they had been boarding with William Bradburn and attending school. Lilburne had not paid Bradburn the agreed sum of $150 for the year and a half the girls had been with him, and Bradburn sent them home to Lilburne and Letitia.[17]

According to the legends, Letitia was several years younger than Lilburne, and was considered the beautiful belle of the county at the time of her marriage. The legends also portray her as a somewhat spoiled young lady.[18] The arrival of Jane and Lucy, whom she scarcely knew, would have added to her household responsibilities and, moreover, the timing could not have pleased Letitia, for she was two months pregnant with her first child, a circumstance that could cause her increasing inconvenience, if not discomfort. The atmosphere must have been tense at Rocky Hill. Almost every aspect of Lilburne's life at this time, both personal and public, was going so badly for him that he was under unrelenting stress. The legends say that Lilburne began to drink rather heavily as the year drew to a close. This has not been proved, but it is plausible.

Another member of the Lewis family who returned to Livingston County that year was Isham. In April of the previous year, while in Natchez he had borrowed $235 from a man who died shortly thereafter. Isham was sued when he did not repay the money to the man's estate. In October of 1811, when the suit was scheduled, "Isham Lewis, the said defendant although solemnly required, came not, but made default."[19] Isham had absconded to Livingston County, a fugitive vagrant, ill qualified to fill Randolph's vacant place in the family circle. The Lewis dynasty was deteriorating rapidly.

·24·

ANNUS MIRABILIS

IN WEST Kentucky, 1811 was a year of portents so strange and unnatural that it was thought the very earth and sky were trying to give forewarning of impending doom. Early in the spring there was a severe flood, and the Ohio bottom lands were covered over vast areas. Crop planting was delayed and unprecedented sickness followed.[1] The great comet of 1811 first appeared in the northern sky in April, and began its long climb across the heavens toward the south. It was clearly visible throughout most of the rest of the year, reaching its brightest intensity in October. As has been the case throughout history with other comets, this one was thought by the uneducated to forewarn of some disaster.[2]

A Lexington paper reported in 1811 that "during the summer months the heat was, in many places, the most intense that was ever known," and in many areas the crops were destroyed by drought.[3] In the eastern section of the country, tornadoes and hurricanes ravaged the land from Maine to Georgia, and a reporter wrote, "The ocean has been the subject of Volcanic terror; and new islands have arisen therefrom."[4]

In August the mighty Indian chief, Tecumseh, accompanied by twenty of his warriors, passed by Rocky Hill and Smithland in their canoes. They had come from a tempestuous conference with Governor William H. Harrison in Vincennes, and were on their way down the Ohio and Mississippi to attempt a confederation of southern tribes to fight the intruding white settlers. The Indians were reluctant to join him, and Tecumseh warned them that when he returned to Detroit he would stamp his foot, and the earth would tremble and their houses would fall to the ground.[5]

The bizarre nature of that year was evident even in the behavior of the wild animals:

> A spirit of change and a restlessness seemed to pervade the very inhabitants of the forest. A countless multitude of squirrels, obeying some great and universal impulse, which none can know but the Spirit that gives them being, left their reckless and gambolling

248

life, and their ancient places of retreat in the north, and were seen pressing foreward by tens of thousands in a deep and sober pha-lanx to the South. No obstacles seemed to check this extraordinary and concerted movement: the word had been given them to go forth, and they obeyed it, though multitudes perished in the broad Ohio, which lay in their path.[6]

At that same time, the awesome flocks of passenger pigeons were feeding in the Ohio Valley, consuming uncountable tons of mast as they swept the forests clean of the natural food of wild herbivores. They stayed until the food was gone, and then moved on to other parts of the continent. Their presence in a given area was infrequent enough to cause great amazement at their almost incredible numbers.[7]

On September 17 of the "Annus Mirabilis," as that year was called, there was an almost total eclipse of the sun. The *Lexington Gazette* reported: "The day was remarkably serene, and the skies entirely clear of clouds, so that its appearance was the most solemn and impressive that we could conceive."[8] In November, Tecumseh's unstable half-brother, the Prophet, provoked his tribesmen to attack an army led by Governor Harrison. Tecumseh was still in the south and the Prophet was defeated in the battle of Tippecanoe, but many Kentuckians lost their lives there. It was discovered that the British had armed the Indian warriors; anger flamed throughout the state, and war was recognized to be inevitable and near at hand.

The climax of this year of dire events came in mid-December with the first terrible shocks of the New Madrid earthquake, the most severe in the recorded history of the North American continent. Tecumseh had stamped his foot. The epicenter of this catastrophe was only seventy-five miles southwest of Rocky Hill. The following summary of this disaster, written years later by a scientist, is more dispassionate than the numerous eyewit-ness accounts, but its accuracy is unquestionable.

It is fairly well established that immediately before the earthquake unusual warmth and a thick oppressive atmosphere with occasional rain and unseasonable thunder showers prevailed over a wide area of country.[9] . . . A little after 2 o'clock on the morning of December 16, the inhabitants of the region were suddenly awakened by the groaning, creaking, and cracking of the timbers of the houses or cabins in which they were sleeping, by the rattle of furniture thrown down, and by the crash of falling chimneys. In fear and

trembling they hurriedly groped their way from their houses to escape the falling debris, and remained shivering in the winter air
until morning, the repeated shocks at intervals during the night
keeping them from returning to their weakened or tottering dwellings. Daylight brought little improvement to their situation, for
early in the morning another shock, preceded by a low rumbling
and fully as severe as the first, was experienced. The ground rose
and fell as earth waves, like the long, low swell of the sea, passed
across its surface, tilting the trees until their branches interlocked
and opening the soil in deep cracks as the surface was bent. Land-
slides swept down the steeper bluffs and hillsides; considerable
areas were uplifted, and still larger areas sunk and became covered
with water emerging from below through fissures or little
"craterlets" or accumulating from the obstruction of the surface
drainage. On the Mississippi great waves were created, which
overwhelmed many boats and washed others high upon the shore,
the return current breaking off thousands of trees and carrying
them out into the river. High banks caved and were precipitated
into the river, sand bars and points of islands gave way, and whole
islands disappeared.

During December 16 and 17 shocks continued at short intervals
but gradually diminished in intensity. They occurred at longer intervals until January 23, when there was another shock, similar in
intensity and destructiveness to the first. This shock was followed
by about two weeks of quiescence, but on February 7 there were
several alarming and destructive shocks, the last equaling or surpassing any previous disturbance, and for several days the earth
was in a nearly constant tremor.

For fully a year from this date small shocks occurred at intervals
of a few days.[10]

The tremors of the earthquake were felt from Upper Canada
to the Gulf of Mexico and from Boston to the Rocky Mountains.
In parts of Missouri, Arkansas, and the far western parts of Tennessee and Kentucky, huge areas, covering thousands of acres,
sank as much as twenty-five feet or more, and near these locations the rivers ran backwards as the depressions filled with
water. Reelfoot Lake in western Tennessee is the most famous of
these, but in Missouri and Arkansas a lake was formed that was
over fifty miles long.[11]

Strange and fearful phenomena accompanied the shocks. The
noise, which was most often described as a thunder-like rumbling, was heard as far away as the Atlantic Coast. In west
Kentucky the sounds were more varied and intense. "The

vertical shocks were accompanied by 'explosions and a terrible mixture of noises.'" The phenomena began with "distant rumbling sounds, succeeded by discharges, as if a thousand pieces of artillery were suddenly exploded." Roaring, whistling, and hissing sounds were heard, and all observers agreed that the tumult was essentially unlike any sound they had ever heard before.[12]

Although the first shock came during the night, in subsequent daytime shocks the atmosphere was darkened by a smoke or fog that persisted several hours after the vibrations ceased. These vapors carried the noxious odor of burning brimstone and sulfurous decay. They rose from the numerous fissures in the earth and contaminated the water so that it was unfit to use as far as 150 miles from the epicenter.[13] During the shocks that occurred at night, weird lights and flashes were frequently seen ascending from the earth like explosions of gas or like lighting low on the horizon. As one observer in Livingston County noted, before a later severe shock the atmosphere "was remarkably luminous, objects being visible for considerable distances, although there was no moon. On this occasion the brightness was general, and did not proceed from any point or spot in the heavens. It was broad and expanded, reaching from the zenith on every side toward the horizon. It exhibited no flashes nor coruscations, but as long as it lasted, was a diffused illumination of the atmosphere on all sides."[14]

Because of the sparse population west of the Mississippi at this time, it is doubtful that there were many deaths among the settlers there, but the boatmen who were traveling on the rivers during the earthquake were in great danger. Some of the most vivid accounts of the upheaval were written by these voyagers, and they leave no doubt that there were many crewmen and passengers who drowned. The writhings and distortions of the Mississippi River were almost beyond belief. Above New Madrid the river bottom rose and formed a six foot waterfall that stretched entirely across the river. Boats were swept over this barrier until it, in turn, was wiped away by the currents. Other boats were tossed about by freak waves that rose thirty feet above the normal water level.[15]

> As soon as it was light enough to distinguish objects, the crews were all up making ready to depart. Directly a loud roaring and hissing was heard, like the escape of steam from a boiler, accompanied by

251

the most violent agitation of the shores and tremendous boiling up of the waters of the Mississippi in huge swells, rolling the waters below back on the descending stream, and tossing the boats about so violently that the men with difficulty could keep on their feet. The sandbars and points of the island gave way, swallowed up in the tumultuous bosom of the river; carrying down with them the cottonwood trees, cracking and crashing, tossing their arms to and fro, as if sensible of their danger, while they disappeared beneath the flood.

The water of the river, which the day before was tolerably clear, being rather low, changed to a reddish hue, and became thick with mud thrown up from its bottom; while the surface, lashed violently by the agitation of the earth beneath, was covered with foam, which, gathering into masses the size of a barrel, floated along on the trembling surface. The earth on the shores opened in wide fissures, and closing again, threw the water, sand, and mud, in huge jets, higher than the tops of the trees. The atmosphere was filled with a thick vapor or gas, to which the light imparted a purple tinge, altogether different in appearance from the autumnal haze of Indian summer, or that of smoke. From the temporary check to the current, by the heaving up of the bottom, the sinking of the banks and sandbars into the bed of the stream, the river rose in a few minutes five or six feet; and, impatient of the restraint, again rushed forward with redoubled impetuosity, hurrying along the boats, now set loose by the horror-struck boatmen, as in less danger on the water than at the shore, where the banks threatened every moment to destroy them by the falling earth, or carry them down in the vortexes of the sinking masses.

Many boats were overwhelmed in this manner, and their crews perished with them. It required the utmost exertions of the men to keep the boat, of which my informant was the owner, in the middle of the river, as far from the shores, sandbars, and islands as they could. Numerous boats wrecked on the snags and old trees thrown up from the bottom of the Mississippi, where they had quietly rested for ages, while others were sunk or stranded on the sandbars and islands. At New Madrid several boats were carried by the reflux of the current into a small stream that puts into the river just above the town, and left on the ground by the returning water a considerable distance from the Mississippi.[16]

As if the stunning impact of the earthquake and the foreboding events that preceded it were not enough for the people of Livingston County, there was yet another apparently miraculous event before the year ended. Most of the citizens had not heard the slightest rumor that the first steamboat to travel the Ohio was on its way downstream to New Orleans, the city for which it was named.

The *New Orleans* was launched in March of 1811 at Pittsburgh. The paddle-wheeler was nearly 140 feet long and twenty-six and a half feet in beam. She had some features of a sailing craft— portholes and an eight foot bowsprit—and was painted the improbable color of sky blue.[17] These odd features, along with her paddle wheel and belching smoke stack, guaranteed that she was the most curious if not frightening apparition that had ever come down the Ohio. The vessel began her trip in late autumn, cleared the falls at Louisville after a delay, and was in the vicinity of Yellow Banks, or Owensboro, when the earthquake struck. She landed at Henderson, and a day or two later churned her way past Livingston County.

The *New Orleans* caused amazement and consternation throughout the length of the Ohio Valley. Latrobe described her reception at Louisville:

> The novel appearance of the vessel, and the fearful rapidity with which it made its passage over the broad reaches of the river, excited a mixture of terror and surprise among many of the settlers on the banks, whom the rumour of such an invention had never reached; and it is related that on the unexpected arrival of the boat before Louisville, in the course of a fine still moonlight night, the extraordinary sound which filled the air as the pent-up steam was suffered to escape from the valves on rounding to, produced a general alarm, and multitudes in the town rose from their beds to ascertain the cause. I have heard that the general impression among the good Kentuckians was, that the comet had fallen into the Ohio.[18]

The citizens of Henderson reacted in much the same way, for "many thought that the devil incarnate had actually arrived, and was shaking the earth with his great wheel. Some took to the woods, while others stood in motionless stupor, victims of absolute fright."[19]

The astonishing sequence of wonders that occurred in 1811 was thought by some to be a warning that God was going to return to earth and punish the wicked. Others thought that halfway measure would not be enough, and that God's intention was to bring about the end of the world in the near future. An editor in Lexington warned: "These are no common events and without incurring the charge of superstition they may be deemed portentous of still greater events. Surely so many extraordinary occurrences in the course of a few months ought to excite something of meditation and reflection."[20] A rival editor was more vehement. "The great scale upon which Nature is operating should be a solemn admonition to men, (or those animals in the shape of men) to abandon the pitiful grovelling, schemes of venality and corruption in the prosecution of which they are so ardently engaged. An *honest heart,* alone, can view those great events, with composure. The political *swindler,* the *assassin of reputation,* must feel severely, the visitations of conscience, at such momentous periods, when Nature appears, in spasmodic fury, no longer to tolerate the moral turpitude of man."[21]

If these events could move newspapermen to editorialize about spiritual matters, then surely the blood-and-thunder frontier preachers must have been transported into a religious frenzy. In New Madrid, a group of tatterdemalion, filthy, unshaven fanatics appeared and, with solemn faces, marched about the town, in and out of houses, intoning "Praise God and Repent." Some of the residents were not impressed, and noted that "more repulsive, ill-timed visitors a hospitable community never had."[22]

Among the westerners a renewed wave of religious interest was apparent after the earthquake. In the affected area of the West, membership in the Methodist Church leaped by fifty percent in one year, and Reverend James B. Finley noted that in Kentucky the youth had given up dancing and drinking in favor of prayer meetings. While many of these conversions stuck, some of the people, known as "earthquake Christians" left the church after the tremors finally ceased.[23]

A legend about Louisville written in 1814 states that following the first shocks of the earthquake the fearful citizens of Louisville subscribed a thousand dollars to build a church. After a while interest in the project waned, until another tremor jarred a second thousand into the collection. The cycle was repeated for a third time, after which the earthquakes stopped for good. Reasoning that the wrath of God had somehow been placated, the keepers of the fund used the three thousand dollars to build a theater.[24]

Like many of the whites and most of the negroes, the Indians also believed that the earthquake was a purposeful act of warning or punishment from God. In the Rocky Mountains, trappers had murdered an Indian who was supposedly under the special protection of the Great Spirit. The tribesmen believed that the tremors had been sent to punish the murderers.[25]

This was not the only killing to become associated with the earthquake. In Livingston County, immediately before the earthquake struck, a ghastly murder had been committed.

·25·

THE MURDER

AMONG Lilburne's slaves was one seventeen-year-old boy by the name of George. Unfortunately, almost no traces remain of his life except a few sketchy comments written in the legend sources, and a comment or two about him handed down verbally as part of the Rutter family tradition. These sources relate that George was an "ill-grown, ill-thrived" boy who served Lilburne as a house servant, errand boy, and general handy man. It was George who made the many trips to Dr. Campbell's house for medicine in 1809. George was, reportedly, rather ugly to look at, had a large scar over one of his eyes, and was of an independent nature. Occasionally George was insolent to Lilburne, but when Lilburne was drinking, George feared him and kept his distance.[1]

At the end of October all the patrollers in Livingston County were discharged "from any longer serving as padrollers,"[2] probably in preparation for the expected war. As a result of this step, there was no organized system to prevent slaves from sneaking away from their owners for short visits to other plantations, or, in fact, from running away entirely. Across the river from Rocky Hill in Illinois lay free territory, and in the Ohio River at that point was a shallow sand bar that stretched from shore to shore. In low water this bar was only three feet under the surface.[3] Escape should have been simple, but the dismissal of the patrol indicates that, for the most part, the slaves in Livingston were orderly, if not contented.

At Rocky Hill, however, the family was apprehensive. Since Lilburne's marriage to Letitia, his business and community activities had all gone wrong, and his family had suffered tragedy and heartbreak. Lilburne was under fearful stress. Lilburne and Letitia, who was eight months pregnant with her first child, had not been especially happy together. Lilburne, whose pride and self-confidence were being undermined by his own flaws and by misfortune as well, began to show signs of character disintegration. It was said that earlier he had been a fair but firm master, but in 1811 he became oppressive and unreasonable with his slaves, and began to drink heavily.[4]

256

Driven by either resentment or fear of Lilburne, George took advantage of the absence of the patrol and ran off on a skulking spell. In a day or two George was either caught or returned voluntarily to Rocky Hill. On Sunday, December 15, shortly after his return, George was sent to fetch water from the spring at the foot of the steep north slope of Rocky Hill. He was given a pitcher in which to carry the water, and on this errand somehow or other he broke the pitcher, which supposedly had been Lucy's. In a transport of drunken rage, Lilburne, with Isham's help, dragged George into the kitchen cabin that stood near the residence, stretched him out on the floor and bound him securely. They next assembled the other slaves in the room and had them build up a roaring fire in the fireplace. It was late at night, and in the eerie light of the flames, Lilburne bolted the door and told the terrified slaves that he was going to teach them a lesson about disobeying his orders. He took up an axe and with a full two-handed swing sank it deep into George's neck. It was a mortal and nearly decapitating blow three inches deep and four inches wide.[5] If the spine was severed, and it probably was, then George's death was instantaneous. If it was not, and the carotid and jugular blood vessels were cut, then George would have remained conscious from ten to forty seconds, and it would have taken nearly a minute before George's heart pumped out most of the four or five quarts of his blood onto the cabin floor.

Lilburne and Isham then forced one of the negro men to take the axe and dismember George's body. The pieces were cast on the fire so there would be no evidence of the crime. It would have required several hours for a body to be consumed completely on a kitchen fireplace. While the grisly cremation was under way, it is said that Lilburne lectured his horror-stricken slaves, and warned them that if they told anyone about George's death, they could expect the same treatment. It was shortly after two o'clock on Monday morning when the first mighty shock of the earthquake struck. The chimney immediately collapsed on top of the fire and George's sizzling remains, smothered the flames, and brought the dreadful last rites to a halt.

Just after daylight came additional tremendous shocks from the earthquake, and although the tremors moderated after eight o'clock, there were not ten minutes during all of Monday when the earth was still.[6] In this supernatural setting Lilburne supervised his slaves in rebuilding the fireplace and the

257

chimney. As the rocks were put in place, most of the unburned pieces of bone and flesh were raked out of the ashes and hidden in the masonry.

This account of George's murder may well be inaccurate. None of the available sources are, at the same time, both detailed and of unquestionable reliability. The four major sources of information about the murder contradict each other on so many points that a true and factual description of George's death will probably never be achieved. This reconstruction of the crime is a combination of what appear to be the most plausible parts of the four written statements that are quoted and discussed below.

In order to examine the most credible source of information, it is necessary to reveal prematurely that the crime of Lilburne and Isham was eventually discovered and the brothers were indicted. The wording of the indictment is illuminating.

In the name and by the authority of the Commonwealth of Kentucky Livingston County set At the March term of the circuit Court held for said County in the year Eighteen hundred and twelve—The grand jury inpannelled and Sworn for the body of the county aforesaid upon their oath present Lilbourn Lewis senior, farmer late of said County and Isham Lewis yeoman late of said County not having the fear of God before their Eyes, But being moved & seduced by the Instigation of the Devil—on the fifteenth day of December Eighteen hundred and Eleven at the house of said Lilbourn Lewis senior in said County & within the Jurisdiction of the said Court with force and arms in & upon the body of a certain Negro Boy called George a slave the property of said Lilbourn Lewis senior of the county aforesaid in the peace of god & this commonwealth then and there living—feloniously wilfully violently and of their malice aforethought an assault did make— and that he the said Lilbourn Lewis senior with a certain ax there & then had & held in both his hands of the Value of two dollars did strike cut and penetrate in & upon the neck of him the said Negro Boy George giving to the said Negro Boy, George then & there with the ax aforesaid in and upon the neck of him the said Negro Boy George one Mortal wound of the Breadth of four inches and of the Depth of three inches of which said mortal wound he the said Negro Boy George Instantly did die in the county of Livingston aforesaid and that the said Isham Lewis then & there feloniously wilfully Violently and of his malice aforethought was present aiding helping abetting comforting assisting and maintaining the said Lilbourn Lewis senior the felony and murder aforesaid in manner and form aforesaid to do and Commit, and so the Jurors

aforesaid upon their oath aforesaid do say that the said Lilbourn
Lewis and Isham Lewis feloniously wilfully Volentarily out of their
malice aforethought him the said Negro Boy George then & there
in manner and form aforesaid did kill and Murder, contrary to the
statute in such case made and provided and against the peace and
Dignity of the said Commonwealth of Kentucky

John Gray atty, for
the Commonwealth[7]

The essence of attorney John Gray's indictment is that Lilburne himself swung the axe and cut a three-by-four-inch gash
in George's neck, from which George "instantly did die." The
meaning of the word "instantly" as used here may be misin-
terpreted. In this context, and at that time, the usual meaning of
"instantly" was "consequently," or "as a result of." Miss Reba
Smith, the present circuit clerk of Livingston, uncovered records
of another murder case of that era in which the victim "did
instantly die in a space of two hours." In any event, it seems
fairly certain that George died quickly from an axe wound in the
neck, and not slowly from a series of lesser wounds, as the next
source claims.

Thirteen years after George was murdered, the Reverend
William Dickey, the Lewis family pastor, wrote a letter describing the crime in lurid detail. Dickey was then the minister of the
Presbyterian church in Bloomingburg, Ohio, and had become
passionately interested in the abolition of slavery. It should be
remembered that Dickey was a highly emotional preacher, and a
person of impressive skill in working his audience into a religious "glow." It is clear that Dickey was using the same talent
when he wrote this letter in behalf of abolition. The same creative imagination that he used to describe the delights of heaven
and the horrors of hell is obvious in this letter, which describes a
thirteen-year-old crime he did not witness.

In the county of Livingston, Ky. near the mouth of the Cumberland, lived Lilburn Lewis, a sister's son of the venerable Jefferson.
He, who "suckled at fair Freedom's breast" was the wealthy owner
of a considerable number of slaves, whom he drove constantly, fed
sparingly and lashed severely. The consequence was, they would
run away. This must have given to a man of spirit and a man of
business great anxieties until he found them or until they had
starved out and returned. Among the rest was an ill grown boy
about seventeen, who having just returned from a skulking spell,
was sent to the spring for water, and in returning let fall an elegant

259

pitcher. It was dashed to shivers upon the rocks. This was the occasion. It was night, and the slaves all at home. The master had them collected into the most roomy negrohouse, and a rousing fire made. When the door was secured, that none might escape, either through fear of him or sympathy with George, he opened the design of the interview, namely, that they might be effectually taught to stay at home and obey his orders. All things being now in train, he called up George, who approached his master with the most unreserved submission. He bound him with cords, and by the assistance of his younger brother, laid him on the broad bench, or meat block. He now proceeded to WHANG off George by the ancles!! It was with the broad axe! — In vain did the unhappy victim SCREAM AND ROAR. He was completely in his master's power. Not a hand amongst so many durst interfere. Casting the feet into the fire, he lectured them at some length. He WHACKED HIM OFF below the knees! George roaring out, and praying his master to BEGIN AT THE OTHER END! He admonished them again, throwing the legs into the fire! Then above the knees, tossing the joints into the fire! He again lectured them at leisure. The next stroke severed the thighs from the body. These were also committed to the flames. And so off the arms, head and trunk, until all was in the fire! Still protracting the intervals with lectures, and threatenings of like punishment, in case of disobedience, and running away, or disclosure of this tragedy. Nothing now remained but to consume the flesh and bones; and for this purpose the fire was briskly stirred, until two hours after midnight, when, as though the earth would cover out of sight the nefarious scene, and as though the great master in Heaven would put a mark of displeasure upon such monstrous cruelty, a sudden and surprising shock of earthquake overturned the coarse and heavy back wall, composed of rock and clay, which completely covered the fire, and the remains of George. This put an end to the amusement of the evening. The negroes were now permitted to disperse, with charges to keep this matter among themselves, and never to whisper it in the neighborhood, under the penalty of a like punishment. When he retired, the lady exclaimed, "O! Mr. Lewis, where have you been and what have you done!" She had heard a strange pounding, and dreadful screams, and had smelled something like fresh meat burning! He said that he had never enjoyed himself at a ball so well as he had enjoyed himself that evening. Next morning he ordered the negroes to rebuild the back wall, and he himself superintended the work, throwing the pieces of flesh that still remained with the bones, behind it as it went up, thus hoping to conceal the matter.[8]

260

Dickey's version states that Lilburne personally and leisurely cut George to bits, beginning with the feet, and pictures the boy's death as protracted. The next source, *Chronicles of a Kentucky Settlement,* agrees that George was murdered in this fashion, but says that one of the slave men was forced to wield the axe.

There were many strange and contradictory rumors about Lilburne and his second wife. There were those who said that, owing to his dissipation and cruelty to his slaves, his young and beautiful wife was not only thoroughly miserable, but was in constant apprehension lest her husband should do herself some personal violence. On the other hand, there were those who said that Lilburne, during the lifetime of his first wife, was a temperate man, a kind husband, and a strict but not unkind master, and that his cold, proud, and scornful young wife—his "cruel Letitia," as he was known to have once called her—was the cause of most of the troubles into which he fell.

About a year after Lilburne Lewis's second marriage, and when his wife was confined to her bed—she having a few days before given birth to a child,—a negro boy named George, a kind of general house servant, suddenly disappeared, and, after remaining secreted for a few days, was arrested and bound with chains in one of the cabins near the residence. That night, horrible to relate, Lilburne Lewis and his younger brother, Isham, caused most of the slaves on the farm to assemble in the cabin where George was bound, flat upon the floor, with each limb extended, and, with drawn pistols, forced one of the negro men to literally chop the bound boy to pieces, and, as joint by joint and limb by limb were severed from the body, they were cast into a roaring fire prepared for the purpose of consuming every trace of the body. When the hellish work was done, the assembled slaves were given to understand that such a fate as George's awaited any of them who should ever whisper a word about George's fate; and, if questioned regarding his disappearance, they were to answer that he had run away and had never been heard from. The cowed slaves were further told that should any of them ever run away they would, when captured, be treated as George had been.

When the two drunken and fiendish brothers left the cabin and were returning to their house, a sudden and terrific rumbling noise was heard, and soon the surface of the earth seemed to rise and fall—rise and fall again like quick succeeding waves. To add to the horror of the phenomena, what appeared like a great blazing ball of fire darted hissing through the heavens, apparently close by, and

261

by its brilliancy momentarily lighting up every object around, which but a moment before was shrouded in dense darkness. The drunken brothers were each prostrated upon the ground by the violence of the earthquake shock (for such it was), and one of them, Isham, in his horrible affright, cried out: "My God! my God!! what is this?" The reply of the beastly brother by his side was: "It's only the devil in h--l rejoicing over having got hold of George!"[9]

The author of this account, William Courtney Watts, was born in Salem, Kentucky, in 1830, nineteen years after George was murdered. In his later years Watts wrote *Chronicles of a Kentucky Settlement.* This 490-page book, his only literary work, was published in 1897. Discussing the historical accuracy of this book, Watts wrote in his preface: "The book, however, is not, as some may infer from its title, a Local History. I endeavored to make it of interest to general readers. . . . To make my work the more interesting, I wove it into the form of a continuous story. The incidents, however, are not arranged strictly in chronological order, but as suited the exigencies of the tales I had to tell." Respected historians have held this book in high regard, even though it contains many factual errors.[10]

Watts did not consult the court records in preparing his book. He relied entirely on local traditions, which were seventy years old when he began to write *Chronicles.* No doubt there is much truth in his account of George's death, but it is certain that some, and perhaps many, of the details are incorrect. For example, Letitia's baby was not born just before George was murdered, but rather forty-seven days afterward. In Watts's version of the murder, George died as a result of being chopped to pieces joint by joint. This agrees with Dickey's letter, but Watts says the axe was swung not by Lilburne, but by a slave man who was forced to do so at the point of Lilburne's gun.

Another element of the crime is the subject of conflicting reports in these three sources: was Lilburne drinking at the time of the murder? The indictment simply stated that the Lewis brothers were "moved and seduced by the instigation of the devil," a routine phrase in felony indictments. Dickey's account did not mention alcohol at all in connection with the crime. Watts, however, said that for some time Lilburne had not been "temperate," and further, that the brothers were drunk on the night of the murder. Later accounts of the murder, although based on the above sources, are so inaccurate that they are nearly useless as sources of historical fact. Nevertheless, some of these make the not unreasonable claim that Lilburne was drinking heavily on that night.[11]

William H. Townsend, a respected Kentucky historian and raconteur of national reputation, was known for his byword, "Never let facts stand in the way of a good story!" It appears that this precept was being followed to some degree by both Dickey and Watts when they wrote their accounts of George's murder. In Dickey's case, the more depraved he could make Lilburne's crime appear, the better his crusade for abolition would be served. As for Watts's *Chronicles,* the more horribly dramatic the story, the greater would be his reader's interest. Both Dickey and Watts were inaccurate in some of the statements in their accounts. In addition, their versions of the crime did not agree in every respect. It is interesting that while Watts did not purport to tell the exact facts of the case, the Reverend William Dickey did present his version as factual. It was not completely so.

The fourth useful source of information contains very little information about the murder itself. It is a one-paragraph newspaper article that appeared in the *Kentucky Gazette* of May 12, 1812. Datelined, "Russellville, April 22," and under the headline, "Murder! Horrid Murder!" the article reported that "Capt. Lilburne and Isham Lewis" had been taken to court "for murdering a negro boy, (the property of the former) and burning him on a kitchen fire."[12]

This brief statement raises some question as to where the murder and cremation actually took place. Watts said it was in one of the cabins near the residence. Dickey said it was "in the most roomy negrohouse." The indictment stated the crime occurred "at the house of said Lilburne Lewis," and the newspaper reported simply that the negro boy had been burned "on a kitchen fire." On many of the west Kentucky farms or plantations at that time the cooking was done in a cabin building near but separate from the main house. Three of the four sources quoted above admit the possibility that the scene of George's death was Lilburne's own kitchen cabin. If these three sources are combined, it appears George was murdered "at the house of said Lilburne Lewis," "in one of the cabins near the residence," and was burned "on a kitchen fire." Only Dickey's letter disagrees with this, claiming that George's death occurred "in the most roomy negrohouse." The exact location of the crime is probably not important, except that if the deed was done in the kitchen cabin next to or near the residence, then it is unlikely that Letitia and the other occupants of the house slept through that fearful night undisturbed until two o'clock, when the earthquake struck.

If George was murdered in the nearby kitchen, and if Letitia and the others in the house were awakened by the sounds and odors of the scene, as seems likely, then they became witnesses to the crime, not eyewitnesses, but witnesses nonetheless. The point has some relevance. Although the murder room was crowded with Lilburne's slaves at the time George died, there were no legal witnesses to the murder in that room other than Lilburne and Isham. The laws of the Commonwealth of Kentucky prohibited negroes from testifying against whites in court.[13]

In this nearly inconceivable episode, Lilburne approached the nadir of his life. Lawyer James McLaughlan's curse upon Lilburne, "God damn your soul," had come to pass.

The people of Rocky Hill were not alone in their anguish for long. A few weeks later, early in the dreadful spring of 1812, a final tragedy came to Randolph's family. Mary, Randolph's beloved widow, the last surviving adult in that home, died at the age of thirty-six. The cause of her death is unknown. The Reverend William Dickey, having been invited to preach at their home, was there on the day she died. Writing of this sad occasion, he noted that Mary had passed away shortly before he arrived, and added that she had been a widow about one year. She probably died sometime in February. The family was bereft. Dickey remembered the grief of the old slave, Frank, who "lamented the loss of his pious Massa & Missis. . . . Solemnity appeared in his face, and a few big tears tumbled down his sable & withered cheeks."[14]

Mary left eight orphans. Warner, the youngest, was not yet two years old. Five of the children were under twelve. The oldest, Charles Lilburne (also called Lilburne Lewis, Jr.) who was in his twentieth year, might have taken the full burden of the family on his shoulders. His two brothers, Howell and Tucker, could have been some help, but the prospect of these three boys raising five young children, and running a plantation as well, was not encouraging.* They could expect absolutely no help from Lilburne and Letitia, for their life at Rocky Hill was in utter shambles, and the situation of Colonel Lewis and his three daughters was very little better. Nevertheless, the remnants of Randolph's family clustered around their grandfather and his three daughters during this time of emergency, and cared for each other as best they could. It was an unworkable expedient, but it had to suffice until the estate could be sold and other arrangements made. Perhaps, in February, they still hoped that Lilburne would survive his troubles and come to their aid in some way. For the moment they were a pathetic little flock without leadership or direction.

---

*It appears that Randolph had some reservations about his son Charles. In his will Randolph left Charles a one-eighth part of his estate during Charles's natural life. At Charles's death that portion was to return to the estate, whether or not Charles had heirs. The other seven children could pass on their portions of Randolph's estate to their heirs. The reason for this distinction between Charles and the other children is unknown.

· 26 ·

AFTER THE MURDER

IN THE MONTHS following the murder there was scarcely one hour when the earth did not tremble. Near the end of January, on the twenty-third, there was another shock, which over a five minute period increased to tremendous intensity. It was equal in force to the first upheaval that collapsed the kitchen chimney at Rocky Hill.[1] In Louisville houses were badly damaged and boatmen on the river found themselves in great danger. "This is a disastrous time for navigators of the Ohio who happen to be hereabout upon the river, seven Boats have been seen passing on the falls to day; some with and some without crews on board; no human power can afford relief to the sufferers, nor can they help themselves but drift on until chance may decide their fate; . . . much howling and lamentation were heard from a boat entering the falls this night, voices of men women and children."[2]

Nine days of comparative quiet passed and then, during the first week of February, the tremors rose gradually in a slow crescendo to a climax of violence in the dark early hours of the morning of the seventh. It was the most severe disturbance of the year-long span of the earthquake, the worst single shock ever recorded on the North American continent.[3] Lilburne's kitchen chimney probably fell in again.

At the end of January, in the time between these two great disturbances, there was a period of relative calmness, during which Letitia gave birth to her first child. It was a son, whom she named after her father, James Rutter Lewis.

Those weeks must have been a period of numbing horror for Letitia and the children. It seems inconceivable that the knowledge of the murder could have been hidden from them for longer than a few hours. They learned of what the two brothers had done and fear settled over them; fear for their own safety, and fear for their futures if Lilburne were tried and taken from them. Without doubt Lilburne kept the slaves in strict isolation on the plantation. At least one of the legends reports that he also kept Letitia confined and under close observation.[4] Lilburne could have controlled the people at

Rocky Hill, but he would have had no way to restrict the movements of Randolph's family and his slaves, or his sisters and the old colonel, who lived two miles up the river. It seems probable that rumors were abroad in the neighborhood before the first tangible and grisly piece of evidence was made known to the public.

When Lilburne rebuilt the chimney after the first convulsion of the earthquake, he concealed the unburned pieces of George's body behind the stones of the chimney. During one or the other of the two subsequent shocks of January twenty-third and February seventh, the chimney apparently collapsed again and exposed George's pitiful remains. Unknown to Lilburne, a dog chanced by and carried off George's head, which had not been consumed in the fire. The dog may have been Lilburne's own dog, Nero. Sometime afterward a neighbor of Lilburne's, passing near Rocky Hill, discovered the dog eating George's head. This information and, no doubt, the gory evidence as well, was carried to the local authorities.

The identity of the man who found George's head is not known precisely, for the discovery is attributed to different men in the various sources. One man who is said to have found the head is Jonah Hibbs, whose farm joined the Rocky Hill plantation along parts of the north and east boundaries. Mrs. Martha G. Purcell, relating the incident in 1923, presents this version of the discovery. "One day as Mr. Jonah Hibbs (this account was given the writer [Mrs. Purcell] by Mr. Jonah Hibbs's son, the Hon. Lacy Hibbs, who represented Livingston County in the State Legislature) was enroute to Smithland when he noticed a dog gnawing a peculiar looking bone and on examination it proved to be a human skull. He reported it to the authorities."[5]

The other person who is given credit for finding the head was Dickson Hurley, the son of Moses Hurley, who owned a 200-acre farm on Bayou Creek.[6] The location of Hurley's farm is not known, but at the closest point, Rocky Hill is three miles from Bayou Creek and at the farthest, about six miles away. Mr. Grady Rutter, the great-grandson of Letitia's brother, James, gave the following verbal account of the discovery of George's head:

> Dick Hurley was a neighbor of the Lewis family. He lived between Birdsville and Salem. It was Dick Hurley who found

George's head. My grandfather told me that Hurley was riding his horse on the road to Salem and saw a dog gnawing on the head which was lying near a cattle trough in the field by the road. He recognized the head because George had a large scar over one of his eyes. Hurley was the one who reported it to the law.

Several years ago one of my relatives was traveling in Memphis, Tennessee, and saw a restaurant sign that said Dick Hurley was the owner. This member of my family went in and asked the proprietor whether he knew anything about Livingston County, Kentucky. Mr. Hurley smiled and said: "Yes, I do. It was my grandfather who found the head and he told me about it."[7]

It may have been either Hurley or Hibbs who found the head, or perhaps both of them together, but in any event, it then became a matter for the law to handle. If the brothers were convicted of deliberate murder they would be hung. The law was clear when it stated the principle, as follows: "Any person, his or her aiders, abettors or counselors, who shall be guilty of murder, and shall perpetrate the same by means of poison, or by laying in wait, or by any other kind of willful, deliberate, and premeditated killing . . . shall be deemed a felon; and every other kind or species of killing, which shall be committed with malice aforethought, either express or implied, shall be deemed felony, and shall be punished with death."[8]

If a person were convicted of a killing done "without malice aforethought" the sentence specified was from six months to six years in the penitentiary. There was no punishment for killing by accident or in self-defense.[9] Both the verdict and the sentence were to be decided by a jury.[10] The jury could direct that Lilburne and Isham be hung, or could send them to the penitentiary for as long as six years, or could let them go free. Since there were no legal eyewitnesses other than Lilburne and Isham, the brothers may have intended to claim that they were punishing George and accidentally killed him. With the discovery of George's partially burned head, however, it became evident that George's death had not been reported, nor had a coroner's inquest been held, and finally, it was clear that someone had decapitated George and tried to burn the body. Someone at Rocky Hill had suppressed evidence, and suspicion of manslaughter, at the very least, was unavoidable.

The penalty for killing a slave had become more severe in the South as the decades passed. The early colonial statutes imposed very light punishment, or none at all.[11] Burnaby, writing of Virginia in 1760, said that it was almost impossible to bring to justice a white who had murdered a negro. If the murderer were indicted, the petit jury would bring in the verdict of not guilty. Burnaby cited two Virginia laws that made it almost impossible to convict a white man of killing a negro. One was the statute, which Kentucky later adopted, prohibiting a negro from giving testimony in court in a trial involving whites. The other colonial Virginia law stipulated that if a white were indicted for the willful and malicious murder of a slave, and upon trial if the jury found him guilty of manslaughter rather than murder, then the defendant could not "incur any forfeiture or punishment for such offence or misfortune."[12]

After the Revolution this lenient policy underwent a radical change. For example, by 1791 in both Virginia and North Carolina, the murderer of a slave was subject to the same penalty as if he had murdered a free man.[13] This was also the situation in Kentucky in 1812, in law, at least. In actual practice, however, the citizens of Kentucky who served on juries tended to avoid giving the death sentence in cases where a white murdered a slave.

An example of this is found in the case of one Zaba Campfield, a resident of Boone County, Kentucky, who murdered his own mulatto slave boy in 1807. Campfield was indicted and held in jail for several months pending trial. The court docket book reveals that Campfield was indicted for murder, and the court minute book shows that Campfield pleaded not guilty. The jury returned a verdict finding Campfield guilty of manslaughter, not murder, and the prisoner was ordered to be remanded to custody to serve a sentence of confinement in the penitentiary for four years.[14]

Although the jury had found Campfield guilty, they had reduced the charge from murder to manslaughter. Instead of a death sentence, he was given four years in prison, and he was pardoned by the governor after serving three years of that term because, as the prosecuting attorney admitted, "the proof was only presumptive and light."[15]

The details of the manner in which Campfield murdered his slave boy have not been found, but it is unlikely that his crime was more bizarre and shocking than Lilburne's. Juries vary in their sentiments, and it cannot be concluded that Lilburne would necessarily have received the same verdict and sentence in Livingston County that Campfield was given at the other end of the state in Boone County. Lilburne's and Isham's jury would be drawn from the citizens of Livingston, a county whose population was not homogeneous, and whose inhabitants varied widely in their feelings about the crime. The brutal and ignorant element of the community, the river men and the drunken brawlers, might have been indifferent or even amused. James McCawley and Richard Ferguson of Smithland, who had beaten the negro, Bob, nearly to death, were public officials and higher on the social scale, but still they might have sympathized with their friend, Lilburne.

The majority of citizens, on the other hand, would have been shocked almost beyond belief. Certainly those many people who had sincere religious convictions would have been horrified and revolted, and any citizen with the least trace of respect for humanity or the law would have felt the same. The upper-class families no doubt were nearly unanimous in their dismay, and in the case of the Rutters and the Rices, who were related to the Lewises by marriage, chagrin would have added to their stunned incredulity.

As has been discussed earlier, the institution of slavery was more benevolent in Kentucky than in most other states, and in the early part of the 1800s it was less oppressive than it was after the 1820s. There is some reason to believe that in West Kentucky at this time, slaves were generally treated with more kindness than in the older eastern and central sections of the state.

On December eleventh, just four days before George's murder, a bill was introduced in the state senate entitled, "A bill to regulate the conduct of masters toward their slaves." The preamble of the bill read as follows: "WHEREAS, it is represented to the present General Assembly, that certain citizens of this Commonwealth possessing slaves, do treat them with inhumanity and cruelty: ... for remedy whereof, be it enacted ...."[16] Certain "cruel and inhuman" practices of slave owners were then listed. The new bill forbade such treatment of slaves as beating or otherwise torturing and abusing, burning, cutting, maiming, and withholding necessary clothing and provision. The bill required that any justice of the peace who was informed of such an incident, must try the offender in his local magistrate's court and, if he found the culprit guilty, bind him over for jury trial by the circuit court. If the circuit court jury found the person guilty of burning, cutting, or maiming, it was to sentence him to three months in jail; and if it found him guilty of a lesser cruelty, he was to be fined $100. Upon a second conviction for the same crime, the owner was to lose possession of his slave, who was then sold to a new owner.[17]

However lenient the bill appears in restricting cruelty to slaves, it was better than no law at all. It is further surprising to find that when this bill came to a vote on February 1, 1812, it was defeated by a vote of seven yeas to nineteen nays.[18] The seven westernmost counties in the state were voted in favor of the passage of this bill by their senators, Young Ewing from Christian and Muhlenberg, and Gen. Samuel Hopkins from Henderson, Union, Hopkins, Caldwell, and Livingston. The other five senators who voted for the bill represented districts that were scattered at random across the rest of the state. The only sizable area of the state that voted for this legislation to protect slaves from inhuman treatment was the far western section, which included Livingston.

The bill was introduced by the senator from Barren County, which lies in the south-central part of the state. If the bill had been introduced by the senator from Livingston, then one might assume that slaves in his western district were treated so badly that the situation there inspired the bill. But this was not the case, and the affirmative vote of the two far-western senators probably reflected the humanitarian feelings their constituents held toward their slaves. If these suppositions are accurate, then George's murder appears even more singularly shocking, because it happened in an area where slaves were treated kindly by most of the citizens.

Although this bill regarding cruelty to slaves was introduced before George's murder, it is possible that the final vote may have been influenced by the killing. Forty-four days elapsed between the murder and the final vote on the bill. This was ample time for rumors of the crime to circulate and reach the senators in Frankfort. It is speculation, but still possible, that Senators Hopkins and Ewing were swayed in their votes by rumors that reached them from Livingston County, that George had been murdered.

The sources of legend unanimously agree that, with few exceptions, the county was outraged by the crime. Watts relates that "what had been whispered suspicions rose into a loud cry for vengeance," and Reverend William Dickey wrote that Lilburne "sunk under the accumulated load of public odium."[19]

In view of this reported attitude, it appears that Commonwealth's Attorney John Gray had strong support in his attempt to indict Lilburne and Isham. Gray's first task would be to convince the grand jury. The attitudes and character of the people who were chosen to serve on the grand jury would determine whether or not Lilburne and Isham would stand trial at all. The selection of the grand jurors, in turn, depend entirely upon the whim and discretion of the amiable, profane, alcoholic Sheriff Robert Kirk. Kirk could pick anyone he wanted without interference from any other person or public official. There was no provision for drawing names at random. Kirk's choice of jurors was final, and could not be revoked. The jury would be impartial only if Sheriff Kirk was impartial in its selection.[20]

If it were to turn out that the grand jury indicted Lilburne and Isham, and Sheriff Kirk's petit jury found them guilty, it is likely that the brothers would be sentenced to no more than a term in the penitentiary for manslaughter. Of the 160 convicts who had been in the penitentiary prior to 1813, three of them were from Livingston County: Essex Casshaw, serving two years of a five-year sentence for a murder done in 1805; William Trimble, who served a mere two-year sentence for the cold-blooded murder in 1807 of John Gooch, a respected citizen; and Samuel Moore, who was given two years in 1806 for felony.[21]

Lilburne's pride could not have survived the penitentiary. The penal code of Kentucky specified that the inmates were to have their heads and beards shaved once a week; to be fed bread, corn meal, "or other inferior food at the discretion of the Inspectors; to have two meals of coarse meat every week, and to be kept at hard labor." The institution was expected to show a profit, and the inmates were rented out as laborers or worked in the prison shops where various things were manufactured for sale: nails, shoes, cut or crushed stone, chains, and other articles.[22]

There were several crimes that Kentuckians regarded as more offensive than manslaughter. Many of these involved property rights rather than personal rights. They are listed here in the order of the severity of the prison sentence: arson of public property, seven to twenty-one years; counterfeiting coin or bank notes, four to fifteen years; forging deeds, bonds, etc., two to ten years; stealing a slave, two to nine years; horse stealing, two to seven years; breaking and entering to rob (more than four dollars), one to seven years.[23]

All six of these crimes against property rights carried a higher penalty than manslaughter, which could be punished by no more than six years of imprisonment. In fact, if a person deliberately burned up his neighbor's corn crib or haystack, the penalty was the same as if he had committed manslaughter. There were also a few crimes against an individual's personal rights (as opposed to his property rights) that were regarded as more serious than manslaughter: polygamy, rape, selling or stealing a free person as if he were a slave, and deliberate murder.[24]

An examination of the penitentiary records for the years prior to 1813 shows, almost without exception, that the inmates were serving less than the maximum sentences allowable. The average term being served for manslaughter was only three years and nine months.[25] Even though Lilburne's and Isham's crime was one of rare depravity, the community was outraged, and Lilburne was resented or disliked by some of the citizens for other reasons—it still seems more probable that the brothers would be sentenced to prison for manslaughter, than that they would be hung for murder.

It was also possible that they might escape punishment entirely. If Lilburne and Isham agreed together to lie in giving their testimony, being the only legal eyewitnesses, they might have been able to blame the murder of George on one or more of the other slaves. As Reverend William Dickey put it, Lilburne "might have eventually so managed the matter as to make the sentence fall upon the heads of his slaves."[26]

John Gray intended to prevent this by proving the charge against the Lewis brothers, murder in the highest degree, "wilful, violent, and with malice aforethought."

·27·

THE FIRST GRAND JURY

Sec. 8. *And be it further enacted,* That each circuit court shall consist of one circuit judge and two assistant judges, which assistant judges shall be residents of the county in which the circuit court shall be held to which they shall be appointed. The circuit judge, or the two assistant judges, or the circuit judge and one assistant, shall be sufficient to constitute a court.[1]

THE FATE of Lilburne and Isham lay in the hands of the law and its officials. The character and ability of the judges, lawyers, and jurymen would determine whether the brothers were to be punished or set free. Honorable William Wallace, a competent, respected, and learned man, was the regular circuit judge of the Livingston court. There had been several terms of the Livingston court at which Judge Wallace was not present; his place had been temporarily filled by Judge Henry Broadnax, whose assigned district adjoined Wallace's district. Broadnax was imperious and severe, and conducted his court with strict, if sometimes high-tempered dignity. His cases were seldom reversed.[2] Either one of these judges would have insisted that the conduct of Lilburne's and Isham's trial observe the letter of the law and be free from personal influence or legal error. The ability and integrity of these two men from Russellville were above suspicion.

The two assistant circuit judges were residents of Livingston County. As was the case in most counties, these assistant judges had little or no legal training, but they were persons of intelligence who had some political experience and influence. One of the assistant judges was Jesse Ford, a veteran of the Revolution, and one of the earliest settlers of the region.[3] After 1800 he became a justice of the peace, performed many marriages in the county, and in 1805, when Smithland was incorporated, he was appointed to be one of the four trustees. In 1806 Ford represented Livingston County in the state legislature and in 1809 was appointed assistant circuit judge by Governor Scott.[4] Jesse Ford was fairly prosperous by the standards of the county, for he owned seven slaves. He and his wife had five young

274

children. Judge Ford had been partially crippled in 1811, when he was shot in the hip by James M. Young during a deer hunt. Apparently Ford thought the shooting was intentional, for he sued Young for $5,000 in a plea of trespass, assault, and battery, and petitioned Judge Wallace for a change of venue to try the suit in another circuit.[5] Ford was well acquainted with Lilburne, having served as one of the three commissioners who divided the 1,000-acre tract on the Ohio River jointly owned by Randolph and Lilburne.

The other assistant circuit judge, Dickson Given, had been a member of the court for about a year when George's murder was discovered.[6] Dickson Given was a strikingly handsome young man, twenty-eight years old at this time. A portrait still in existence depicts him with dark hair and eyes (see Figure 3). His forehead was tall and the chin very strong and masculine, offsetting the almost gentle warmth of his eyes and the pleasing symmetry of his other features. The portrait gives the impression that Given was a young man of strong character, but mature understanding.[7]

Given had married Nancy Davis of Fayette County in 1807, when she was sixteen, and in the next four years they had two children, Esther and Henry. Three slaves completed their growing household. At the time of his marriage, Given was twenty-three years old and held the job of deputy sheriff, the first of many official positions that would eventually lead him to the state senate and an impressive business career.[8]

In spite of his obvious abilities, Given must have been aware that he was not fully trained in the intricacies of legal procedure. Four years after Lilburne and Isham were indicted, Given wrote the following passage into his own will: "I wish my children to have a complete education if it should take the chief part of their patrimony *to doe it*— I *doe* not wish them to labor under the same disadvantages that I *doe* my mind being as good as many others that is call[d] men of tallents yet language is deny[d] me to convey my *Eides* for the lack of education both male & female I wish completely educated."[9]

By coincidence, Given had a slave boy who bore the same name as Lilburne's dog, Nero. Given felt quite differently about his boy Nero than Lilburne did about George. In one section of his will Given said that he did not want his slaves to be sold in order to settle his estate, but rather he wished them to be divided

275

Figure 3. Dickson Given.
(Courtesy of Mrs. Lee L. Davis,
Hilton Head, S.C.)

among his heirs, and then he added, "I wish my negro boy Nero to live with my wife during her widowhood to manage and take care for her and if she marry I wish him to be set free . . . he has been a faithful servant to me and I would hate he should now be abused."[10]

These were the men who were to conduct the trial of the Lewis brothers: Wallace, or, in his absence, Broadnax, both highly qualified judges, and Assistant Judges Jesse Ford and Dickson Given, energetic men, prominent in local affairs and politics, even though they were indifferently educated in the law. They were probably typical of Kentucky assistant circuit judges. If neither of the senior judges, Wallace or Broadnax, was able to be present at Lilburne's and Isham's hearing and trial, then the assistant judges, Ford and Given, presiding together, would have full authority to conduct the business of the circuit court without the presence of a senior judge. If they took their oaths seriously, then the Lewis brothers would have had impartial judges. Ford and Given had sworn to "administer justice without respect of persons, and do equal right to the poor and the rich."[11]

The most powerful county official was Sheriff Robert Kirk, whose office and deputies were at the disposal of the circuit court. Kirk had stepped up from the county court to succeed James Johnson early the previous year.[12] In 1809, an attempt had been made to have Kirk impeached by the legislature and removed from his position as justice of the peace. The charges were dismissed by the house committee, which noted that, although Kirk did act in his official position while intoxicated, nonetheless "few men could have sustained a more amiable character, both official and private, then Mr. Kirk." The report said that Kirk was uniformly esteemed as an independent and intelligent officer even though "he several times drank too much spirits." The committee concluded its decision with this endorsement: "His usefulness as an officer is not at all impaired thereby; nor is he more liable to become intoxicated now than when he accepted the appointment."[13] Kirk ran an official inspection station for tobacco, hemp, and flour at his property on Mill Creek near present-day Marion. The friendly and esteemed sheriff on several occasions had been indicted for profanity, once for "swearing 'By God' fifteen times at his house."[14]

Kirk's deputies were the men who actually did the more

difficult work of the office, making long trips on horseback, often in bad weather or at night, to deliver official papers, make arrests, and other such tasks. One deputy, having ridden eighteen miles to bring in a prisoner, was allowed twenty-five cents by the court, and had to wait five years before he actually got the money.[15]

James Hodge, who kept a tavern in his home, was one of Kirk's deputies.[16] Another was Christopher Haynes, who had been a hatter by trade, and a justice of the peace. Haynes, who had a large family and seven slaves, resigned as magistrate to become a deputy sheriff in 1811.[17] The third deputy was Thomas Champion, a man who, by the end of 1812, had held almost every minor political job in the county: constable, keeper of the stray pen, tax collector, patroller, magistrate at Salem, trustee of Salem, deputy sheriff, and jailer. Champion lived in the county seat, Salem, where he kept a tavern in his home.[18]

The job of coroner of Livingston was held by one of the more colorful personalities in the county, John Dorroh, a farmer, who was also the ferryman where the road from Smithland to Centerville crossed the Cumberland at the present site of Dycusburg. John Dorroh was a native of Ireland who had come to America as a young man. He had lived in South Carolina for a number of years and then, sometime before 1806, he moved to Livingston County and settled seventeen miles above Smithland on the Cumberland River. By 1810 Dorroh's family consisted of five girls and three boys. There were no slaves in his household.[19]

Dorroh was not a poor man, for in addition to the income from his farm and ferryboat, he kept a tavern in his home, and had received some fees as constable, a job he was given in 1809.[20] During this period, a lunatic, one Shemiah Watson, was assigned to Dorroh's care for six months by the circuit court. Dorroh was to be paid $100 to clothe and care for Watson, and was given authority to "restrain and confine the said lunatic" to keep him out of mischief.[21]

Coroner John Dorroh was not a polished gentleman, by any means. On the contrary, he fit rather well into the traditional stereotype of a hard-drinking, profane, and high-tempered Irish immigrant. Dorroh had been indicted for profanity at least once, and usually more often, in each of the five previous years. Among Dorroh's better efforts in the practice of imprecation was this masterpiece, which cost him a five-shilling fine: "God damn you, you half made son of a bitch."[22] On another occasion Dorroh visited the tavern whorehouse of James Ivy and addressed the group there with his sentiments of the moment, "God damn you all!"[23] Dorroh was indicted several times for drunkenness, and on at least two occasions he was fined four dollars for "contempt of court by fighting in the presence of said court."[24]

To summarize the character of the county officials assigned to deal with crimes and violence in Livingston: Sheriff Kirk was an "amiable, uniformly esteemed," moderately profane alcoholic; the three deputies were competent men from families that were respected in the county; and Coroner Dorroh, somewhat less amiable than the sheriff, was a high-tempered drinker and a master of invective.[25] Although some of these five men may have had personal shortcomings, none of them was riff-raff. They all had property and sources of income other than their official jobs. Although three of them kept taverns in their homes, keeping a tavern was as acceptable as any other business, if it were run in an orderly way. In most taverns food and lodging were available, and the term "innkeeper" might better describe this occupation.

From the night in December when George was murdered, it would be ninety-one days before the circuit court was scheduled to meet again. It is not known exactly when, during this period, George's head was discovered at the roadside. It was probably sometime after the most violent earthquake shock on February seventh, the tremor that no doubt wrecked Lilburne's kitchen chimney for a second time and disclosed the unburned pieces of George's body. If so, the grand jury was to meet sometime less than five weeks after the head was found. There is one very peculiar circumstance that suggests that the head was not found until immediately before the circuit court opened its session on March sixteenth. The puzzling fact is that Coroner John Dorroh did not hold an inquest to investigate George's death.

It was clearly the main function of the coroner's office "to come and enquire upon the view of *any* person slain, drowned, or otherwise by misadventure suddenly dead." The statutes required the coroner to summon "at least twelve of the most respectable house keepers of the vicinage or county to appear before him . . . with all convenient speed." These men were then sworn in and taken to the scene where the violence was discovered or presumably done. They were then to inquire where the person was slain, who was culpable, and "who were present, either man or woman, and of what age soever they be."[26] The cause of death was also to be ascertained: "All wounds ought to be viewed, the length, breadth and deepness, and with what weapons, and in what part of the body the wound or hurt is, and how many be culpable, and how many wounds there be, and who gave the wounds; all which things must be enrolled in the roll of the coroners."[27] After these steps were taken, the body was then to be buried immediately. If this investigation disclosed a presumed culprit, he was put in jail by the sheriff until a lower court was convened either by a justice of the peace or by the coroner himself "for the investigation of such offender." After this inquest, or hearing of the lower court, if the evidence appeared strong enough, it was written down and held as material for subsequent court action, the witnesses were put under bond to testify later, and the suspect and his accessories were put in jail pending trial. If the offenders could not be found, warrants were to be issued for their arrest.[28]

It is not likely that Dorroh would fail in his duties, for there was a penalty involved. "If any coroner be remiss and make not inquisition upon a view of the body slain or murdered, or shall not endeavor to do his office upon *any* person dead by misadventure, . . . he shall for every such offence, forfeit the sum of ninety pounds . . . one half thereof to the use of the informer, and the other half to the use of the commonwealth."[29] Even though it was eleven miles from Rocky Hill to Salem, and ten miles more to Dorroh's home on the Cumberland, it is difficult to believe that Dorroh did not learn about the discovery of George's head within a day or two after it was found. He could not afford to ignore the information, considering the public mood and the penalty of well over two hundred dollars that he would certainly have to pay. The only logical explanation for Dorroh's failure to hold a coroner's inquest is that he did not have time to do so before the opening day of the circuit court on Monday the sixteenth. The head must have been found no more than a day or two before the grand jury convened, and when it did convene, the circuit court and the grand jury could perform the functions that the coroner and his jury of inquest would ordinarily have done had there been enough time.

280

At the beginning of February, Lilburne probably did not think that he would be indicted for murder six weeks later, but he did know his three sisters would have to appear in court during that March term. On the same day that Lilburne's son James was born, Deputy Christopher Haynes was given a summons containing these orders: "You are hereby commanded to attach Lucy Lewis, Patsy Lewis, and Nancy Lewis and them safely keep so that you have their bodies before the judges of our Livingston circuit court on the second day of our next March term to answer concerning a certain contempt by them to this court offered by not appearing as witnesses at June term 1811 in behalf of Arthur Campbell against Lilburne Lewis."[30] The efforts of Lilburne's sisters to delay the settlement of Dr. Campbell's suit had landed them in court on a charge of contempt. It is possible that Lilburne had prevailed upon them to be absent from court the previous June. The other members of his family were becoming entangled in the wreckage of his life.

On Monday morning the circuit court opened its session in Salem. It had rained intermittently for the previous two days, but on Monday the clouds began to clear. The temperature was in the low fifties and for an hour after court convened, between nine and ten o'clock, there were moderate earthquake tremors. On the trees and shrubs the buds were beginning to swell and burst open.[31] Neither Judge Wallace nor Judge Broadnax was present at court, and Assistant Judges Given and Ford were presiding.

The grand jury panel had been chosen and summoned by Sheriff Kirk, and they assembled in the twenty-four-foot square main room of the hewn log courthouse. According to law, Sheriff Kirk was required to summon twenty-four of the "most discrete housekeepers" in the district. A minimum of sixteen housekeepers was required to compose a lawful grand jury.[32] In this case twenty-one men* showed up and were sworn in by Enoch Prince, the court clerk.[33] Drury Champion was made foreman, and they retired to one of the three smaller rooms that opened off of the courtroom. There they would discuss the

---

*Drury Champion, James Rutter, William Anderson, George Robertson, William Elder, James Strickland, John Rentfro, John Ramage, William Brown, Amos Watson, Jesse Gibson, James Anderson, Robert Boyd, Benjamin Coffield, Bolen Thompson, William Henry, Champion Terry, Elijah Flannery, John Brown, William McKlesky, and James Brown.

presentments and evidence prepared by Commonwealth Attorney John Gray, and also any charges presented by other citizens. If the grand jury felt the case under discussion to be a strong one that deserved to be tried, the indictment was labeled true bill, and the case was sent to a petit jury for trial and then sentencing, providing the verdict of the petit jury was guilty.

The majority of the jurymen appear to have been yeoman farmers and more or less average citizens, for their names seldom appear in the county records. In relation to George's murder case, however, two of the jurymen require comment. In 1809 Lilburne had been a member of a grand jury that indicted William Brown for trespass, assault, and battery,[34] and now William Brown was a member of the grand jury before which Lilburne stood presented for murder. If Brown were a vindictive man, then Lilburne had at least one enemy on the jury. The other juryman of special interest to Lilburne was his own father-in-law, James Rutter, Sr.[35] It is not known how much Rutter knew about the murder or, in fact, if Letitia had been able to get in touch with him at all; nor is it known what Rutter's opinion was of Lilburne as a man and son-in-law. In addition to these questions, there is another, which has no answer: was Rutter opposed to indicting Lilburne, or did he support the indictment? There is no possibility of uncovering all that went on in that jury room during the two and one-half days the jurors spent there.

While the grand jury was meeting to consider its various presentments, the other business of the circuit court went on. On Monday a lawyer was admitted to practice, two fugitive burglars were outlawed, a few cases from the previous term were postponed, one was settled amicably, and a few others were tried. On Tuesday the seventeenth, court business continued pretty much the same as it had on Monday. The sky was clear all day and there were some earthquake tremors for an hour, beginning as the court opened at nine o'clock in the morning. The temperature rose gradually from about forty degrees in the morning to the low fifties by evening.[36] The senior judge of the court was still not present, and the two assistant judges were behind the bar of justice. This was the day that Lilburne's three sisters had been ordered to appear in court on a charge of contempt for not appearing as witnesses for Dr. Arthur Campbell. There is no mention of them in the records of Tuesday's court proceedings. Apparently they had ignored the summons again.[37] The other business of the court was routine; one case was tried and a few others were settled, dismissed, or continued to the next term.

The final action of the day was the release of schoolteacher Patrick O'Connell from jail on bond. O'Connell had spent the previous six months in confinement for sending a challenge to fight a duel to one Timothy O'Neal, who had declined the invitation.[38] After O'Connell was released, court was adjourned until the next day, when the grand jury would return its indictments.

At about eight o'clock Wednesday morning, earthquake rumblings began and continued fitfully all day and into the evening. There was a shock of considerable force at 9:00 P.M. The day was fair and calm otherwise, and toward nighttime the sky became overcast.[39] Throughout the morning nearly twenty cases were brought before the court. A few judgments were rendered, but most of the cases were continued to the next term. This may have been done because the senior circuit judge was not present and the assistant judges were unwilling to depend upon their own meager legal experience. In the afternoon the grand jury returned into court with their presentments and indictments. Fifteen men were accused of minor offenses, among them Coroner Dorroh for drunkenness, and Sheriff Kirk for swearing. One man was charged with a felony and two others with assault and battery. The last indictment was one charging Lilburne with the murder of George.[40] At that point it appeared that there was no more work for the grand jury, and it was discharged. The court then issued a warrant for Lilburne's arrest, "returnable forthwith."[41]

This indictment did not charge Isham with being an accessory to the murder. In wording and form the document was similar to the indictment John Gray wrote later, naming both the brothers. In this first indictment, however, Gray did not say that Lilburne had been "moved and seduced by the instigation of the Devil," as was customary in felony indictments, nor did he comment that the axe was worth two dollars, but he did describe the wound in George's neck as being four, rather than three, inches deep.

Lilburne was in Salem that day, awaiting the decision of the grand jury. Earlier in the day, his friend, Justice of the Peace Richard Ferguson of Smithland, had been involved in a suit concerning seventy dollars. Lilburne signed Ferguson's $100 bond as security, and Ferguson's case was held over.[42] Immediately after Lilburne's indictment was given to the court, the assistant judges ordered clerk Enoch Prince to issue a warrant for Lilburne and to "have his body before the Judges" on that same day in order to answer those things for which he stood indicted.[43] Deputy Christopher Haynes served the warrant on Lilburne, who straightway presented himself to the court. It was well into the afternoon by this time, too late to take up the charges against Lilburne. Lilburne was not held in jail that night, but was released with $1,000 securing his appearance in court the next morning.[44]

The five men who signed Lilburne's bond as securities were among the most influential in the county: Jonathan Ramsey, general of the militia, and Lilburne's commanding officer; William Rutter, Mark Phillips, and William C. Rodgers, Lilburne's brothers-in-law; and lastly, James Rutter, Sr., Lilburne's father-in-law, who had been a member of the grand jury that returned the indictment. The fact that these men were willing to pledge their own "goods, lands, and tenements" against Lilburne's appearance in court on the next day, indicates they still had some confidence in Lilburne, and that they were not afraid for Letitia's safety if Lilburne were to spend that night at Rocky Hill. One might also guess that James Rutter, Sr., when serving on the jury, had voted against the indictment of Lilburne.

The afternoon was wearing on when Lilburne was released, and there was little time left for other court business. However, John Dorroh was present with Shemiah Watson, the lunatic. Dorroh was discharged as committee "for the safekeeping and taking care of the said Shemiah Watson," and the job was given to another man.[45] Two other cases were quickly settled. Coroner Dorroh and Sheriff Kirk and a few others paid their five-shilling fines for drunkenness and profanity, and then the last business of the day was brought before the court by Commonwealth Attorney John Gray. Gray made the highly unusual legal request that a second grand jury be summoned to appear the next day at 10:00 A.M. The judges ordered that it be done and adjourned until 9:00 A.M. on Thursday.

Sometime during that afternoon, following the dismissal of the grand jury, John Gray had learned that Isham was also involved in George's murder.

·28·

THE TRUE BILL

ON THURSDAY the nineteenth there was a high cloud cover, through which the sun shone dimly. There was little wind and the temperature was in the mid-fifties during most of the day. Earthquake vibrations were felt from about eight o'clock on through the day. Shortly before noon there were large tremors that lasted for five minutes. The motion was very irregular, with the impulses coming from "curious directions, changing each few seconds."[1]

At nine o'clock, in the absence of the senior judge, Jesse Ford and Dickson Given again convened the court and, during the next hour, ten cases were handled. Most of them were postponed in order to obtain depositions and, at ten o'clock, the second grand jury was sworn in. As was the case with the previous grand jury, twenty-one veniremen took the oath and retired to the juryroom.[2] Again, most of the jurymen were yeoman farmers, apparently with no special connections to the Lewis family.* Three of them, however, had served with Lilburne on other juries, and one of them, James Trimble, had been indicted for unlawfully selling whiskey two years before. Lilburne had been foreman of the jury that indicted Trimble, and now the situation was reversed. Two of the jurymen had been officers in the militia, one was a trustee of Salem, and several of the men were slave owners. One of the jurymen, John McDaniel, had the unusual, if irrelevant, distinction of being "noted in his day as the ugliest man short of old 'Virginny.' "[3]

With the exception of James H. Rice, this was not an unusual jury. It appears to have represented a cross section of the citizens of the county. James H. Rice, however, did have a special connection to Lilburne, for Rice's brother, Patrick, had married Sally Rutter, one of Letitia's four sisters. Lilburne's connection

*Elisha Rees, forman, Jacob Houts, John Dunn, Jacob Craft, John Reed, John Harrington, James H. Rice, Thomas Hodge, John Hardin, Moses Hutson, James Trimble, Robert Coffield, Isam Briant, Abraham Fulkerson, John Pickens, Evan Shelby, John McDaniel, Benjamin Pippin, William Pippin, Henry Ewen, William Hodge.

to James H. Rice was not as close as his family connection on the previous grand jury, his father-in-law, James Rutter, Sr. Nevertheless, the Lewis family was intertwined with the Rices as well as the Rutters. They shared not only the intermarriages, but also religious persuasion, social position, Virginia background, and education. Whether Lilburne expected Rice to exert influence in his behalf is unknown, but one thing is certain: the new evidence that John Gray presented to the second grand jury in the attempt to indict both Isham and Lilburne, was all heard by James H. Rice. After the second grand jury was dismissed he, no doubt, passed on what he had heard to the rest of his family, and to the Rutters as well.

The second grand jury did not deliberate as long as the first one. While they were out of the courtroom one suit was dismissed, another continued, and a third was settled with a restraining order. Then the grand jury returned to court with three charges: one for profane swearing, one indicting James McCawley for assault and battery against a member of the jury panel, and one against "Lilburn Lewis and Isham Lewis for murder, a true bill." Having nothing further to present, the second grand jury was then dismissed.[4]

The court records give no hint of what evidence was presented to the second grand jury, but certain events indicate that far more was revealed to the second grand jury than to the first.[5] Isham's complicity was revealed, to be sure, but there was more than that. The six witnesses who had testified before the second grand jury, "Lilburne Lewis Junr," Archibald Cannon, and William Dyer, were placed under bond to appear in court on Friday to give evidence; and, whereas Lilburne had been let out on bail the day before, there was now some question as to whether the same offence was bailable now that new evidence had been heard and both brothers were involved. There was not time to settle the question on Thursday. The decision was scheduled for the next day, and Lilburne and Isham were committed into custody and spent that night in jail.[6]

The Lilburne Lewis, Jr. who testified was probably Charles Lilburne Lewis, Lilburne's nephew, the eldest son of Randolph. He was approaching his twenty-first birthday.[7] The court records show also that three additional witnesses were summoned to testify on Friday. John Menees, Francis Hollingshead, and John Bolen were placed "under the penalty of 100 pounds" against their appearance.[8] There is some reason to believe that all six of these witnesses lived in the general vicinity of Rocky Hill, but what they knew about the murder that was relevant remains a mystery.

In general, the witnesses appear to have been average citizens. They did not hold any public offices, nor had their names appeared on public records in connection with any trouble with the law. There is no indication that they had any special affiliation or dealings with the Lewises, except for Lilburne Lewis, Jr., who was a member of the family.

At the end of that day, with Lilburne and Isham in jail, one important question remained to be settled: would the brothers be tried immediately, or would their case be continued to the next term of court in June? There was not much time to try the case, since the regular term of court, which lasted for six judicial days if necessary, could not be extended. Any court business that had not been completed in a given term had to be continued to the next scheduled session.[9] Thus, after court adjourned on Thursday, two more days remained in that term of court. There were eight or ten cases left on the docket that would have to be disposed of before Lilburne's could be heard. It was a tight schedule in which to try a case as sensational as this murder indictment. Moreover, it was obvious by now that William Wallace, the senior circuit judge, or his occasional substitute, Judge Henry P. Broadnax, would not be in attendance this term. The full responsibility would fall on Assistant Circuit Judges Ford and Given. They must have felt uneasy about the prospect of trying Lilburne's and Isham's case themselves, without a senior judge being present. On the other hand, Henry F. Delany, the attorney for Lilburne and Isham, might have felt he could do more for this clients without the experienced and stern senior judge behind the bench.[10]

Friday dawned dull and overcast. The temperature hovered around fifty degrees all day and, toward evening, rain began and continued all night. Early in the morning there were slight earthquake tremors, but about the time Lilburne and Isham were led into court at 9:20, earthquake recording instruments began a "smart motion" and were "in almost constant action till 12 o'clock."[11]

During the week in which Lilburne and Isham were indicted, more earthquake shocks were recorded than in any other previous week except the last seven days of February. These were not shocks of the greatest intensity, but a few were said to be generally alarming to people. The lesser shocks were described as "often causing a strange sort of sensation, absence, and sometimes giddiness."[12] Such was the setting when Sheriff Kirk took Lilburne and Isham out of jail and led them into the courtroom on Friday. After hearing evidence, Judges Ford and Given decided to admit the brothers to bail in the sum of $1,000 for Lilburne and $500 for Isham. Next, lawyer Delany petitioned the court to try the case immediately, but the judges decided that the trial would have to be held at the next term of court, three months later. The witnesses were then placed on $200 bond to be present at that time.[13]

At this point Lilburne and Isham had to find five men who would sign their bail bond as securities. Failure to obtain these signatures would mean that they would spend the next eighty-six days in jail waiting for the June term of court to open. If they obtained the signatures but failed to show up in court, then the total bail of $1,500 would be forfeited to the court and taken out of the Lewis brothers' property. If there were not enough value there to cover the bail, then the men who signed the bond would have to make up the difference out of their own pockets.

After the first grand jury had indicted Lilburne, General Ramsey and the Rutters had signed Lilburne's bond; this time they did not. They could have if they had wanted to, for they all lived in or near Salem. Evidently they had learned something, perhaps from juryman James H. Rice, or perhaps from Letitia, which turned them against Lilburne.

Five other men were found who were willing to act as securities. William C. Rodgers, the surveyor, was one of them. The other four men who signed for Lilburne and Isham, strangely enough, were witnesses for the commonwealth in this same case.

> Lilburn Lewis, William C. Rodgers, Francis Hollingshead, Archibald Cannon, John Bolen, and William Dyer acknowledged themselves severally indebted to the commonwealth the said Lewis in the sum of one thousand Dollars and said Rodgers, Hollingshead, Cannon, Bolen, and Dyer Jointly in the sum of one thousand dollars to be levied of their goods chattells land tenements respectively to be void on condition that the said Lilburn Lewis shall appear here on the first day of the next June term of this court to answer a bill of

indictment found by the grand Jury against him at this Term and not depart without the leave of the court.[14]

The same men signed Isham's bail in the amount of $500. The personal relationship between these men and the Lewis brothers is unknown. One can only guess at the reasons that influenced them to become securities for Lilburne and Isham.

After this business was completed a few more cases were heard in court. Thomas Champion, the deputy sheriff and jailer, was paid five dollars for tending the jail that week, and then the two judges adjourned the court until June. In spite of lawyer Delany's request, the court did not meet on Saturday, the last day of that term.

Lilburne and Isham went home to Rocky Hill after being admitted to bail. Lilburne's relationship to Letitia had, no doubt, been extremely tense since the murder of George. The sources of legend recount that Lilburne kept Letitia under observation and was her constant shadow, and further state that she had full knowledge of the crime, having been awakened by the ghastly sounds and the odor of burning flesh.[15] The fact that Letitia's father and brother signed Lilburne's bail bond after the first indictment for murder on March eighteenth, indicates that they did not have all the facts, or they may not have believed what they had heard. It is clear that they did not think Letitia would be in danger from Lilburne or Isham. After the second indictment, however, which included Isham, they evidently felt quite differently, for they did not sign as security for the Lewis brothers, implying that they preferred to have them in jail rather than at Rocky Hill.

A central issue in this situation was Letitia's role as witness to the crime. There is no doubt whatever that Letitia would not be allowed to testify against Lilburne, for it is a common-law rule of remote antiquity that neither the husband nor the wife can be a witness either for or against the other in a criminal prosecution. This rule is so old that its origin is well-nigh undiscoverable.[16] As for Isham, however, there was no rule of this sort to protect him from Letitia's testimony. After the first indictment, Lilburne had little to fear from his wife, but after Isham was indicted too, then she became a certain threat to Isham and a possible danger to Lilburne as well.

Letitia fled to safety. She left Rocky Hill with her two-month old baby, James R., and found sanctuary in her father's home at Salem. A newspaper account written later states that Letitia "made her escape to save her life, as it was feared that her evidence would be admitted against Isham, as an aider and abettor of the horrid deed with which her husband stood charged."[17]

Some of the sources of legend are more elaborate in their versions of Letitia's escape. They are unanimous that she fled for her safety's sake, but disagree on points of detail, and especially on the timing of her flight. It seems more reasonable that she fled after Isham was indicted, rather than before. The most lurid account, as might be expected, came from the pen of William Dickey, the rabid abolitionist.

> In the interim, other articles of evidence leaked out. That of Mrs. Lewis hearing a pounding, and screaming, and her smelling fresh meat burning, for not till now had this come out. He was offended with her for disclosing these things, alleging that they might have some weight against him at the pending trial.
>
> In connection with this is another item, full of horror. Mrs. Lewis, or her girl, in making her bed one morning after this, found, under her bolster, a *keen* BUTCHER KNIFE! The appalling discovery forced from her the confession that she considered her life in jeopardy. Messrs. Rice and Phillips, whose wives were sisters, went to see her and to bring her away if she wished it. Mr. Lewis received them with all the expressions of *Virginia hospitality*. As soon as they were seated they said, "Well, Letitia, we supposed that you might be unhappy here, and afraid for your life; and we have come to-day to take you to your father's, if you desire it." She said, "Thank you, kind brothers, I am indeed afraid for my life."— We need not interrupt the story to tell how much surprised he affected to be with this strange procedure of his brothers-in-law, and with this declaration of his wife. But all his professions of fondness for her, to the contrary notwithstanding, they rode off with her before his eyes.—He followed and overtook, and went with them to her father's; but she was locked up from him, with her own consent, and he returned home.[18]

Another of the sources claims that before her flight Letitia had been able to slip a note asking for help to some of her family who had come to visit her.[19] These could have been her brothers-in-law, Mark Phillips and Patrick H. Rice, who were mentioned by Reverend William Dickey. It seems certain that the men who actually came to Rocky Hill and took her back to Salem with them were her father, her brother James, and two of their friends, James M. Young and Thomas Terry. A short time after Letitia left, Lilburne paid his lawyer, Henry F. Delany, a fee of $67.50, cash in advance, to prosecute these four men for trespass.[20] Lilburne wanted to be sure Delany pressed the trespass charges, and when he gave Delany the fee, he demanded a note in return for the full amount, which was to fall due on Christmas day of that year. Presumably, if Delany prosecuted the men during the eight months left before Christmas, then Lilburne would destroy the note, otherwise Delany would have to return the fee in exchange for the note.[21] Lilburne wanted revenge against these men, but that would not bring Letitia back. The suit for trespass was never prosecuted.

Good Friday, and then Easter, came and passed at the end of March. The earth still trembled intermittently and the nights were cool with light frost evident in the mornings.[22] By April first, twelve days after the circuit court adjourned, the schedule of militia musters for that year was in the hands of all the men in Lilburne's company. War with England was imminent and musters were not taken lightly. The first muster of the year was scheduled in April, and Lilburne, as captain, would have to lead and drill his company.[23] He was, no doubt, by then the most notorious object of morbid curiosity in the county. The pending muster could not have been anticipated with pleasure by the man Dickey described as a proud Virginian.

On April second, the remnants of Lilburne's fragile self-esteem received another blow. The five men who had signed Lilburne's and Isham's bail as securities came to the brothers and demanded a mortgage on seven of Lilburne's slaves. They obviously were fearful that one or both of the brothers would run off before their trial in June, and that they, the five men, would be held accountable for the bail. The mortgage on the slaves was to be void if both brothers appeared in court as directed. The five securities obviously felt that the case against the brothers was so strong that Lilburne or Isham would be tempted to flee. Letitia may have told them what she knew, and may have said further that she would testify against Isham. The demand for the mortgage was a clear expression of mistrust on the part of the five men, who had previously thought well enough of the brothers to sign their bail. The mortgage document itself was prepared by Henry F. Delany, and witnessed by him and Samuel C. Harkins.[24]

Lilburne had become a pariah. He had lost all of the things that make up a sense of identity and worth in a man; his prestige was gone. The nature of Lilburne's crime was so heinous that he could expect sympathy from no one except the lowest class of social scum. He, who was now the eldest son, who should have been the effective head of all three of the Lewis households, had seen these families decimated by death and debt. The dreams of a West Kentucky dynasty, for which the Lewises had left Virginia, had blown away. He was the defendant in two unsettled court cases, one for a substantial debt, and another for murder. His own nephew was to testify against him, and his wife might implicate his brother. He had lost his political influence and could not even obtain the position of justice of the peace. His wife, whom he loved, had deserted him out of fear and taken their infant son away with her. The last blow was the mortgage of his slaves; five men who had trusted him, the bondsmen, had finally repudiated him. William Dickey described Lilburne's feelings: "Now he saw that his character was gone, his respectable friends believed that he had massacred George; but, worst of all, he saw that they considered the life of the harmless Letitia was in danger from his perfidious hands. It was too much for his chivalry to sustain. The proud Virginian sunk under the accumulated load of public odium."[25]

There was not one aspect of Lilburne's life that remained intact, not one corner of his personality where his tortured mind could rest. He had come face to face with his failure, and he could think of no place to go to avoid the intolerable realization. Except one.

· 29 ·

THE GRAVEYARD

SOMETIME during the next week Lilburne decided to kill himself. He prevailed upon Isham, and they formed a suicide pact. Thursday, the ninth, was a gloomy day with the temperature in the mid-fifties. Earthquake vibrations were barely perceptible. On this day Lilburne wrote his will, one of the most unusual documents ever admitted to public record.

In the name of God Amen. This my last Will & c

1st. It's my desire that all my just debts be paid & then my property both real & personal be equally divided between my children Jane W. Lewis, Lucy J. Lewis, Lilburne L. Lewis, Elizabeth Lewis, Robert Lewis & James R. Lewis, reserving to my beloved but cruel wife Letitia G. Lewis her lawful part of said property during her natural life—

2d. It's my desire that my beloved Father Chas L. Lewis be possessed of the riding Horse which I purchaised of Hurley, my Rifle & Shott bag during his natural life also my walking cane & that my beloved Sisters Martha C. Lewis, Lucy B. Lewis & Nancy M. Lewis may be comforted from the perquisites of s'd Estate by my Executors as prudence may require, or in other words, so as to do my children & themselves entire justice.

3d. I do hereby constitute my beloved Father Chas L. Lewis, the Revd. Wm. Woods near Salem, Saml C. Harkins, James McCawley, & Richd Furgison my Executors, whom I must remind that Henry F. Delaney has received a fee from me for the prosecution in a Trespass against James Rutter Senr, James Rutter, Junr. James Young & Tho. Terry. Given under my hand this (& revoking all & every other will heretofore made) ninth day of Apl. Eighteen hundred and twelve.

Lilburne Lewis.

N. B. My dog Nero I do hereby bequethe to my beloved Father.

L. L.[1]

Lilburne wrote this will on one side of two sheets of paper, each approximately eight by thirteen inches in size (see Figure 4). When finished he folded the sheets once in the center, and then again in the same direction, reducing the size of the packet

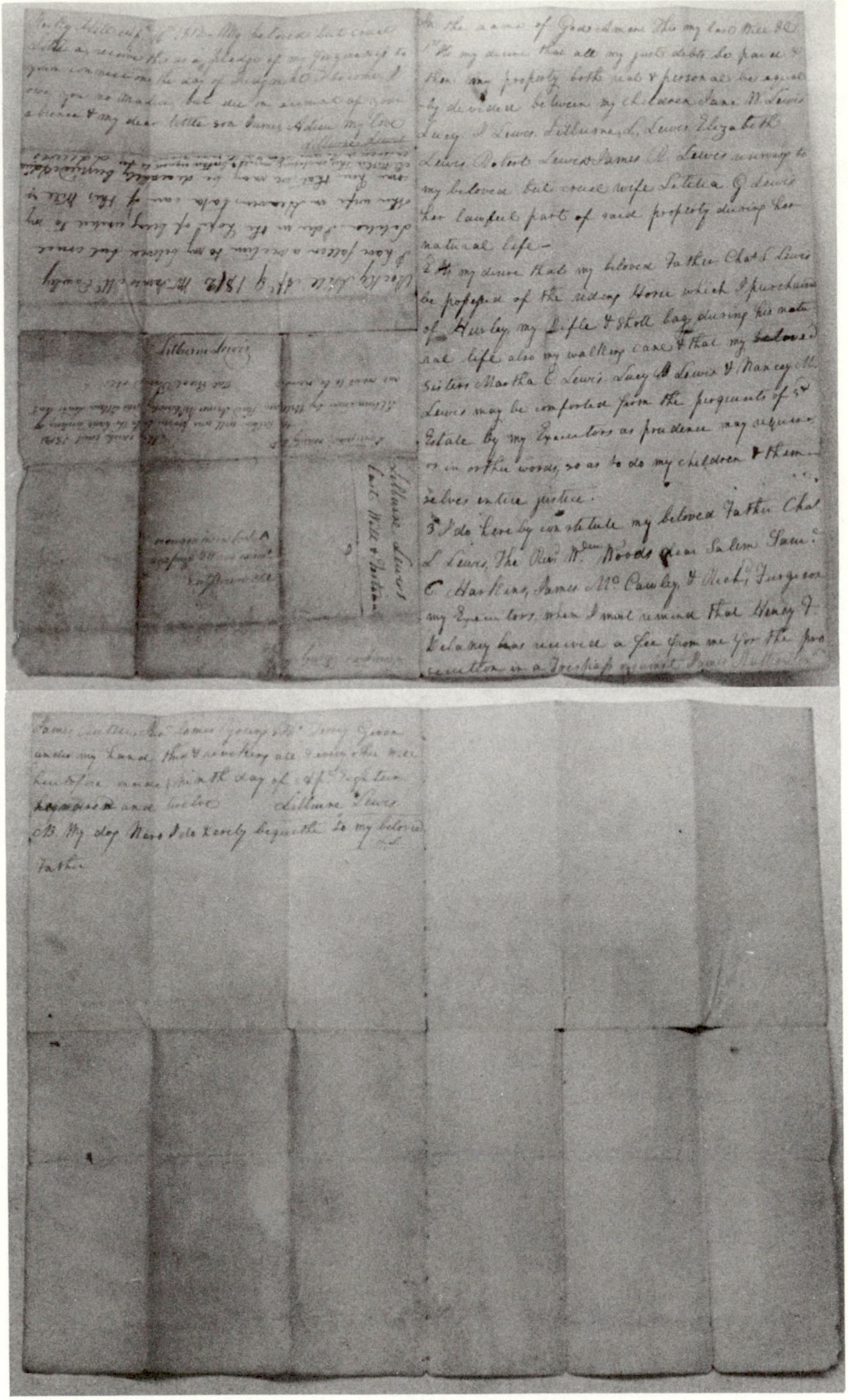

Figure 4. The Will. *(Photo by John Lucas.)*

to about three by eight inches, with a blank face outward on both the front and back of the folded document. On one side of the folded will Lilburne wrote the following message to his friend in Smithland: "Rocky Hill Apl. 9, 1812. Mr. James McCawley I have fallen a victim to my beloved but cruel Letitia. I die in the hope of being united to my other wife in Heaven. Take care of this Will & come here that we may be deceantly burried. Adieu. L. Lewis" The suicide pact was to be consummated the next day.

The weather on Friday was gloomy and overcast. The bottom lands between Rocky Hill and the bank of the river had been flooded for a week and upstream in Henderson, where there was much flat land, Judge Henry Broadnax discharged the grand jury so that those living near the river might go to their homes and save their property from the high water.[2] Shortly before noon on Friday there was a tremulous shaking of the ground, not a severe tremor, but it was accompanied by an unusual disturbance of the earth's magnetic field. During a period of ten minutes compass needles did not point to the north.[3]

At Rocky Hill Lilburne and Isham took two guns and went to the graveyard where Lilburne's first wife, Elizabeth, lay buried alone inside the thirty-foot square plot of ground. Their plan was to stand facing each other across the cemetery, each with his back to the inside of the cedar rail fence that kept the livestock from trampling Elizabeth's grave. They would then raise their guns, aim at the other's breast, and fire simultaneously on the count of three.

Lilburne had brought his will to the graveyard and put it nearby on the ground, where it would be found. Just before coming to the graveyard he had written a message to Letitia on the blank outside back fold of the paper. "Rocky Hill Apl. 10th—1812—My beloved but cruel Letitia, receive this as a pledge of my forgiveness to your connections, the day of Judgment is to come. I owe you no malice, but die on account of your absence & my dear little son James, Adieu my love. Lilburne Lewis." He had then turned the packet over and in the cramped space below the message to James McCawley he scrawled the following last request to his friend: "N. B. Within this inclosure myself & brother request to be entered in the same coffin & in the same grave." His handwriting, which once was fluid and graceful, had become as chaotic and disorderly as his mind.

While standing there in the grave yard, one of them, probably

Isham, commented that perhaps one of the guns might misfire, as flintlocks occasionally did. In that case only one of the brothers would be shot, but Lilburne explained to Isham how the survivor could kill himself and complete their pact. Lilburne told Isham, that if his gun did not fire, to re-prime the gun, cock the hammer, and then showed him how to position the rifle. Lilburne rested the butt on the ground and held the weapon at an angle with the muzzle pointed directly at the center of his own chest. Lilburne told Isham to get a small branch and cut it off about two feet long, which he did, and handed it to Lilburne. Lilburne then leaned forward slightly, holding the stick in his other hand, and, in the process of showing Isham how he could push the trigger with the stick, he inadvertently touched the trigger and fired the gun upward into his own heart. He had botched the macabre ceremony which was to be the last act of his life. He fell to the ground before Isham who, stunned and horrified, saw Lilburne's blood cover the ground by Elizabeth's grave. It was over. Stricken by the ghastly sight of Lilburne's death, Isham could not bring himself to re-enact such a scene. He left the graveyard.

The news spread rapidly, and by the next day had reached Coroner John Dorroh more than twenty miles away at his home on the Cumberland. Although Dorroh had not held an inquest for George's murder, he acted quickly in the matter of Lilburne's suicide, and assembled a coroner's jury at Rocky Hill on Saturday the eleventh.

Commonwealth of Kentucky)   To any sheriff or Constable in
)
Livingston County   )   sd. County to execute—

Whereas information is made to me John Dorro, coroner in & for sd. County, that Lilburne Lewis has by some means unknown been killed, or otherwise came to his death, These are therefore to command you to summon twelve good & lawfull housekeepers of the vicinage to appear before me at the late dwelling of the deceased on this day for the purpose of investigating such facts & circumstances attending the death of the aforementioned Lilburne Lewis as may be given them in charge and this shall be your warrant for do doing.
Given under my hand this
11th day of April 1812.   John Dorroh[4]

296

Eight of the twelve coroner's jurymen who were summoned to Rocky Hill had had special connections with Lilburne. Richard Ferguson, Lilburne's friend from Smithland, was named as executor in the will. Mark Phillips and William Rutter were his brothers-in-law. Two other men were Lilburne's partners in the Westwood real estate promotion; John Bolen and Francis Hollinshead were bonded to testify against Lilburne and had signed the bail bond for the Lewis brothers; and William Pippin had been on the grand jury that indicted Lilburne and Isham. James McCawley's name had been on the list, but for some reason it was scratched out and replaced by another.[5]

During the inquest Isham's sworn statement was heard and written down as follows: "Isham Lewis before the Jury. and saith upon oath that him self and Lilbourn Lewis agreed to present a gun at each others breast and fire at a word with an intention of killing each other—but that Lilbourn in trying an experiment accidentally shot himself dead. Sworn to before John Dorroh, Coroner L. C. April 11th, 1812."

The report was folded and the verdict was written on the outside. "We of the Jury are of the opinion that Lilburn Lewis Did murder him self on the 10th Day of April 1812 on his own plantation and Isham Lewis present and acessary to the murder. Wm. Rutter foremn—."[6]

The next step, required by law, was for Coroner Dorroh or a justice of the peace to convene a court of inquiry.[7] Isham would have to be turned over to the sheriff and held in jail until this step was taken. Dorroh wasted no time, however, and on that same Saturday took Isham into the presence of Justice of the Peace William ("Baptist Billy") Woods in Salem. William Woods was an old friend of the Lewis family. Lilburne had named him as one of his executors. Woods had left Albemarle County, Virginia, about a year before and settled near Salem. Having read the report of the coroner's jury, Woods wrote his decision across the top of the coroner's report: "At a court held for the coroner's inquest of Isham Lewis charged with being accessory to the murder of Lilburne Lewis, ordered that said Isham Lewis be acquitted, Given under my hand this 11th day of Apl. 1812. Wm. Woods." Even though he had been a justice of the peace for only a little over three months, Baptist Billy must have known that he had stretched the law rather thin in Isham's behalf.[8] At that point Isham was free from the charge of accessory to Lilburne's self-destruction.

Baptist Billy Woods was about sixty-four years old at this time, and had come by his nickname years before in Albemarle, where there were three residents of the county by the name of William Woods. In order to distinguish among them one was nicknamed Surveyor Billy, another Beaver Creek Billy, and the friend of the Lewises was called Baptist Billy because he was a minister in the Baptist Church. In Virginia the Reverend William Woods was regarded as an independent person of "real ability and genuine magnetism." It is said that in his younger days he was tall and handsome and that he long retained his manly beauty. He was considered wealthy, and always rode a splendid horse accompanied by his faithful body servant, Ben.[9] His worldly appearance and independent ways sometimes disturbed the stricter members of his church. Occasionally he was called to account for denominational errors, but was always acquitted. Once, although he was exonerated from a charge of drunkenness, it was recognized that he drank "too freely."[10]

On another occasion, during the Revolution, Baptist Billy had lent his horses and wagons to move military supplies on Sunday. Upon being called to account for Sabbath breaking, Woods replied that in great emergencies he knew no difference between his patriotism and his religion. Woods and Thomas Jefferson were warm personal friends who exchanged frequent visits, Woods at Monticello, and Jefferson at Woods's church a mile west of Charlottesville. Both men were staunch Republicans in sentiment, and it was at Jefferson's insistence that Baptist Billy temporarily resigned the ministry in order to enter politics. He was popular in Albemarle and was elected to the Virginia legislature.[11]

It is clear that there was very little justification for the action taken by Baptist Billy in Isham's behalf. His reasoning is difficult to understand, but the fact is, he let Isham go free on the charge of accessory to suicide. He may have wanted to do a favor for a relative of his old friend, Thomas Jefferson; or, on the other hand, Isham may have lied to Baptist Billy. There were other members of the county court in Livingston who thought that Woods had acted improperly. On the next day, Sunday the twelfth, Justice of the Peace Gen. Jonathan Ramsey issued a warrant for the re-arrest of Isham:

298

Commonwealth of Kentucky
Livingston County
  Whereas human inquest lately held on the body of Lilburne
Lewis, found dead. The Jurors on their oaths having returned, that
the said Lilburne murdered himself and that Isham Lewis was
present foloniously aiding and abetting the said Lilburn in the said
murder, these and therefore to command you in the name of the
commonwealth to take the body of said Isham Lewis if to be found
and him safely keep so that you have him before me so that the
above charge may be further inquired into and be further dealt
with agreeable to law herein fail not given under my hand and seal
this 12th day of April 1812.

J. Ramsey[12]

  General Ramsey gave the warrant to Deputy Sheriff Thomas
Champion, who served it on Isham and brought him before
General Ramsey and another justice of the peace, Joseph Reed,
for reexamination. Joseph Reed was the senior member of the
county court, and would replace Robert Kirk as sheriff when
Kirk's term in office expired eight months later.[13] Ramsey and
Reed, acting within their authority as members of the county
court to institute criminal proceedings, examined Isham.[14] They
reached their decision, scratched out the order of acquittal that
Baptist Billy had written on the report of the coroner's jury, and
wrote their findings on the back of the warrant for Isham's arrest.

  We certify that an examining into the charge contained in the
  within warrent the said Isham Lewis acknowledged in our presence
  that he was present when Lilburn Lewis killed himself and that he
  had consented to kill said Lilburn himself and went to the graveyard for that purpose and that he cut the stick and brought to said
  Lilburn with which he pushed the trigger when he killed himself.
            Given under our hands and seals this
            12th April 1812   J. Ramsey J. P.
                                                    Jos. Reed J. P.[15]

  The next step taken by Ramsey and Reed followed the statute
law exactly. "Two justices shall enquire into the truth thereof,
and if they shall be of opinion that the accused ought to be tried
before the circuit court, the said justices shall, by a warrent
under their hands, commit the person so charged to the jail of
his county . . . there to remain until the first day of the next circuit court."[16] Isham was handed over to Thomas Champion,

who took him over to the hewn log jail, put him inside, and locked the door.

Isham was now held as accomplice in two killings, George's murder and Lilburne's suicide. It seems likely that the reason Justices of the Peace Ramsey and Reed sent Isham to jail was not to ensure that he would stand trial for Lilburne's suicide, but rather to be certain of his presence at his trial for the murder of George, the charge upon which he had been released on bail.

Baptist Billy, deliberately or not, had given Isham a chance to flee—only one night, as it turned out—but Isham had not made use of the opportunity. There were sixty-four days left before the circuit court was to convene again on June fifteenth. It appeared that Isham would stand trial.

At this same time the earthquake was fading away. On the day after Isham was put in jail, the scientist, Jared Brooks, wrote in his notebook: "This is the 120th day of the continuance of the earthquakes, and, from the manner of moderating, it is to be hoped they will soon cease and let the earth repose again."[17] The murder of George and the subsequent stumblings of the law toward justice coincided almost exactly in time and duration with the paroxysms of the earthquake. In both of these events, however, there remained a few more tremors.

The foregoing reconstruction of Lilburne's suicide and Isham's legal difficulties is based primarily on the court records. There are two other sources that give somewhat variant accounts of the suicide. One is the short news article in the *Kentucky Gazette:*

> Capt. Lilbourn and Isham Lewis ... mutually agreed, the week before last, to destroy each other, and met with their rifles for that purpose on the plantation of Cap. Lilburn Lewis. Lilburn stood on his first wife's grave—Isham a few steps from him—Lilburn received a ball through his heart and fell without discharging his gun, which was found cocked and loaded on the ground with him. ... Isham is confined in Salem jail, where it is said he confessed the above particulars, but at present denies them.[18]

The other version of the suicide pact comes from the letter of Reverend William Dickey, parts of which have been quoted earlier.

> He proposed to his brother Isham, who had been his accomplice in the George affair, that they should finish the play of life with a still

300

deeper tragedy. The plan was, that they would shoot one another. Having made the hot-brained bargain, they repaired with their guns to the graveyard, which was on an eminence in the midst of his plantation. It was inclosed with a railing, say thirty feet square. One was to stand at one railing, and the other over against him at the other. They were to make ready, take aim, and count deliberately 1, 2, 3, and then fire. Lilburn's will was written, and thrown down open beside him. They cocked their guns and raised them to their faces; but the peradventure occurring that one of the guns might miss fire, Isham was sent for a rod, and when it was brought, Lilburn cut it off at about the length of two feet, and was showing his brother how the survivor might do, provided one of the guns should fail; (for they were determined upon going together;) but forgetting, perhaps, in the perturbation of the moment that the gun was cocked, when he touched the trigger with the rod the gun fired, and he fell, and died in a few minutes—and was with George in the eternal world, where *the slave is free from his master.* But poor Isham was so terrified with this unexpected occurrence and so confounded by the awful contortions of his brother's face, that he had not nerve enough to follow up the play, and finish the plan as was intended, but suffered Lilburn to go alone. The negroes came running to see what it meant that a gun should be fired in the grave-yard. There lay their master, dead! They ran for the neighbors. Isham still remained on the spot. The neighbors at first charged him with the murder of his brother. But he, though as if he had lost more than half his mind, told the whole story; and the course or range of the ball in the dead man's body agreeing with his statement, Isham was not farther charged with Lilburn's death.[19]

Dickey was mistaken in at least one point in the above version, for Isham was "farther" charged in Lilburne's death. It is highly probable that Dickey's account contains other errors. There is no question that this version of his is based on hearsay. Furthermore, it was written twenty-five years after the event.[20] Evaluating sources of this kind, where obvious error and apparent truth are found in the same short paragraph, is uncertain work. For example, near the end of the letter, Dickey used his imagination with abandon. "The Court sat—Isham was judged to be guilty of a capital crime in the affair of George. He was to be hanged at Salem. The day was set. My good old father visited him in the prison—two or three times talked and prayed with him; I visited him once myself. We fondly hoped that he was a sincere penitent. Before the day of execution came, by some means, I never knew what, Isham was *missing.*"

In this quotation the errors are: Isham was not judged to be guilty; he was not sentenced to be hung; the day was not set. The statements that appear to be credible are that Dickey and his father visited Isham in jail, prayed with him, and hoped that he was a sincere penitent. The one statement that is undisputed fact is that when the circuit court convened in June, Isham was missing. He had somehow or other escaped from the Salem jail. Isham was only one of many who had carried off that particular feat in Livingston County.

The circuit court order book contains the following terse entry: "Ordered that Thomas Champion be allowed seventy-five cents per day for guarding the Jail of said county twenty-three days while Isham Lewis was confined therein for murder and that the same be certified to the County Court of Livingston."[21] It is possible that Champion was suspected of complicity in Isham's escape. For some reason the county court did not pay Champion his $17.25 for guard duty, at least not at once, for a year later the circuit court again ordered the county court to pay this fee.[22]

However he accomplished it, Isham did make good his escape on May fifth, forty-one days before his case was scheduled to be heard. He fled the county. There is no indication that he ever returned. In July, Justice of the Peace James Henderson was ordered by the court to repair the locks of the jail.[23]

· 30 ·

THE ORPHANS

WHEN THE three Lewis families had come to Livingston County in 1808, full of hope for the future, there were, altogether, six adults, twelve children, Lucy's three unmarried daughters, and about twenty-four slaves. Four years later, in the spring of 1812, of the white adults there remained only the oldest, Col. Charles L. Lewis. There were thirteen grandchildren and the colonel's three daughters, who had not yet married. Randolph's slaves were still with the family, as were Colonel Lewis's old domestics, without whom he would have been "in infinite distress, without any aid or means of subsistance."[1] He had not lost his slaves, but his burdens and troubles had multiplied beyond imagination. He, the patriarch of the family, fifty-nine years old, with few means and little help, faced the nearly impossible task of taking care of and providing for his daughters and grandchildren.

When Randolph wrote his will he assumed that his wife, Mary, together with his two administrators, Lilburne and Colonel Lewis, would be able to manage his estate and care for his children. After Mary died early in 1812, and the children were orphaned, Colonel Lewis and his daughters kept Randolph's family together as best they could without much, if any, help from Lilburne. As executor and administrator, Colonel Lewis could collect and spend funds from Randolph's estate in behalf of the orphans. But after Lilburne's suicide, Colonel Lewis was unable to cope with all the new problems. The family had almost no cash on hand, and it became necessary to sell the possessions of Randolph's family at auction in order to provide for the children.

The preliminaries of this step were taken at a meeting of the county court held just eleven days after Lilburne shot himself. Colonel Lewis gave up control of Randolph's estate and Amos Persons and Mark Phillips were then appointed administrators.[2] At this same session of county court the inventory and appraisal of Randolph's estate, which had been made almost a year before, was entered in the court records. It was not a detailed accounting, and did not list Randolph's land holdings, but his other possessions, including slaves and livestock, were evaluated at $2,746.[3] Persons and Phillips, who had taken over Randolph's estate from Colonel Lewis, scheduled the sale for May 12, three weeks later.

In two respects Randolph's and Mary's orphans were lucky. Almost all the information about Randolph's old neighbor, Amos Persons, and Lilburne's brother-in-law, Mark Phillips, indicates that these two men were well thought of and competent. The children were also more fortunate than other orphans whose parents had left them too little or no property at all. There was a law to cover such cases:

> Every orphan who hath no estate, or not sufficient for maintenance out of the profits, shall, by order of the court of the county in which he or she resides, be bound apprentice until the age of twenty-one years, if a boy, or of sixteen years, if a girl, to some master or mistress, who shall covenant to teach the apprentice some art, trade or business, to be particularized in the indenture, as also reading and writing, and, if a boy, common arithmetic, including the rule of three, and to pay him or her three pounds and ten shillings, and a decent new suit of clothes, at the expiration of the time; which indenture shall be approved by the court and recorded.[4]

Bound apprenticeship for orphans was not unknown in Livingston County. About six months before Persons and Phillips took over as administrators of Randolph's estate, a young boy was so indentured by the county court. "Ordered that William Robeson, a poor orphant, be bound to Michael Stout to learn the trade, art, or mistery of farming untill he becomes 21 years of age, being three years of age the 25th of September last."[5]

Statute law gave full power and authority in all matters concerning orphans to the county courts, except when a parent's will had made specific provisions for the custody of children.[6] In cases where the orphans were not destitute and the court appointed guardians, the law was rather detailed in describing the duties and powers given to the guardian, with most attention being given to the guardian's handling of the orphan's share of the parent's estate. Far less was said about the way the orphan was to be cared for and treated. In short, the guardian controlled the orphans, body, soul, and pocketbook. The guardian was bonded, and could be replaced if the court disapproved of his conduct, but in the case of Randolph's children the guardians appeared to have been men of acceptable character.

On the day of Randolph's auction his family was broken up forever. In the sale the administrators held back some of the items which the children would have to have in order to survive: furniture, some cooking utensils, and personal items such as clothes. All that remained was sold: the livestock; the cooking, cloth-making, and farming equipment; and the slaves were rented out to the highest bidder.[7] Of the twenty-three different persons who bought things at the sale, the largest purchaser was Randolph's oldest son, Charles, who had turned twenty-one by that time.[8] He rented his father's farm and slave man, Andrew, and bought enough of the livestock and tools to farm on a small scale.[9] Evidently he intended to keep house for himself, as best he could, with the other items he bought: a featherbed, counterpane, a large iron kettle, candle mold, and three chairs. Where he got the money for these items is unknown, but it is apparent he had some money of his own apart from his father's estate. Charles did not buy any of the books of his father's library, which were sold that day.

Colonel Lewis bought some bed clothes and a few small items. The Rice brothers, Patrick and William, each bought a few books and counterpanes and quilts. These three men, Colonel Lewis and the Rices, had agreed to take on the responsibility of acting as guardians for Randolph's children, and bought the few extra items they would need for the orphans. About a week after the sale the county court met again and directed that Howell, Randolph's second son, be given into the care of William Rice, who had posted a $500 guardian bond.[10] The same procedure was repeated with Randolph's third son, Tucker, who chose Patrick Rice as his guardian. The remaining five of Randolph's children—Mary, Lucy, Susannah, Robert R. (called Randolph), and Warner— went to live with their grandfather and his three grown daughters. The oldest of these children, Mary, was about eleven, and Warner, the baby, was not yet two. Colonel Lewis's daughters were in their early twenties. There were now nine members of Colonel Lewis's household, with only his old servants to aid them. Randolph's slaves had all been rented out at the auction for the remainder of that year.[11] The hardship that the colonel's household experienced from that time on is apparent in a request for money that Colonel Lewis submitted to the "worshipfull Court of Livingston County" a year or two later. He asked the court to repay him for a pair of shoes, two hats, a spelling book, a pair of cotton stockings, and several yards of domestic cloth. Below this list Colonel Lewis wrote the following explanation:

> My Daughters made all the clothing for five of the Dis[ts] children for near twelve months—they could illy spair their time being oblidged to work for their living without compensation. . . .They are of the opinion that the clothing made for them is worth ten dollars if they had not made them I must of hired the making in that event I think the court could not think I should afford it out of my purse. We think the requisition reasonable but at same time submit it to your worships.
>
> Chas. L. Lewis Exctor
for Randolph Lewis Dis[t12]

Sometime prior to this, Colonel Lewis and his daughters had moved to Salem. They may have moved shortly after Lucy's death; the exact timing of the move is unknown, but following Mary's death and the sale of Randolph's things, it is certain that they left the farm on the river. The auction had brought in $462.59. The rental of the land and slaves would continue to bring a little more money into the estate, which Mark Phillips and Amos Persons were to administer. This, and the goodness of the guardians, was all that stood between Randolph's children and indentured service.

As 1812 drew to a close, two events occurred that took some of the pressure off of Colonel Lewis's family in Salem. His daughter, Nancy (Ann M.), sold some property in Virginia for $250, and her sister, Lucy, married a resident of the county, Washington A. Griffin.[13] The property that Nancy sold was the 224-acre tract on the north side of the Rivanna that she had obtained from Isham in 1807.[14] This was the last piece of property in Virginia owned by Colonel Lewis or his children. The sale had come at a good time, but it was not very much.

Not only were the lives of the Lewises at a low ebb, but the War of 1812, which began that June, brought widespread hardship to Kentucky as a whole. A Methodist church historian, writing of the winter of 1812–1813 in Kentucky, recalled:

> Besides that moral lapse so general at such times, the financial condition of the country was deplorable. Jacob Young says: "We began to feel the effects of hard times. War between the United States and Great Britain was progressing. Provisions of all kinds were very high. Flour in some parts of the district was 16 dollars per barrel,

and other provisions in proportion. . . . Winter months came on—
snow fell deep, weather extremely cold—sometimes we had not
much to eat, and suffered greatly at night for bedclothes." Those
who had supplies were much given to extortion from their poorer
neighbors. Some sold corn at two dollars per bushel. . . . A money
madness seized the people, and a mania for wild speculation
prevailed.[15]

While Randolph's children and estate were being cared for by
Colonel Lewis as best he could in Salem, the situation at Rocky
Hill following Lilburne's suicide was even more heart-breaking.
Colonel Lewis was overburdened with Randolph's children and
could not possibly help with Lilburne's five orphans. The oldest
of these, Jane, was fourteen, and Robert, the youngest, was five.
Letitia had left these children a month or more before, and taking her infant son, James, had gone to her father's home in
Salem. There was no one to care for these children at Rocky Hill
except the slaves, who probably did all they could to help in spite
of the nightmarish events through which they had suffered.

In response to this emergency, various neighbors and friends
voluntarily took Lilburne's children into their homes. It was
several weeks before the county court appointed other willing
housekeepers to the job, and authorized payment for the
children's care. A year would pass before legal guardians were
appointed. In the meantime, James McCawley took five-year-old
Robert into his tavern home in Smithland, and Mark Phillips
took Lucy and young Lilburne, aged twelve and ten, into his
home.[16] James Henderson, a blacksmith and justice of the peace
from Salem neighborhood, provided for the oldest girl, Jane,
during this period, and Hamlet Ferguson of Smithland apparently looked after eight-year-old Elizabeth.[17] At various
times during this emergency, other people helped care for Lilburne's orphans. These people who kept the children were paid
two dollars a month per child by the county court.[18]

While Lilburne's children were scattered in different
households, the county court took steps to bring some order into
Lilburne's estate. Letitia's brother, James Rutter, Jr., posted
bond and was appointed curator to collect, take care of, and inventory the property.[19] This was done eleven days after the suicide. In the same court session, the subject of Lilburne's will was
brought up. "It being suggested in court that Lilburn Lewis
decd. had made a last will and Testament and has named execu-

tors in said Will, it's therefore ordered that William Woods, Richard Ferguson, James McCawley, Charles L. Lewis, and Samuel C. Harkins be summoned to Appear at next county court to inform the court whether they intend to qualify as executors to said will of said Lilburn Lewis deceased if any there be."[20]

About a month later, in mid-May, the county court met again and "a paper was exhibited in court purporting to be the last will and testament of Lilburn Lewis." Since no witnesses had signed the will, it was necessary for Colonel Lewis, James McCawley, and William Rice to swear that the shaky handwriting was, in fact, Lilburne's. This satisfied the court, and the will was ordered to be recorded.[21] After this it was necessary to qualify Lilburne's executors. At this point all of the executors named by Lilburne "declared they would not take upon themselves the burden of the administrator or executorship of said decedent's estate." They were evidently either embarrassed by, or fed up with, the whole affair. Baptist Billy Woods not only refused to serve as executor, but also resigned his commission as justice of the peace. He may have received some criticism after Isham's escape from jail two weeks before.

The next step taken that day was to appoint an administrator for the estate. James Rutter, Jr., posted $5,000 bond and was given the job. His securities were his father, his brother William, Mark Phillips, and William Rice. If it were not for the members and in-laws of the Rutter and Rice families, the Lewis children would have been in desperate condition. After James Rutter, Jr., was appointed administrator, the court then picked four commissioners, who appraised Lilburne's estate and turned in their appraisal on June 1, the day before Lilburne's family possessions were to be put on the auction block for public sale.[22] The last business of the May county court in dealing with Lilburne's estate was the motion made by Letitia to appoint three commissioners "to assign, set apart, and make over to the said widow her right of dower in her deceased husband's estate." It was so ordered.[23]

The auction of Lilburne's estate took place at Rocky Hill and lasted for two days. There was a large crowd present, with some seventy different actual buyers taking part. The sale bill, unlike Randolph's, indicates that nearly everything in the house and on the plantation was sold or rented out, except a few head of stray livestock. Lilburne's clothes were sold: "1 pair of small cloaths," his shirts, stockings, waistcoats, "sassamore pantaloons & breeches," and even his militia uniform, "1 military hat, 1 military coat." His "spectakles" were sold, as were his backgammon box, pocket compass, two shot guns, and his library, which must have been one of the better collections of books in the county. All the furniture and dining accessories were put under the hammer, as were the kitchen and farm equipment, horses, cattle, sheep, hogs, geese, ducks, and beehives. The quilts, sheets, pillows, and featherbeds—all were sold, everything down to four fishhooks, which brought twelve and one-half cents. It is likely that sometime before the sale Colonel Lewis, the "beloved" father, had taken possession of Lilburne's special bequests, the things so dear to a Virginia gentleman—his riding horse, his rifle and shot bag, his walking cane, and the dog, Nero.

At the sale Colonel Lewis bought nothing except some gear for the horse Lilburne had given him: a saddle, "sirsengle," bridle, and blanket, all for the cost of $3.96. Letitia was there, too. She spent more than anyone else, nearly ninety dollars, primarily on domestic items: bed sheets and covers, tableware, bedroom furnishings, cruets, candlesticks, and so on. She bid on nothing else except to hire the negro girl, Mary. These items that Letitia bought may have been articles of her dowry which she had taken to Rocky Hill after she married Lilburne.

The total income from the sale was $994.78, more than twice the amount realized at Randolph's auction.[24] Lilburne's slaves and land, which were not sold at this time, made up by far the most valuable part of his estate. The appraised total value of the slaves was listed later as $3,065.[25] Lilburne had mortgaged seven of these slaves to his and Isham's bail securities, and now it appeared that because of Isham's flight, his $500 bond would be forfeited. Lilburne's suicide had voided his own $1,000 bail bond, and his murder suit was abated by the circuit court on June 15.[26] Isham's $500 bond, however, would have to be paid out of Lilburne's estate if there was enough money and, if not, the securities who had signed the bail bond would have to pay. In that event they could exercise their mortgage on the slaves. Even though the slaves were subject to this mortgage, they were rented out at the auction for the remaining seven months of that year. About two months later, after the June term of circuit court met and Isham did not appear, the slave mortgage was recorded in the county court.[27] William C. Rodgers and the other mortgage holders evidently intended to protect themselves.

The estate administrator, James Rutter, Jr., was well aware of this sizable claim against the estate and, at the end of September, he circulated a petition that asked the newly reelected Governor Isaac Shelby to remit the $500 bond.[28] Governor Shelby, who had previously served as Kentucky's first governor, was the brother of Livingston County resident Moses Shelby, who may have been one of the signers of this petition. When the petition was completed, James Rutter, Jr. gave it to Gen. Jonathan Ramsey to deliver to the governor. General Ramsey had been reelected to the Kentucky House of Representatives that August, and would soon be making the trip to Frankfort for the term of legislature that began in early December. Ramsey delivered the petition and the governor's decision was recorded in his journal.

> December 16th, 1812
> The Governor remitted a recognizance and Judgment against William C. Rogers, John Bolen, William Dyer, Francis Hollinshead, and Archibald Cannon, securities for Lilburne and Isham Lewis's appearance before the Livingston Circuit Court at the last June term, which recognizance was forfeited and a Judgment rendered thereon at the last September Term amounting to five hundred dollars which same was likely to be made out of the estate of the Orphan Children of the said Lilburne Lewis who murdered himself before the day for his trial, and the said children being Motherless, and likely to suffer for support if the amount of the said judgment was made out of their estate.[29]

It was a decision that should have pleased everyone. For a while, at least, there was enough money in the estate to care for the children.

There were a few other loose ends of Lilburne's past life that were straightened out that year. On the same day that he was to have stood trial for George's murder, his vacancy in the militia was filled.[30] Three days later war was declared against England. About a month later, Lilburne's vacant position as trustee of Westwood was also filled.[31]

The lawsuit by Dr. Arthur Campbell, which was pending against Lilburne for debt, had dragged on for two years and was not yet decided. Dr. Campbell still pressed his claim against the estate, and finally in the spring of 1814, four years after it had begun, the suit was settled by a jury that awarded Dr. Campbell $19.50, far less than he had earned.[32] There was one more unsettled claim against Lilburne's estate. It was the money Lilburne owed William C. Bradburn of Harrodsburg for boarding Lilburne's two daughters, Lucy and Jane, for a year and a half. Lilburne had paid nothing on the account, and, in the spring of 1813, Henry F. Delany took the case and sued the estate for $300. In the document Delany claimed that Lilburne, his former client, had "contrived and fraudulently intended to cheat" Bradburn out of the money. It may have been true but, on the other hand, legal phraseology can be self-serving. In any event, the suit was settled out of court that fall.[33]

· 31 ·

DURING THE WAR

THE NEWS OF the declaration of war was received with great joy in Kentucky. The citizens in the western counties had been harassed by Indians long enough, they felt, and now they could convert their anger into action. Things had not gone well at first. Hull's surrender of his army to the British in Canada without a fight was a disgrace that cried for revenge, and the killing of a number of families near the Ohio River in the Indiana territory had frightened the settlers there so much that hundreds of them fled south into Kentucky.[1]

In Livingston County, Moses Shelby, the governor's brother, was given command of a mounted company in the First Regiment of Kentucky Mounted Militia.[2] The seventy men of this company from west Kentucky volunteered on September 18 to serve under Gen. Samuel Hopkins north of the Ohio as part of an expedition to destroy Indian villages and winter supplies. This foray of two thousand men was poorly organized and supplied, and turned out to be a fiasco, which was described with disgust by William C. Rodgers in a letter to the editor of the Lexington *Reporter*.[3]

From time to time during the previous four years, in fact ever since the Lewises had come to Livingston, militia units had patrolled intermittently along the east bank of the Tennessee River in Livingston and Caldwell counties, where the more isolated settlers had a genuine fear of Indian raids.[4] By 1812 hostile Indian activities on the borders of Livingston County had increased alarmingly. In the spring Gen. Jonathan Ramsey, "knowing it to be indispensably necessary for the peace and security of the frontier neighborhood," called out militia units to guard the citizens and continued the patrols all through that summer in Livingston and Caldwell counties. The cost of this activity was nearly $3,500, which General Ramsey requested from the legislature.[5]

Again, in the next year, county residents petitioned the governor for protection along the frontier of the Chickasaw hunting grounds.[6] Governor Shelby wrote to General Ramsey and asked him to confer with his regimental commanders to determine if another patrol was necessary. The cost of such militia patrols to the state treasury caused the governor some concern. Ramsey sent the decision of his officers to the governor: "We give it as our decided opinion that a guard on the aforesaid frontier, is essential and necessary, as nothing short of a measure of that kind will, in our opinion, prevent the settlements between the Tennessee and Cumberland Rivers from breaking up; many have moved away. We are also of opinion that there ought to be at least forty men ordered as a guard, or more if the governor's instructions would have authorized it."[7] The governor approved, and the militia was called out again in Livingston. Even though the people in Smithland and Salem were not immediately threatened, it was a time of some excitement in the county.

For the members of the Lewis family, simple survival was more of an issue than protection from Indian raids. In the Kentucky legislature, newly elected Senator John Gray, who had prosecuted Lilburne and Isham, proposed a bill to amend the law respecting executors, administrators, and heirs. This bill, which passed the house in January, permitted the circuit court in certain cases to sell the real estate and slaves of infants.[8] Gray probably had the situation of the Lewis orphans in mind here, but it did not become necessary to sell Randolph's or Lilburne's land in order to support the children. Nonetheless, the burden on Colonel Lewis's family in Salem was great. In April 1813, the county court gave Colonel Lewis nearly $100 out of Randolph's estate for taking care of Randolph's five youngest children during the previous year. It was at this time that two of Randolph's children, Mary and Susannah, were sent back to Virginia to live, presumably with some of their many relatives.[9] The other three struggled on with Colonel Lewis and his daughters for another year, until finally Colonel Lewis was forced to ask the county court to take them off his hands. "The two oldest of the children I have brought to court for the purpose of the court to take charge of, my situation being such as not to atherize my keeping any longer. The youngest, with the permission of the court, I am willing to keep longer."[10]

The aging colonel was now utterly desperate and, conspiring with his daughters, concocted a scheme to bilk his own son-in-law, Craven Peyton, out of the 650-acre Buck Island in Albemarle. The plan was as dishonest as it was intricate. Most surprising of all is the fact that Craven Peyton, the intended victim of the swindle, had for years treated the Lewis family with the greatest generosity, and had come to their rescue time after time. The background of this scheme is discussed in some detail in chapter six, but briefly, it began in 1802, when Colonel Lewis gave his son, Charles, lifetime control of the 650-acre tract. If Charles married he was to have the tract in fee simple, but if Charles died unmarried it was to be divided among the colonel's daughters. The involvement of the daughters in this document of transfer to Charles was kept a secret from Craven Peyton, who subsequently bought out all of Charles's interest for $5,000 and then paid Colonel Lewis $5,000 more for the same land. Colonel Lewis told Peyton that the gift of the land to Charles was "conditional," but he lied about the conditions, saying that he held an interest in the property. He did not tell Peyton what the true conditions were, hence Peyton paid twice for the land. Now, twelve years later, Colonel Lewis intended to prove that his daughters owned the 650-acre tract because his son, Charles, had died single.[11]

Colonel Lewis's three daughters had lived in Peyton's home for five years during their childhood. As their mother, Lucy, had told Jefferson, "Mr. Peyton has been . . . to my daughters as long as they were undar his guidance, as the most just and affectionate farthar." In return for Peyton's kindness, the three daughters joined their father, Colonel Lewis, in the conspiracy and retained as their agent Thomas Jefferson, Jr., the son of Randolph Jefferson and namesake nephew of the retired president. Thomas Jefferson, Jr. was also the first cousin and brother-in-law of the three Lewis sisters who lived in Kentucky. He had married their older sister, Mary, and now they were all scheming to get the 650 acres away from Craven Peyton and his wife, Jane, who was the eldest of the five Lewis sisters. It was an almost unbelievable family tangle of greed and deception.

The three sisters in Livingston County recorded their power of attorney in the court house at Salem.

> Know all men by these presents that we Washington A. Griffin, and Lucy His wife, formerly Lucy Lewis, Martha C. Lewis, Ann M. Lewis of the state of Kentucky have constituted and by these presents do constitute Thomas Jefferson junior esq. of the state of Virginia our attorney to prosecute for us any suit . . . to recover any

lands to which we may be legally entitled ... and especially to
reduce to possession for us our interest respectively in an estate of
Buck Island containing 650 acres of land situated in the county of
Albemarle in the state of Virginia aforesaid now in the occupancy
of a certain Craven Peyton and claimed by us by virtue of a deed
executed by Charles L. Lewis and Lucy his wife bearing date of
30th July 1802 and duly recorded in the court of the county aforesaid.[12]

Craven Peyton must have been horrified when he learned of
this scheme. He asked his aging friend, Jefferson, for an opinion
on the case, and the reply came from Monticello that the deed
from Colonel Lewis to Peyton was binding on Colonel Lewis,
even though it had not been recorded within the prescribed time
limit. Although there was some question about this delay, Jefferson felt that Peyton's deed became good when Peyton finally
recorded it.[13] In spite of Jefferson's opinion, Colonel Lewis and
his daughters persisted in their efforts, and two years later
Peyton received an opinion from two Virginia lawyers saying
that Peyton had a strong case. Peyton then wrote again to his old
friend and business partner at Monticello, asking for his evalua-
tion of Peyton's position:

Dear Sir   Monteagle June 26–17
You was so good as to say you woud give me your opinion, On the
Deed from Lewis to Lewis, I have therefore sent a copy by my son
with the opinions of Messrs Markham & Wirt they appear to
entartain no doubt, indeed if the case was a doubtful one I woud
endeavor to compromise, Your goodness in complying with my
wishes in this case, will lay me, undar the greatest obligation to you,
with Sincere Esteem yrs

                                            C. Peyton[14]

After Jefferson received this letter he jotted down some notes
on the back referring to some of the legal technicalities involved
in the controversy, and then he wrote down several strong
points that he thought were in Peyton's favor. Briefly, they note
that Peyton was a bona fide purchaser and that he had paid full
and valuable consideration for the land. Jefferson further wrote
that the daughters had participated in a fraudulent silence. Of
Colonel Lewis's actions Jefferson said, "Not only the silence of
C. L. Lewis on executing the deed to Peyton, but the import of
that deed itself convicts him of gros fraud & disqualifies him
from being a witness."[15]

315

In time the controversy was either settled or abandoned, for Peyton still owned the land at his death many years later. This incident can leave no doubt about the nature of the personal feelings of Thomas Jefferson at this time. The son of his brother and the husband and daughters of his sister had conspired basely to defraud one of his own most loyal friends.

Back in Livingston County, when Randolph's oldest son, Charles, became of age, he began proceedings to obtain his share of his father's estate. The April county court appointed commissioners to set aside his part. This procedure dragged on for a year, and then Charles sued his brothers and sisters, a necessary legal step for the division of the estate.[16] At this time guardians were appointed to represent Randolph's orphans in court, and the slaves belonging to the estate were ordered to be sold.[17] Notice was posted and the sale was held in January. It appears from the court records that feeble old Frank, who had been converted into the church by Reverend William Dickey, was sold away from his wife, Sarah:

Negro Judy to Jesse Roberts at $455.56¼
Negro Andrew to Jesse Roberts at $450.56¼
Negro Matilda and old Sarah to Aaron Threlkeld $431.56¼
Negro Frank to John Mott at $19.00
Negro Aggie to William Gordon & Company $400.00
Total $1,756.68¾
William Rice Commissioner[18]

In the spring of 1815 the court ordered the proceeds of the slave sale to be divided equally among the eight children. They each received nearly $220. In the case of the minor children the money was given to the legal guardians. A year later fifty acres were measured off of Randolph's farm and given to Charles as his portion of his father's plantation.[19] This tract, which fronted on the Ohio, Charles kept for a year or two and then sold for $100, about a third less than his father had paid for the same land ten years earlier.[20]

One of the more intriguing questions about the members of the Lewis family is what happened to Isham after he escaped from jail in 1812. The only certain answer is that he disappeared. Reverend William Dickey's letter, written in 1837, gives one version of Isham's adventures. Even though Dickey's account is presented as fact, it is probably not entirely accurate.

Dickey closed his letter with this paragraph about Isham: "About two years after, we learned that he had gone down to Natchez, and had married a lady of some refinement and piety. I saw her letters to his sisters, who were worthy members of the church of which I was pastor. The last letter told of his death. He was in Jackson's army, and fell in the famous battle of New Orleans."[21] Dickey's statement about Isham's fate was accepted as true and used in subsequent recountings of the Lewis story, notably Watts's *Chronicles of a Kentucky Settlement* and the Atlanta H. T. Pool newspaper article published in the *Louisville Courier-Journal,* June 10, 1894. Both of these accounts add one detail to Dickey's version. They state that Isham enlisted in the army under an assumed name. That Isham took an alias seems reasonable, but there is some doubt about his service in the army.

Shortly after its publication, the Pool newspaper article was reprinted in the Lewis family genealogical publication, *Lewisiana.* The reprinting of Pool's article drew a highly critical letter from a reader of *Lewisiana,* John M. McAllister, a genealogist and lawyer who was distantly related to the Lewises of Livingston County.[22] There is no question that Pool's article is riddled with factual errors and speculations, but, on the other hand, it also appears that Mr. McAllister may have been trying to shield the reputation of his distant relatives, the Lewises.

By J. M. McAllister Atlanta, Ga.

I have read in a late number of LEWISIANA what purports to be, an account of the tragic end of Lilburn and Isham Lewis by Atlanta H. Taylor Pool. That there is enough truth in this to give colour to the fiction there can be no doubt, but as a whole, it is a sensational "newspaper story." The record of the indictment and the tradition of the suicide of Lilburn Lewis, are no doubt true, the balance is fiction pure and simple, built upon these facts. Nor is there anything, except the imagination of the writer, to sustain the theory that the indictment had any foundation, or in any way gave rise to the suicide. What "Pool" says in regard to the suicide and its causes, is entitled to the same credit, as is his account of Isham Lewis after the suicide and no more, and this latter is absolutely incredible.

My uncle, Robert Lewis Cobbs, was surgeon of Coffee's Brigade at the Battle of New Orleans. He attended all the wounded and saw all the dead. There were only thirteen (six were killed) altogether. Isham Lewis was not there. My uncle had been in Ky. with his Lewis relatives and knew Isham personally. He [the uncle] spent

317

the last eight years of his life at my mother's in Va. and from time to time gave me most minute accounts of the battle.

It is not my intention to come to the defence of any one, in contravention of history, but in the interest of the "truth of history" to combat fiction as far as possible. The whole history of this affair is that Lilburn and Isham Lewis were indicted, that Lilburn suicided and that Isham was never brought to trial.[23]

Reverend William Dickey and the sources of legend claim that Isham was killed in the Battle of New Orleans, and Mr. McAllister denies it. Adding some substance to Dickey's statement is a short entry in the Livingston circuit court order book dated March 20, 1815, a little over two months after the battle: "The Commonwealth—Plaintiff, against Isham Lewis—Defendant, On an indictment for murder: Ordered that this suit abate by the death of the defendant."[24] Someone had told the court that Isham was dead, and the officers of the court apparently believed it.

There is no way at this time to prove what actually happened to Isham after his escape. It seems doubtful that he would go to Natchez, even under an alias, for he was known in the city and there was a court judgment outstanding against him for a debt of over $250.[25]

This paragraph is offered as one theory of what happened to Isham. It is guesswork. After fleeing Livingston, he assumed an alias and went south, possibly to New Orleans, where he found some employment and married. His wife corresponded with Isham's sisters from time to time. When the Battle of New Orleans occurred, Isham took advantage of the situation to have his murder indictment quashed. The false news of his death was reported back to Livingston in a letter from Isham's wife, or perhaps by some returning Livingston County soldiers who knew Isham and joined in his scheme. The indictment was dismissed, and Isham Lewis was never heard from again in Livingston.

A month after Isham's indictment was dismissed, Isham's sister, Martha, married a Livingston man by the name of Daniel Monroe. Monroe, a cabinet maker, had lost all his possessions in a fire a few days before the wedding and he and Martha were in great need of help. As her father and most of her brothers and sisters had done at various times before, she turned to her uncle,

Thomas Jefferson, and in a piteous letter asked him for assistance.

Salem Kentucky August 6th, 1815

My Dear Uncle

Some time has elapsed since we have been favored with a line from you, or indeed any of our friends, except my Father. Feeling quite anxious to hear from you, And at the same time knowing it to be my duty to write to you as an Uncle, I take the liberty of forwarding a few lines by my friend. Yea and a friend to Mankind Mr. Woods who has promised to deliver it himself. I have written Cousin Martha Randolph three times and have not received a line from you since I have been in Kentucky, it is dear Uncle a maval impossible for me to describe to you the heart rending troubles we have experienced since we left virginia. I dare say you are not unapprised of some of it, However since the 21 of April last I have been somewhat happier, as on the evening of that day, I married a man who has been as Kind to me as you can possibly conceive, we are quite poor but happy. Mr. Woods can tell you as much or more than I can write concerning him. Mr. Woods dear Uncle the last time he was in virginia suggested that you wished to send some money for our benefits, If so you will be so good as to send by Mr. Woods my friend as there will be certainty of receiving what you send. A few days before Marriage my husband met with a loss to loose all he owned by fire, therefore I can not show our circumstances more plainly. With due Respect I remain your affectionate

M.A.C. Monroe[26]

The coolness of Jefferson and his daughter, Martha Randolph, toward the Lewises is evident in this letter from Colonel Lewis's daughter, who had written her cousin three times without receiving an answer. However distant Martha Randolph wished to remain, it seems that her father, Thomas Jefferson, had some compassion for the Lewises, for at one time he intended for Baptist Billy to deliver a gift of money to them.

By the time Martha Lewis Monroe wrote this letter, her father had returned to Virginia to live. The last record of the colonel's presence in Livingston was in June of the previous year.[27] After Randolph's children had been put in guardians' hands and two of the colonel's three daughters had married, there was little left for him in Kentucky.

In the fall of 1815, the guardianship of five-year-old Warner, Randolph's youngest child, was transferred to Martha and her

319

husband, Daniel Monroe, and when they moved to New Orleans shortly afterward they took the child with them.[28] Randolph's family of ten was completely broken up. Both parents had died, four of the children had returned to Virginia, one was in New Orleans, two were in the care of guardians in Salem, and the oldest son was engaged in subsistence farming a few miles from Smithland. If Randolph had lived he would have been forty-two years old.

During this period the remnants of Lilburne's family, while not so widely dispersed, were in an equally unfortunate situation. Prior to 1813, the children had been boarding at various homes in Livingston. In May the court ordered that they be bound out to legal guardians, which was done before the end of the year.[29] In December Lilburne's estate was split up by court order so that Letitia could receive her portion. The ten slaves were appraised and four of them, equal to one-third of the total value, were assigned to Letitia.[30] The six remaining slaves, valued at $2,045, were rented out from year to year to provide income for the estate. Sometime during the next year and a half Letitia remarried, and in August of 1815 her new husband, Christopher G. Houts, the ex-deputy sheriff, was made legal guardian of Lilburne's youngest child, James.[31]

For the several years following 1813 the county order books list payments to the guardians of Lilburne's orphans for the childrens' board and keep. One of these was an entry involving James McCawley, guardian of seven-year-old Robert: "May 16, 1814. Ordered that James McCawley, Guardian to Robert Lewis, infant orphan of Lilburne Lewis decd. be allowed $19.50 per acct. filed and sworn to in open court; for boarding and burial expenses to said infant." McCawley had carried the boy's body to Rocky Hill and laid him to rest beside his parents, Elizabeth and Lilburne. This was the third and last grave to be dug in the lonesome plot on Rocky Hill.[32]

Lilburne's other children grew up in Livingston County, and years later three of them, Lilburne, Elizabeth, and James, moved to Missouri.[33] Their sister, Lucy, remained in Livingston County and died there before she reached the age of twenty-seven. Jane eventually returned to Albemarle and married her first cousin, Peter Field Jefferson. This was the third successive, direct-line, first cousin marriage between the Lewis and Jefferson families.[34] With the possible exception of the Randolphs of Virginia, no family was as intricately intermarried with the Jeffersons as were the Lewises of Albemarle and Livingston.

The tragedy of the families was now complete. The Lewises had come to West Kentucky in 1808 comparatively well-to-do and with high hopes and excellent prospects. In the course of the next six years the unity of the family was gradually, inexorably, and utterly destroyed. The causes of their downfall lay partly in the time and the place, but most of all in themselves.

· 32 ·

THE AFTEREFFECTS

In Livingston County the crime had a profound effect on the surviving members of the Lewis family, as has been shown. As for the other citizens, a few of them found their lives changed, as well. One such person was Dickson Given, the assistant circuit judge. Given was deeply disturbed by the way the county court handled the affairs of the Lewis orphans. The court had clearly acted within the provisions of the law regarding orphans, and Colonel Lewis had voluntarily relinquished three of his grandchildren into the court's care, but, nevertheless, the plight of the Lewis children made Given fearful for the future of his own children if he should die. One legal step that could be taken to prevent orphans from falling under the jurisdiction of the county court was for a person to make specific provision for the guardianship of his own children in a will.[1] Given took this step and wrote his will in 1816, when he was thirty-two years of age. It was unusual at that time for a will to be written except when death appeared imminent, but Given, if he did not anticipate death, feared it for his children's sake. He lived fourteen years after writing these provisions into his bequest:

> Frankfort 12th July 1816
>
> In the name of God Amen. I Dickson Given of the County of Livingston and State of Kentucky now on a lengthy journey and sound in mind, memory, etc. but knowing the uncertainty of human life. If I never should return from s^d. journey to Philadelphia make this my last will and testament. . . . [Three routine provisions deleted].
>
> 4th. I wish my ever beloved Brother Joseph R. Given, my present partner and only brother, to be my executor to take charge of all my earthly efects and I wish him not to be bound in any security. I further wish him, in case my beloved wife should ever marry again, a thing I think likely as she is yet young, to take charge of my children and put them out to school and not suffer them to live with a step father, as step fathers are so apt to abuse children. I wish here to observe, for fear my ever dear wife may think this hard as she has suffered many pains and fatigues in raising those children, that I have the utmost confidence in her and, if I should never see her more, I will here observe that I believe I have been

blessed with one of the most affectionate and beloved companions that ever man was blessed with; but if her 2nd husband was to go to abuse my children what could a womans arm do to hinder such abuse; and my blood runs cold now in my *veighens* to think of my little darling Babes receiving the stripes from a step father,—I should be glad if my wife could reconcile it to herself to never marry, and raise our little darlings, and her and my dear Brother conduct their education, both male & female; but this, from the common corse of things, I could hardly expect as she is young. She may now think she will never marry, but I fear will get out of that notion.

5th. . . . I wish my dear wife to have and keep my portrait remembering, at same time, that is the resemblance of a man who was dearly attached to her, and if in the other world we should ever meet and be known to each other, it would be gratifying to me in the extreme to see the partner of all my pleasures and griefs and know at same time she had well done her part below with our dear babes, which lies heaviest on my mind, that and parting with my friends here below. . . .

6th I wish here to observe that one principle reason for making my will at this time is that, if I never should return, I do not wish the County court of Livingston to have any management of my children as I have always thought it was unwisely done by them. I do not wish to hurt the feelings of said court, many, and indeed the most, of them I venerate as men of a great deal of goodness of heart not surpassed by any, but merely the difference of opinion between them and me. . . .

I certify to the world this is my handwriting for above purpose,

Dickson Given[2]

Dickson Given died fourteen years later, in 1830, and two years after that his brother and executor, Joseph, died. In that same year, 1832, Dickson Given's widow, Nancy, as predicted, "got out of the notion" of remaining a widow and married Jonathan Ramsey.[3]

The other assistant circuit judge, Jesse Ford, also made a change in his life. Shortly after Lilburne's suicide, Ford vacated his office and moved out of Livingston County.[4] Ford and Given would have been on the bench if the Lewis brothers' trial had been held. Ford's reason for leaving Livingston County is not known. One could speculate that the Lewis tragedy may have had something to do with his move.

It appears that the only person who benefited from the Lewises' calamity was Commonwealth Attorney John Gray. He

323

had won some recognition for his efforts to prosecute Lilburne and Isham, and, in August 1812, he was elected state senator from Livingston and Caldwell counties.[5]

As for Coroner John Dorroh, there was evidently some controversy over his performance of his official duties. Ten days after Lilburne's suicide, Dorroh's presence in the county court was noted in the following entry: "April 20, 1812, ordered that John Dorroh be fined four dollars for a contempt by him to this court offered by fighting in the presence of said court." Dorroh continued as coroner for three months longer and then resigned.[6]

Like Gray and Dorroh, James McCawley's life was not the same after he became involved with Lilburne. In March, while the first grand jury was debating Lilburne's indictment, McCawley had gotten into an argument with John Harrington, and finally assaulted him "so that his life was greatly dispaired of." The subject of the argument is unknown, but it may have been Lilburne. Two days later Harrington was sworn in as a member of the second grand jury, which indicted both the Lewis brothers. This grand jury also indicted McCawley for his assault on Harrington. McCawley's assault case was tried in June and the jury found him guilty and fined him sixty cents.[7]

On the afternoon of the same day that he was fined sixty cents for assault, McCawley served on a petit jury to try the case of Francis Hollingshead, who was charged with the theft of an iron clivis, worth fifty cents. Hollingshead was one of the bail securities for the Lewis brothers and had been on the coroner's jury to investigate Lilburne's suicide. At this same time Hollingshead held a mortgage on Patsy, one of Lilburne's slaves who had been rented by McCawley. McCawley and the rest of the jury found Hollingshead guilty and sentenced him to receive fourteen lashes on his bare back. The court record then continued; "Whereupon it is ordered that the sheriff take the defd. to the whipping post, if any, if not to any convenient place on the public square and execute the above sentence immediately and that the said defd. be committed until he pay the cost of his prosecution."[8]

The disparity of the sentence McCawley received for assault, a sixty-cent fine, and the one he meted out for a fifty-cent theft, fourteen lashes, is an interesting example of the relative im-

324

portance placed on property rights as opposed to personal rights.

Before this incident, James McCawley had been in the middle of the furor resulting from Lilburne's suicide. Presumably he had honored Lilburne's request to come and bury him. He had proved the handwriting on the will, and then refused to serve as Lilburne's executor. At the same time he resigned as trustee of Smithland.[9] During this period Lilburne's five-year-old son, Robert, came to live at the tavern home of this brutal and contentious man. Robert died two years later of unknown causes. McCawley was a member of the county court that entrusted Robert to his care and paid for the child's upkeep.[10]

Another Livingston resident, Lilburne's lawyer, Henry F. Delany, appears to have been so influenced by the murder that he altered the plans for his life. In 1816 Delany moved out of Livingston to Union County, Kentucky, where two years later he professed religion, renounced the practice of law, and entered the ministry.[11] Delany was converted at a Cumberland Presbyterian camp meeting at the Piney Ford church under the preaching of Reverend Finis Ewing. Three years later Delany was licensed as a minister. It is said that while he was a good lawyer for his time, he became a great preacher, whose piety was deep and uniform, and whose eloquence was engaging and impressive. Probably the most unusual aspect of Delany's pastorate, at least unusual in western Kentucky at that time, is the fact that he became a strong advocate of temperance. His was the first voice raised against alcoholic liquors in the councils of the Cumberland Presbyterian church.[12] Another minister who was present on that occasion, Dr. Richard Beard, described the long-lasting effect of Delany's support of temperance:

> The Cumberland Presbyterian Church is known as a temperance Church. She has, in late years, expressed herself in no uncertain words on this subject; but the introduction of the question was inauspicious. In the course of the sessions of the Synod . . . Rev. Henry F. Delany . . . introduced a resolution about equivalent to the old temperance pledge. It was prefaced by some pertinent and strong remarks on the utter incongruity of intemperance in any form, especially in dram-drinking, with the self-denying work of a minister of Christ. His manner was exceedingly impressive, and his argument seemed to be overwhelming. . . . My own conversion was

deep and abiding. . . . Some of my brethren mildly reproached me
for my new ideas, and occasionally good sisters cracked a joke at my
expense and offered me a toddy, but I held on and kept my field.
At the next Synod . . . I had acquired vigor enough to introduce
the subject myself, and by the aid of two or three older brethren,
the resolution was passed without division.[13]

There is nothing particularly unusual in the fact that Delany
became a preacher. Others in Livingston County, such as the ex-
sheriff, James Johnson, joined the ministry. What is notable is
that it was Delany who introduced the temperance movement
into his church, a policy it has endorsed ever since.

One wonders what caused Delany's antipathy to alcohol. The
murder of George by the drunken Lewis brothers must have
had a tremendous impact on him. As their lawyer, Delany knew
nearly every detail of the crime, and, among its causes, the
excessive use of alcohol is conspicuous. The fact that slavery
existed in Kentucky was another inescapable element in the
crime, but, for understandable reasons, Delany chose to ignore
it. During his entire adult life he was himself a slave owner. In
1810 he owned three slaves, and by the time of his death late in
1830, he had increased this number to twenty.[14]

It appears that Delany, who died a rich man, was not entirely
relaxed about his ownership of slaves. In his will there is an
unusual paragraph in which he urges his wife to make the moral
decision he had neglected himself: "It is my will and wish that if
my family wish it, lands should be purchased in some state
where slavery is not tolerated, where they may settle & I hereby
authorize my executors to do & my wife to remove with the
estate or any part of it she may deem proper to such state."[15]

Delany, who espoused temperance, did not move to a state
where slavery was not tolerated, nor did Rhoda, his wife. She
stayed in Union County and remarried three years later.[16]

Another minister closely involved with the Lewises did move
to a free state. During 1816, the same year that Delany went to
Union County, the pastor of the Lewis family, Reverend William
Dickey, moved to Bloomingburg, Ohio, where he spent the remainder of his life.[17] While Delany preached temperance in
Kentucky, Dickey preached abolition in Ohio, both men
probably motivated, in part, by different aspects of the same
grim episode with which they were so familiar.

What was Jefferson's reaction when he learned what his

nephews had done? No evidence has been discovered to date indicating that Jefferson ever wrote or spoke a word directly concerning this crime, or that it changed his life or attitudes.

Jefferson genuinely detested slavery. His opposition to the institution is well known. Even though most southerners felt that blacks were an inferior race, this opinion was only a "suspicion" in Jefferson's mind, and, at that, one he "hazarded with great diffidence." Furthermore, he insisted that blacks had rights.[18] The problem of negro slavery in America was a source of anguish to him all his life. The news that his nephews had maliciously slaughtered a slave boy surely must have sharpened Jefferson's despair and stirred his anxiety for the future of his nation. As to the deed itself, how could he cope with this evident depravity in his own kin? There was only one answer he could find that was emotionally and reasonably acceptable to him. He believed his nephews were insane at the time of the murder. He did not say so outright, but one of his writings leaves little doubt.

In 1813, about a year after Lilburne's suicide, Jefferson wrote a brief sketch of the life and suicide of his ex-secretary, Meriwether Lewis, attributing the suicide of Meriwether to "hypochondriacal affections." Jefferson continued, "It was a constitutional disposition in all the nearer branches of the family of his name."[19] Jefferson had no doubt that such traits could be passed within families from generation to generation. About two months after Jefferson mentioned the "hypochondriacal affections" in the Lewis family, he wrote to John Adams, saying, "Experience proves that the moral and physical qualities of man, whether good or evil, are transmitted in a certain degree from father to son."[20]

Jefferson's timing, when he wrote this short biography of Meriwether, is intriguing. Meriwether had killed himself four years before Jefferson wrote the account of it. Three years after Meriwether's suicide, another member of that "branch of the family," Jefferson's own nephew, Lilburne Lewis, had destroyed himself after committing an incomprehensible crime. It appears that, although Meriwether was the subject of Jefferson's statement, Lilburne's fate and the family "constitutional disposition" were very much on Jefferson's mind.

It is not known how Jefferson learned the news of the murder and Lilburne's suicide. Baptist Billy or some other of Jefferson's acquaintances in Kentucky might have carried the information to him. On the other hand, the news may have come to Jefferson by mail. If it did, there is no trace of the letter in Jefferson's records.[21]

In spite of its notoriety, this murder had no noticeable impact on the institution of slavery as a whole, probably because the crime did not change the one almost universal conviction that made the existence of slavery possible. This conviction was the seldom-questioned belief that, inherently and by nature, the negro race was inferior to the white race. The dilemma posed by this assumption was stated succinctly by Alexis de Tocqueville long before the Civil War. He said of the problems faced by slaves who had been given their freedom: "To induce the whites to abandon the opinion they have conceived of the moral and intellectual inferiority of their former slaves, the negro must change; but as long as this opinion subsists, to change is impossible."[22]

· 33 ·

THE EPILOGUE

IN TRYING TO understand how this tragedy could have happened one cannot avoid the most important fact that there was an inbred strain of mental instability in Lilburne's family. Jefferson referred to it as "hypochondriacal affections," and stated it was a "constitutional disposition in all the nearer branches of the family." He said further that this was a fact "for whose truth I have no hesitation to make myself responsible." There seems little doubt that at the time of the murder Lilburne was not only deeply disturbed, but drunk as well. This is enough to explain the murder.

The other aspects of the situation—the time, the place, and the circumstances of Lilburne's life—merely set the scene, and were passive elements in the tragedy; nevertheless they deserve some discussion. They cannot all be determined with certainty, for too much of the evidence is missing. The conclusions that follow are therefore based on the author's opinion and should not necessarily be accepted as proven facts.

It was the American frontier, with its siren song of natural wealth, that drew the Lewises into the tide of people migrating to Kentucky. Each emigree had his reason. The rambler wanted room, the hunter wanted pelts, the fugitive wanted anonymity, and bankrupts and debtors wanted a new start. Rich speculators in land wanted greater wealth, young lawyers wanted clients, sons of the influential hoped to found new dynasties, and the multitude of destitute poor wanted a life of some dignity and hope. The frontier was settled by people who had been more or less discontented east of the mountains. The poor had had no chance and the rich were still covetous. The planter had mined out his soil and used up his credit, and the criminal feared the day of his accounting to the law. As long as the frontier existed, Americans could be prodigal. They could find new farms in the west to use up after they had destroyed their ancestral lands in the east. Errors or sloth in business did not mean final ruin as long as the west lay empty. As long as the frontier existed, judgment was suspended for the profligate and incompetent. The

329

awareness of this amnesty of natural wealth is basic in the traditional character of Americans.

Among the multitude of settlers on the frontier was a disproportionate number of social misfits, failures, highwaymen and river pirates, keelboat roughnecks, gamblers, land swindlers, and men who turned to violence for reasons of pleasure or vanity, who fought among themselves as eagerly as they volunteered to wipe out the hated Indians. Violence was a conspicuous frontier reaction to many problems: boredom, personal vanity, child discipline, and the subjugation of slaves, Indians, and law-breakers.

Violence as a characteristic of life in Kentucky was still evident nearly a century after George's murder. A respected Kentucky historian and scholar, discussing the thirty-year period that ended the nineteenth century, said that "one of the most notable features of the period in Kentucky was violence, lawlessness and crime. This was perhaps brought about by war, hatreds, general public callousness and ignorance; by weak-kneed, often venal officials. . . . Kentucky's record in the field of crime was so glaring as to be notorious and disgraceful in the eyes of the nation."[1]

Another factor in the background of Lilburne's crime was the state of his own business affairs. Although there was a severe depression in America, which lasted all during the short remainder of Lilburne's life in Kentucky, nevertheless many if not most businessmen survived it. In Lilburne's case, however, suits for debt were a regular feature of the court docket. He was under constant stress from money troubles.

An equal, if not greater, blow to Lilburne was the death of his first wife, his older brother, and his mother, in less than a two-year period. At that time in the South the family was regarded as a clan, and was cherished far more than in the North. There was a loyalty and sense of mutual obligation which included even the distantly related "kissing cousins."[2] These deaths, which shattered the Lewis family in Livingston, seriously upset the pattern of Lilburne's life. As far as is known, these deaths were not violent or self-inflicted, and it is natural to suppose that if frontier medicine had been less primitive these people might have lived on, sources of strength and reassurance for Lilburne.

The existence of American chattel slavery is perhaps the most important secondary element in this tragedy. Reverend William Dickey, at least, felt that it was. "It is certain, that the state, by making men ... [Lilburne's] property, gave him the opportunity of perpetrating the horrid deed, and therefore it stands first in the list of crimes!"[3] There can be no doubt that slavery supplied the victim and shaped the character of the murderers.

The abject plight of the slaves themselves is perhaps better known than the corrosive effect that the institution had on the character of many slave owners. Jefferson spoke eloquently about this moral erosion:

> There must doubtless be an unhappy influence on the manners of our people produced by the existence of slavery among us. The whole commerce between master and slave is a perpetual exercise of the most boisterous passions, the most unremitting despotism on the one part, and degrading submissions on the other. Our children see this, and learn to imitate it; for man is an imitative animal. . . . The parent storms, the child looks on, catches the lineaments of wrath, puts on the same airs in the circle of smaller slaves, gives a loose to his worst of passions, and thus nursed, educated, and daily exercised in tyranny, cannot but be stamped by it with odious peculiarities. The man must be a prodigy who can retain his manners and morals undepraved by such circumstances. . . . With the morals of the people, their industry also is destroyed.[4]

De Tocqueville also noted that the children of slave owners were imbued from their earliest years with the despotic notion that they were born to command. In addition, slave owners looked upon themselves as members of a social class superior to that of nonslave owners.[5] Visitors to the South were quick to notice the exaggerated sense of personal pride and honor among the slave owners. This arrogance, frequently the cause of duels, was nourished by slavery, they said.[6]

Another element that may have played a part in setting the scene for the murder was the nature of the relationship between Lilburne and Letitia. There are no reliable descriptions of her personality, but the accounts based on tradition relate that she was not only the beautiful belle of the county, but was also a "cold, proud, scornful, young wife."[7] At the time of the murder, Letitia was in the eighth month of her pregnancy, a fact which, considering the times, may indicate a cessation of sexual relations between Letitia and Lilburne. If so, and even though justified, it was one more frustration in Lilburne's life.

Another factor in the background of the murder is mentioned in Reverend William Dickey's account of the tragedy, in which Dickey stated that because of Lilburne's cruelty, his slaves ran away from time to time. This "gave great anxieties [to Lilburne] until he found them or until they had starved out and returned."[8]

The scene was now set for an explosion. A proud, unstable, and haughty self-styled aristocrat had been stripped of nearly everything he valued, seemingly by an unjust and malevolent fate alone. Death had broken up the family leadership and the dreams of a Kentucky empire. Lilburne's inability to cope with his business affairs during an economic depression had wiped out his wealth and exposed his debts to public view. His political influence had been vitiated by local politicians and he was not able to control his slaves.

Lilburne's state of mental anguish anticipates the final ingredient, alcohol. It could bring forgetfulness, blunt the pain, and hide the truth. On the night of December 15. Lilburne's drunken rage found an outlet in George's fragile life. Lilburne's insane outbreak of anger seems almost predictable, although there was no way to tell what form it would take. At that time he might have killed Letitia, or himself. A few elements were still missing, however, before he would lay aside his alcohol in favor of suicide and complete oblivion.

Although Lilburne had vented his wrath on George, the murder had only compounded his problems. Letitia's subsequent flight to the safety of her father's home, about two months after the birth of their son James, was, no doubt, wise and necessary. To Lilburne, however, it probably appeared to be an unmistakable and public rejection. In his will Lilburne gave this as the reason for killing himself. His phrase, "beloved but cruel Letitia," could be interpreted as having sexual implications.

It is a surprising fact, apparent in the will, that Lilburne did not show the slightest trace of guilt over the murder of George, nor did he recognize the murder and subsequent indictment as causes for his suicide.[9] Lilburne showed every expectation of going to heaven and being reunited with his first wife, Elizabeth. This was an unusual interpretation of religious doctrine, for murderers were generally thought to be consigned to hell, along with the suicides. Perhaps, as a Presbyterian, he felt he was one of the elect, and predestined to go to heaven. As for his suicide, he evidently felt that, since he had "fallen victim to his beloved but cruel Letitia," he was blameless. He probably convinced himself that in all his other troubles he was also an innocent victim.

The most puzzling statement in the will is the sentence in which Lilburne pledged Letitia his "forgiveness to your connections." If Lilburne thought that Letitia intended to testify against Isham in his murder trial and thereby implicate Lilburne, he should have said "intentions," instead of "connections." It is possible that in the word "connections" he was referring to her family, the Rutters, who had come and taken her away from him.

Of all the people involved in this incident, Isham is the most mysterious. Very little is known about him. At the time of Lilburne's suicide, Isham was about twenty-six, ten years younger than Lilburne. He had no home of his own and no roots anywhere. In 1809, when Jefferson recommended Isham for a job in Mississippi, he had praised Isham's character. In spite of Isham's defective education, Jefferson said Isham was "worthy of . . . entire confidence" and was "a young man of excellent disposition, correct conduct, and good understanding."[10] Jefferson may have been overly sanguine in this recommendation, for when Isham got to Mississippi, if he ever found a job surveying, he did not hold it for long, and finally fled the area, leaving a sizable bad debt behind him. One other aspect of Isham's personality is obvious in the letter Isham wrote to Jefferson when he asked his uncle to help him find employment. Isham placed all the blame for his situation on his father, whose "foibles, neglect, and false promises of wealth" were at fault, he said. Isham's resentment is clear, and so are his own feelings of self-righteousness. Isham's writing style in the letter was wordy and pretentious in contrast to the precise and beautiful phraseology of Jefferson's reply. Like Lilburne, Isham felt that his troubles were in no way his own fault.

The intensity of Isham's resentment and frustration at the time of the murder and suicide cannot be determined. He was the only one of Colonel Lewis's four sons who had not been deeded substantial gifts of property. He had no title or occupation. His father was "colonel," Lilburne was "captain," Randolph was "farmer," and he was a "yeoman," which, in prestige, was

333

equivalent to "nobody." In the relationship between Isham and Lilburne, it appears, at first, that Lilburne was the dominant personality, even during the time of his final derangement. It is still difficult to imagine how Lilburne could have persuaded Isham to join him in George's murder and then a suicide pact, unless Isham was willing, or drunk, on both occasions. It does not seem probable that both brothers reached the same acute stage of mental breakdown simultaneously. The bizarre final request in Lilburne's will that both of them be buried in the same coffin, appears to have originated in Lilburne's mind. Isham did not write a will, and he did not kill himself. He may never have intended to, but went along with Lilburne's plans until the last moment. At this time Isham was no longer a "young man of excellent disposition," but at least his sense of survival was still intact. The suicide appears to have been Lilburne's idea. The few facts that are known about Isham do not indicate that his own situation in life had changed appreciably for the worse in the previous year or two. However shadowy his personality must remain, the role of willing suicide seems inconsistent for Isham.

Isham's part in the murder of George is a different matter. The one surviving relic of Isham's life, the letter he wrote to Jefferson, reveals the resentment which was so evident in his personality. He felt that he had been cheated out of his rightful inheritance through no fault of his own. Lilburne had received his share in plenty, for which Isham may have envied him. Given this possible relationship between Isham and Lilburne, one might guess that Isham, full of liquor, resentment, and envy, had egged on his drunken and distraught older brother to murder George, knowing that the punishment, if it came at all, would fall more heavily on Lilburne than on himself. A few months later, when life had become intolerable for Lilburne and he decided to commit suicide, Isham may have encouraged him, never intending to fulfill his own part of the pact.

Immediately following Lilburne's suicide there was some suspicion that Isham had shot Lilburne. Reverend William Dickey's account of the suicide mentions this. "The neighbors at first charged him with the murder of his brother. But he, though as if he had lost more than half his mind, told the whole story; and the course or range of the ball in the dead man's body agreeing with his statement, Isham was not farther charged with Lilburne's death."[11] There is little doubt that the bullet that killed

Lilburne was fired upward into his chest. At the moment he was shot, Lilburne was showing Isham how to hold the muzzle to his chest and push the trigger with a stick. At that instant Isham could have reached out and tripped the trigger just as easily as Lilburne. If he did, no one will ever know. This casting of Isham as Cain in the Lewis tragedy is supposition only. Other guesses about the relationship between Lilburne and Isham might be closer to the truth.

In summary, these are the background elements of the tragedy: slavery and its degrading effect on both master and slave; the natural wealth of the western frontier, and the ubiquity of physical violence during its settlement; the deaths of the most stable elders of the Lewis family; Lilburne's failure to control his business affairs and his slaves; unhappiness between himself and Letitia. These things cannot be said to have caused Lilburne's breakdown by themselves. Everyone in Livingston County was influenced more or less by the natural resources and the violence of the frontier, and by the institution of slavery as well. It was not uncommon for slaves to run away. There were deaths and some unhappiness in every family. Financial difficulties were widespread there at that time, as was heavy drinking. These things did not cause an outbreak of insanity in Livingston. Apparently almost all the citizens survived these hard times with resigned perseverance, while certain of the Lewises, at the same time and place, did not.

Jefferson described Meriwether Lewis as intelligent, capable, energetic, and courageous. There is no reason to think that these characteristics could not have been applied to Lilburne prior to his move to Kentucky. Jefferson noted that under a certain situation of continued stress Meriwether's personality became deranged. It appears that the same thing happened to Lilburne.

APPENDIXES

APPENDIX 1

NOTES ON LEWIS

GENEALOGY

Section 1. The Charles Lewises of Albemarle

Even the most astute genealogists and scholars have been confused by the plethora of Charles Lewises living in Virginia between 1750 and 1800. The frequent intermarriage of cousins in this family has made it difficult to unravel the lines of descent. To compound the confusion, many of the Charles Lewises were colonels and married ladies whose first names were either Mary or Lucy. In any event, the direct family line that is the subject of this book is as follows:

1. Col. Charles Lewis of The Byrd, St. James–Northam Parish, Goochland County, 1696–1779. He married Mary Howell and was the father of
2. Col. Charles Lewis, Jr., of Buck Island, Fredericksville Parish, Albemarle County, 1721–1782. He married Mary Randolph and was the father of
3. Col. Charles Lilburne Lewis of Monteagle, St. Anne's Parish, Albemarle County, 1747–1831. He married Lucy Jefferson and was the father of Randolph, Lilburne, Charles, Isham, and six daughters: Jane, Mary, Lucy, Martha, Ann, and Elizabeth.

Section 2. Charles Lewis of North Garden

Col. Charles Lewis, Jr. of Buck Island has frequently been confused with Charles Lewis of North Garden.[1] They were both colonels, their wives were named Mary, they lived in Albemarle County at the same time, and possessed land, slaves, and wealth sufficient to qualify them as gentrymen. Charles Lewis of North Garden married his cousin, Mary R. Lewis, the daughter of Charles Lewis, Jr. of Buck Island. Both these branches of the Lewis family were ardent in their patriotism, but Charles Lewis of North Garden was more active in military matters during the

339

Revolution than Charles Lewis, Jr. of Buck Island. The author has seen no reliable records to indicate that Charles Lewis, Jr. of Buck Island, who was fifty-five years old in 1776, ever served in a military capacity during the Revolution. His rank of colonel must have been earned in military service prior to the Revolution.[2]

The military career of Charles Lewis of North Garden was a distinguished one. He commanded the Albemarle volunteer company of minutemen that marched to Williamsburg to demand restitution from Lord Dunmore in 1775. About a year later his rank was raised to colonel, and he led a regiment that served in North Carolina and the Potomac area of Virginia. In the fall of 1776 he served in the campaign that broke the power of the Cherokee Indians, and shortly afterwards was given command of the Fourteenth Virginia Regiment, which was part of the continental line. This unit fought in the battles of Brandywine and Germantown. In March 1778, he resigned the command of the Fourteenth Virginia Regiment and returned to Albemarle, being obliged to do so by concern for the care of his large family, and perhaps by poor health. That December, he was appointed to command a regiment assigned to guard the British and German prisoners taken at Saratoga. They were to be quartered at the barracks outside Charlottesville. Col. Charles Lewis of North Garden died on February 26, 1779, shortly after the prisoners arrived.[3]

Jefferson thought highly of Charles Lewis of North Garden. In 1813 Jefferson said of him:

> Charles was one of the early patriots who stepped forward in the commencement of the Revolution and commanded one of the regiments first raised in Virginia and placed on continental establishment. Happily situated at home, with a wife and young family, and a fortune placing him at ease, he left all to aid in the liberation of his country from foreign usurpations, then first unmasking their ultimate end and aim. His good sense, integrity, bravery, enterprise, and remarkable bodily powers, marked him as an officer of great promise; but he, unfortunately, died early in the Revolution.[4]

In addition to his military service, Charles Lewis of North garden served for about a year as one of the two delegates from Albemarle to the second, third, and fourth sessions of the Virginia Convention, which met in Richmond.[5]

SECTION 3. A MISTAKEN TITLE

For more than seventy-five years there has existed a persistent false belief that Col. Charles L. Lewis of Monteagle was a doctor. In all of the letters, court records, and genealogies that compose the primary source material of this book, Charles Lilburne Lewis is spoken of as colonel, mister, or esquire, but never as doctor. Nevertheless, in both Watts's *Chronicles of a Kentucky Settlement,* published in 1897, and A. H. T. Pool's newspaper article of 1894, Charles L. Lewis is said to have been a doctor. These two accounts of the Lewis tragedy contain many errors of fact, and were based largely on local tradition handed down and distorted through eighty years of time. During this period someone who repeated the legend evidently decommissioned Col. Charles L. Lewis and awarded him a medical doctor's degree instead, by which title he has since been known in various newspaper feature articles and other versions of the Lewis tragedy.

This might be explained by a peculiar coincidence. During the last half of the 1800s there lived in Owensboro, Kentucky, the family of Dr. Charles Cadwallader Lewis, an entirely different branch from the Charles L. Lewis family that lived in Livingston County. These two branches of the Lewis family, the Charles L. Lewis line, and the Charles C. Lewis line, had the following things in common:

1. Both families had lived near the Ohio River in west Kentucky decades before Watts and Poole printed the Lewis story in the 1890s.
2. Both families were of aristocratic background.
3. Both families had the same last name, and the first name of Charles appears in at least three successive generations of both families.
4. Both families moved to Kentucky from Virginia.
5. Both families were connected by marriage to Virginia statesmen of the highest distinction.
6. An older son in each line married a girl named Letitia.

It appears that sometime during the three generations or more that the Lewis legend was handed down by mouth, the identity of Col. Charles L. Lewis became confused with that of Dr. Charles C. Lewis.[6]

Another possible explanation is that the use of this erroneous title sprang from careless reading of the tax records in Albemarle County, Virginia. In 1782 Nicholas Hamner was sheriff of Albemarle. The book in which he kept the records of his tax collections is so arranged that the abbreviations for debit and credit appear to be part of the taxpayer's name. For example, the heading under which Col. Charles L. Lewis's tax returns are listed reads as follows: "Dr. Charles L. Lewis Colo. Cr."[7] Even though all the names in Hamner's account book are prefaced by "Dr.," a hasty reader may have confused the abbreviation of debit with the abbreviation of doctor.

SECTION 4. DESCENDANTS OF LUCY AND COL. CHARLES L. LEWIS

The author has not attempted to trace the lives of Lucy's children and grandchildren in Kentucky later than 1815; however, the following material may be of some interest.

A. Daughters of Colonel and Lucy Lewis

Lucy B. Lewis married Washington Griffin in Livingston County in 1813. They moved to Shelby County, Kentucky, shortly afterward and then, in 1830, removed to New Albany, Indiana. They had nine children. Martha A. C. Lewis married Daniel Monroe in Livingston County in 1815. They became guardians of Randolph's youngest son, Warner, and took Warner to New Orleans when they moved to that city to live. Ann M. (Nancy) Lewis died an old maid at her sister Martha's home in New Orleans.[8]

B. Children of Randolph Lewis

In July 1833, Randolph's surviving heirs sold all their undivided interest in their father's land in west Kentucky to Robert C. Bigham, the Livingston County court clerk. Robert R. Lewis, who still lived in Livingston County, had been given power of attorney by his surviving brothers and sisters and, acting for them all, he sold Bigham all their interest in 3,833 ⅓ acres. The tracts that had been set aside at an earlier time for Randolph's oldest son were not part of this transaction. Bigham paid the unbelievably low sum of $500 for the land, which had cost Randolph over $9,000 twenty-five years before.[9] The disparity between these two sums suggests that some of the land had been sold earlier, or that there were other claims against the property.

The several powers of attorney gathered for this transaction reveal the places of residence of Randolph's children in 1832. Warner lived in New Orleans. He moved to Missouri at a later time. Howell lived in Fluvanna County, Virginia. Susannah, who had married William H. Douthat, lived in Rockbridge County, Virginia. Mary Jane, who had married Charles Palmer of Richmond, Virginia, had died before 1832. Lucy J. had died prior to this time, and was not involved in the transaction. In 1822 Tucker was a resident of Goochland County, Virginia, and Charles was still a resident of Livingston County.[10] Sometime after this sale was made, Robert moved to Labe County, Tennessee, where he died in 1859.

C. Children of Lilburne Lewis

In 1827 Lilburne's land in Kentucky was divided among his four surviving children.[11] Robert had died in 1814, and Lucy had died sometime between 1819 and 1827. Prior to 1827 Elizabeth had married Richard Phillips, and Jane had married her first cousin, Peter Field Jefferson. The land to be divided lay in two tracts, 1,000 acres at Rocky Hill and 500 acres located two miles up the Ohio, facing Stewart Island. Each tract was divided into four equal parcels, with frontage on the river. The parcels were distributed by lot among the heirs, each one receiving a total of 375 acres.

A few years after this division of land, Lilburne, his sister, Elizabeth, and her husband, Richard Phillips, moved to New Madrid, Missouri. James, Letitia's son, moved to Scott County, Missouri, at about the same time. Jane, who had lived in Albemarle County, Virginia, after her marriage in 1819, spent the rest of her life there.

By 1832 all of Lilburne's sisters and his four surviving children had moved out of Kentucky, and all but two of Randolph's children had done the same. As far as can be determined the descendants of Randolph and Lilburne lived praiseworthy lives, many of them achieving distinction in their chosen fields.

SECTION 5. GENEALOGICAL CHARTS

1. JEFFERSON

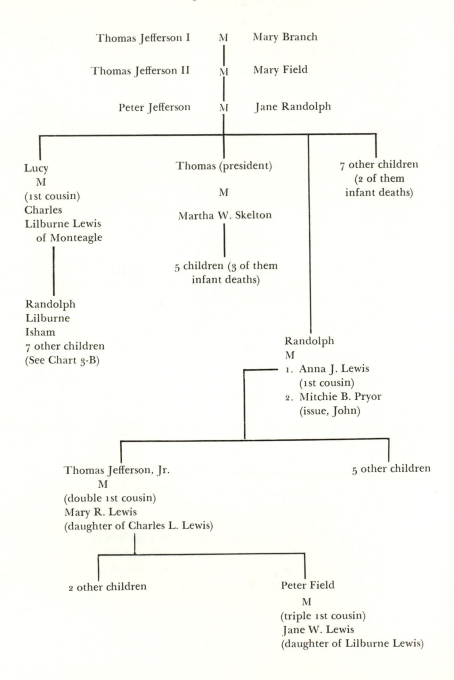

Thomas Jefferson I   M   Mary Branch

Thomas Jefferson II   M   Mary Field

Peter Jefferson   M   Jane Randolph

Lucy
M
(1st cousin)
Charles
Lilburne Lewis
of Monteagle

Thomas (president)

M

Martha W. Skelton

7 other children
(2 of them
infant deaths)

5 children (3 of them
infant deaths)

Randolph
Lilburne
Isham
7 other children
(See Chart 3-B)

Randolph
M
1. Anna J. Lewis
(1st cousin)
2. Mitchie B. Pryor
(issue, John)

Thomas Jefferson, Jr.
M
(double 1st cousin)
Mary R. Lewis
(daughter of Charles L. Lewis)

5 other children

2 other children

Peter Field
M
(triple 1st cousin)
Jane W. Lewis
(daughter of Lilburne Lewis)

2. ISHAM – RANDOLPH

Henry Isham (descendant of Plantagenet kings)

M

Catherine (window of James Royal)

|

Mary Isham of Bermuda Hundred

M

William Randolph of Turkey Island (1651–1711)

|

Isham Randolph of Dungeness (1685–1742)

M

Jane Rogers

Jane (1720–1776)	7 other children	Mary (1725–1803)
M		M
Peter Jefferson		Charles Lewis, Jr. of Buck Island

7 other children	Thomas (president)	Lucy Jefferson	M	Charles Lilburne Lewis of Monteagle		6 other children

(See Chart 4)

Randolph Jefferson M Anna J. Lewis

(*The Randolphs of Virginia* by Jonathan Daniels is a comprehensive study of the family.)

3. LEWIS

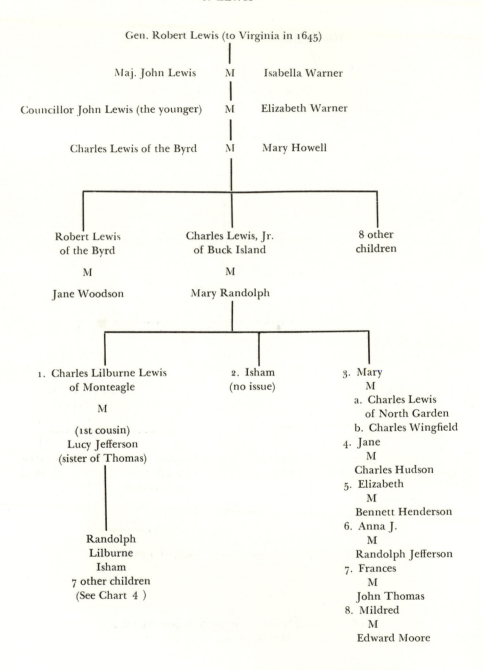

Gen. Robert Lewis (to Virginia in 1645)

Maj. John Lewis   M   Isabella Warner

Councillor John Lewis (the younger)   M   Elizabeth Warner

Charles Lewis of the Byrd   M   Mary Howell

Robert Lewis of the Byrd	Charles Lewis, Jr. of Buck Island	8 other children
M	M	
Jane Woodson	Mary Randolph	

1. Charles Lilburne Lewis of Monteagle

M

(1st cousin)
Lucy Jefferson
(sister of Thomas)

Randolph
Lilburne
Isham
7 other children
(See Chart 4)

2. Isham
(no issue)

3. Mary
   M
   a. Charles Lewis
     of North Garden
   b. Charles Wingfield
4. Jane
   M
   Charles Hudson
5. Elizabeth
   M
   Bennett Henderson
6. Anna J.
   M
   Randolph Jefferson
7. Frances
   M
   John Thomas
8. Mildred
   M
   Edward Moore

4. LEWIS OF MONTEAGLE

Charles Lilburne Lewis of Monteagle (1747–1831)

M (1st cousin)

Lucy Jefferson (1752–1810)

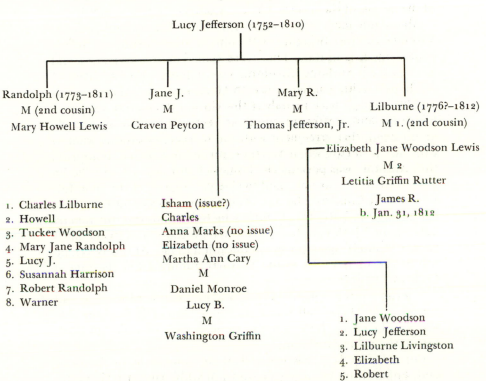

Randolph (1773–1811)
M (2nd cousin)
Mary Howell Lewis

Jane J.
M
Craven Peyton

Mary R.
M
Thomas Jefferson, Jr.

Lilburne (1776?–1812)
M 1. (2nd cousin)

Elizabeth Jane Woodson Lewis
M 2
Letitia Griffin Rutter
James R.
b. Jan. 31, 1812

1. Charles Lilburne
2. Howell
3. Tucker Woodson
4. Mary Jane Randolph
5. Lucy J.
6. Susannah Harrison
7. Robert Randolph
8. Warner

Isham (issue?)
Charles
Anna Marks (no issue)
Elizabeth (no issue)
Martha Ann Cary
M
Daniel Monroe
Lucy B.
M
Washington Griffin

1. Jane Woodson
2. Lucy Jefferson
3. Lilburne Livingston
4. Elizabeth
5. Robert

APPENDIX 2
THE COLLE SALE

THE background of the dispute over the sale of Colle and some of the details of the transaction are discussed in this appendix.

About nineteen years before this time, Mazzei had come to Virginia to live, bringing with him a small group of fellow countrymen from Italy. They were skilled in various trades, and one, named Anthony Gianinni, was a horticulturist.[1] Part of Anthony's written agreement with Mazzei was that Mazzei was to pay his passage back to Italy if the vintner decided to return to his homeland. Jefferson stood as security for, or personally guaranteed, this agreement with the worker.[2] Anthony went to work for Jefferson when Mazzei returned to Europe. It appears that Anthony was periodically homesick, for as early as 1780 he wished to return to Italy, and twelve years later, at the time Jefferson sold Colle to Thomas, Anthony was pressing his claims for passage and also for clothing which, he said, was due him by agreement.[3] Jefferson had persuaded Anthony not to sue Mazzei and himself, since Jefferson intended to pay Anthony's claim out of the money that would be forthcoming from the sale of Colle to Thomas.[4]

Another of the Italian craftsmen who came to Albemarle and stayed after Mazzei left was a gardener named Giovannini. He was employed by Jefferson for some period of time, and Jefferson thought well of him.

Col. Charles L. Lewis learned of the intentions of Anthony and, apparently confusing Giovannini with Anthony Gianinni, mistakenly feared that both Italians planned to place an attachment on Colle and sue for their money. Colonel Lewis wrote a letter to Jefferson.[5] Thomas and his security, Colonel Lewis, were then six months overdue in paying for Colle, which did not surprise Jefferson, but the news that Giovannini was to claim money from Mazzei's estate did shock him, as is evident in Jefferson's reply to the colonel's letter:

Philadelphia June 4, 1793

Dear Sir

The constant calls of public business which scarcely ever permit me to turn to what is private, will I hope apologize for my late acknolegement of your letter of March 22. on the subject of the claims of Anthony & Giovannini against Mr. Mazzei. With respect to Anthony, I always assured him that whenever I should have any money of Mr. Mazzei's in my hands, I would ... [assist?] him in referring his claim to any impartial judge, and do him justice as far as in my power. I am still of the same purpose. With respect to Giovannini, I have known him ... 16 or 18 years. He lived a considerable time in my family. I have enjoyed his confidence & I believe his esteem, and never before heard of his having any claim against Mazzei. I have too much regard for him not to hope he will avoid the risk of any unfounded claim. However when I come home this fall I will hear what he has to say & do for him whatever justice & my powers will authorize.

I have little of news to add to what the newspaper will give you. We have a good prospect of preserving our neutrality. Consequently we may hope open markets for our productions. I am afraid it will be difficult to quiet the Creek Indians; & an open war with whom will be expensive & hazardous. Be so good as to present my ... love to my sister & the family, & to be assured of the esteem of Dear Sir

Colo. C. L. Lewis

Your friend & servt
TH: Jefferson[6]

What Charles L. Lewis said to Jefferson in his letter of March 22, which prompted the above reply from Jefferson, is unknown, for the letter has not been found to date. One can only guess that Lewis asked Jefferson what he intended to do about the claims since they clouded the title to Colle. Lewis may well have told Jefferson that as security for Mr. Thomas, he, Lewis, would not pay for Colle until Anthony and Giovannini had been satisfied, their claims settled, and the title to Colle cleared. If so, it was a perfect three-way standoff: Anthony would not clear the title of Colle until he had been paid, Jefferson could not pay the Italian until he got the money for Colle from Lewis, and Lewis would not pay for Colle until he could get a clear title.

Jefferson broke this stalemate two years later by taking Thomas and Lewis to court. He reported to Mazzei: "In regard to the purchase money of Colle £250. I got a judgement lately for it, but by the present execution laws, the money will hardly be got till next spring."[7] The sale of Colle to Thomas was nearly settled. Six months more, and Jefferson would have the money in hand. It had been four years in process, during which Thomas (and perhaps Lewis) had used the value of Mazzei's property with no money of their own invested. In fact, Thomas made a profit of £125, for he had resold Colle six months before he finally paid Jefferson for it. Jefferson noted this resale of Colle in a letter to James Monroe, who was interested in buying land in that neighborhood: "Monticello May 26, 1795. . . . Colle is lately sold for £375 to a Mr. Catlet, a farmer, whom I do not know. It is very possible it will be for sale again."[8]

In the summer of 1796, the four-year imbroglio over the sale of Colle came to an end. With the help of arbitrators, Jefferson and Anthony had tried to reach an agreement, but Anthony, who rejected the arbitrator's decision, had taken his claims to court and was awarded a settlement.[9] As for the claims of Giovannini against Mazzei, Lewis was evidently mistaken, for there is no record of such claims by him. Colle was but a small part of Mazzei's estate in America. The power of attorney, which Jefferson held for his old friend, was an agonizing problem that Jefferson still had not settled as late as 1820.[10]

APPENDIX 3

THE INTERVIEW WITH

MATILDA

THE following newspaper article was reprinted November 19, 1954, in *The Crittenden Press,* published in Marion, Kentucky. It was first published in *The Crittenden Press* on December 22, 1880. The author has not been able to locate the copy of *The Cumberland Wave* that contains Matilda's version of the Lewis tragedy.

Matilda was mistaken in one point: Charles, who died in 1806, did not emigrate to Kentucky. When the slaves belonging to Randolph's estate were sold in January 1815, Matilda was bought by Aaron Threlkeld.

History of Crittenden County
This Story is the 16th in a series of
The History of Crittenden County
Published through the courtesy of
The Marion Woman's Club.

———

A Niece of Thos. Jefferson

———

(A Copy from The Crittenden Press
of December 22, 1880)

In the quiet little village of Marion, where the eyes of the people have never fallen upon a President from father Washington down to Jas. A. Garfield and where the vistage of the lineage of either of the illustrious has never been knowingly looked upon, the discovery of a descendant of the "Sage of Monticello" might awaken a riffle of astonishment.

Yet within the walls of a poorly chinked, ill constructed log cabin in the suburbs of our out-of-the-way village may be found an ancient woman through whose veins the blood of Thos. Jefferson is slowly ebbing. "Aunt" Matilda Threlkeld is verging upon the age of four scores. And old Tim has pressed his blighting fingers upon her, until the aged woman can no more leave the miserable hovel, she calls home. According to her own statement she was born in Albermarle County, Virginia, and is a daughter of Charles Lewis whose mother was a sister of Thos. Jefferson. The brothers, Randolph, Charles and Lilburn, emigranted to this State when "Aunt"

351

Matilda was but a child. After remaining in Gallatin County for a short time, they permanently settled in Livingston County, where "Aunt" Matilda was raised, being hired out as a servant girl. Subsequently she came to Marion which has since been her home.

Fluent in conversation, with an active mind and a memory unshattered by time, she relates many historical events in a well delineated manner that indicates a parentage above the mediocrity. She remembers well the soldiers of General Jackson, and can relate incidents connected with the war of 1812. She told the writer which illustrates the longevity of her mind about as follows:

When Jackson was fighting, I was living in Old Salem, a number of soldiers took dinner at my masters one day, when whiskey was being served, one of the soldiers drank during the meal, thirty cups of coffee. I remember distinctly of handing him that number for I was waiting upon the table and counted every cup. My arms ached when I was done passing it. Among other things she remembers the Lewis tragedy that occurred about five miles from Smithland, when she was twelve years old, an account of which was published in the Cumberland Wave some seven years ago, and which we will republish if a file of the Wave containing it can be obtained. . . .

The article continued at some length with a rehash of William Courtney Watts's version of the Lewis story, as found in *Chronicles of a Kentucky Settlement.*

APPENDIX 4

MEDICAL NOTES

1809

May 23	laxative for slave Isaac, $.50	$ .50
June 14	opium for sleep or pain, $1.25	1.25
June 16	opium for sleep or pain, $2.00	2.00
June 16	liver or bile pill, $.50	.50
June 16	bleeding slave Isaac, $.50	.50
June 18	laxative for Lilburne Lewis, $.50	.50
June 18	laxative for Lilburne Lewis, $.25	.25
June 19	visit slave at Daniels, $.50; for bleeding, $.50; liver pill, $.50	1.50
July 30	laxative for negro at McCawley's, $.50; quinine for malaria, $1.00	1.50
August 2	one box pills, $1.00; blue ointment for lice, $.50	1.50
August 5	visit Nancy, sister of Lilburne, a night call, $3.00; bleeding, $.50; laxative, $.50	4.00
August 7	quinine for malaria, $1.00; sedative, $.37½	1.37½
August 13	bleeding slave Frank, $.50	.50
August 18	pills for sisters, $1.00; antimony to cause sweat and vomiting, $1.00	2.00
August 20	night call on sisters, $3.00; ague pills, $1.00; quinine for malaria, $2.00	6.00
August 21	visit family, $2.00; laxative for child, $.25; paregoric for diarrhea and cramps, $.50; sweet spirits of niter for stomach pain and nausea, $.75	3.50
August 22	visit family, $2.00; 3 childs' doses of laxative, $.75	2.75
August 23	sweet spirits of niter for stomach pain and nausea, $1.00; laxative, $.50; quinine, $1.00	2.50
August 25	visit family, $2.00	2.00
August 26	quinine for malaria, $2.00; ague pill for Isham Lewis, $.50	2.50
August 27	visit family, $2.00; quinine, $2.00	4.00
August 29	laxative, $.50; quinine, $2.00	2.50
August 30	visit family, $2.00	2.00
August 31	visit family, $2.00	2.00

September 1	laxative, $.50; laxative, $.25; ammoniated liniment for aches, pains, and sore throat, $.50	1.25
September 3	quinine, $1.00	1.00
September 5	laxative for Lilburne Lewis, $.50	.50
September 8	quinine, $1.00	1.00
September 11	visit to negro, $2.00; two doses of laxative, $1.00; quinine, $1.00	4.00
September 13	two doses laxative for children, $.75; gum camphor for fever or spasms, $.25	1.00
September 16	sweet spirits of niter for stomach pain and nausea, to increase urine flow, $.50; liver pill, $.50	1.00
September 25	visit to son, $2.00; visit daughter at Randolph Lewis's, $2.00; ether for cramps, fever, or asthma taken internally, or as vapor for whooping cough, $.75	4.75
October 1	visit family, $2.00; two doses laxative for Lilburne Lewis, $.50; castor oil for slave Carter, $.37½	3.37½

1810

January 7	visit slave Ursula at Erwin's (in Smithland) and opening breast (boil or tumor), $1.50	1.50

Credit on this bill—

By hire of negroes £3.18 ($13.00)
By cash in Danville £3.00 ($10.00)
Balance due £13.10 ($43.50)

SECTION 2. DISEASES IN THE OHIO VALLEY

In 1819 Dr. Henry McMurtrie published *Sketches of Louisville and Its Environs.* In this book Dr. McMurtrie described the city, its people, their way of life, and some economic and other aspects of the time and locality. Among these essays is a section on diseases prevalent in Louisville and the Ohio Valley at that time. Excerpts from this section (pp. 146–52) are quoted below. His failure to distinguish between malaria and yellow fever is understandable.

The nature of those diseases incident to any particular spot, may be deduced with great certainty, from the climate and physical topography of the surrounding country. This being the case, the reader will naturally suppose that bilious, remitting, and intermitting fevers must be common in this place. . . .

The most fatal complaint among adults, (exclusive of small pox), is a bilious remitting fever, whose symptoms are often sufficiently aggravated to entitle it to the name of *yellow fever,* and unless some speedy change be made in the internal regulations of the town, and an efficient police established, in room of the nominal one existing at present, that pestilent foe may be expected to make his appearance every summer, as a native born citizen of the place. It is vain and useless to talk of establishing lazarettoes and quarantines, to prevent the importation of this fell destroyer from abroad, while we are accumulating at home, the sources whence he springs. During the months of July, August, and September, so strongly are the inhabitants of this and the adjacent towns, *predisposed* to this disease, by the joint influence of climate, and the miasm of marshes, and decayed and decaying vegetable and animal matter, that they may be compared to piles of combustibles, which need but the application of a single spark to rouse them into flame! Let me not be accused of alarming people unnecessarily, for I write this under a solemn conviction in my own mind, that unless greater attention be paid to *cleanliness,* in every possible way, Louisville cannot long escape a signal visitation from this destroying angel. I have repeatedly seen sporadic cases of it, but fortunately at a time of year when there existed the least danger of its spreading.

Hepatic complaints, the usual sequents of badly treated intermittents, or, indeed, of any other kind of fever, are common, accompanied with splenitis and other obstructions of the glandular system, which together annually deprive us of some members of our society.

In 1817, the small pox ravaged the town, and although every endeavour to cut short its progress by vaccination and preventing all intercourse between the sick and the well, was made by the faculty, yet, from the slothful negligence of the civil authorities, it was impossible to prevent its inoculating the place for each succeeding year.

The proportion of children to that of adults, who are annually transported to "that bourne from which no traveller returns," is as two to one. This awful difference is principally occasioned by the prevalence of cholera infantum and of worms. Every child is troubled with the latter more or less, which, by inducing convulsions or tabes mesenterica, destroy a great portion of them. Diarrhoea, rheumatism, cholera morbus are frequent; consumption not so much so. If to these we add those diseases that *at times* occur every where, we have the list complete.

355

To affirm that Louisville is a healthy city, would be absurd, but it is much more so than the thousand tongues of fame would make us believe, and as many of the causes which prevent it from becoming perfectly so, can be removed, a few years hence may find the favorable alterations accomplished, and do away the general impression of its being the grave yard of the western country.

As no better opportunity offers than the present of touching upon a subject which certainly does not add to the credit of the place, I must be permitted to embrace it. I allude to the want of an hospital, or dispensary, within whose walls the indigent victim of disease or accident might find relief. Not a hut or shelter of any kind is provided for him, and should he be destitute of a home, unless an individual withdraws him from the street, there must he perish. . . .

[Emigrants should] rely upon a strict attention to their diet, upon wearing *flannel next their skin,* upon avoiding the *early morning air and evening dews,* by the *moderate* use of *sound wine* or *good malt liquor,* and, if possible, upon removing, for the first year to two, into the higher country, during the months of July, August, and September.

Sketches of Louisville and its Environs has been reproduced recently in a 1,000-copy edition by the J. R. Clark Press of Louisville. A scholarly discussion of Dr. McMurtrie and his book may be found in Thomas and Conner, "Henry McMurtrie, M. D."

An extensive study of the practice of frontier medicine, containing numerous bibliographical aids, is Pickard and Buley, *The Midwest Pioneer.*

Section 3.   A Case History

The case history described below was printed in a medical textbook published in 1815 (Hamilton, *Observations on the Utility and Administration of Purgative Medicines,* pp. 208–12). The patient was a three-year-old child who, during a twelve-day period early in 1811, was treated for an unidentified complaint of the digestive tract. This child's horrifying experience is recounted here because many of the medicines given to the infant were the same ones used by the Lewises in 1809. The descriptions of the drugs used below were taken from Jonathan Pereira's two-volume *Elements of Materia Medica.*

2d Jan. 1811.—John F———, three years of age, was attacked after breakfast, with vomiting, which has continued at intervals all the forenoon. Pulse 100, countenance dejected, eye dim, tongue white, belly tense and hard. He has been unusually cross for the last two days. Has had a stool, in general, every day, except one, last week, when a dose of magnesia produced a proper effect; yet for the last three months he has often complained of his belly.

Let five grains of calomel be given immediately. [Calomel is an irritant purgative made from the poisonous element, mercury.]

3d.—Vomited much during the night; no stool; other symptoms as yesterday. . . . [On January 3, a concoction of castor oil, jalap and senna was given to John every two hours. Jalap is a powerful cathartic "operating with great promptness and often causing much pain." Senna is a cathartic "disagreeable and nauseous to the taste."]

4th Jan —Has taken all the medicine; had a small dark coloured watery stool after the first spoonful, and again during the night, but without any appearance of feces. No sleep; complains much of his belly. Has not vomited; other symptoms as before. . . . [John was dosed with jalap and sugar water every two hours until seven that night, when he was given an enema. There were no results, so the jalap and sugar water was resumed.]

5th. —Has taken all the medicine; no stool; appears worse; passed a very restless night, with some approach to delirium. Pulse very quick. . . . [The infant was taken off of jalap and put back on senna, a somewhat milder purgative.]

6th. —Has been restless all night. Took all the decoction without effect.

Let six grains of calomel be given now, and ten grains of jalap in the evening.

7th Jan. — . . . slept a little in the night; had again an inclination to stool, without passing anything but a very little dark coloured fluid. As antimonials, after producing their full emetic effect, having often been observed to operate by stool also, he took this day a saline mixture, with tartrite of antimony. A great quantity of dark coloured bile was thrown up, and a little of a thinner dark fluid passed by stool, both without any feces.

8th. —Last evening, at seven, he was kept ten minutes in the warm bath; after which he started much and screamed wildly; in the night he slept little, and was completely delirious, making frequent attempts to bite his left arm, seemingly insensible of the pain produced by his teeth, though the marks were evident. . . . [A medicine containing colocynth and aloes was promptly given to the child. Aloes is a cathartic with a bitter and disagreeable taste, while colocynth is a violent cathartic "acting sometimes very harshly even in small doses, and in overdoses producing dangerous, and occasionally fatal enteric inflammation." Later in the day John was given senna and jalap again.]

9th. —Yesterday's medicines produced little or no effect. The

357

warm bath again aggravated all the symptoms, as it did this day, when it was thought unadvisable to persist in it; strength much exhausted; has several times fallen suddenly and profoundly asleep in the midst of the most violent struggles. Has slept from the commencement of his illness, with his eyes half open. His sight appears much impaired. . . . [The treatment with colocynth and aloes was repeated, a blistering poultice, or plaster, was applied between John's shoulder blades, and he was given an enema.]

10th Jan. —The clyster was returned nearly as injected; no stool; about six hours after the blister was applied became calm, and slept well till morning. Is evidently much easier, though no change of consequence has been produced on his bowels from the beginning of his illness to the present hour. . . . [A tablespoon of castor oil and senna was administered every two hours for three days in a row!]

11th. —Symptoms as yesterday; has taken all the mixture without effect.

Let it be repeated.

12th. —Still no effect, though the medicine has again been all given.

Let it be repeated.

13th. —The mixture has been all taken; some trifling evacuation, but no real feces.

Let him take a tea-spoonful of calcined magnesia three or four times a day.

The three-year-old child had lain for twelve days in a stupor, when not screaming, delirious, or vomiting. It even appeared that he was losing his eyesight, when Dr. King, the attending Scottish physician, reported that the twelve days' accumulation of laxatives in John's body had finally "begun to produce some good effects."

14th. —Several doses of calcined magnesia were given at intervals yesterday; and at length the purgative medicines, thus accumulated, have begun to produce some good effects. He has had several large stools of green glutinous matter, mixed with dry hardened feces in round compact balls, amounting in all to a large quantity, sufficient to account for all the symptoms: and however singular it may appear, I have no hesitation in avowing my belief, that the feces evacuated on the 12th or 13th day were, from the commencement, lodged in some part of the intestines.

From the time that his bowels began to act, the purgative plan was continued till all the symptoms were removed. Particular directions were given to attend to the state of his evacuations, and he now continues in perfect health.

APPENDIX 5

LILBURNE LEWIS'S ESTATE

SECTION 1. THE AUCTION SALE RECORDS

Livingston County June 2nd 1812
The following is the sale Bill of the Estate
of Lilburn Lewis deceas'd (to wit)

Names	*Articles*	
Geo Robison	1 Plow	.50
Moses Hurly	1 Do	1.41
J. Ramsey	1 pair of haims and chains	2.75
Do	1 pair of Do and Do	2.00
H. F. Delaney	1 hoe	.37½
J. Ramsey	1 axe	1.37½
Geo. Robison	1 hoe	1.10
Enoch Fliece	1 Do	.12½
Do	1 axe	.62½
J. Ramsey	1 Do	.75
J. Rutter, Jr.	1 Do	1.75
Jno. Menees	1 Veleas	.55
S. C. Harkins	1 Book Case	5.00
Chrt. Haynes	1 Bureau	5.25
E. L. Head	1 Backgammon Box	2.00
L. Lewis	1 Trunk	3.50
Moses Hurly	Timothy seed	.38½
Jno. Menees	1 pocket compass	.50
Jesse Roberts	1 Brass lock	.37½
Enoch Trinar	1 Military hat	.75
J. Rounsovall	1 pair of spectakles	.50
Jas. Hodge	1 padlock	.75
Geo. Robison	1 Do	.25
Jno. Daniel	4 fish hooks	.12½
David Fort	1 brush	.25
Thos. Terry	1 hammer shears & some other trifles	.37½
Robt. Hodge	1 inkstand and chane	.13¾
E. Flease	1 Do & gimblits	.34
J. C. Hicks	1 Military Coat	7.00
Do	1 pair of sasamore pantaloons	5.62½
J. Ramsey	1 pair of pantaloons & Breeches	.50
Geo. Robison	1 Broad Cloath Coat	8.79
		55.76¼

Names	Articles	
A. Persons	1 Waist coat	.81
Wm. Rice	1 Do Do	.12½
Mark Phillips	1 Do Do	.81¾
Geo. Robison	1 pair cotton stockins	.76
Archer	1 shirt	.75
Joshua Gross	2 Waistcoats	1.00
Charles	1 shirt and pair of overalls	.50
J. Rutter Sr.	2 Waistcoats	.26
Do	1 pair of small cloaths and coat	2.01
E. Fliece	1 pair of stockins & 1 pair of socks	.13½
Jas. Hodge	1 spear and walking cane	1.25
G. Robison	1 skillet	1.00
J. C. Hicks	1 bake oven	2.25
Lewis Barlow	1 kettle	5.00
Robt. Hodge	1 small table	3.00
Jas. Hodge	1 coffy mill	4.00
Joseph Ray	1 pair of flatt irons	1.06¼
Jno. Caldwell	1 shott gun	9.00
Moses Hurly	1 Do	6.75
Thos. Champion	1 gridiron	.50
Do	6 chairs	4.25
Jas. Henderson	1 sifter	1.25
Enoch Fliece	1 straner	.51
J. C. Hicks	1 Lantern & Coffy pot	.65
H. F. Delany	1 pair of hand irons	4.56¼
David Rice	1 Churn and 1 pail	1.00
Do	1 set of chairs	5.00
J. Rutter Jr.	2 Crocks	.68
Joseph Reed	1 Do	.18¼
Enoch Prince	1 jar	.75
Do	1 Do	.100
G. Thrailkill	1 pitcher	.37½
Enoch Fliece	1 jar	.37½
A. Persons	1 spice mortar	1.62½
J. Rutter Sr.	1 jug	.70
Joseph Reed Sr.	1 piggon 1 cooler & pan	.42
J. Ray	1 pair of Stilirds	2.81
Geo. Robison	1 Trunk	.30
		67.42

Names	Articles	
David Rice	1 Cotton Wheel	1.10
Peggy Wilson	1 Reel	1.00
A. Persons	Shovel and tongs	2.02
James Hodge	1 Demijohn	3.63
Joseph Ray	1 Negro boy Frank hired	38.12½
Jas. McCawley	1 Negro boy Isaac hired	36.00
Jones Mencer	1 Negro boy Carter hired	36.68¾
Mark Phillips	1 Negro boy Archer hired	39.01
Lettisha Lewis	1 Negro girl Mary hired	2.12½
James McCawley	1 Do Do Cely hired	.87½
J. C. Hicks	1 Feather Bed	18.25
Jacob Houts	1 Negro Boy William fed & cloathed)	
	7 years & 11 Months for what he)	
	will do in that time)	
Jno. Morgan	A Feather Bed	10.59¼
Wm. H. Ramsey	1 Do Do	17.13½
Geo. V. Lusk	1 Do Do	10.00
Thos. Champeon	1 Do Do	25.00
H. F. Delaney	8 Spectator Vol.	4.25
Wm. Rice	1 Book	1.01
John Garth	2 Books	2.37½
A. Parsons	1 Counterpain	7.00
Thos. Champeon	1 Dish	1.87½
J. Rutter, Jr.	2 plates	.31¼
Thos. Champeon	2 Do	.25
J. C. Hicks	10 Do	1.31
Wm. Padon	5 Do	.66
Robert Hodge	1 Dish	1.50
Enoch Fliece	1 Do	.87½
J. C. Hicks	1 Do	.80
P. H. Rice	1 Do	.25
Jas. Hodge	1 table & furniture	2.52
Mark Stallcup	1 Gray horse	31.12½
Champion Terry	1 Sorrel Mare	30.00
Wm. Rice	1 Bay Mare	48.00
Jno. Delaney	2 Books	2.50
A. Persons	2 Do Franklin works	1.57¼
P. H. Rice	10 pounds of wool	2.70
Enoch Fleece	10 Do Do	2.51
		384.85½

PAGE 4

Names	*Articles*	
Robert Hodge	2 Books	1.12½
Jno. Menees	1 Do	3.56
Wm. Pippin	1 Do	.56
Enoch Fliece	1 Do	.76
Geo. V. Lusk	1 Do	.40
Moses Hurley	10 Pounds of wool	3.01
Jas. Hodge	1 Book	1.37½
David Rice	1 pair of cotton cards	.81
Robt. Hodge	4 Sheep 1st choice	9.25
Do	4 Do 2nd Do	8.00
Do	4 Do 3rd Do	6.87½
Do	4 Do 4th Do	6.00
Enoch Prince	1 Case of Bottles	3.12½
Jno. Berry	1 Cow and Calf	10.31½
Jas. Rutter Sr.	1 Conk Shell	.51
J. C. Hicks	1 Bed quilt	3.83
Jas. Henderson	1 Coverlid	4.55
Willis Champeon	1 Kettle	2.53
Jas. Rutter Sr.	1 Basket	.25
		66.83½

PAGE 5

Names	*Articles*	
Mark Phillips	1 Vol of Gutherys Grammer	2.51
Jas. Henderson	1 Counterpain	6.50
Thos. Champeon	2 Sheets	3.37
J. C. Hicks	2 Pillows	1.00
Do	2 Sheets	1.52
David Rice	1 Dictionary Ent	.25
J. C. Hicks	1 Bedquilt	1.25
Jno. Donakey	1 Do	3.25
Thos. Champeon	2 Pillows	1.00
Jno. Donakey	1 Bedquilt	4.40
H. F. Delaney	2 Candlesticks	2.51
Geo. V. Lusk	the life of Washington	.75
W. A. Griffin	1 Inkstand	.06¼
Wm. Hosick	1 Book Virginia revised code	1.10
Mark Phillips	1 set of iron teaspoons	.28
Do	1 Counterpain	4.25
Wm. Hosick	1 Do	4.63
Jno. Donakey	1 Book	.20

Enoch Fliece	1 Table cloath	.15½
S. C. Harkins	1 Do	2.18¼
Wm. Rice	1 Do	2.76
Thos. Champeon	2 pillow cases	.31
Jno. Dunn	2 Vols. of morses universal geography	5.00
Thos. Champeon	1 Counterpain	6.32
Jas. Henderson	1 Sheet	1.31
Jas. Rutter Jr.	1 Table cloath	2.00
Mark Phillips	1 Bureau tilet	.50
Jno. Donakey	2 pillow cases	.37½
David Mahhan	1 Bureau tilet	1.06¼
Wm. Rice	1 Counterpain	6.96
Lettisha Lewis	1 Bureau 1 table & cover 1 dressing)	
	glass 1 Dressing Box 1 small trunk)	
	6 pictures fraims & profiles 1 Caster) 31.00	
	of Crewits 1 glass picher and cream pot)	
	2 wine glasses & 1 goblet 2 phials)	
	4 tea spoons 1 soop spoon 1 pair)	
	of sugar tongs & 2 Candlesticks)	
Jno. Delaney	1 Book	.25
J. Ray	1 Do Bartrams travels	.51
S. Lamkin	1 Do History of America	.50

PAGE 6

Names	Articles	
J. Gross	100 wt. of seed cotton	2.88½
J. Rutter Jr.	100 wt. of Do	2.80
		105.26¼

PAGE 7

Names	Articles	
Gabriel Thrailkile	100 wt. of seed cotton	2.81
James Rutter Sr.	The Balance of the seed cotton at	
	2½ pr. lb.	3.02
James Rutter Jr.	Caster of Crewits	2.00
Micajah Phelps	1 Saddle Blanket	1.00
D. Kirk	1 Book practical navigator	.28
J. Rutter Jr.	1 tea canister	.37½
H. F. Delaney	1 Clevis	.30
Micajah Phelps	14 phials	1.00
Wm. Rice	4 puter spoons	.25
J. Rutter Sr.	1 trivet	.08
J. Ray	1 pair of candle snuffers	.06¼

363

D. Kirk	1 Book of Jeffersons notes	1.26
Wm. Pippin	some old peices of books	.25
D. Kirk	a pacel of peices of old books	1.02
Do	1 Book	.13½
G. Thrailkill	2 Books	.12½
D. Kirk	2 Do	.15
Thos. Champeon	1 Bedstead	.56
Do	1 Bedcord	.59
Wm. Rice	1 Do	.53
E. Fliece	1 Do	.13
J. Rutter Sr.	2 Bedsteads	.38
Do	1 Bedcord	.26
Jno. Manees	1 Beehive	1.05
P. Caldhoon	1 Do	1.31
D. Fort	1 Do	1.02
Jno. Menees	1 Do	.77
Archabald Cannon	1 Iron wedge	.70
Do	1 padlock	.12½
C. Buckler	20 Bushels of corn	6.81¼
W. A. Griffin	20 Do Do	6.31¼
A. Cannon	20 Do Do	6.04
Thos. Salsberry	20 Do Do	6.05
W. A. Griffin	20 Do Do	6.17
H. F. Delany	1 pair of candle snuffers	.37½
Wm. Pipin	1 Book	.25
D. Kirk	1 Book	.52
E. Fliece	1 teacanister	.15½
J. Rutter Sr.	1 Do	.12½
		54.35½

PAGE 8

Names	Articles	
H. Davis	10½ Bushels of corn	3.55
F. Hollenshead	7 Do Do	2.12½
H. Davis	30 cents per bushell for the Balance of the corn	
Jno. Menees	Green wheat	22.50
C. L. Lewis Sr.	1 mans saddle without a pad	
	1 sirsengle	2.00
Jas. McCawley	1 spur	.31
Jas. Rutter Sr.	669 feet of poplar plank	6.00
C. L. Lewis Sr.	1 bridle	.26
Wm. Boggs	1 cotton wheel	1.30
C. L. Lewis Sr.	1 Blanket	1.70

Moses Hurly	1 Grindstone	.75
Jno. Menees	1 Bedstead	.80
J. Gross	1 Do	1.00
Jas. McCawley	1 Do	2.12½
Joseph Daniel	1 Horse	16.28
Jno. Killingsworth	1 Horse	15.12½
Jas. Rutter Sr.	1 padlock	.06¼
Jno. Menees	2 Barrels	.50
Do	1 Do & some Buck Wheat	.12½
P. Caldhoon	2 Gees	.80
Mark Phillips	1 stone jar	.08
Geo. Robison	1 Bridle Bit	.15
Joseph Daniel	1 Do Do 1 latch 1 fork & other trifles	.81¼
Jno. Menees	All the hogs belonging to the Estate	32.50
Do	1 Cow and calf	11.18¾
D. Mullin	1 Do Do	7.00
David Fort	1 Do Do	7.39
Wm. Boggs	6 yearlings	15.01
Jno. Menees	1 Cow	9.12½
H. Davis	1 Heifer	4.25
J. Gross	1 Cow	8.01
J. Menees	1 Do	7.25
J. Boling	1 Table	.25
A. Cannon	the plantation rented	2.00
D. Fort	7 Barrels	2.00
		183.22¾
Betsy Rodgers	4 Ducks	.50

PAGE 9

Names	*Articles*	
Jas. Rutter Jr.	3 Coarse coverlids	5.00
Do	1 set of knives and forks	2.00
Do	1 pair of saddle bags	2.00
Do	4 spoons	.68
Do	1 pair of candle snuffers	.37½
Do	1 basket with some blue cotton in it	.50
Do	1 Book Columbian orator	.75
Lettisha Lewis	1 Bed 4 counterpains 4 sheets	)
	2 peast covers 1 blanket 2 coverlids	)
	2 table cloaths 3 pillow cases 3 Bureau	)
	tilets & 3 glass covers	) 50.25
Do	1 set of knives and forks	) 1.50
Lettisha Lewis	2 sets of cups and saucers & a server	3.50

Do	1 Book the letter writer	.50
Patrick H. Rice	money scales	1.00
Robt. Boid	1 small book	.37½
Burrell Phillips	Leather	.75
James Rutter Jr.	1 pair panteloons not made up	1.00
Robt. Boid	1 Ink Bottle	.25
Jno. Daniel	1 pair bridle leathers	.37½
Thos. Elden	1 mattack	1.12½
Geo. Robison	1 axe	.50
Wm. Rutter	1 small jug	.12½
H. David	1 Bolster	.25
P. H. Rice	1 Do	.75
James Rutter Sr.	tallow	1.00
		76.55½

The sale bill of the personal Estate of Lilburn Lewis decd. also the hire of the slaves of said Estate

James Rutter Adminis.

Section 2. Estate Appraisal

Livingston County June 1, 1812

We Joseph Reed James Henderson George Robison and Patrick H. Rice being first duly sworn proceeded to appraise the goods Chattles and slaves of the Estate of Lilburn Lewis deceased
According to order of May Court
James Henderson George Robison and Patrick H. Rice
    Sworn Before me
Joseph Reed sworn Before me

1 Bed, 4 Counterpains, 4 sheets, 2 peast covers, 1 Blanket 2 Coverlids, 2 table cloaths, 3 pair pillow cases 3 Bureau tilets 3 glass covers	105.00	Paleys Philosophy 2 volums	7.75	
Jeffersons notes	2.00	first volum of Scotts Gazette—Nicholson Philosophy	3.00	
8 volumes of the Spectator	4.00	Constitution Columbian Orator & the History of America	2.25	
2 volumes of Guthries Grammer	5.00	Smiths moral sentiment & practical navigator	1.50	
2 volumes of Bartrams travels	2.00	Morses geography & revised code	3.25	
		Elements of morality letter writer & Life of Washington	1.50	

Flowers of History 2 volums	.75
Robison Crusoe & Wises companion	1.00
Morses Geography	1.00
Stuben	.50
Enticks Dictionary 2 of them	.75
Franklins Works 2 volums	1.50
a view of the Executive of the United States & a sketch of the History of America	1.12½
2 Spelling Books part of Bible and a prise book	.62½
Washingtons Letters	.37½
a number of peices of old Books & an old map	1.11½
4 Candlesticks	6.00
1 glass picher cream pot sugar tongs scop spoon & 4 teaspoons	13.50
1 Backgammon table	3.00
2 Casters of Crewits	5.00
3 glasses & 1 tumbler	1.12½
2 sets of cups and saucers and a server	3.50
12 phials	1.25
3 Do	.37½
1 Dressing glass	5.00
1 Dressing Box	1.25
1 small trunk	.75
1 Bureau	12.00
2 sets of Knives & forks 1 set at $2 the other at $1.50	3.50
4 table spoons 4 shillings 1 set of teaspoons 3 shillings	1.17
4 tablespoons	.37½
3 pair of candle snuffers	1.00
money scales	2.50
3 tea canisters	1.00

2 padlocks and several other old articles	3.25
1 pocket compass and 1 pair of spectakles	1.50
1 Conkshell	.50
part of a case of Bottles	5.00
profiles of Washington and Bonapart	1.50
Picture fraims	1.25
1 pair of casamore overalls	10.00
1 pair of casamore smallclothes $3 1 pair of nankeen Do. 75 cents	3.75
2 pair of overalls	.75
1 Broad Cloath coat	12.00
1 Military Do	13.50
1 Broadcloath Do	2.00
7 Waistcoats	5.00
1 Military hat	1.00
timothy seeds	.50
2 shirts	1.50
1 pair of cotton stockings	1.50
1 pair of old socks and stockins	.12½
1 Bureau	4.00
1 jug	1.00
1 Demijohn	3.00
1 pair of saddle bags	2.00
1 shott gun	5.00
1 Do Do	3.00
Seed cotton	16.50
1 Folding leaf table	9.00
1 small Do	2.50
1 table cover	1.00
3 Bedcords	1.25
2 pair of harnes and trace chains	4.00
3 axes	4.00
2 hoes and a mattick	2.00
2 plows	2.00
1 portmanteau	3.00
1 trunk	4.00

1 Bookcase	5.00	1 Do	3.75
31 pounds of wool	9.50	1 Counterpain	10.00
some blue cotton & a		1 peast bedcover	2.00
basket	.50	3 Coverlids	5.00
1 pair of cotton cards	1.00	1 table cloath	.50
a spear and walking		1 Do	2.00
stick	1.50	1 Do	1.50
2 bedsteads	1.50	1 Do	2.50
1 Do	1.50	2 sheets	4.00
12 chairs	6.00	1 Do	2.25
2 smothing irons	1.00	2 Do	1.50
1 Bake oven	2.00	1 Counterpain	9.50
1 Churn	.50	1 Do	11.50
1 Skillet	1.00	1 Do	10.00
2 piggons & a cooler	.75	1 Do	9.00
1 sifter	1.00	1 Do	10.00
1 piggon	.25	1 tilet	1.00
1 reel and 1 cotton		1 Do	2.00
wheel	3.00	3 pair of pillow cases	1.75
1 pair of Dog irons	3.00	1 axe $2.50 — 2 kettles	
1 shovel & tongs	2.00	$8 — 1 hoe $1	11.50
1 pair of stilards	3.00	Tallow	1.00
8 crocks and jars	4.25	16 sheep	30.00
1 spice martar	2.50	1 Bay mare	60.00
1 straner and coffy pot	.75	1 sorrel Do	25.00
1 lantern	.50	1 gray horse	35.00
1 coffy mill	3.00	1 cow and calf	10.00
1 basket 1 pitcher &		1 negro man Isaac	400.00
plates	4.00	1 negro man Frank	450.00
6 saucers 1 tea canister		1 Do Carter	400.00
& tea cup	.50	1 Do Archer	450.00
5 dishes	5.00	1 negro woman Aggy &	
1 gridiron & tribit	.75	child	425.00
1 pair of skeats	1.00	1 negro girl Mary	250.00
1 small table	1.00	1 Do Do Celey	175.00
1 small trunk	1.00	1 negro boy William	112.50
5 Beds the 1st $9 the		3 Bee hives	4.50
2nd $12 the 3rd $20		1 Do Do	2.00
the 4th $8 the 5th $11	60.00	2 Bridle Bits and clips	.50
2 pairs of pillows and		1 set little irons wedge	
two bolsters	4.00	etc.	1.25
2 Blankets	2.00	1 rifle gun and shott bag	22.00
1 Coverlid	6.00	1 walking staff	1.00
1 Bedquilt	4.00	1 Walnut bedstead	2.50
1 peast cover	2.50	1 Trundle Do	1.50

1 Bedstead	1.00		1 padlock	.25
1 Crib of corn	56.00		1 pair bridle bits	.25
1 Field of Wheat	18.00		1 cow and calf	10.00
1 Horse	50.00		1 Do Do	7.00
1 Saddle	5.00		3 cows $10 each	30.00
1 Grindstone	1.50		1 Do	10.00
1 small pickling jar	.25		1 Heifer	4.00
669 feet of poplar plank	10.00		6 yearlings	12.00
1 table	.50		17 large hogs	35.00
2 Gees	1.00		52 small shoats	26.00
1 pair of hand mill-			40 sows and shoats	30.00
stones	3.00		1 small jug	.50
1 spur	.25		1 Iron wedge	.75
1 Bridle	.50		1 axe	.62½
1 Cotton wheel	2.50		1 Ink Bottle	.25
1 sorrel Horse	16.50		1 Black grain piece of	
1 sorrel Do	15.00		Leather	.75
4 meat tubs large	2.00		2½ yds. Cotton lining	.25
6 small meat tubs	.87½		1 pair Bridle leathers	.37½
1 whiskey barrel	.75		4 Ducks	.50

Patrick H. Rice   )
George Robertson)   appraisers
Jos. Reed   )

James Rutter Administrator
L. Lewis app bill

SECTION 3. ESTATE EXPENSES FOR 1812

The Estate of Lilburn Lewis decd. dn. to James Rutter administrator of sd. Estate for services done and money Expended in the year 1812

To 2 days in wrighting notes advertisements & distributing them	$2
June 1st 1 day attending on the appraisers	1
June 2nd and 3rd 2 days attendance on the sale	2
June the 4th & 6th 2 days in casting up accounts and taking notes	2
June 11th & 13th 2 days in Copying appraisement & Sale bills and examining papers	2
June 15th & 16th 2 days attendance at Court on business belonging to said estate	2
June 22nd 1 day in going to and coming from Mark Phillips and setling with the adm. of Randolph Lewis Decd.	1

369

July 11th 1 day in going after two men indebted to the Estate
   who was reported to be about to abscond themselves and taking new security   1
July 20th 1 day at Court to give in the appraisement & Sale bill
   etc.   1
3 days in going to and coming from the Salem lick on business
   of the Estate (to wit) the 25th 26th & 27th days of July   3
August 17th 1 day in a settlement with Randolph Lewis's adm.   1
Sept. 24th 1 day spent in getting signers to a petition to the
   Governor for the benefit of sd. Estate   1
Sept. 25th & 26th 2 days in going to Smithland on business
   belonging to sd. Estate and hunting cattle that was not sold at
   the sale   2
Nov. 27th 1 day in seling a Cow at Wm. Rices   1
Expenses in the trip to the Lick   1.50
4 Dollars & 50 cents paid to Wm. H. Ramsey for crying the
   Estate for two days   4.50
four appraisers two days at 75 cents per day Each   6
75 cents paid to Joseph Reed Exqr. for qualifying three appraisers   ·75
1 Dollar 75 cents paid for whiskey at the Sales   1.75
6 Dollars paid Archabald Cannon for collecting of stock previous to the sale feeding hogs etc.   6
2 Dollars paid James Rutter Senr. for his attendance on appraisement and sales   2
                                                 $44.50
To paper   .25

                                             $44.75

                 Rutter   )
)
            vs.   )   Acct.
)
         L. Lewis Dec.)

                     Oct–Nov–Dec

NOTES

Key to Location Symbols

DLC – Library of Congress
Ky Hi – Kentucky Historical Society, Frankfort
Liv. Cir. Ct. – Livingston Circuit Court Clerk's Office,
            Smithland, Kentucky
Liv. Co. – Livingston County Court Clerk's Office,
            Smithland, Kentucky
M Hi – Massachusetts Historical Society, Boston
Mo SHi – Missouri Historical Society, St. Louis
Presb Hi – Presbyterian Historical Society, Philadelphia
Vi – Virginia State Library, Richmond
Vi Hi – Virginia Historical Society, Richmond
Vi U – University of Virginia Library, Charlottesville
T McG Lib. – Tracy W. McGregor Library, Vi U
MSS Dept. – Manuscripts Department, Vi U

Key to Other Abbreviations

The publications and periodicals listed below are those most frequently cited throughout this book, and are cited consistently in the abbreviated form given here. Other works are referred to by author and short title; the full reference may be found in the bibliography.

Census 1810 – Third Census, 1810, Livingston County, Kentucky, National Archives Microfilm Publications, microcopy 252, roll 7.

Filson Quarterly – Filson Club History Quarterly, Louisville, Ky., 1926–.

Ky. H. J. – *Journal of the House of Representatives of the Commonwealth of Kentucky,* Frankfort, state printer, 1792–.

Ky. S. J. – *Journal of the Senate of the Commonwealth of Kentucky,* Frankfort, state printer, 1792–.

Littell – William Littell, *The Statute Law of Kentucky, with Notes, Praelections, and Observations on the Public Acts,* 5 vols., Frankfort, 1809–1819.

Mag. Alb. Hist. – *Magazine of Albemarle County History,* Charlottesville, Va., 1940–.

Register – Register of the Kentucky Historical Society, Frankfort, 1903–.

TBCF – Constance E. Thurlow, Francis L. Berkeley, Jr., John Casteen, and Anne Freudenberg, comps., *The Jefferson Papers of the University of Virginia,* Charlottesville, 1973. This book catalogues in chronological order all of the Jefferson papers at the University of Virginia. Each of the more than three thousand items is described, summarized, located in the collection of which it is a part, and numbered. These numbers are used in the footnotes below, following the symbol TBCF, in order to establish precise identification of the document cited.

Vi. Hist. Mag. – *Virginia Magazine of History and Biography,* Richmond, 1893–.

W. M. Quarterly – *William and Mary College Quarterly Historical Magazine,* Williamsburg, Va., 1892–.

BUNDLES

The use of the word "bundles" in citations of the circuit court records refers to the legal documents that pertained to any given case put on the court docket. When the case was settled and went off the docket these documents were assembled and folded into a small bundle about two by six and one-half inches. The bundle of a complicated case might contain depositions, subpoenas, indictments, bills, notes, letters, and any other written evidence or court orders pertaining to the case. At the end of the court term the individual case bundles were gathered together, labeled, tied with a string or ribbon, and filed in boxes as part of the court records.

In the county court, all documents pertaining to court business transacted at any given session of the county court were folded and tied into bundles similar to those of the circuit court. These bundles were boxed and filed in the county court clerk's office. A great variety of documents may be found in the county bundles: estate settlements, requisitions, tavern bonds, commissioners' and appraisers' reports, and many other papers concerning official county business.

In many Kentucky courthouses the filing of old bundles was haphazard at best. Often it is difficult to find certain papers. Almost without exception, the papers that compose these bundles are extremely fragile, and faded as well. They contain information found nowhere else and should not be handled casually.

1. COLONIAL DAYS

1. Bergman, *Chronological History of the Negro,* p. 10.

2. Col. Charles Lewis of the Byrd, also known as Charles Lewis of Goochland and Parish of St. James Northam, was born in Abingdon Parish, Gloucester County, September 3, 1696. He was the second son of Councillor John Lewis ("the younger") of Warner Hall, and Elizabeth Warner Lewis. On May 28, 1717, Charles Lewis of the Byrd married Mary Howell, daughter of John Howell. In 1756 Charles Lewis of the Byrd served on the vestry of St. James Parish (*W. M. Quarterly,* 1st ser. 15 July 1906, p. 24). He is listed in the *D.A.R. Patriot Index* as having

rendered patriotic service to Virginia. "Patriotic service" is a broad classification that includes civic as well as military duty.

3. Hening, *Statutes at Large*, 3:305–12, 81–83; W. M. Dabney, "Jefferson's Albemarle," pp. 14–19; C. W. Watts, "Colonial Albemarle," pp. 24–37.

4. Hening, *Statutes at Large*, 3:306; Watts, "Colonial Albemarle," pp. 24–25. This law limiting patent size was later relaxed, and larger grants were made in Albemarle County.

5. Ayres, "Albemarle County," p. 48. By 1775 the average sale price for land near the headwaters of the James River had risen to fifty cents per acre.

6. Patent Book 14 (1728–1732), p. 375, Land Office, Vi; Woods, *Albemarle*, p. 251. As was often the case in issuing patents, there was confusion with the claims of other men as to the location and priority of this grant to Charles Lewis of the Byrd. This was not cleared up until eight years had passed, when the patent council, on Lewis's petition, ordered that the land be surveyed in Lewis's name. It was not until late in 1739 that Lewis was free to open the Buck Island plantation (*Vi. Hist. Mag.* 14 [April 1907]: 338–39).

The part of the Buck Island grant which lay south of the Rivanna is today bounded on the south by the lower section of Buck Island Creek, on the southwest by Virginia Route 53, on the southeast and northeast by the Rivanna River. Most of the land owned by Mr. and Mrs. Schuyler M. Harris lies in the tract, as does the eastern section of the land owned by Mr. and Mrs. Stephen Sweeney of Albemarle County.

7. Ayres, "Albemarle County," pp. 45–47.

8. On p. 251 of his history of Albemarle County, Edgar Woods states that Charles Lewis of the Byrd built and resided at the home, Monteagle, south of the Rivanna in Albemarle County. The author can find no evidence to support this statement. The deed books of Goochland County confirm Lewis's residence at the Byrd during the years of 1741, 1756, 1760, 1767, 1768 and 1779.

9. Full title to these lands was not deeded to Charles Lewis, Jr. by his father until 1766 and 1767.

10. Dabney, "Jefferson's Albemarle," pp. 28–29.

11. Rosenberger, *Jefferson Reader*, p. 32.

12. Ibid., p. 43.

13. Ayres, "Albemarle County," pp. 39–43; Brown, *The Cabels and Their Kin*, p. 53, quoted in Schachner, *Thomas Jefferson*, p. 11.

14. Albemarle County Surveyor's Book 1 (1744–1755), Part 1, pp. 121, 161, Charlottesville, Va. (hereafter cited as Albemarle Surveyor's Book). The 400-acre tract was described in 1749 as being located on the Lime Kiln Branch, presently called Limestone Creek. It appears that the burning of lime to make mortar was one of the crafts practiced in the neighborhood prior to 1749.

15. Albemarle County Deed Book 4, pp. 260, 385, Charlottesville, Va. (hereafter cited as Albemarle Deed Book).

16. Albemarle County Will Book 2, pp. 403–405, Charlottesville, Va. (hereafter cited as Albemarle Will Book).

17. Eli Whitney did not invent the improved cotton gin until 1793. The cotton "ginn" mentioned in the inventory of Charles Lewis, Jr. was an earlier form of the gin, which used two counter-rotating rollers to tear the fiber from the seed. See Anburey, *Travels,* 2:246.

18. Stampp, *The Peculiar Institution,* p. 282.

19. Gilmer, "Papers," p. 119. A slave named Frank, who had served four generations of the Charles Lewis family, stated in an interview at the age of ninety that he had always been healthy and had almost never been sick in his life. Evidently the Lewises provided a balanced diet for their slaves (William Dickey to James H. Dickey, June 29, 1812, MS 81008, Presb Hi).

20. Albemarle Will Book 2, pp. 403–405.

21. Rawlings, "Albemarle County Court, Order Book," p. 16.

22. Malone, *Jefferson,* pp. 3–32; Schachner, *Thomas Jefferson,* pp. 1–19.

23. Schachner, *Thomas Jefferson,* pp. 20–21; Albemarle Will Book 2, pp. 32–34.

24. Mayo, *Thomas Jefferson and Randolph,* pp. 7–8.

2. THE FIGHT FOR FREEDOM

1. Sullivan, "The Gentry and the Association," pp. 35–44.

2. Gilmer, "Papers," pp. 75, 82.

3. Ibid., p. 80. The captain of this company was Charles Lewis of North Garden, the brother-in-law of Charles Lilburne Lewis.

4. Malone, *Jefferson,* p. 215; Gilmer, "Papers," p. 103.

5. Gilmer, "Papers," p. 81.

6. Branchi, "Memoirs of Doctor Philip Mazzei," pp. 172–73; Mazzei, *Memoirs,* pp. 209–12.

7. Gilmer, "Papers," pp. 81–82. This letter was dated June 2, 1775.

8. Dabney, "Jefferson's Ablemarle," p. 39.

9. Gilmer, "Papers," pp. 86–89.

10. George Gilmer to Jefferson, July 26 or 27, 1775, in Boyd, *Papers,* 1:237; Gilmer, "Papers," p. 89.

11. Boyd, *Papers,* 1:237.

12. Gilmer, "Papers," pp. 92–93.

13. Boyd, *Papers,* 1:237; Gilmer, "Papers," pp. 99, 107–108.

14. Gilmer, "Papers," pp. 108–10.

15. Hening, *Statutes at Large,* 9:198.

16. Eaton, *A History of the Old South,* p. 63.

17. Boyd, *Papers,* 1:268, 4:45–46, 5:263n, 6:56–57.

18. Gilmer, "Papers," pp. 111–13; Woods, *Albemarle*, p. 30; "Virginia Legislative Papers," *Vi. Hist. Mag.*, 17 (1909): 58. The commanding officer of the Albemarle regiment during its training period at Rockfish Gap and the subsequent tour of duty in the Hampton and Potomac areas during the summer of 1776 was Col. Charles Lewis of North Garden. Prompted, perhaps, by the epidemic sickness in the coastal areas, or by the imminence of combat, he wrote his will on June 11, 1776. His brothers-in-law, Charles L. Lewis and Bennett Henderson, who were evidently serving with the Albemarle regiment, signed the will as witnesses and were named therein as executors (Albemarle Will Book 2, p. 374). See also Appendix 1, sec. 2.

19. While on the Cherokee campaign, Col. Charles Lewis of North Garden wrote a codicil to his will. Charles L. Lewis, executor and witness to the original will, did not sign the codicil as witness. This probably indicates that he was not with the regiment at that time.

20. The vestry of the Episcopal church managed many of the charity, welfare, and other secular problems in the various parishes. For example, the church wardens indentured or bound out orphans in St. Ann's parish to learn and work as apprentices until they reached the age of twenty-one. In many cases the vestrymen were not Episcopalians. (Meade, *Old Churches, Ministers, and Families of Virginia*, 2:49; Vestry Book, "Parish of St. Ann's 1782–1785," pp. 1, 8 Vi).

21. Woods, *Albemarle*, pp. 130–31; Dabney, "Jefferson's Albemarle," p. 171.

22. Estate Inventory of Charles Lewis, Jr., Albemarle Will Book 2, p. 403.

23. Bishop, *History of the Church*, p. 54.

24. Jefferson, *Autobiography*, pp. 52–53.

25. Stanard, "Virginia Legislative Papers," *Vi. Hist. Mag.* 13 (July 1905): 40–45; Boyd, *Papers*, 1:586.

26. Stanard, "Virginia Legislative Papers," *Vi. Hist. Mag.* 18 (1910): 255–58. Extracts from this petition give the general tone of these documents:

Your Memorialists have never been on an equal footing with the other good people of this Colony in respect of religious Privileges, having been obliged by Law to the support of the Established Church, while at the same Time, they were moved from a Principle of Conscience to support that church of which they are called themselves members; Yet . . . for the sake of good order, they have patiently submitted to their Grievances, continuing to be peasable and loyal subjects. . . . When it became necessary that the Form of Government should be new moddled, in consequence of our having thrown off our Dependance on the Crown & Parliament of great Britan, your Memorialists cannot disguise their real concern . . . to put every religious Denomination on an equal Footing, to be supported by themselves, independent of one another.... It would not only be a just and reasonable mode of Government, but would most certainly have an happy Influence on the greater Purity of the several churches; on their more free and friendly Intercourse with one another; on suppressing anything like Feuds and animosities amongst the People, and on warmly attaching all of every Denomination to Government. Such a mode of government is all that your Memorialists desire.

27. Boyd, *Papers,* 1:586–89.

28. In 1775 dissenters were relieved from the levies collected for the Episcopal church, and were released from the oppressive laws of Parliamentary origin. Certain other restrictions remained unsolved. Little pertinent law was written until Jefferson's Bill for Establishing Religious Freedom was passed in 1786. Jefferson had written the bill nine years before, at a time when its passage appeared unlikely, but even then his intention was to "extinguish forever the ambitious hope of making laws for the human mind" (Boyd, *Papers,* 1:274–80, 525–29; 2:545–53). Jefferson regarded this law as equal in importance to the Declaration of Independence, and considered it to be one of the three of his greatest achievements. Since then thoughtful men have considered it an "ineffaceable landmark of human liberty" (Malone, *Jefferson,* pp. 274–80).

3. A Colonel in the Militia

1. Gilmer, "Papers," pp. 134–37; Boyd, *Papers,* 2:130n.

2. Gilmer, "Papers," pp. 73, 138.

3. Dabney, "Jefferson's Albemarle," pp. 52–61.

4. James Wood to Jefferson, June 15, 1780, Boyd, *Papers,* 3:449–50.

5. Albemarle Will Book 2, pp. 374–75; Albemarle Will Book 5, pp. 50–56.

6. Woods, *Albemarle,* pp. 47–48.

7. Albemarle Surveyor's Book 1, part 2 (1756–1790), p. 120.

8. Robert, *Tobacco in America,* p. 25.

9. Brief biographical notes concerning the other three candidates for the legislature may be found in Woods, *Albemarle:* Isaac Davis, pp. 175–76; James Marks, p. 262; George Twyman, p. 333.

10. George Gilmer to Jefferson, April 13, 1781, Boyd, *Papers,* 5:430–31.

11. Malone, *Jefferson,* p. 367.

12. George Gilmer to Jefferson, April 13, 1781, Boyd, *Papers,* 5:430–31.

13. Jefferson to David Jameson, April 16, 1781, Boyd, *Papers,* 5:468–69.

14. Reuben Lindsay to Jefferson, April 25, 1781, Boyd, *Papers,* 5:554–55.

15. Dabney, "Jefferson's Albemarle," p. 67; Jefferson to William Davies, May 31, 1781, Boyd, *Papers,* 6:48–49n.

16. Girardin, *History of Virginia,* 4:497.

17. V. Dabney, "Jack Jouett's Ride," p. 57.

18. A comprehensive bibliography of published material regarding Tarleton's Raid and Jouett's Ride is Wyllie's "Writings about Jack Jouett and Tarleton's Raid."

19. Wyllie, "Daniel Boone's Adventures," pp. 13, 16n, 23.

20. Woods, *Albemarle,* p. 45.

21. Tarleton, *History of the Campaigns of 1780 and 1781,* p. 304.

22. Girardin, *History of Virginia,* pp. 500–501.

23. Wyllie, "Daniel Boone's Adventures," pp. 6–20; Girardin, *History of Virginia,* p. 501.

24. Boyd, *Papers,* 4:278–79.

25. Ibid., pp. 400–403.

26. Schachner, *Thomas Jefferson,* p. 217.

27. Boyd, *Papers,* 6:77–79n.

28. Malone, *Jefferson,* pp. 358–66; Boyd, *Papers,* 6:135–36.

29. Schachner, *Thomas Jefferson,* p. 216.

30. Jefferson to Isaac Zane, December 24, 1781, Boyd, *Papers,* 6:143; Jefferson to George Rogers Clark, November 26, 1782, Boyd, *Papers,* 6:205; Malone, *Jefferson,* p. 361.

31. Col. William Fleming to Jefferson, June 14, 1781, Boyd, *Papers,* 6:93.

32. Palmer, *Calendar of Virginia State Papers,* 3:262. The editor of this work was a great-grandson of Col. Charles L. Lewis.

4. PROSPERITY

1. Anburey, *Travels,* pp. 248–49, 231.

2. James Wood to Jefferson, February 20, 1781, Boyd, *Papers,* 4:672.

3. Dabney, "Jefferson's Albemarle," p. 77.

4. Du Roi, *Journal,* p. 155.

5. Ibid., p. 153.

6. Dabney, "Jefferson's Albemarle," pp. 58, 62–63.

7. The personal property tax rolls of Albemarle County in 1782, Vi, list Charles Lewis, Jr. of Buck Island as owning 58 slaves, 14 horses and mules, and nearly 100 head of cattle.

8. Albemarle Will Book 2, pp. 399–405.

9. Dabney, "Jefferson's Albemarle," pp. 207–208.

10. Account Book of Sheriff Nicholas Hamner, 1782–1783, Vi U.

11. Just three years before, in 1779, the father of Charles Lewis, Jr., Charles Lewis of the Byrd, had died in Goochland in the eighty-third

year of his life. He left the remaining 400 acres he owned at Buck Island to Charles Lewis, Jr. (Goochland County Will Book 13, September 21, 1779, pp. 13–15, Goochland, Virginia).

12. Albemarle Will Book 2, p. 399. Isham, the second son, was left 1,400 acres on the north fork of the Hardware River, and one of the daughters inherited 1,000 acres on Ivy Creek. Another daughter, Mildred, was left 750 ounces of silver or its equivalent in gold. Each of the six daughters inherited a slave girl, and the nine eldest grandchildren were given a slave boy or girl between the ages of four and seven.

13. Albemarle Will Book 3, pp. 52, 111.

14. Jefferson to Charles L. Lewis, September 11, 1795, private collection of Mrs. Charles W. Biggs, Lewisburg, West Virginia.

15. Albemarle Deed Book 10, pp. 111, 113. At his father's death, Isham had inherited title to 1,400 acres on the north fork of the Hardware River. Isham managed this tract for his mother since, as at Buck Island, she held a life interest in it. At Isham's death she "leased and let to farm" the Hardware River tract to Edward Moore, her son-in-law.

16. Hening, *Statutes at Large,* 13:87. Howell was the son of Charles Lewis of North Garden.

17. Woods, *Albemarle,* p. 57.

18. Ibid., pp. 166, 336, 384. Edward Carter and Wilson C. Nicholas were legislators. William Clark had been sheriff and magistrate, and Francis Walker became a member of the legislature.

19. Albemarle County Personal Property Tax Rolls, Book A, 1790–1793, Vi.

20. Presently identified as Virginia State Route 616.

21. Wyllie, "Daniel Boone's Adventures," p. 17.

22. Albemarle County Personal Property Tax Rolls, Book A, 1790–1793, Vi; Wilkerson, *Thomas Duckett Boyd,* p. 10. In 1806, Col. Charles L. Lewis gave this tract of land to his son, Isham. At that time the land was described as being in the possession of Thomas D. Boyd, evidently on a rental arrangement (Albemarle Deed Book 15, pp. 290–91; Book 16, pp. 282–83).

23. Jefferson to Philip Mazzei, January 7, 1792, Maruzzi Archives, Pisa, Italy, published in Marraro, "Unpublished Correspondence," pp. 119–20.

24. At the present time this house and approximately 300 acres of the Monteagle tract are owned by Mr. and Mrs. Schuyler Marshall Harris of Albemarle County. They have made extensive alterations in the original home.

25. Anburey, *Travels,* p. 187.

26. The exact date of the completion of Monteagle is unknown. The evidence at hand indicates that the house was built prior to 1785. It is still standing and is owned and occupied by Mr. and Mrs. Stephen

Sweeney. They have kept the house in good repair (it has been restored since 1937, when the photograph in Figure 1 was taken), and have made only minor alterations in the basic structure. The Sweeneys also own nearly 600 acres of the original Monteagle tract south of the Rivanna.

27. Jefferson had reservations about Virginia architecture. In 1786 he wrote that in "Virginia . . . it is worse than in any other part of America, which I have seen." (Jefferson to John Page, May 4, 1786, Boyd, *Papers,* 9:445).

28. "Mount Eagle" [*Monteagle*]: Albemarle County Home, W.P.A. Historical Project, 1937, 5-A of Bulletin 3400, Archives Division, Vi.

29. United States Bureau of the Census, *Heads of Families,* p. 81.

30. One of these slave houses is still standing on the Schuyler M. Harris tract. The two others, no longer in existence, stood on the Stephen Sweeney tract. The ceiling joists of this cabin were sawed five-by-nine-inch timbers, and the loft was floored with one-by-six-inch heart pine planks. The rafters were three-by-four-inch sawed timber, and the decking was rough-edged plank over two feet wide, and spaced about five inches apart. The roof was shingled. The floor of the cabin was about two feet off the ground and the walls of the cabin, up to the loft floor level, were made of huge hand-hewn timbers, beautifully fitted at the corners in chamfer-and-notch style to shed rain. These timbers were spaced about four inches apart, and the spaces were chinked with a friable hair mortar daubed in between small split pieces of wood, which were placed in the chinking space to save mortar.

31. Martha was called "Patsy," and Ann was called "Nancy."

32. Martha J. Randolph to Jefferson, March 22, 1791, Boyd, *Papers,* 19:599.

33. Albemarle County Personal Property Tax Rolls, Book A, 1789–1793, Vi.

34. Albemarle Deed Book 11, pp. 145–48.

35. Ayres, "Albemarle County," pp. 45–50.

5. THE VIRGINIA PLANTER

1. Jefferson to Charles L. Lewis, February 22, 1790, Boyd, *Papers,* 16:192.

2. Ibid.; Charles Lewis to Jefferson, September 25, 1801, M Hi.

3. Albemarle County Personal Property Tax Rolls, Book A, 1789–1803, Vi. There is no record of the sons' attendance at William and Mary College.

4. One notable exception is Jefferson's *Notes on the State of Virginia.*

5. Thomas and Connor, "Henry McMurtrie," p. 311.

6. Burnaby, *Travels,* pp. 53–58.

7. Du Roi, *Journal,* p. 160.

8. Anburey, *Travels*, pp. 190–91, 215–18.

9. Chastellux, *Travels in North America*, 2:429, 434–42, 533.

10. Ibid., p. 603, n. 14.

11. Jefferson to Chastellux, September 2, 1785, Boyd, *Papers*, 8:467–69.

12. Smyth, *A Tour in the United States of America*, 1:41–43; Warville, *New Travels in the United States*, pp. 231, 347–49, 359.

6. The Shipwreck of the Fortunes

1. Jefferson to Gideon Fitch, May 23, 1809, M Hi.

2. Alexander Hamilton's policies for funding and assuming the debts of the several states had greatly enhanced the value of the obligations, and persons with access to advanced information realized immense fortunes. At the same time, speculation in bank stocks and land was epidemic, with overextension of credit a common practice. The failure of a few entailed failures of many "and severe losses to more; a shock to business confidence affecting seriously mercantile activities themselves entirely unconnected with speculation; a tumble of prices not only of securities, but also of real estate and commodities" (Smith and Cole, *Fluctuations in American Business*, pp. 12–13).

3. Wynes, "Banking in Virginia," pp. 35–36.

4. McMaster, *History of the People of the United States*, 1:593. For a discussion of Jefferson's role, see Boyd, *Papers*, 18:611–88; Miller, *The Federalist Era*, pp. 51–52.

5. Nettels, *Emergence of a National Economy*, p. 125.

6. Smith and Cole, *Fluctuations*, pp. 14, 17.

7. Albemarle County Personal Property Tax Rolls, 1799–1812, Vi.

8. Eaves, *Virginia Tobacco*, p. 12 (quoting Craven, *Soil Exhaustion*, p. 20).

9. Jefferson, *Notes*, pp. 166–68.

10. Betts, *Garden Book*, pp. 241–42, quoting La Rochefoucauld-Liancourt, *Travels*. Today, with the use of improved seed, machinery, chemicals, and techniques, it is not uncommon to realize six or seven times these yields year after year on the same ground.

11. Dabney, "Jefferson's Albemarle," p. 98, quoting John H. Craven to the journal, *Farmer's Register*, 1:150.

12. Anburey, *Travels*, pp. 234, 238. In addition, it was a common practice at this time to burn over woods annually to promote the growth of grass for cattle (Boyd, *Papers*, 17:325n).

13. Betts, *Garden Book*, pp. 178, 219; Betts, *Farm Book*, pp. 203, 230.

14. Betts, *Garden Book*, pp. 237–38.

15. Betts, *Farm Book*, p. 314.

16. Ibid., p. 230.

17. Betts, *Garden Book*, pp. 267, 354.

18. Betts, *Farm Book,* pp. 272, 274.

19. Randolph, *Domestic Life,* p. 208.

20. Jefferson to Eliza Trist, December 15, 1786, Boyd, *Papers,* 10:600.

21. Woods, *Albemarle,* pp. 386–95.

22. Colonel Lewis's brother-in-law, Bennett Henderson, once well-to-do and influential, had died shortly before Lewis lost possession of, or gave up, the tavern and stage line. It may have been that these businesses were interlocked with, or depended upon, the Henderson enterprises at Milton. Two years after Henderson's death, his widow, who was Colonel Lewis's sister, and her children were "absolutely pennyless" (Betts, *Farm Book,* p. 352).

23. The corn shortage of 1796, and the threat of famine that attended it, may have been one cause for this sale of slaves. Unless in extremity, compassionate slave owners seldom broke up families by a sale.

24. Eaves, *Virginia Tobacco,* p. 21.

25. *Lewisiana,* book 35, chap. 68, p. 22.

26. Charles Lewis to Jefferson, April 29, 1806, M Hi.

27. Lucy Lewis to Jefferson, May 26, 1806, TBCF #959, Vi U, MSS Dept.

28. Haynes, "History of Crittenden County" (reproduced in Appendix 3 below); Anburey, *Travels,* p. 223.

29. Anburey, *Travels,* pp. 190–91; Burnaby, *Travels,* p. 53. Thoughtful landowners were well aware of the dangers of using the type of overseer usually found in Virginia. Thomas M. Randolph, Jr. wrote to Jefferson, bemoaning the fact that he did not have a New England farmer to manage his own estate. "Ignorance of Agriculture is so evident in our common Virginia overseers that it must decrease in value every day under the management of them" (Boyd, *Papers,* 16:442).

30. Albemarle Deed Book 14, p. 402. This gift of land to Lilburne was made in late 1799 or early 1800. The deed was not recorded, but the change in ownership is shown in the tax rolls, and the property is described in a deed made a few years later (Albemarle Deed Book 15, p. 332).

31. Albemarle County Court Order Books: Book 1793–1795, pp. 39, 262, 478; Book 1795–1798, pp. 57, 203, 323; Book 1798–1800, pp. 91, 232; Book 1801–1802, p. 56.

32. The statements in this chapter concerning the property of Colonel Lewis and his sons are based on the Albemarle County real and personal property tax rolls from 1792 to 1812, Vi.

33. Bowers, *Jefferson and Hamilton,* p. 97.

34. Albemarle Deed Book 14, p. 231. This tract of land lay on the south side of the Rivanna, adjoining and upstream from the tract where the Monteagle home stood. Of the 400 acres, about one-quarter was bottom land.

35. Albemarle Deed Book 14, pp. 506–507. This tract included the fertile land east of present Route 53, which is now owned by Schuyler M. Harris, and the poor timberland west of Route 53, including the Mount Eagle Church site. The timberland section west of Route 53 was part of 985 acres bought by Charles L. Lewis in 1776. The Harris section east of Route 53 was part of the 350 acres (actually 500) Charles L. Lewis was given by his father in 1770. The Monteagle home site now owned by Stephen Sweeney was not part of the land given to Charles.

This gift may have been made in anticipation of Charles's marriage. A year before Charles was given the property, Jefferson, in a letter to his son-in-law, John W. Eppes, remarked that "Nancy Jefferson is said to be about marrying Charles Lewis." (Jefferson to John W. Eppes, April 8, 1801, TBCF #698, Vi U, property of Luther Ely Smith). Nancy Jefferson was the daughter of Randolph Jefferson, the president's brother, and had the marriage taken place, it would have been between first cousins, a common thing in those families. Something or someone intervened, however, for Charles did not marry his cousin Anna S. (Nancy) Jefferson.

36. Charles L. Lewis Family Bible Records, Vi U. These records give October 31, 1803 as the date of Mary Lewis's death. Merrow E. Sorley, in his impressive *Lewis of Warner Hall,* may have transposed figures when he gave the date as October 13, 1803.

37. Albemarle Deed Book 14, p. 402.

38. At an earlier time, when Col. Charles L. Lewis's sister, Elizabeth Henderson, was in financial trouble following the death of her husband, Bennett Henderson, Colonel Lewis had bought her portion of her father's estate, thus giving him two shares. Colonel Lewis's portion, which he sold to Craven Peyton, included twelve slaves.

39. Sometimes during the two-year period following the gift of the 650-acre tract, Charles sold or mortgaged it to John and Matthew Henderson. This sale was not recorded in the court records, but it was made, for on July 17, 1804, two years after he was given the tract by his parents, Charles bought back "all their right, title, and interest in" the same tract from John and Matthew Henderson, for the sum of 1,000 pounds (Albemarle Deed Book 15, p. 28). The day after this repurchase from the Hendersons, Charles sold all his right, title, and interest in this same 650-acre tract to Craven Peyton for 1,500 pounds (Albemarle Deed Book 15, p. 33).

40. Albemarle Deed Book 15, p. 30.

41. Albemarle Deed Book 15, pp. 408–409; Albemarle Deed Book 16, p. 144. Peyton sold this tract to Brown Rives & Co., of Milton.

42. Albemarle Deed Book 15, pp. 409–10.

43. Ibid., p. 409.

44. Albemarle Deed Book 15, pp. 290–291; Albemarle Deed Book 16, pp. 181–83; Mead, *Historic Homes,* pp. 271–4; Woods, *Albemarle,* pp. 260–62.

45. Albemarle County Real Estate Tax Rolls, Book B, Vi; Albermarle Deed Book 18, pp. 234–36.

46. Isham Lewis to Jefferson, April 27, 1809, M Hi.

47. Lucy Lewis to Jefferson, November 19, 1807, TBCF #1014, Vi U, MSS Dept.

7. CRAVEN PEYTON, THOMAS JEFFERSON,
AND THE HENDERSONS

1. Boyd, *Papers,* 16:51.

2. Ibid., 1:87.

3. Ibid., 1:88n.

4. Bear, "Thomas Jefferson's Account Books," pp. 94, 651; Wertenbaker, "Rivanna," p. 4.

5. Betts, *Garden Book,* p. 315.

6. Rawlings, *Albemarle of Other Days,* p. 112.

7. Betts, *Farm Book,* p. 257; Thomas Jefferson, *Notes,* p. 6.

8. Betts, *Farm Book,* p. 349.

9. Sorley, *Lewis,* pp. 371–72; Jillson, *Kentucky Land Grants,* Part 1:62; Virginia Grants, Book 7, p. 445, Office of the Secretary of State, Frankfort, Kentucky. This grant of 2,351 acres was listed as being in the "county of Jefferson at east fork of Plum Creek." The value of Henderson's grant was about $940, Virginia currency. Evidently Henderson's term of service was longer than Charles L. Lewis's, for Lewis did not receive a land grant.

10. Woods, *Albemarle,* p. 376. The Bennett Henderson family is not known to have any connection with Richard Henderson of North Carolina and the Transylvania Company.

11. Betts, *Garden Book,* p. 291; Wertenbaker, "Rivanna," p. 3.

12. Anburey, *Travels,* p. 205.

13. Wertenbaker, "Rivanna," p. 3.

14. Hening, *Statutes at Large,* 13:87; William Woods, surveyor, Plat of the Division of Land Belonging to the Legatees of Bennett Henderson, November, 1801, TBCF #753, Vi U. Of the more than 20 lots finally sold, one went to Randolph, Charles L. Lewis's eldest son. It was lot no. 18, and was sold in 1792 for 15 pounds, 10 shillings (Albemarle Deed Book 10, p. 366).

15. Craven Peyton to Jefferson, October 16, 1801, TBCF #741, Vi U, T McG Lib.; Betts, *Farm Book,* p. 351.

16. Betts, *Garden Book,* p. 294.

17. Randolph, *Domestic Life,* pp. 341–45; Schachner, *Thomas Jefferson,* p. 516.

18. Schachner, *Thomas Jefferson,* pp. 577–80; Garlick, *Philip Mazzei,* pp. 133–37.

19. Thomas Jefferson's Account with Craven Peyton, January 7, 1811, ser. r 194: 34556–9, reel 75, DLC.

20. A detailed discussion of Jefferson's mills and Rivanna projects may be found in Betts, *Farm Book,* pp. 341–411.

21. Woods, *Albemarle,* p. 295; Sorley, *Lewis,* p. 352.

22. Woods, *Albemarle,* pp. 58, 295; Palmer, *Calendar,* 6:655; Albemarle County Real Estate Tax Rolls, 1782–1800, Vi. In 1793 a disgruntled contractor wrote to Virginia officials complaining that the bids were let in secret and that Craven Peyton and two other men had gotten the contract for eight pence, the highest ever paid, whereas the complainant would have bid six pence if he had had a chance (Palmer, *Calendar,* p. 655).

23. Jefferson to Craven Peyton, May 7, 1814, M Hi; Jefferson to Craven Peyton, May 8, 1814, DLC.

24. Jefferson to David Michie, March 22, 1817, M Hi.

25. Jefferson to Craven Peyton, October 25, 1807, TBCF #1010, Vi U, T McG Lib. Edmund Bacon was Jefferson's farm manager at Monticello for twenty years, beginning in 1806. Later, he became the primary source for Hamilton W. Pierson's *Jefferson at Monticello.*

26. Jefferson to Craven Peyton, January 15, 1801. TBCF #677, Vi U, T McG Lib. See also Craven Peyton to Jefferson, September 25, 1801, TBCF #734, Vi U.

27. Randolph, *Domestic Life,* pp. 228–29.

28. Mazzei, *Memoirs,* pp. 214–17.

29. Craven Peyton vs. John Henderson. Court Record, 1804–1812, p. 13, TBCF #907, Vi U, T McG Lib; Schachner, *Thomas Jefferson,* p. 743.

30. Schachner, *Thomas Jefferson,* pp. 784, 901.

31. Betts, *Farm Book,* p. 352.

32. Craven Peyton to Jefferson, November 6, 1801, TBCF #750, Vi U, T McG Lib.

33. Betts, *Garden Book,* p. 270.

34. Betts, *Farm Book,* pp. 166–68; Craven Peyton to Jefferson, November 6, 1801, TBCF #750, Vi U, T McG Lib.; Craven Peyton to Jefferson, October 16, 1801, TBCF #741, Vi U, T McG Lib.

35. Jefferson's Account with Peyton, ser. r 194:34556, DLC; Albemarle Personal Property Tax Rolls, 1801, Vi.

36. Craven Peyton to Jefferson, October 3, 1801, TBCF #1008, Vi U, T McG Lib.

37. William Woods, Plat of the Division, TBCF #753, Vi U. For example, one son, James Henderson, drew lot 9 between Milton and the Rivanna, lot 7 downstream from Milton, lot 2 in the timberland behind Milton, and lot 9 upstream from Milton. The parcels within each of the four areas were all of the same size; in front of Milton 2 acres, behind Milton 102 acres, upstream 5 acres, and downstream five and three-quarter acres.

38. Craven Peyton to Jefferson, October 3, 1801, TBCF #1008, Vi

U, T McG Lib.; Jefferson's Account with Peyton, ser. r. 194:34557, DLC.

39. Craven Peyton to Jefferson, October 3, 1801, TBCF #1008, Vi U, T McG Lib.

40. Jefferson to Craven Peyton, October 28, 1812, M Hi; Jefferson's Account with Peyton, ser. r 194:34556-9, DLC.

41. Craven Peyton to Jefferson, October 3, 1801, TBCF #1008, Vi U, T McG Lib. The Lewis mentioned in the letter was James Lewis, who was not closely related to Charles L. Lewis.

42. Jefferson's Account with Peyton, ser. r 194:34556-9, DLC. The six pages of accounts concerning Jefferson's and Peyton's agreement were described by Jefferson in a letter to Peyton (October 28, 1812, M Hi). "I made very full entries in my book. I send you a copy of the statement of them. They consist in fact of 4 accounts, all of which you will find very exactly stated & balanced. The 1st is the Shadwell account as settled & signed by ourselves. The 2d is that of the purchases of the lands of the Hendersons. The 3d is our corn-contract as far as it was carried into execution. The 4th is chiefly of the rents & profits of the lands bought while under your direction."

43. Bennett Henderson to Craven Peyton, Deed, June 28, 1804, TBCF #897, Vi U; Craven Peyton's bill of petition to George Wythe, judge of the High Court of Chancery in Thomas Jefferson's handwriting, submitted May 12, 1804, TBCF #908, p. 1, Vi U; Elizabeth Henderson Deposition, December 25, 1813, TBCF #1264, Vi U.

44. Craven Peyton to Jefferson, October 16, 1807, TBCF #741, Vi U, T McG Lib.; Jefferson to Craven Peyton, October 25, 1807, TBCF #1010, Vi U, T McG Lib.

45. TBCF #907, #908, #909, Vi U, T McG Lib.

46. Peyton vs. Henderson, Court Record, pp. 1–3, 33, TBCF #907, Vi U, T McG Lib.

47. Craven Peyton, Bill of Petition, TBCF #908, Vi U.

48. Peyton vs. Henderson, Court Record, p. 13, TBCF #907, Vi U, T McG Lib.

49. Ibid., pp. 25–27.

50. Craven Peyton to Jefferson, June 25, 1802, date received (listed in TBCF as 1805), TBCF #937, Vi U.

51. Peyton vs. Henderson, Court Record, pp. 22–23, TBCF #907, Vi U, T McG Lib.

52. Jefferson to Craven Peyton, May 7, 1814, M Hi.

53. Craven Peyton to Jefferson, August 6, 1809, TBCF #1061, Vi U, T McG Lib.

54. Albemarle Deed Book 17, p. 405.

55. Jefferson's Account with Peyton, ser. r 194:3455-9, DLC.

56. Betts, *Farm Book*, p. 335.

57. Albemarle Deed Book 10, p. 366.

58. Jefferson to Craven Peyton, August 10, 1813, Vi Hi; Craven Peyton to Jefferson, October 16, 1801, TBCF #741, Vi U, T McG Lib. (mentions receipt of $1,240 from Jefferson, not identified as remuneration).

59. Jefferson to David Michie, March 22, 1817, M Hi; Jefferson to Craven Peyton, January 15, 1801, TBCF #677, Vi U, T McG Lib. Jefferson's Summary of Henderson land purchases 1799 to 1803, 2 pp., TBCF #909, Vi U, T McG Lib. Notations under most of the deeds listed here indicate they were not recorded.

60. B. Perkins, *Prologue to War*, pp. 177–79. The closing days of Jefferson's term as governor of Virginia were likewise something less than glorious.

61. Betts, *Farm Book*, p. 45; Jefferson to Craven Peyton, August 12, 1821, TBCF #2994-a, Vi U.

8. JEFFERSON AND THE LEWISES

1. Mayo, *Jefferson and Randolph*, p. 8.
2. Malone, *Jefferson*, p. 45.
3. Boyd, *Papers*, 6:374.
4. Ibid., 14:427–28.
5. Mayo, *Jefferson and Randolph*, p. 10.
6. Boyd, *Papers*, 14:427–28, 433–34.
7. Ibid., 16:93.
8. Albemarle Will Book 2, pp. 403–405. Jefferson did not serve as an executor of the estate of Charles Lewis, Jr. His duties in Congress and his wife's last illness demanded his attention at that time.

9. Boyd, *Papers*, 16:191–92. The pedigree of the horse, Caractacus, is listed in Betts, *Farm Book*, p. 92.

10. Jefferson to Philip Mazzei, January 7, 1792, Maruzzi Archives, Pisa, Italy, published in Marraro, "Unpublished Correspondence" pp. 119–20. It is difficult to identify the Mr. Thomas mentioned here. He was probably John Thomas, who married Charles L. Lewis's sister, Frances, but he may have been Michael Thomas, past magistrate and sheriff of Albemarle County (Woods, *Albemarle*, pp. 284, 327). Woods reports that Michael Thomas was greatly harassed by suits brought against him as sheriff, largely because of the maladministration of his two deputies. One of these dubious deputies was Edward Moore, who was married to Charles L. Lewis's sister, Mildred. Deputy Moore had once been prominent, but because of "unfortunate habits" he became overwhelmed with debt, lost his property, and eventually was declared insane.

11. See Appendix 2 for further discussion of the sale of Colle.

12. Jefferson to Craven Peyton, November 1, 1801, TBCF #748, Vi U, T McG Lib.

13. Craven Peyton to Jefferson, November 6, 1801, TBCF #750, Vi U, T McG Lib.

14. Charles Lewis to Jefferson, September 25, 1801, M Hi.

15. Charles Lewis to Thomas M. Randolph, September 27, 1801, M Hi.

16. Betts and Bear, *Family Letters,* pp. 204–205. Aunt Carr, mentioned in this letter, was the president's sister, Martha, a widow who lived at Monticello for several years.

17. Betts and Bear, *Family Letters,* pp. 4–13.

18. Ten years later, Jefferson was still having trouble obtaining stockings. He wrote to Martha from Philadelphia: "The cold of this place has made me wish for some stockings of cotton and hair's fur knit together. I do not recall whether Bet can knit. If she can do it well, it might be a good employment for her sometimes. If she cannot, I wish a good knitter could be found in the neighborhood to knit some for me. They should be very large" (Boyd, *Papers,* 18:580).

19. C. W. Campbell, *Memoirs of a Monticello Slave,* reproduced in Bear, *Jefferson at Monticello,* pp. 3–24.

20. Boyd, *Papers,* 15:634; Randolph, *Domestic Life,* p. 104.

21. Martha J. Carr to Jefferson, December 3, 1787, Boyd, *Papers,* 15:639–40.

22. Boyd, *Papers,* 13:350–51.

23. Ibid., 9:397.

24. Jefferson to Mazzei, January 7, 1792, Maruzzi Archives.

25. Woods, *Albemarle,* p. 284; Jefferson to Charles L. Lewis, September 11, 1795, private collection of Mrs. Charles W. Biggs, Lewisburg, West Virginia. The unfortunate brother-in-law was Edward Moore, who married Mildred Lewis.

26. Jefferson, *Notes,* p. 157.

27. Lipscomb and Bergh, *Writings,* 15:243.

28. Ibid., pp. 403–404.

29. Jefferson to Charles L. Lewis, September 11, 1795, private collection of Mrs. Charles W. Briggs, Lewisburg, West Virginia. The Isham Lewis mentioned here was the brother, not the son, of Col. Charles L. Lewis.

30. On August 5, 1799, Jefferson sold his plantation, Elkhill, in Goochland County, to one Thomas A. Taylor. Among the five men who were present at the transaction and signed the deed as witnesses were Lilburne and Randolph Lewis. This deed (TBCF #636 Vi U) was recorded in Goochland on January 20, 1800, having been "proved" by Randolph Lewis's oath.

31. Schachner, *Thomas Jefferson,* p. 65; Randolph, *Domestic Life,* p. 104.

32. Betts and Bear, *Family Letters,* pp. 252–53. The aunt whose children had convulsions was not identified. Martha had many aunts, including Lucy Lewis.

33. Pierson, *Jefferson at Monticello,* reproduced in Bear, *Jefferson at Monticello,* pp. 89, 93–94.

34. Betts and Bear, *Family Letters,* p. 360.

35. Biddle, "Scandal," p. 12.

36. Bradford, *Damaged Souls,* p. 151.

37. Biddle, "Scandal," pp. 10–13, 79–82.

38. Jefferson, *Autobiography,* p. 19.

39. Boyd, *Papers,* 1:409.

40. Schachner, *Thomas Jefferson,* p. 88.

41. Boyd, *Papers,* 1:34–35.

42. Malone, *Jefferson,* pp. 37, 216.

43. Dos Passos, *Head and Heart,* pp. 69, 75.

44. Ford, *Works,* 11:343–440.

45. Randall, *Life,* 3:673.

46. Ford, *Works,* 11:343–44.

9. THE PLAN TO EMIGRATE

1. Charles Lewis to Jefferson, April 29, 1806, M Hi.

2. See Appendix 3.

3. Bill of Sales and Hire—Estate of Randolph Lewis, January 1, 1813, January bundles, Liv. Co.

4. Rosenberger, *Jefferson Reader,* pp. 51–52, quoting La Rochefoucauld-Liancourt, *Travels.*

5. Jefferson to John W. Eppes, April 8, 1801, TBCF #698, Vi U, property of Luther Ely Smith. Anna Scott (Nancy) Jefferson was the daughter of Randolph Jefferson, the president's brother. At a later time, Nancy married Zacharia Nevil of Nelson County, Virginia.

6. Charles Lewis to Jefferson, May 1, 1806, M Hi.

7. Jefferson to Mrs. Lucy Lewis, May 26, 1806, M Hi.

8. Lucy Lewis to Jefferson, May 26, 1806, TBCF #959, Vi U, MSS Dept.

9. Jefferson to Col. Charles L. Lewis, October 6, 1806, M Hi.

10. Craven Peyton to Jefferson, October 9, 1806, TBCF #791, Vi U, T McG Lib.

11. Albemarle Personal Property Tax Rolls, Vi.

12. In later years Nelson became speaker of the Virginia House of Delegates, judge of the Federal court, presidential elector in 1809, member of Congress from 1811 to 1823, and finally, minister to Spain. He was the son of Virginia governor Thomas Nelson, and became a trusted friend and advisor of Jefferson. The popular and courtly Nelson married into the Walker family of Belvoir, where he entertained sumptuously. His wealth was considerable. In 1810, he offered 100 slaves to be auctioned in Albemarle on court day (Woods, *Albemarle,* p.

289; Mead, *Historic Homes,* pp. 163–64; Dabney, "Jefferson's Albemarle," pp. 132–33; Albemarle Deed Book 19, pp. 132–33).

13. Statement of Randolph Lewis's debts, Carr family business papers #4869a, box 1, Vi U, MSS Dept.

14. Albemarle Deed Book 15, pp. 213–14; Woods, *Albemarle,* pp. 275, 381.

15. Jillson, *Pioneer Kentucky,* pp. 9–10.

16. Clark, *Rampaging Frontier,* p. 20, quoting Francois A. Michaux, *Travels to the Westward of the Allegheny Mountains,* p. 70.

17. While in Kentucky, Lilburne borrowed $275 from a man named Lynch Brooks. The records of the subsequent courtroom efforts of Brooks to regain his money attest to Lilburne's presence in Livingston County in 1806.

18. When Lilburne had sold his portion of Buck Island to Hugh Nelson, more than two years before, Nelson had not recorded the deed in the county court deed books. In Virginia at that time, when persons of substance were generally acquainted and their affairs more or less known to each other, it was common that documents not be routinely recorded. However, if one of the principals were planning to leave the area, or had died or was expected to die, or if there were some question about the transaction, then the buyer would record the deed as soon as he could. After holding Lilburne's deed for over two years, Hugh Nelson recorded it at the end of March, 1806. Evidently this was when Nelson learned that Lilburne was going to leave Virginia for good.

19. Randolph Lewis to Jefferson, April 20, 1807, TBCF #991, Vi U, MSS Dept.

20. Betts, *Farm Book,* p. 5.

21. Jefferson to Randolph Lewis, April 23, 1807, M Hi.

22. Jefferson to Walter Key, April 29, 1807, M Hi; Randolph Lewis to Jefferson, April 30, 1807, M Hi.

23. Betts, *Farm Book,* p. 27.

24. George Pickett was one of the original supervisors of the Bank of Richmond, founded in 1792. During the Revolution he had been a contractor to the Culpepper Minute Battalion, supplying food and equipment, thus laying the foundation for his fortune. At the same time he served as drummer in the "Silver Greys," a volunteer guard company formed at Richmond to free militia units for other duty. Two of Pickett's grandsons became Confederate generals in the Civil War: Gen. Henry Heth, and Gen. George E. Pickett of Gettysburg fame (Weeks, "Snowden," p. 27; Palmer, *Calendar,* 8:157 and 9:547, 590; *Vi. Hist. Mag.* 2:190; Hening, *Statutes at Large,* 13:599).

25. Liv. Co. Deed Book B, pp. 195–200, 204–207.

26. The location of this letter from Peyton to Jefferson is unknown.

27. Jefferson to Craven Peyton, August 10, 1807, TBCF #1001, Vi U, T McG Lib.

28. Albemarle Deed Book 16, pp. 585–86.

29. Lucy Lewis to Jefferson, November 19, 1807, TBCF #1014, Vi U, MSS Dept.

10. THE TRIP TO KENTUCKY

1. For more than a decade prior to 1807, the Wilderness Road had been open for wagons. The commissioners had claimed, "Waggons loaded with a ton weight, may pass with ease, with four good horses" (Kincade, *Wilderness Road,* p. 191).

2. Filson, *Discovery,* p. 12.

3. McMeekin, *Louisville,* p. 53.

4. Hartley, *Ohio River Navigation,* p. 15.

5. Some of the Lewises and their slaves may have gone to Kentucky in advance of the main party, but no information has been found to indicate that this was done. It does seem reasonable to assume that the Lewises would have made some preparations in Kentucky for their arrival.

6. Clark, *Rampaging Frontier,* p. 80.

7. Sale Bill of the Estate of Lilburne Lewis, June 2, 1812, Liv. Co. Bundles, October–December, 1812, box 1811–1813. See Appendix 5.

8. Banta, *Ohio,* p. 265. For discussion of early roads in Virginia and Kentucky, see Nettels, *National Economy,* p. 161; Jillson, *Pioneer Kentucky,* pp. 37–65. An interview with one of Randolph's slaves, Matilda, was published many decades after the trip west was completed. She recalled the journey and mentioned a layover in Gallatin County on the Ohio River. See Appendix 3.

9. Leahy, *Who's Who,* p. 79; Sale Bill of Lilburne Lewis, Appendix, 5.

10. Leahy, *Who's Who,* p. 94, quoting Zadok Cramer, *The Navigator* (1814).

11. Hall, *Letters,* pp. 33–35.

12. Nettels, *National Economy,* p. 307.

13. Ambler, *Transportation,* pp. 83, 94.

14. Ibid., pp. 40–43; Havighurst, *Voices,* p. 33.

15. Starling, *Henderson County,* p. 127.

16. Donovan, *River Boats,* p. 127; Nettels, *National Economy,* p. 306.

17. Ambler, *Transportation,* p. 42; McMeekin, *Louisville,* p. 53; Banta, *Ohio,* p. 284; Hall, *Letters,* pp. 323–24. There were many variables affecting the speed at which keelboats traveled; including the crew, the cargo, the depth and speed of the current, and the size and shape of the boat itself. The following keelboat trips and times have been recorded: the Shakespeare from New Orleans upstream to Nashville in a record sixty-seven days; the regular keelboat packet service, round trip between Pittsburgh and Cincinnati, one month; Pittsburgh to New Orleans, four to six weeks, returning upstream in four to six months;

Cincinnati to New Orleans and back, four to six months (Byrd Douglas, *Steamboatin' on the Cumberland*, p. 16; Ambler, *Transportation*, p. 44; Donovan, *River Boats*, p. 25; Hartley, *Ohio River Navigation*, p. 15).

18. Jones, "Ohio River," p. 219.

19. Leahy, *Who's Who*, p. 94, quoting Cramer, *The Navigator* (1814).

20. Staples, *Lexington*, p. 216.

21. Latrobe, *Steamboat Voyage*, p. 24.

22. Leahy, *Who's Who*, pp. 53–54, quoting *Centennial of the Northwest Territory*, January 11, 1794.

23. Harrison, *John Breckinridge*, pp. 40, 45n 111; Ambler, *Transportation*, p. 46.

24. Parton, *Aaron Burr*, p. 387.

25. Betts and Bear, *Family Letters*, p. 331.

26. See Appendix 3. Carroll County was formed out of Gallatin County in 1836.

27. Leahy, *Who's Who*, pp. 47–48; Collins, *History*, 2:118, 286.

28. Harlow, *Weep No More, My Lady*, pp. 167–68, quoting John Melish, *Travels in the United States of America*.

29. Jefferson to Craven Peyton, August 22, 1814, Tennessee Historical Society, Nashville.

30. Cramer, *The Navigator* (1808), p. 71.

31. Leahy, *Who's Who*, p. 61.

32. Hall, *Letters*, pp. 184–86.

33. Cramer, *The Navigator* (1808), p. 73.

34. Book, "Audubon," p. 189.

35. Audubon, *Delineations*, pp. 92–96.

36. McMeekin, *Louisville*, pp. 43, 45.

37. Clark, *Rampaging Frontier*, p. 30.

38. Leahy, *Who's Who*, p. 79.

39. McMeekin, *Louisville*, pp. 41, 55; Clark, *Rampaging Frontier*, p. 34.

40. Leahy, *Who's Who*, p. 48; Starling, *Henderson County*, p. 129.

41. Cramer, *The Navigator* (1808), p. 137; Ambler, *Transportation*, pp. 73, 76.

42. Snively and Furbee, *Satan's Ferryman*, pp. 35–43.

43. Cramer, *The Navigator* (1808), p. 80.

44. Ibid.

11. THE LAND AND TOWNS

1. Charles L. Lewis to Jefferson, September 17, 1810, TBCF #2795-a, Vi U, MSS Dept. Some punctuation and capitalization supplied.

2. O'Malley, *Union County*, pp. 13–14; Starling, *Henderson County*, p. 138; Rothert, *Muhlenberg County*, pp. 114–15.

3. Liv. Co. Order Books C, 1807–1808; D, 1808–1809; E, 1810–1816.

4. Liv. Co. Order Book D, 1808–1809, November 29, 1809.

5. Audubon, *Birds of America,* 4:306–10. The Carolina paroquet is now extinct.

6. Ibid., 5:25–35.

7. By 1808 Livingston County had been part of at least seven Virginia counties, ranging back through Lincoln, Kentucky, Fincastle, Botetourt, Augusta, and Orange, to Spottsylvania in 1720, and others before that time. After Kentucky became a state, Livingston's parent counties had been in turn the Kentucky counties of Lincoln, Logan, and Christian. This process of subdividing counties continued after the Lewises came to west Kentucky. Less than two years after their arrival, the southern half of Livingston was formed into Caldwell County. From the Livingston County of 1808 eventually would be formed all or parts of Caldwell, Lyon, Crittenden, and Trigg (Rone, *Atlas,* pp. B6, B10, C4–C12).

8. Robertson, "Paducah," p. 109.

9. It appears that at least part of this land had been owned by one David Walker, for in 1798, the year before Lyon bought the tract, the Kentucky legislature had established an official inspection station for tobacco, hemp, and flour, "on the lands of David Walker at the place called Eddyville on the Cumberland River" (Littell, 2:213).

10. Campbell, *Two Fighters,* p. 101.

11. Collins, *History,* 2:489.

12. Cramer, *The Navigator* (1808), p. 140; Sprague, "Louisville Canal," p. 77.

13. Liv. Co. Order Book A, p. 285. Apparently the county and circuit courts of Livingston continued to meet at Eddyville after Centerville had been designated the county seat. In November 1804, the legislature passed an act to "compel the circuit and county courts for Livingston to hold their respective courts at the place fixed by the commissioners for erecting the Public Buildings for Livingston County" (Littell, 3:165).

14. Jillson, *Pioneer Kentucky,* pp. 58–59.

15. Groom, "Presbyterian Church," p. 9.

16. Census 1810; Liv. Cir. Ct., August 9, 1808, August Bundles; Liv. Cir. Ct. Order Book 1807–1810, p. 187.

17. Liv. Co. Order Book C, April 5, 1808.

18. Liv. Cir. Ct. Bundles, September 1809.

19. Ibid.

20. Liv. Cir. Ct. Bundles, August 1808.

21. Clift, *"Corn Stalk" Militia,* p. 114.

22. Liv. Co. Order Book C, 1807–1808, May 5, 1808.

23. Liv. Cir. Ct. Order Book 1807–1810, March 11, 1808, p. 95.

24. Liv. Cir. Ct. Bundles, August 1808, Commonwealth Judgments.

25. Littell, 2:391.

26. On maps drawn between 1840 and 1850, this town was called

Cookseyville. This same town, presently named Tolu, is still in existence.

27. Snively and Furbee, *Satan's Ferryman,* p. 62.

28. Cramer, *The Navigator* (1808), p. 80.

29. Snively and Furbee, *Satan's Ferryman,* p. 42.

30. S. W. Thomas, "William Croghan, Sr.," pp. 51–52.

31. Schultz, *Travels,* quoted in Rothert, "Lewis Brothers," p. 258.

32. Cuming, *Western Country,* quoted in Rothert, "Lewis Brothers," p. 258.

33. Census 1810; Hall, *Letters,* p. 229.

12. HOUSES AND CROPS

1. Stampp, *Peculiar Institution,* pp. 50–51.

2. Census 1810.

3. Appraisal of Randolph Lewis estate, February 20, 1812. Liv. Co. Bundles, Box 1813–1814; Appraisal of Lilburne Lewis estate, June 1, 1812, Liv. Co. Bundles, October–December 1812, Box 1811–1813; Liv. Co. Tax Records, 1810.

4. O'Malley, *Union County,* pp. 95–96.

5. Rothert, *Muhlenberg County,* p. 113.

6. Hall, *Letters,* p. 188.

7. "James Gay's Bacon and Pork Recipe," 1802, Draper MSS, 12ZZ324, The State Historical Society of Wisconsin, Madison. The pork was dipped in boiling brine in order to kill "skippers," small black beetles whose larvae infested and destroyed the meat.

8. Lilburne Lewis estate sale records (see Appendix 5). An excellent discussion of frontier home life, implements, food, and clothing, may be found in Harriette S. Arnow's *Seedtime on the Cumberland,* pp. 343–425.

9. Charles L. Lewis to Jefferson, September 17, 1810, TBCF #2795-a, Vi U, MSS Dept. Some punctuation and capitalization supplied.

10. Appraisals of estates of Randolph and Lilburne Lewis, Liv. Co. Bundles, Box 1811–1813, Box 1813–1814.

11. See Appendix 5.

12. In 1970, sections of Lilburne's farm were owned by Mr. William Lucas, Mr. Rayford Dees, the family of Mr. Roy Dunn, Mrs. Odell Bradley, Mr. Boynton Merrill, Jr., and Mr. William H. Spencer.

13. Hall, *Letters,* p. 228.

14. Today the small town of Birdsville stands in this general area, partly on the bluff, with a few houses and a store at its foot. A few more houses stand just north of Randolph's property line, near the river. Most of the rest of Randolph's farm is presently owned by the Lula Hibbs estate.

15. O'Malley, *Union County,* pp. 26–27.

16. The whipsaw was in common use in west Kentucky as late as 1820. The whipsaw was shaped like a common, long, two-man crosscut saw. A log was put on a trestle, and the power, applied by two men, one above and one below, drove the saw along from one end to the other, guided by a line that had been made by snapping a cord on the surface of the log. This line was generally colored with pokeberry juice or charcoal dust made into a paint with water. Using a whipsaw was a tedious process, but the weatherboarding and framing timbers for all the houses built in Henderson prior to 1818 were sawed in this way (Starling, *Henderson County*, p. 122).

17. See Appendix 5.

18. See Chapter 20, p. 218.

19. Interview, June 30, 1970. James Lacey Hibbs was the son of Zacharia and Sally Hibbs. Zacharia was the son of Jonah Hibbs, neighbor of Randolph and Lilburne Lewis (Westerfield, *Biography*, 4:119, quoting Perrin, Battle, and Kniffin, *Kentucky*.

13. The Smithland Neighbors

1. At that time the name of the creek was spelled "Bio" and pronounced, as it is today, "By-oh."

2. Knox, *Amos Persons*, pp. 7–9; Liv. Co. Tax Rolls, 1811.

3. Westerfield, *Biography*, p. 119.

4. Liv. Co. Plat Book C, certificate #1282, p. 112; Liv. Co. Deed Book HH, pp. 517–18; Liv. Co. Plat Book A, p. 91; Liv. Co. Locations Plat Book 1801–1804, No. 560, p. 109; Liv. Co. Plat Book 1819–1854, certificate #1528, p. 20.

5. Cypress Run is now known as Phelps Creek.

6. Durrett, "Early Banking," pp. 2–9.

7. Ibid., p. 8.

8. Hulbert, "Western Ship Building," p. 722; Ambler, *Transportation*, p. 73.

9. Ambler, *Transportation*, p. 87; Starling, *Henderson County*, p. 120.

10. Hulbert, "Western Ship Building," pp. 726–27, 730.

11. Littell, 3:239.

12. Ibid., 3:237.

13. Liv. Cir. Ct. Bundles, June, 1812. Tippling was not the drinking of illegal liquor, but rather the sale of spirituous liquors without a license.

14. Liv. Cir. Ct. Bundles, September 1809; Liv. Cir. Ct. Bundles, June 1811; Liv. Cir. Ct. Order Book 1810–1814, June 26, 1811, p. 196.

15. Liv. Co. Order Book D, February 27, 1810.

16. Census 1810. Three years later, on August 16, 1813, McCawley posted a marriage bond of $500. One of the three slaves in McCawley's possession was Patty, whom McCawley had rented from Lilburne.

17. Liv. Cir. Ct. Bundles, March 1810; Liv. Cir. Ct. Order Book 1807–1810, pp. 413, 432.

18. The Livingston court records from 1801–1811 clearly show that Isaac Bullard was the county champion at drunkenness and profanity. In addition, although he had a family and owned property, his suits for debt were so numerous it appears probable that Bullard, whose occupation was listed variously as farmer, ferryman, and tavern keeper, was also a note shaver, or dealer in discounted notes.

19. Liv. Cir. Ct. Bundles, June 1810.

20. Liv. Cir. Ct. (Court of Quarter Sessions) Order Book B, February 25, 1801, pp. 10–11.

21. Clift, *"Corn Stalk" Militia*, pp. 14, 172; Liv. Co. Order Book D, August 29, 1809.

22. Ireland, *County Courts*, p. 305.

23. Littell and Swigert, *Digest*, 2:1150.

24. Ibid., pp. 1160–61.

25. Fidelio was the brother of the famous and brilliant lawyer, Solomon P. Sharp, who was stabbed to death in Frankfort, Kentucky, by Jereboam Beauchamp in 1825.

26. Liv. Cir. Ct. Bundles, June 1810.

14. ISSUES IN WEST KENTUCKY, 1808

1. Dale Van Every states that the West had its own foreign policy, which was at some variance with the aims of the national government. Westerners wanted three things: more land, free trade on the Mississippi, and the removal or extermination of all Indians (Van Every, *Final Challenge*, p. 119).

2. North, *Economic Growth*, p. 36; Smith and Cole, *Fluctuations*, pp. 16–18.

3. North, *Economic Growth*, p. 37.

4. Perkins, *Prologue to War*, pp. 170–71.

5. Nettels, *National Economy*, pp. 327–29.

6. Bryant, *Embargo*, pp. 36–40.

7. One exception to this, an interest group of westerners who opposed Jefferson's embargo, were the river men whose livelihood depended directly on shipping. When the shipbuilding business at Marietta, Ohio, was forced to close down completely, a local poet complained in verse:

Our ships all in motion
Once whitened the ocean
They sailed and returned with a cargo;
Now doomed to decay
They have fallen a prey
To Jefferson, worms, and embargo.

(Hulbert, "Western Ship Building," p. 720).

8. Ky. H. J., 1808–1809, December 16, 1808, pp. 30–31.

9. Ibid., pp. 31–33.

10. *Kentucky Gazette*, July 11, 1809.

11. J. H. Perkins, *Annals*, pp. 510–11.

12. Van Deusen, *Henry Clay*, p. 74.

13. Col. Arthur Campbell to Jefferson, October 10, 1807, 30274, DLC.

14. Matthew Lyon to Jefferson, February 9, 1808, 30931, DLC.

15. "An Act for the Benefit of Certain Militia Men of the 55th Regiment," February 11, 1809, Enrolled Bills of Gov. Charles Scott, 1808–1810, Ky Hi; Ky. H. J., 1808–1809, p. 274.

16. Enrolled Bills of Gov. Charles Scott, 1808–1810, January 17, 1809, Ky Hi; Ky. H. J., 1808–1809, p. 111.

17. Ky. H. J., 1808–1809, February 11, 1809, p. 327.

18. Ky. H. J., 1811–1812, pp. 170–71.

19. The 24th Regiment was composed of men from the area now contained in Livingston and Crittenden counties, and the 55th Regiment was made up of men from the area now contained in the counties of Lyon, Caldwell, and parts of Trigg. The patrolling militiamen came from the 55th Regiment (Clift, *"Corn Stalk" Militia*, pp. 113–16).

20. Kephart, *Southern Highlanders*, pp. 152–59.

21. Furnas, *The Americans*, pp. 263–64.

22. Miyakawa, *Protestants and Pioneers*, pp. 99–117.

23. Quisenberry, *Humphrey Marshall*, pp. 71–72; Watlington, *Partisan Spirit*, pp. 42–43.

24. Crockett's wife was Elizabeth Moore, a sister-in-law of Charles L. Lewis. Polly, a daughter of Crockett, married into the Bennett Henderson family, forming another in-law tie. Col. Joseph Crockett had been a commissioner of the Wilderness Road, one of the founding trustees of Transylvania University and of the towns of Frankfort and New Market (Young, *Jessamine County*, pp. 23–29; Littell, 1:688, 2:231, 3:557, 560).

25. Joseph Crockett to Jefferson, January 9, 1807, 23761, DLC. It was Colonel Crockett himself who arrested Aaron Burr. The author has not been able to discover any connection, not even a casual contact, between Aaron Burr and any members of the Charles L. Lewis family.

26. Jefferson to Mrs. Lucy Lewis, April 19, 1808, Mo S Hi.

27. In April, 1808, in Charlottesville, Isham recorded the deed to the 230-acre tract which his father had given him, and which he had subsequently transferred to his sister, Nancy. Isham was living in Goochland County at this time, probably at the Byrd (Albemarle Deed Book 17, pp. 282–83; Albemarle Real Estate Tax Rolls, 1807, Book B, Vi).

28. Lipscomb and Bergh, *Writings*, 12:147.

29. Ibid., 12:99–100.

15. THE COUNTY COURT

1. Ireland, "Aristocrats All," pp. 365–66.

2. Ibid., p. 366.

3. Ireland, "Sale of Public Office," p. 265.

4. Littell and Swigert, *Digest*, 2:691–95.

5. Ibid., 1:290.

6. *Acts Passed at the Forth-Fourth General Assembly*, pp. 487–94.

7. "To serve a summons, twenty-five cents each; to summon a witness, twelve and one-half cents each; to summon jurymen, thirty-three and one-third cents each" (Ky. S. J., 1811–1812, p. 156).

8. Second Constitution of Kentucky, Art. 3, Sec. 31 (Young, *Three Constitutions*, pp. 44–45).

9. Ireland, *County Courts*, p. 9.

10. Starling, *Henderson County*, p. 120.

11. Ireland, "Sale of Public Office," pp. 267–74. In larger counties, such as Fayette or Jefferson, the sale price of the sheriff's office was from two to four thousand dollars.

12. Ireland, *County Courts*, pp. 93–95.

13. Liv. Co. Records: 1807, George Brown and Wiley Davis; 1808, John Beardon; 1809, James Johnson; 1810, Thomas G. Davis; 1811, Robert Kirk; 1812, Joseph Reed; 1813, Robert Kirk (again).

14. Ky. H. J., 1810–1811, p. 37. In November 1810, Livingston County owed the fifth highest total of back taxes. Only one other county, the desperately poor Greenup, had been delinquent for all of the preceeding four years. The tax delinquency of Livingston County was the highest in the state in 1806, second in 1807, and fourth in 1808. In 1809, the last year of the embargo, 38 out of 49 Kentucky counties were delinquent in tax collections. Livingston was tenth highest in taxes owed in that year.

15. Ireland, "Sale of Public Office," pp. 262–64.

16. Ireland, *County Courts*, p. 5.

17. The county court appointed town trustees until the town reached the size of fifteen occupied lots, after which the trustees were elected by the residents of the town (Littell, 2:1214–15).

18. Ireland, "Sale of Public Office," p. 267.

19. Ford, *Works*, 11:530–31.

20. The author has not found any evidence that bribes or blackmail were used to influence the members of the Livingston County court.

21. Starling, *Henderson County*, p. 122.

22. Liv. Cir. Ct. Order Book 1810–1814, June 26, 1811, p. 98; Liv. Cir. Ct. Order Book 1807–1810, p. 425; Liv. Cir. Ct. Bundles, August 1808, March 1810.

23. Snively and Furbee, *Satan's Ferryman*, p. 35; Liv. Cir. Ct. Order Book 1807–1810, p. 96.

24. Liv. Cir. Ct. Bundles, June 1810, September 1810.

25. Ibid., September 1809.

26. Ibid., August 1808.

27. Kirk had run an official inspection station for tobacco, hemp, and flour for the previous eight years. This station was located on his land on the Mill Creek branch of Hurricane Creek, which is located north of present-day Marion (Littell, 2:391). A member of the Lusk family, James, had run a similar inspection station on the Ohio River since 1802 (Littell, 3:23). Bad feelings may have arisen over these competing inspection stations, but that is at best a guess.

28. Ky. H. J., 1809–1810, pp. 170–71.

29. Ibid., pp. 190–92.

30. Ibid., pp. 63–64.

31. Liv. Cir. Ct. Bundles, March 1812.

32. Liv. Cir. Ct. Order Book 1810–1814, March 17, 1812, p. 279.

33. McDonald, *Echoes of Yesteryear*, p. 3.

34. Clift, *"Corn Stalk" Militia*, p. 195.

35. Ky. H. J., 1808–1809, p. 76.

36. "An Act for the Payment of Witnesses," December 23, 1809, Enrolled Bills of Gov. Charles Scott, 1808–1809, Ky. Hi.

37. Second Constitution of Kentucky, Art. 5 (Young, *Three Constitutions*, p. 47).

38. J. W. Coleman, Jr., *Famous Kentucky Duels*, pp. 32–43; Hopkins, *Henry Clay*, 1:391–402; Ky. H. J., 1808–1809, pp. 90, 98–99, 202, 315–16. Neither man was seriously wounded.

39. Ky. H. J., 1808–1809, p. 79; Ky. S. J., 1809–1810, pp. 53–54.

40. In 1842 Livingston County was further divided by the formation of Crittenden County. Caldwell County was later reduced in size by the formation of Trigg County in 1820 and Lyon County in 1854 (Rone, *Atlas*, pp. C9–C12).

41. Ky. H. J., 1808–1809, pp. 75, 92.

42. Littell, 4:22–24; Liv. Co. Order Book D, November 29, 1809.

43. Liv. Co. Order Book A, March 21, 1800, pp. 31–32.

44. Liv. Co. Order Book D, April 24, 1809 (punctuation supplied).

45. Ibid., February 6, 1809, May 23, 1809, January 10, 1810, February 26, 1810.

46. Liv. Co. Order Book D, May 23, 1809.

47. Liv. Cir. Ct. Order Book, 1807–1810, June 26, 1809, p. 312.

48. Liv. Co. Order Book D, February 26, 1810. The trustees were John Gordon, Samuel Larkin, William Rutter, Samuel C. Harkins, and William Thompson.

49. Liv. Co. Order Book D, January 23, 1810.

50. Liv. Cir. Ct. Bundles, March, 1812. Lilburne Lewis was the foreman of the grand jury that indicted these two thieves. The cloth stolen was listed as cotton velvet, black silk florentine, Irish linen, olive

color cotton, black velveteen, dove colored cotton velveteen, grey mixed Bennett's cord, and striped silk moleskin.

16. THE YEAR OF TROUBLE, 1809

1. *Lewisiana*, Book 35, ch. 68, p. 22.

2. This young doctor should not be confused with the irascible Col. Arthur Campbell, who was one of the earliest and most politically influencial settlers of Kentucky. The colonel was well educated, and was active in military, business, and political affairs in Virginia and Kentucky. The author does not know if the doctor and the colonel were related. See Kincaid, *Wilderness Road*, pp. 82–90, 93, 132, 134, 144, 163. See also Williams, *Franklin*.

3. These notes, the medical bills, and the other documents concerned with the suit over the payment of the bills, are all to be found in Liv. Cir. Ct. Bundles, March 1814. An edited copy of the Lewises' bill may be found in Appendix 4.

4. Pereira, *Materia Medica and Therapeutics*.

5. Blue ointment (ungt. merc.), which was prescribed in this case, was also to treat the lesions of syphilis. Other diseases common in the Ohio Valley at that time are discussed in Appendix 4.

6. "To visit Miss N Per Noct, 18/ven sect 3/cath 1 3/."

7. Liv. Co. Deed Book B, p. 386; Liv. Cir. Ct. Bundles, March 1814.

8. See Appendix 5.

9. Ky. H. J., 1809–1810, p. 72.

10. Campbell had married Catherine, daughter of Edward B. West, in Lexington on July 11, 1809 (Clift, *Kentucky Marriages*, p. 10).

11. For biographical material on Col. Joseph Crockett see Young, *Jessamine County*, pp. 23–26. Col. Joseph Crockett was not closely related, if related at all, to his far less distinguished namesake, Davy Crockett. Joseph Crockett's daughter, Josephine, married Bennett H. Henderson III, who was the first cousin of Lilburne Lewis.

12. Liv. Cir. Ct. Bundles A to H, 1813.

13. Liv. Cir. Ct. Bundles, June 1810, and March 1814.

14. Durrett, "Early Banking," p. 11.

15. *Russellville Farmer's Friend*, October 27, 1809.

16. Boaz (rhymes with rose) Station, which Lilburne spelled phonetically as "Beau Station," was in Livingston County. The author is not certain, but believes it was located at or near the present site of Boaz School, two and one-half miles north of Dycusburg, Kentucky. Lynch Brooks was married, had eight children, owned five slaves, and was a resident of Madison County, Kentucky, in 1810 (Census 1810).

17. Swem, "Kentuckians at William and Mary," pp. 179–90.

18. Daniels, *Devil's Backbone*, pp. 61–62; Wilson, ed., *Letter*, p. 17n 19.

19. *Lexington Kentucky Gazette,* March 6, 1790, quoted in Hopkins, *Hemp Industry,* pp. 71–72.
20. Hamlin, "Peyton Short," p. 3.
21. Ky. H. J., 1809–1810, pp. 121, 152. This was not the George James Trotter who became famous as an editor and duelist; he was only two years old in 1810. See J. W. Coleman, Jr., *Duels,* pp. 45, 76–87.
22. Liv. Cir. Ct. Bundles A to G, March 1811.
23. Ibid.
24. Collins, *History,* 1:514; Sneed, *Kentucky Penitentiary,* p. 26.
25. Sneed, *Kentucky Penitentiary,* p. 16; Harrison, *John Breckinridge,* pp. 85–87.
26. This crowded document and others on the Lynch Brooks case may be found in Liv. Cir. Ct. Bundles A to G, March 1811.
27. Liv. Cir. Ct. Bundles A to G, March 1811.
28. Martha C. Lewis, Lucy B. Lewis, Ann M. Lewis (written by Charles L. Lewis) to Jefferson, September 17, 1810, TBCF #2795-a, Vi U, MSS Dept.

17. LILBURNE ENTERS PUBLIC LIFE

1. Liv. Circ. Ct. Order Book 1807–1810, p. 312.
2. McDonald, *Echoes,* pp. 97–98.
3. Census 1810.
4. McDonald, *Echoes,* p. 196; Draper, *Kings Mountain,* pp. 417, 577.
5. Liv. Cir. Ct. Order Book 1807–1810, p. 312.
6. The two districts that included all of Kentucky lying south and west of Hardinsburg, Leitchfield, and Glasgow have since been divided into about thirteen counties each (not including the Purchase area). It was a huge territory for one man to travel.
7. Littell, 3:37–41.
8. Ibid., 5:346; Littell and Swigert, *Digest,* 1:371. In 1816 the office of assistant judge was abolished.
9. Littell and Swigert, *Digest,* 2:691.
10. Levin, *Lawyers,* p. 463; *Russellville Mirror,* January 9, 1807, October 18, 1808.
11. *W. M. Quarterly,* 1st ser. 14 (1905–1906):52–58, 135–38; Mary S. Payne letter, 1874, Misc. folder, Box 2 L–R, Starling Papers, Kentucky Library, Bowling Green.
12. A. Coleman, *John J. Crittenden,* 1:18.
13. Starling, *Henderson County,* p. 130.
14. Taylor, *Ohio County,* pp. 21–24.
15. Coffman, *Russellville,* p. 21.
16. Liv. Cir. Ct. Order Book 1807–1810, pp. 399–400, 406.
17. Ibid., pp. 349, 370, 443.
18. Clift, *"Corn Stalk" Militia,* preface, p. 3.

19. Littell, 3:410.

20. Rothert, *Muhlenberg*, p. 165.

21. Ky. H. J., 1812–1813, pp. 85, 117, 143; Enrolled bills of Gov. Charles Scott 1808–1810; February 11, 1809, "An Act for the Benefit of Certain Militia Men of the 55th Regiment," Ky. Hi.

22. Littell, 4:403. A list of Lilburne's property written in 1812, noted "1 military coat, $7.00, 1 military hat, 75¢," and a volume of "Stuben," probably the military drill manual.

23. Thacker, "Kentucky Militia," p. 70.

24. Littell, 3:517.

25. Ky. H. J., 1809–1810, pp. 27–30; Ky. S. J., 1809–1810, p. 44. Jereboam Beauchamp was executed for the murder of Solomon P. Sharp in Frankfort, Kentucky, in 1825.

26. Weir, *Lonz Powers*, quoted in Rothert, *Muhlenberg*, pp. 170–75.

27. Clift, *"Corn Stalk" Militia*, p. 171.

28. Liv. Co. Deed Book HH, pp. 517–18; Liv. Co. Plat Book 1819–1854, certificate 1528, p. 20.

29. Isham Lewis to Jefferson, April 27, 1809, M Hi.

30. Jefferson to Isham Lewis, May 1, 1809, Mo S Hi, quoted in Padover, *Jefferson Profile*, pp. 186–87.

31. Jefferson to George Jefferson, March 27, 1801, Ford, *Works*, 9:238.

32. Jefferson to J. Garland Jefferson, January 25, 1810, Ford, *Works*, 11:133.

33. Jefferson to Gideon Fitch, May 23, 1809, M. Hi.

34. Jefferson to Seth Pease, May 23, 1809, M Hi.

35. Bear, "Account Books," p. 823.

36. *The Farmer's Friend*, June 1809–December 1809. The North Fork of the Tradewater River is in the general area of Sturgis, Kentucky. This tract of land, which Randolph advertised as being "of the first rate," was actually described in the tax rolls as "of the third rate."

37. Liv. Co. Deed Book B, pp. 204–208. Either Randolph or Isham could have made the trip to Frankfort. Lilburne was sick at the time.

38. Liv. Co. Deed Book D, August 28, 1809.

39. McDonald, *Echoes*, p. 5; Collins, *History*, 2:776.

40. Liv. Co. Deed Book FF, p. 321.

18. THE CHURCH IN WEST KENTUCKY

1. Dann, reviewer, "The Great Revival," by John B. Boles. Discussing the works of Clement Eaton, Albert D. Kirwan observed that the combination of slavery and the religious orthodoxy that followed the Great Revival effectively banished freedom of thought in the antebellum South (Albert D. Kirwan, ed., *The Civilization of the Old South: Writings of Clement Eaton*, p. xii). For a discussion of the effects of slavery on ante-

bellum southern intellectual development, see Elkins, *Slavery*, pp. 206–22. The institution of slavery, which can hardly be called an "event," is generally thought to be the most tragic and deleterious element in the American experience.

2. Cartwright, *Autobiography*, pp. 24–25. In 1793 Logan County included the entire southwest third of Kentucky, which was sometimes called the Green River country. Livingston County, formed in 1799, was almost sixty miles west of Russellville.

3. Groom, *Salem Church*, pp. 27, 43. Copies of this 112-page study may be found in the libraries of the Filson Club, Ky Hi, and various Presbyterian theological seminaries and historical societies.

4. Boles, *Revival*, p. 87.

5. Groom, *Salem Church*, p. 32.

6. Presbyterian ministers William Hodge, John Rankin, William McGee, and Methodist John McGee.

7. Boles, *Revival*, pp. 51–58.

8. McMaster, *History*, 2:579–82.

9. Rogers, *Cane Ridge*, p. 157; Cartwright, *Autobiography*, p. 30.

10. Boles, *Revival*, pp. xi, 54, 64–69.

11. Ibid., pp. 88–89. After 1810 the Cumberland Presbyterian church made wide use of the camp meeting.

12. Starling, *Henderson County*, p. 34; J. Smith, *Christian Church*, p. 642; Cossitt, *Finis Ewing*, p. 27.

13. Groom, *Salem Church*, p. 27.

14. McVey, *Gates Open Slowly*, p. 49.

15. Eaton, *Mind*, pp. 204–205.

16. Bishop, *History*, pp. 307–308. Out of the total population of Kentucky in 1820, only about one in ten of the citizens attended public worship. The Catholic church was important in the early settlement of Kentucky, especially in the Bardstown area. In far west Kentucky, however, like the Episcopal church it had few members and was not influenced by the Revival.

17. Z. F. Smith, *The History of Kentucky*, pp. 535–38.

18. Finis Ewing to James B. Porter, December 8, 1809, Groom, *Salem Church*, p. 54; Cossitt, *Finis Ewing*, p. 191.

19. William Dickey to James H. Dickey, June 29, 1812, MS 81008, Presb Hi; Rothert, "Lewis Brothers," p. 240.

20. Cartwright, *Autobiography*, pp. 31–32.

21. Harlow, *Weep No More, My Lady*, p. 61.

22. Miyakawa, *Protestants and Pioneers*, p. 127.

23. Sonne, *Liberal Kentucky*, pp. 4–5, 18–19.

24. Miyakawa, *Protestants and Pioneers*, p. 22; Sonne, *Liberal Kentucky*, pp. 14–15.

25. Miyakawa, *Protestants and Pioneers*, pp. 31, 79; Sonne, *Liberal Kentucky*, pp. 110–11.

26. Ky. H. J. 1810–1811, December 27, 1810, p. 75; Ky. H. J. 1805–1806, December 25, 1805, p. 154.

27. For a discussion of education and the churches see Posey, *Frontier Mission,* pp. 257–302.

28. Miyakawa, *Protestants and Pioneers,* pp. 30, 85, 99.

29. Ibid., pp. 88–90.

30. Ibid., pp. 90–91, 112–15.

31. Ibid., pp. 15–16, 112–15, 236.

32. Moore, *Frontier Mind.*

33. Hofstadter, *Anti-Intellectualism,* p. 80.

34. Miyakawa, *Protestants and Pioneers,* pp. 174–75, 180; Posey, *Frontier Mission,* pp. 327–51.

35. Miyakawa, *Protestants and Pioneers,* pp. 180–81.

36. Ibid., pp. 190–91, 222–23.

37. Hofstadter, *Anti-Intellectualism,* p. 300.

38. Miyakawa, *Protestants and Pioneers,* p. 199; Sonne, *Liberal Kentucky,* pp. 21, 110–11.

39. Sonne, *Liberal Kentucky,* p. 3; see ch. 8, notes 26, 27, 28.

40. Miyakawa, *Protestants and Pioneers,* p. 199.

41. Pool, "Tragedies in Livingston."

42. Robert, *Tobacco,* p. 25.

43. Watts, *Chronicles,* pp. 224, 384–86.

19. THE PRESBYTERIAN LEWISES

1. Fellow board members with Rice at this institution were Patrick Henry and James Madison. David Rice was also moderator of the Hanover Presbytery, and author of a famous petition for religious freedom to the Virginia House of Burgesses (*Vi. Hist. Mag.,* 6:176, 13:40–45).

2. Littell, 3:572. On January 1, 1799, this seminary merged with the Kentucky Academy to become Transylvania University (Littell, 2:232).

3. Reprinted in Bishop, *Outline,* pp. 384ff.

4. Young, *Autobiography,* p. 98.

5. Martin, "Father Rice," pp. 328–29.

6. Breckinridge, et al., eds., "The Men of Danville," *Danville Quarterly Review* 4 (June 1864):291.

7. Groom, "Livingston Church," p. 18. This twenty-two page study is available at various Presbyterian seminaries and historical societies.

8. Ibid., p. 1.

9. Bishop, *Outline,* p. 165.

10. Baker, *Caldwell County,* p. 61.

11. Groom, "Livingston Church," pp. 1, 5. Donaldson's in 1798 or 1799, Crooked Creek (later called Bethany church) in 1803, and Salem (later called West Salem) in 1804.

12. Groom, "Livingston Church," p. 11. Bethany church, also called Crooked Creek church, was located about one and a half miles north of present-day Marion, Kentucky. Groom believes that Dickey lived near the church.

13. J. M. Wilson, *Presbyterian Almanac,* p. 112.

14. Ibid., p. 117. In a subsequent marriage Dickey had four more children.

15. Copies of this portrait are on file at Pres Hi.

16. Wilson, *Presbyterian Almanac,* p. 117.

17. Ibid., pp. 115–16.

18. Ibid., pp. 113, 116.

19. Bishop, *Outline,* p. 358.

20. Littleton Groom to author, December 11, 1969.

21. William Dickey to James H. Dickey, June 29, 1812, MS 81008, Presb Hi.

22. Albemarle Deed Book 11, p. 145.

23. Dickey to Dickey, June 29, 1812.

24. Weld, *American Slavery,* p. 94.

25. Perrin, *Christian and Trigg,* pp. 205, 243.

26. In his fine biography, *Meriwether Lewis,* Richard Dillon proposes that Lewis was not a suicide, but was murdered. This theory of murder was put forward and discussed in 1893 by Elliott Coues in *History of the Expedition under the Command of Lewis and Clark,* 1:xv–xlii. Dillon admits that the case for the theory of murder is unproved. The issue will not be argued here, but it is relevant to this work to point out that in 1809 almost everyone, Jefferson included, believed that Lewis died a suicide.

27. Dillon, *Meriwether Lewis,* p. 325.

28. Meriwether Lewis received this appointment to take effect in March 1807 but, for some reason, it was not until a year later that he took up his duties in residence at St. Louis. There he found problems far different from the responsibilities of commanding an expedition that was military in character, if not purpose. Leaders who can inspire their men in battle or exploration often fail to cope with the meanness and compromise of political administration, and Meriwether Lewis, arriving to fill an office vacant for a year, found the subordinate officials entrenched, selfishly resentful, and uncooperative.

29. Coues, *History,* 1:xv–xlii.

30. Ibid., as condensed in Lewis's *Genealogy.*

31. Pool, "Tragedies in Livingston"; Watts, *Chronicles,* p. 224.

20. INSECURITY

1. Liv. Co. Order Book D., January 23, 1810; Liv. Co. Order Book E., 1810–1816, July 23, 1810, pp. 8–9; Liv. Cir. Ct. Order Book 1807–

1810, pp. 312, 370, 502. Bio (Bayou) Creek ran through the land of Amos Persons, just north of Randolph's farm.

2. Liv. Co. Deed Book 3, p. 386; Dr. Arthur Campbell medical bill, Liv. Cir. Ct. Bundles, March 1814, Judgments.

3. After 1815, the state legislature of Illinois permitted slavery in a six-mile-square area in Saline and Gallatin counties, where the large salt industry was centered. Eventually there were three thousand slaves in this area who worked as salt makers, many of them having been rented from Kentuckians. The rental rate for a prime male was about forty dollars a year.

4. Estate Sale Records of Lilburne Lewis, Liv. Co. Bundles, October-November-December 1812. See Appendix 5.

5. Liv. Co. Order Book E 1810–1816, July 22, 1811, pp. 88–89.

6. See Ch. 16, n. 11.

7. Woods, *Albemarle*, pp. 227–28, 284, 356.

8. Ten years earlier, in 1800, there were 2,856 people in the county (Robert Trail, "Livingston County, Kentucky—Stepping Stone to Illinois," Register 69, July 1971:274).

9. The author has seen no other county census report in which a dun for pay was written on the body of the report.

10. Martha C. Lewis, Lucy B. Lewis, Ann M. Lewis (written by Charles L. Lewis) to Jefferson, September 17, 1810, TBCF #2795-a, Vi U, MSS Dept. Some punctuation and capitalization supplied.

11. Pool, "Tragedies in Livingston"; Watts, *Chronicles,* p. 194.

12. Littell and Swigert, *Digest,* 2:878–79.

13. *Lewisiana,* book 35, ch. 68, p. 22.

14. Liv. Co. Order Book D, January 23, 1810.

15. Liv. Co. Plat Book C, 1807–1819, p. 222.

16. Collins, *History,* 1:26; Liv. Cir. Ct. Bundles, September 1811.

17. Liv. Co. Order Book E, February 26, 1811, pp. 71–72.

18. Patrick H. Rice did not move to Livingston County until after the census of 1810 was taken. His brother was a slave owner. His father was an abolitionist.

19. Liv. Co. Will Book A, p. 38.

20. Interview with Mr. Grady Rutter, May 9, 1967.

21. Liv. Co. Will Book A, p. 38.

22. Ireland, *County Courts,* p. 62.

23. Liv. Co. Order Book E, August 27, 1810, pp. 23–24.

24. The census of 1810 records that five slaves lived on Randolph's farm, and the tax rolls show that he owned seven.

25. Liv. Co. Deed Book B, pp. 195–200, 204–207.

26. *The Farmer's Friend,* October 26, 1810. The Salem store of this firm had had its troubles. In August 1809, Vance was indicted for sabbath breaking because he and his hired negroes had worked on Sunday to build a stable. In October his store was burglarized (Liv. Cir. Ct. Bundles, September 1809).

27. Liv. Cir. Ct. Bundles, September 1810; Liv. Cir. Ct. Order Book, 1810–1814, September 26, 1810, p. 102.

28. Liv. Co. Deed Book B, pp. 195–200.

29. Adams County Record of Judgments Book B, November 1802–April 1811, pp. 478–79, Natchez. A careful and extended search in the records of the Mississippi State Land Office (with the kind assistance of Commissioner Watt Carter) reveals no indication that Isham was ever employed by that agency.

30. See Ch. 31, n. 26.

31. Martha C. Lewis, Lucy B. Lewis, Ann M. Lewis (written by Charles L. Lewis) to Jefferson, September 17, 1810, TBCF #2795-a, Vi U, MSS Dept. Some punctuation and capitalization supplied. The first six lines of this letter to Jefferson contained the news of Lucy's death. Colonel Lewis had waited four months to inform Jefferson that his sister was dead, and then wrote, as usual, when he needed help. At the end of the letter, Lewis appended a discussion of the climate, wild life, and richness of the Kentucky frontier (see Ch. 11, p. 112; Ch. 12, p. 126).

32. Jefferson to Craven Peyton, December 6, 1810, M Hi.

33. Liv. Co. Bundles, October 30, 1811.

21. Community Affairs, 1810

1. Ky. S. J. 1809–1810, p. 5; *Lexington Kentucky Gazette,* May 12, 1812.

2. Draper, *King's Mountain,* p. 417. Moses Shelby was a hero of the Revolution who fought in many battles and was wounded at King's Mountain. He was the first colonel commandant of the Livingston militia.

3. Liv. Cir. Ct. Order Book 1803–1805, May 4, 1803, pp. 32–35. The coroner's jury report and the five pages of testimony, all in Matthew Lyon's handwriting, together with the report of Coroner George Robison, may be found in Liv. Cir. Ct. Bundles of May 1803. The murder of Jimmy is mentioned in Warren, *Brother to Dragons,* pp. 136, 219.

4. Ky. S. J. 1809–1810, pp. 9, 14–15.

5. Ky. H. J. 1811–1812, p. 106.

6. Ky. H. J. 1810–1811, p. 202–203.

7. Liv. Cir. Ct. Bundles, March 1810, June 1810, March 1811; Liv. Co. Order Book E, 1810–1816, July 24, 1810, p. 22.

8. William Prince wrote his will in 1808. It was probated August 6, 1810. Henry and Rhoda Delany were executors of this will.

9. "Historier," letter to *Banner of Peace and Cumberland Presbyterian Advocate,* April 25, 1861, Archive Files, Trinity University, San Antonio.

10. Starling, *Henderson County,* p. 120; Baker, *Caldwell County,* p. 149; Liv. Co. Order Book D, January 23, 1810.

11. Liv. Cir. Ct. Order Book 1810–1814, March 30, 1811, p. 177; Liv. Co. Order Book E, November 26, 1810, p. 43.

12. Coffman, *Logan County*, pp. 111, 279. A distinguished leader on the western frontier, Ninian Edwards was a member of the Kentucky legislature from Nelson County in 1796. In 1798 he moved to Russellville, practiced law there, and became rich. In 1802 he was appointed one of the first nine circuit court judges in the state, and four years later became a member of the Kentucky Court of Appeals, and then its chief justice in 1808. A year later President Madison appointed Edwards governor of the Illinois Territory, a post he held for nine years. Later he held the office of United States senator, and then governor of the state of Illinois (Collins, *History,* 2:488).

13. Starling, *Henderson County,* p. 120; Perrin, *Christian and Trigg,* part 1, p. 54; *Russellville Mirror,* October 10, 1807.

14. Liv. Cir. Ct. Order Book 1807–1810, March 28, 1810, pp. 502–503; Liv. Cir. Ct. Order Book 1810–1814, March 16, 1812 p. 276.

15. This was the same Micajah Phelps who sued Gen. Jonathan Ramsey in 1809, agreed to arbitration, and lost the decision. Lilburne was one of the arbitrators.

16. John Reed and George Robertson were the other two jurymen who indicted Lilburne.

17. Liv. Cir. Ct. Order Book 1810–1814, September 25, 1810, p. 82.

18. Harlow, *Weep No More, My Lady,* p. 366.

19. Liv. Cir. Ct. Bundles, September 1810. The William Woods mentioned here was not the Reverend William (Baptist Billy) Woods.

20. Liv. Cir. Ct. Bundles, September 1810; Liv. Cir. Ct. Order Book 1810–1814, September 24, 1810, p. 63.

21. Liv. Co. Order Book D, February 26, 1810. Christopher Haynes became a justice of the peace four months after this incident. Marshal Smelser (*The Democratic Republic 1801–1815,* p. 34) states that public drunkenness and the coarse brutality of rough-and-tumble fighting came to America with the English rural immigrant. It was common in Virginia long before Kentucky was settled.

22. Collins, *History,* 1:434.

22. SLAVERY IN LIVINGSTON

1. Among the more notable of these are: Stampp, *Peculiar Institution* and Elkins, *Slavery.* More regional in scope is J. W. Coleman, Jr., *Slavery Times.*

2. *Mellon, Views,* pp. 31–32.

3. Stampp, *Peculiar Institution,* pp. 8–11; Elkins, *Slavery,* pp. 208, 240.

4. Stampp, *Peculiar Institution,* pp. 134–40, 428; Coleman, *Slavery Times,* pp. 85–95, 112–13.

5. Stampp, *Peculiar Institution,* pp. 350–58.

6. Coleman, *Slavery Times*, pp. 65–66; Hopkins, *Hemp Industry*, pp. 26–27.

7. Eaton, *History*, pp. 276–78; Elkins, *Slavery*, pp. 231–37.

8. Coleman, *Slavery Times*, pp. 54–56.

9. Harrison, "Memories," p. 254.

10. Mathias, "Slavery," p. 4.

11. Young, *Three Constitutions*, part 2, p. 50.

12. Littell and Swigert, *Digest*, 2:1149–53, 1161.

13. Ibid., pp. 1150–51, 1160–61.

14. Ibid., pp. 1154–55.

15. Young, *Three Constitutions*, part 2, p. 50.

16. Ibid., p. 84.

17. Littell and Swigert, *Digest*, 2:980–81.

18. Coleman, *Slavery Times*, pp. 96–98.

19. Ibid., p. 97. In many of the Livingston County official documents, patrol is spelled "pad roll."

20. Census 1810; Liv. Co. Tax Rolls.

21. Snively and Furbee, *Satan's Ferryman*, p. 60.

22. "Inquisition Over Strong's Negroe," Coroner's jury report, September 12, 1804, Liv. Cir. Ct. Bundles, September 1804, quoted in Warren, *Brother to Dragons*, pp. 220–21.

23. Coroner's jury report, December 9, 1804, Liv. Cir. Ct. Bundles, December, 1804.

24. Ky. H. J. 1810–1811, pp. 148–50.

25. Liv. Co. Order Book E, October 28, 1811, p. 99. Since men serving on the patrol were exempt from militia service, the dismissal of the patrol may have been ordered so that the patrollers could bolster the militia ranks. Tension was high then, just seven months before war was declared.

26. Liv. Co. Order Book D, December 25, 1809.

27. Ky. H. J. 1809–1810. p. 83.

23. TREMORS IN THE DYNASTY

1. W. C. Watts, *Chronicles*, p. 154.

2. Liv. Co. Deed Book A, p. 31.

3. Liv. Co. Order Book E, 1810–1816, February 25, 1811, pp. 63–64.

4. Liv. Co. Bundles, Box 1813–1814. The designation, "castings," refers to cast iron kettles, pots, Dutch ovens, and skillets. "Stilyards" is a phonetic spelling of steelyard (beam scales).

5. Liv. Co. Order Book E, 1810–1816, February 25, 1811, p. 65.

6. Ireland, "Aristocrats All," pp. 370–71.

7. Executive Journal of Gov. Charles Scott, May 17, 1811, p. 152, jacket 41–6, Ky Hi.

8. Perrin, *Christian and Trigg*, part 1, pp. 53–54, 193.

9. Liv. Cir. Ct. Order Book 1810–1814, March 28, 1811, p. 149; Liv. Cir. Ct. Bundles A to G, March 1811.

10. Liv. Cir. Ct. Bundles A to G, March 1811.

11. Ibid.

12. A few years later, when Amos Persons died, David Fort married his widow. She had four children at the time.

13. Liv. Cir. Ct. Order Book 1810–1814, pp. 42–44, 178, 194, 236.

14. Liv. Co. Order Book E, 1810–1816, July 22, 1811, pp. 88–89.

15. Littell and Swigert, *Digest,* 2:1213–19.

16. Littell, 3:517–24.

17. Liv. Cir. Ct. Bundles A–H, September 1813.

18. Pool, "Tragedies."

19. Adams County Record of Judgments Book B, November 1802–April 1811, pp. 478–79, Natchez.

24. ANNUS MIRABILIS

1. C. J. Latrobe, *Rambler,* 1:102–103.

2. Nearly one hundred years later, with another comet, this same fear was present and unabated in the Ohio Valley. "The 1910 visit of Halley's comet brought at least one death, mass hysteria, and a sweeping religious fervor to Evansville, Indiana. Uneducated persons were convinced that a collision was imminent, the end of the world was coming, there were poisonous gases in the comet's tail that would kill everyone on earth, rocks would fall from the sky, and fire from heaven would devour the land. Evansville citizens flocked to the churches to pray" (Greer, "Terror of 1910").

3. *Lexington Kentucky Gazette,* May 12, 1812.

4. *Lexington American Statesman,* December 17, 1811.

5. Drake, *Tecumseh,* pp. 141, 144–45.

6. Latrobe, *Rambler,* p. 102.

7. Audubon, *Birds,* 5:25–32.

8. *Lexington Kentucky Gazette,* May 12, 1812.

9. Fuller, "Earthquake," p. 13. This 115-page study is the most comprehensive work that the author has found on this event.

10. Fuller, "Earthquake," pp. 10–11.

11. Ibid., p. 8, map.

12. Ibid., pp. 101–102.

13. Ibid., pp. 44–45.

14. Ibid., p. 46.

15. Viitanen, "Mississippi," pp. 57, 60.

16. Bradbury, *Travels,* pp. 204–10. Quoted in Collins, *History,* 2:283.

17. Ambler, *Transportation,* pp. 111–16. Descriptions of the *New Orleans* vary so greatly that her actual appearance has not been

authenticated. Robert Fulton and Nicholas J. Roosevelt were prominent in the association that financed and built the ship.

18. Latrobe, *Rambler,* pp. 105–106.
19. Starling, *Henderson County,* pp. 136–37.
20. *Lexington Kentucky Gazette,* May 12, 1812.
21. *Lexington American Statesman,* December 17, 1811.
22. Ravenswaay, "Reminiscences," p. 94.
23. Viitanen, "Mississippi," pp. 64, 66.
24. Casseday, *Louisville,* pp. 125–26.
25. Ibid., p. 63.

25. THE MURDER

1. Weld, *American Slavery,* p. 93; interview with Grady Rutter, May 9, 1967.
2. Liv. Co. Order Book E, 1810–1816, October 28, 1811, p. 99.
3. Capt. H. Young, Capt. W. T. Poussin, and Lieut. S. Tuttle, "Reconnoissance of the Mississippi & Ohio Rivers, 1821," map #16, U. S. Army Corps of Engineers, Louisville. This first engineers' survey of the Ohio was made ten years after the earthquake. It is possible that at this bar, number seventeen, the water was deeper before the earthquake. Or it may have been shallower. There is no way to tell now.
4. In one fictional account of the Lewis story, two slaves discuss Lilburne's change of character. "He ain't lak hisse'f, Jim. Ain't nuthin' lak hisse'f."

"I knows 'e ain't, Hanna. An' I'se wondehin' what's gwinter hap'n iffen 'e gits mo' lak what 'e ain't." Baugher, *Wedgwood Pitcher,* p. 301.
5. In one official document the wound was described as being four inches deep and four inches wide (first indictment, Liv. Cir. Ct. Bundles, March 1812).
6. McMurtrie, *Sketches,* p. 234.
7. Liv. Cir. Ct. Bundles, March 1815. Gray's writing style was not unusual in legal circles. At an earlier time Jefferson had commented on this kind of legal gobbledegook: "I thought it would be useful also, in all new drafts, to reform the style . . . of our own Acts of Assembly; which, from their verbosity, their endless tautologies, their involutions of case within case, and parenthesis within parenthesis, and their multiplied efforts at certainty, by *saids* and *aforesaids,* by *ors* and by *ands,* to make them more plain, are really rendered more perplexed and incomprehensible, not only to common readers, but to the lawyers themselves." (Jefferson, *Autobiography,* pp. 57–58).
8. Rankin, *American Slavery,* pp. 62–64, quoting William Dickey to Thomas Rankin, October 8, 1824.
9. Watts, *Chronicles,* pp. 194–95. The actual names of the characters have been substituted here for the pseudonymns used by Watts.

10. Rothert, "Lewis Brothers," p. 232.

11. See the Bibliography for a discussion of these sources.

12. Other sections of this article may be found in Ch. 28, n. 17, and Ch. 29, n. 18.

13. Littell and Swigert, *Digest,* 2:1150. "Sec. 2. No negro or mulatto shall be a witness, except in pleas of the commonwealth against negroes or mulattoes, or in civil pleas where negroes or mulattoes alone shall be parties."

14. William Dickey to James Dickey, June 29, 1812, MS. 81008, Presb Hi.

26. AFTER THE MURDER

1. McMurtrie, *Sketches,* p. 236.

2. Ibid., p. 237.

3. Ibid., p. 239; Fuller, "Earthquake," p. 7.

4. Purcell, *Lucy Jefferson Lewis,* p. 9.

5. Ibid., pp. 9–10.

6. Liv. Co. Tax Rolls; Liv. Co. Will Book B, p. 106.

7. At the time of this interview, May 1967, Mr. Grady Rutter was seventy-three years old and a pleasant man of keen mind. As in Mrs. Purcell's account, there were some factual errors in the remainder of Mr. Rutter's verbal statements. When one considers that 155 years had passed since the murder, this is not surprising. The town of Birdsville mentioned above is located on what was the riverfront portion of Randolph's farm. In a two-day search in Memphis in 1968 the author was unable to find any descendants of Dickson Hurley.

8. Littell, 2:467.

9. Ibid.

10. Sneed, *Kentucky Penitentiary,* p. 19.

11. Stampp, *Peculiar Institution,* p. 218.

12. Burnaby, *Travels,* p. 54.

13. Stampp, *Peculiar Institution,* p. 218.

14. Boone County Circuit Court Minute book A, April 19, 1808, p. 95; Boone County Circuit Court Issue Docket Book A, p. "Commonwealth's causes to April, 1808." As is the case in many Kentucky counties, the early court bundles and records of Boone County (Burlington, Kentucky) are neatly boxed, but are not properly arranged by year. A search of the bundles from 1800 through 1819 did not uncover Campfield's indictment. The requisition for payment of Campfield's prison guards in 1807–1808 was found in the 1816 box, and the record of payment for the expenses of the trip to the penitentiary was found in the box for 1820.

15. Executive Journal of Gov. Charles Scott, January 3, 1811, p. 116, jacket 41–46, Ky Hi.

16. Ky. S. J. 1811–1812, p. 36.
17. Ibid., pp. 184–86.
18. Ibid., p. 186.
19. Watts, *Chronicles,* p. 196; Weld, *American Slavery,* p. 94.
20. See Ch. 15, notes 4–6.
21. Liv. Cir. Ct. Order Book 1807–1810, p. 7; *Russellville Mirror,* March 13, 1807; Sneed, *Kentucky Penitentiary,* pp. 73–75.
22. Sneed, *Kentucky Penitentiary,* pp. 21, 71, 121.
23. Littell, 2:468–74.
24. Ibid., 2:467–71.
25. Sneed, *Kentucky Penitentiary,* pp. 73–75. The prison records list all the manslaughter convictions under the term "murder." The actual charge is clear, even if the wording is misleading.
26. Rankin, *Letters,* p. 65.

27. THE FIRST GRAND JURY

1. Littell, 3:40.
2. See Ch. 17, notes 11–17.
3. McDonald, *Echoes,* p. 5.
4. Collins, *History,* 2:776; Executive Journal of Gov. Charles Scott, February 4, 1809, Ky. Hi. It was not unusual for magistrates to be elected to the legislature and hold both offices concurrently.
5. Liv. Cir. Ct. Bundles, September 1812.
6. Executive Journal of Gov. Charles Scott, January 17, 1811, p. 124, jacket 41–46, Ky Hi. Given replaced David Caldwell, who had moved to Russelville to start a saddling and tannery business (*The Farmer's Friend,* October 26, 1810).
7. Whitley, *Portraiture,* pp. 482–83.
8. Liv. Cir. Ct. Order Book 1807–1810, p. 138; Genealogy papers of Mrs. Clara Lee Whitt, Marion, Kentucky.
9. Liv. Co. Will Book A, p. 131. In 1816 the legislature abolished the office of assistant circuit judge. The fact that poorly educated men did not belong on the bench may have been a factor (Littell and Swigert, *Digest,* 1:371).
10. Liv. Co. Will Book A, p. 131.
11. Littell, 3:41.
12. Liv. Co. Order Book E, 1810–1816, April 22, 1811, p. 78.
13. Ky. H. J. 1809–1810, pp. 170–71.
14. Littell, 2:391; Liv. Cir. Ct. Bundles, August 1808.
15. Liv. Cir. Ct. Order Book E, 1815–1820, September 18, 1815, p. 91.
16. Liv. Co. Order Book D, January 3, 1809.
17. Census 1810.

18. Liv. Co. Order Book E, May 18, 1812, p. 130; Liv. Co. Order Books C and D.

19. Westerfield, 4:113; Census 1810; Liv. Co. Order Book E, July 24, 1810, p. 21.

20. Liv. Co. Order Book E, July 24, 1810, p. 21; Liv. Co. Order Book D, January 2, 1809.

21. Liv. Cir. Ct. Order Book 1810–1814, September 26, 1811, p. 253.

22. Liv. Cir. Ct. Bundles, September 1809.

23. Liv. Cir. Ct. Bundles, March 1808.

24. Liv. Cir. Ct. Order Book 1807–1810, September 27, 1809, p. 432; Liv. Cir. Ct. Order Book 1810–1814, March 18, 1812, p. 289; Liv. Co. Order Book D, February 27, 1810; Liv. Co. Order Book E, April 20, 1812, p. 215.

25. Watt's *Chronicles* indicates that Christopher Haynes was a man of excellent character and high integrity.

26. Littell and Swigert, *Digest,* 1:337. Italics supplied.

27. Littell and Swigert, *Digest,* 1:339.

28. Ibid., p. 239.

29. Ibid., pp. 339–40. Italics supplied.

30. Liv. Cir. Ct. Bundles, March 1814, Judgments.

31. The comments on the weather, earthquake, and vegetation (above and following) are taken from the records of Jared Brooks, a talented engineer and surveyor who lived at that time in Louisville, Kentucky. His records may be found in McMurtrie's *Sketches,* pp. 233–53. Louisville is 150 miles northeast by east of Livingston County. The timing of the earthquake shocks recorded in Louisville would correspond very closely with the time the same shock was felt in Livingston, with perhaps no more than a few minutes difference; but the amplitude would be greater in Livingston County, which was much closer to the epicenter. The growth stage of vegetation in west Kentucky is usually from one to two weeks ahead of the Louisville area. Weather conditions are more of a problem to judge, but as a general rule weather conditions move across Kentucky from the southwest to the northeast with about a day required, on the average, for weather variations to move from west Kentucky to the Louisville area. It is clear that projecting weather conditions found in Louisville backward one day in time and 150 miles in distance to Livingston County is a very speculative procedure. At the present time, supposedly scientific weather forecasts are frequently wrong, and rain or snow are usually predicted with an accompanying percentage figure of probability. Just as a forecast does not purport to be a certainty, neither does the author claim that the weather described herein is in every case historically accurate. He hopes for a hundred percent correspondence, but would expect a somewhat lower figure.

32. Littell and Swigert, *Digest,* 2:691.

33. Liv. Cir. Ct. Order Book 1810–1814, March 16, 1812, p. 275.

34. Liv. Cir. Ct. Order Book 1807–1810, June 30, 1809, p. 399.

35. The title, "Sr." was not used after Rutter's name in the order book, but the assumption was made here that this was not Lilburne's brother-in-law, James Rutter, Jr., but rather the elder James Rutter.

36. McMurtrie, *Sketches,* p. 248.

37. Liv. Cir. Ct. Order Book 1810–1814, March 17, 1812, pp. 279–81.

38. Liv. Cir. Ct. Bundles, March 1812; Liv. Cir. Ct. Order Book 1810–1814, September 23, 1811, p. 227, March 17, 1812, p. 281. O'Connell appears to have been a somewhat disturbed person. He spent the six months in jail because he could not find two men in the entire county who were willing to sign a bond for his good behavior. Two years before this incident, he had been indicted for tippling. Five days after he got out of jail in 1812 he committed suicide (Liv. Cir. Ct. Order Book 1807–1810, September 17, 1809, p. 432; Liv. Cir. Ct. Bundles, June 1812).

39. McMurtrie, *Sketches,* pp. 248–49.

40. Liv. Cir. Ct. Bundles, March 1812.

41. Liv. Cir. Ct. Order Book 1810–1814, March 18, 1812, p. 290.

42. Ibid., p. 282.

43. Liv. Cir. Ct. Bundles, March 1812.

44. Liv. Cir. Ct. Order Book 1810–1814, March 18, 1812, p. 290.

45. Ibid., pp. 290–91.

28. The True Bill

1. McMurtrie, *Sketches,* pp. 248–49.

2. Liv. Cir. Ct. Order Book 1810–1814, March 19, 1812, p. 297.

3. Several years later, McDaniel's hideous appearance became the subject of a wager that ended in an ugliness contest: "On the day mentioned both parties were present with their champion beauties (?), who were carefully blanketed and placed in separate rooms. Judges were appointed, straws drawn for the first show, and the lot fell to Humphreys' man. Grasty was brought out, and during the inspection did what he could to heighten the effect of his native ugliness by all sorts of grimaces and demoniacal contortions of his countenance. And surely it seemed as if no mortal man could be uglier and live. But Cravens, nothing daunted, when the time came, went for his man, and with the injunction: 'Now, Mac, look jist as nateral as you kin; look jist as God A'mighty made you,' placed him before the judges. The result was instantly arrived at when McDaniel had attained his most natural look, and the bet was forthwith and unanimously awarded to the Cravens champion amid the approving plaudits of the standers-by. McDaniel was born, lived, and died in a chapter of accidents: was buried into the ground by

a falling tree, tossed up into the air by another, fell forty-five feet down one well, was blown out of another, and was finally killed by a tub of rocks falling from above in a third." (Perrin, *Christian and Trigg,* part 1, p. 279).

4. Liv. Cir. Ct. Order Book 1810–1814, March 19, 1812, p. 288.

5. There is no record that Jonah Hibbs or Dickson Hurley, one of whom supposedly discovered George's head, testified before the grand juries.

6. Liv. Cir. Ct. Order Book 1810–1814, March 19, 1812, p. 301.

7. Lilburne's oldest son and third oldest child, Lilburne Livingston Lewis, was seven weeks short of his tenth birthday at this time. He may have been called to testify, but it does not seem reasonable that he could post a $200 bond.

8. Liv. Cir. Ct. Bundles, March 1812.

9. Littell, 3:38, 506; Littell and Swigert, *Digest,* 1:570. It was not until 1816 that circuit judges were allowed to call extra terms of court and, at a later time, to extend the length of a regular term (Littell, 5:347).

10. The court records do not mention the name of the defense attorney, but Lilburne retained Delany and paid him a fee in another matter about that time. The author assumes Delany was Lilburne's counsel in this case.

11. McMurtrie, *Sketches,* p. 249. Court opened at 9:00 A.M. One slander case was discussed briefly and dismissed. Then the Lewis brothers were brought in.

12. McMurtrie, *Sketches,* p. 255.

13. Liv. Cir. Ct. Order Book 1810–1814, March 20, 1812, pp. 303–304.

14. Ibid., pp. 305–306. Reverend William Dickey's account of admitting Lilburne to bail is somewhat more dramatic than it is accurate. "And though the dredful wretch was taken upon suspicion, and bound over to court, yet, I apprehend there was little probability of his actually falling under the sentence of the law.... This apprehension is rendered very probable by the fact that the populace actually let him out of prison in order to screen him from justice" (Rankin, *Letters,* p. 65). The populace did not let Lilburne and Isham out on bail. Judges Given and Ford made that decision, and they do not appear to have been men who could have been coerced by public opinion.

15. Purcell, *Lucy Jefferson Lewis,* p. 9; Watts, *Chronicles,* p. 196; Weld, *American Slavery,* p. 93.

16. Oakes and Gulick, *American Jurisprudence,* 58: Witnesses, sec. 175, pp. 124–25.

17. *Lexington Kentucky Gazette,* May 12, 1812 (dateline Russellville, April 22, 1812).

18. Weld, *American Slavery,* pp. 93–94. The butcher knife under Letitia's pillow may not have been put there with malicious intent.

Charles M. Wilson, in his book *Backwoods America* (p. 52), discusses old folk beliefs, one of which is a remedy for nightmares: "Bad dreams are but visitations of the nightmare man. To keep him away, one should wad the keyhole with cotton and sleep with a sharp knife under his pillow." Perhaps one of Letitia's servants was trying to protect her mistress from the nightmare man.

19. Purcell, *Lucy Jefferson Lewis,* p. 9.

20. Liv. Co. Will Book A, p. 34.

21. Lilburne Lewis Estate Inventory "not before returned," Liv. Co. Bundles, December 1812.

22. McMurtrie, *Sketches,* p. 250.

23. Littell, 4:287, 294.

24. Liv. Co. Mortgage Book, July 27, 1812, p. 386. Samuel Harkins lived in Salem and was one of the first trustees of that town. The court met in his house during 1809 and 1810 while the courthouse was under construction. He kept a stable in Salem and had a tavern license for his home.

25. Weld, *American Slavery,* p. 94.

29. The Graveyard

1. Liv. Co. Will Book A, p. 34. The original deed may be found in Liv. Co. Bundles, May 1812. Reverend William Woods was "Baptist Billy," the old friend of the family from Albemarle who had moved to Salem in 1810.

2. Starling, *Henderson County,* p. 138.

3. McMurtrie, *Sketches,* pp. 251–52.

4. Coroner's inquest summons and jury report, April 11, 1812, Liv. Cir. Ct., unmarked bundle.

5. Ibid. The twelve coroner's jurymen were: Mark Phillips, James Minese, Cullin Cook, Francis Hollinshead, Richard Ferguson, John Daniel, John Woods, William Pippin, William Dun, Sr., William Rutter (foreman), John Bolen, and Thomas Roe.

6. Coroner's inquest summons and jury report, April 11, 1812, Liv. Cir. Ct., unmarked bundle.

7. Littell and Swigert, *Digest,* 1:338.

8. Liv. Co. Order Book E, 1810–1816, December 23, 1811, p. 109.

9. Turpin, *Albemarle Baptist,* pp. 25, 30; Woods, *Albemarle,* pp. 353–54, 356. There was another man by the name of William Woods in Livingston County. He had a rather unsavory reputation and lived near the mouth of Hurricane Creek. Baptist Billy lived near Salem.

10. Rawlings, *Albemarle,* pp. 99–100; Turpin, *Albemarle Baptist,* p. 32.

11. Turpin, *Albemarle Baptist,* pp. 26–27, 31.

12. Commonwealth vs. Lewis & Lewis, Liv. Cir. Ct. Bundles, March 1815.

13. Executive Journal of Gov. Isaac Shelby, December 14, 1812, p. 27, jackets 47–55, Ky Hi. Court records show that Robert Kirk was still acting as sheriff in 1813. He evidently bought the office back from Joseph Reed.

14. Littell and Swigert, *Digest,* 1:405.

15. Commonwealth vs. Lewis & Lewis, Liv. Cir. Ct. Bundles, March 1815.

16. Littell and Swigert, 1:405. Under certain conditions bail was permissible.

17. McMurtrie, *Sketches,* p. 252.

18. *Lexington Kentucky Gazette,* May 12, 1812.

19. Weld, *American Slavery,* p. 94.

20. A shorter account of the story was written by Dickey in 1824, thirteen years earlier; Rankin, *Letters,* pp. 53–65.

21. Liv. Cir. Ct. Order Book 1810–1814, September 23, 1812, p. 377.

22. Liv. Cir. Ct. Order Book 1810–1814, September 23, 1813, p. 454.

23. Liv. Co. Order Book E, 1810–1816, July 20, 1812, p. 144.

30. The Orphans

1. Jefferson to Craven Peyton, December 6, 1810, M Hi.

2. Liv. Co. Order Book E, 1810–1816, April 21, 1812, p. 127.

3. Liv. Co. Bundles, April 1812.

4. Littell and Swigert, *Digest,* 1:644.

5. Liv. Co. Order Book E, 1810–1816, October 28, 1811, p. 98.

6. Littell and Swigert, *Digest,* 1:641.

7. Liv. Co. Bundles, August 1813.

8. The clerk's records of this sale were written by two different men. One of them listed Randolph's oldest son as Charles L. Lewis, and the other listed his name as Lilburne Lewis. It is clear that the same person was referred to. Colonel Lewis's name was written here as Charles L. Lewis, senr. by both record keepers.

9. Bill of Sale and Hire of Randolph Lewis Estate, January 1, 1813; Liv. Co. Bundles, August 1813.

10. Liv. Co. Order Book E, 1810–1816, May 18, 1812, p. 136.

11. Matilda ("a yellow girl," Randolph's niece) to Patrick Calhoun, $10.00; Judah to Jacob Houts, $25.12½; Agnes ("a yellow woman") to Samuel C. Harkins, $21.00; old Frank and Sarah to Jesse Roberts, $2.25; Andrew to Randolph's son, Charles, $53.00.

12. Liv. Co. Bundles, May 1814.

13. Liv. Co. Marriage Bonds, December 21, 1812.

14. Albemarle County Real Estate Tax Rolls, 1807, Book B, Vi. It was on this tract that Watson's Ordinary, later called Boyd's Old Tavern, was located next to the Three Chopt Road. Nancy sold the tract to Rev. John B. Magruder, whose son-in-law, Thomas D. Boyd, evi-

dently had a long-term lease on the land and tavern (Albemarle Deed Book 15, p. 190; Wyllie, "Daniel Boone's Adventures," p. 17.

15. Arnold, *Methodism,* 1:370–71.

16. Liv. Co. Order Book E, 1810–1816, August 17, 1812, p. 146, October 19, 1812, p. 149.

17. Liv. Co. Order Book E, 1810–1816, October 19, 1812, p. 149, October 18, 1813, p. 211.

18. Liv. Co. Bundles, 1812–1815.

19. Liv. Co. Order Book E, 1810–1816, April 21, 1812, p. 127.

20. Ibid.; Liv. Co. Will Book A, p. 34.

21. Liv. Co. Order Book E, 1810–1816, May 18, 1812, p. 133.

22. Liv. Co. Bundles, May 1812. See Appendix 5.

23. Joseph Reed, Samuel C. Harkins, and John Mott served as Letitia's commissioners.

24. See Appendix 5.

25. Liv. Co. Order Book E, 1810–1816, December 20, 1813, pp. 229–30.

26. Liv. Cir. Ct. Order Book, 1810–1814, June 15, 1812, pp. 310–11.

27. Liv. Co. Deed Book B, July 27, 1812, p. 386.

28. Report of Administrator of Lilburne Lewis Estate, Liv. Co. Bundles, October–December 1812, box 1811–1813. See Appendix 5.

29. Executive Journal of Gov. Isaac Shelby, December 16, 1812, p. 28, jackets 47–55, Ky Hi. In the left margin of the petition is the notation, "Delivered—General Ramsey."

30. "Minutes of Military Commissions, June 1812–August 1816," MS 1140, pp. 14, 40, Ky Hi. The following nomination was ratified on July 21: "A majority of the field officers and capts. of the 24th Regiment of Kentucky Militia met in the town of Salem on the 15th of June, 1812 and doth anominate William Berry, Lieutenant, in the place of Lilburne Lewis, decesed" (Executive Papers of Gov. Charles Scott Military Appointments, 1812, box 8, jacket 52, Ky Hi).

31. Liv. Co. Order Book E, 1810–1816, July 20, 1812, p. 143.

32. Liv. Cir. Ct. Order Book, 1810–1814, March 22, 1814, p. 458.

33. Ibid., September 21, 1813, p. 435; Liv. Cir. Ct. Bundle A–H, September 1813.

31. During the War

1. Isaac Shelby to William Eustis, September 5, 1812, Ky. H.J. 1812–1813, pp. 17–18.

2. Kentucky Adjutant-General's Office, *Kentucky Soldiers,* p. 304; Collins, *History,* 1:27; Ky. S. J., 1813–1814, pp. 19–20.

3. William C. Rodgers, letter to the editor of *Lexington Reporter,* November 19, 1812, Draper MSS., 5CC32, The State Historical Society of Wisconsin, Madison.

4. The area patrolled lay in the present-day counties of Trigg, Lyon, and Livingston, where they border the Tennessee River or lie under the waters of Kentucky Lake.

5. Ky. H. J. 1812–1813, pp. 60–61, 143.

6. Ky. S. J. 1813–1814, pp. 19–20.

7. Ibid., pp. 20–21.

8. Ky. S. J. 1812–1813, pp. 30–193. Prior to the passage of this bill, executors and administrators were forbidden to sell slaves of the testator except to satisfy debts of the estate (Littell and Swigert, *Digest*, 2:1157).

9. Liv. Co. Order Book E, 1810–1816, April 19, 1813, pp. 174–75; May 16, 1814, p. 255; Liv. Co. Bundles, May 1814.

10. Liv. Co. Bundles, May 1814. Punctuation supplied. Warner, the youngest child, was three years old at this time.

11. The four deeds involved in this deception are recorded in Albemarle Deed Book 14, p. 506; Albemarle Deed Book 15, pp. 28, 30, 33.

12. Liv. Co. Deed Book B, p. 504.

13. Jefferson to Craven Peyton, August 13, 1814, Coolidge Papers, M Hi (typescript copy at Vi U, TBCF #2870–a). The deed referred to is Charles L. Lewis to Craven Peyton, September 29, 1804, Albemarle Deed Book 15, p. 30.

14. Craven Peyton to Jefferson, June 26, 1817, TBCF #1460, Vi U, T McG Lib.

15. Ibid., overleaf.

16. Liv. Co. Order Book E, 1810–1816, April 19, 1813, p. 178; Liv. Cir. Ct. Order Book 1810–1814, pp. 484, 494, 506.

17. Patrick H. Rice, guardian for Tucker, Lucy, Susannah, and Mary; James H. Rice for Warner; and Gabriel Threlkeld for Robert. The second oldest son, Howell, was apparently twenty-one by this time. The absence of his name from all the records indicates he may have returned to Virginia with his two younger sisters in 1813 (Liv. Cir. Ct. Order Book 1810–1814, pp. 484, 506).

18. Liv. Cir. Ct. Order Book E, 1815–1820, March 25, 1815, p. 46.

19. Liv. Co. Deed Book C, p. 326.

20. Ibid., p. 330.

21. Weld, *American Slavery*, p. 94.

22. Sorley, *Lewis of Warner Hall*, pp. 723, 727.

23. *Lewisiana* 5, Book 35, ch. 37, p. 137.

24. Liv. Cir. Ct. Order Book E, 1815–1820, p. 2. It is possible that Isham was killed in the first skirmishes of the Battle of New Orleans, which took place on December 23, 1814, on the west side of the Mississippi. There were several hundred U.S. casualties.

25. Adams County Record of Judgments Book B, October 14, 1811, pp. 478–79, Natchez. A diligent search of the public records in Natchez failed to reveal any indication of Isham's presence there after 1810.

26. Martha A. C. Monroe to Jefferson, August 6, 1815, TBCF #1365, Vi U, MSS Dept. The "friend to mankind, Mr. Woods," was Baptist Billy, who delivered this letter to Jefferson on October third, almost three months after it was written.

27. Liv. Cir. Ct. Order Book 1810–1814, June 23, 1814, p. 506.

28. Liv. Co. Order Book E, 1810–1816, November 21, 1815, p. 346; personal records of Mrs. Marilyn J. Martin, Newtown Square, Pennsylvania.

29. Liv. Co. Order Book E, 1810–1816, July 19, 1813, pp. 197–98 (Jane W. to Gen. Jonathan Ramsey, Lilburne L. to Mark Phillips, James R. to his grandfather James Rutter, Sr.); August 16, 1813, p. 204 (Robert to James McCawley); October 18, 1813, p. 211 (Elizabeth to Hamlet Ferguson); November 15, 1813, p. 217 (Lucy J. to Mark Phillips).

30. Liv. Co. Order Book E, 1810–1816, December 20, 1813, pp. 229–30. Appraisal values: Celia, $150; William, $110; Frank, $435; Ursula, $325.

31. Liv. Co. Order Book E, 1810–1816, August 21, 1815, p. 328.

32. Reliable witnesses are unanimous that there were only three graves in this graveyard, one of them much smaller than the other two, which were the graves of Elizabeth and Lilburne. In spite of the legendary claims, Lucy Lewis cannot be buried there. She probably lies in the graveyard on Randolph's farm, near the top of the hill behind Birdsville, Kentucky.

33. See Appendix 1, sec. 4.

34. (1) Randolph Jefferson, the president's brother, married his first cousin, Anna J. Lewis; (2) their son, Thomas Jefferson, Jr., married Mary R. Lewis, his first cousin, whose parents (Col. Charles L. Lewis and Lucy Jefferson) were first cousins, and also respectively brother and sister to Thomas Jefferson, Jr.'s parents; (3) the son of Thomas Jefferson, Jr. and his wife, Mary R., was Peter Field Jefferson, who married his first cousin, Jane W. Lewis, whose parents (Lilburne and Elizabeth Lewis) were second cousins.

32. THE AFTEREFFECTS

1. Littell and Swigert, Digest, 1:641.

2. Liv. Co. Will Book A, pp. 130–32. Punctuation supplied.

3. Whitley, Kentucky Portraiture, p. 482; genealogy records of Mrs. Clara Lee Whitt, Marion, Kentucky, compiled from Livingston County records. General Ramsey had been a member of the county court that Given thought had acted unwisely in the care of orphans. In 1813 Ramsey had been appointed guardian of Lilburne's daughter, Jane.

4. Ky. S. J. 1812–1813, p. 75. It is said that Jesse Ford moved to Tennessee.

5. Ky. S. J. 1812–1813, December 7, 1812.

6. Liv. Co. Order Book E, 1810–1816, July 20, 1812, p. 138.

7. Liv. Cir. Ct. Bundles, June 1812; Liv. Cir. Ct. Order Book 1810–1814, June 16, 1812, p. 313.

8. Liv. Cir. Ct. Order Book 1810–1814, June 16, 1812, pp. 316–17.

9. Liv. Co. Order Book E, 1810–1816, May 18, 1812, pp. 131–32.

10. Executive Journal of Gov. Charles Scott, August 3, 1812, jackets 47–55, Ky Hi.

11. Union County Deed Book A, p. 304, Morganfield, Kentucky; Beard, *Sketches,* 1st ser., p. 279.

12. Groom, "Henry F. Delany," pp. 6–7.

13. Ibid., quoting Richard Beard, "Address to the General Assembly of the Church," May 21, 1880, Evansville, Indiana. Littleton Groom has compiled extensive material about the history of the Cumberland Presbyterian church.

14. Estate Inventory, Union County Will Book A, April 18, 1831, p. 315, Morganfield, Kentucky.

15. Union County Will Book A, p. 316.

16. Union County Marriage Bonds and Records, June 5, 1834, Morganfield, Kentucky.

17. J. M. Wilson, *Almanac,* p. 112.

18. Jefferson, *Notes,* p. 143; Mellon, *Slavery,* pp. 109, 122.

19. Coues, *Expedition,* 1:xv–xlii.

20. Ford, *Works,* 11:341–43.

21. Jefferson was careful about keeping records of his huge correspondence. When he did not keep the original or verbatim copies he usually recorded brief notes of the letters in his Summary Journal of Letters. It seems inconsistent and unlikely that Jefferson would have destroyed any correspondence regarding the Lewises, either upon receipt of the letters, or at a later time. Jefferson took extraordinary care to maintain the fullest record of his life. In the many years since Jefferson's death, his papers passed through hands far more careless than his in trying to preserve the total record. As a result, several thousand letters written by and to him are missing.

22. Tocqueville, *Democracy,* 1:363n.

33. THE EPILOGUE

1. Tapp, "Kentucky Politics," p. 464.

2. Eaton, *Mind,* p. 292.

3. Rankin, *Letters,* p. 65.

4. Jefferson, *Notes,* pp. 162–63.

5. Mathias, "Slavery," pp. 1–3 (quoting Tocqueville, *Democracy,* 1:400).

6. Eaton, *Mind,* p. 290.

7. Pool, "Tragedies."

8. Rankin, *Letters*, p. 62.

9. John M. McAllister's letter (see pp. 317–18) supports this: "Nor is there anything . . . to sustain the theory that the indictment . . . in any way gave rise to the suicide."

10. Jefferson to Seth Pease, May 23, 1809, M Hi.

11. Weld, *American Slavery*, p. 94.

APPENDIX 1

1. Charles Lewis of Belvoir (his childhood home) and North Garden, was the son of Robert Lewis of Belvoir (see Sorley, *Lewis of Warner Hall*, pp. 345–46).

2. The Albemarle County public records from 1748 to 1781 were destroyed by the British in Tarleton's raid of June 1781.

3. Branchi, "Mazzei," p. 172; "Col. Charles Lewis," p. 194; Gilmer, "Papers," p. 80; Woods, *Albemarle*, p. 30; Edmund Pendleton to Jefferson, May 24, 1776; Boyd, *Papers*, 1:297; Edmund Pendleton to Jefferson, July 29, 1776; Boyd, *Papers*, 1:480; Palmer, *Calendar*, 8:196; Albemarle Will Book 2, pp. 374–75; Albemarle Will Book 5, pp. 50–56; Stanard, "Virginia Legislative Papers," *Vi. Hist. Mag.* 16 (July–December, 1908):170–2, and 17 (July–December, 1809): 52–60.

4. Coues, *Expedition*, 1:xv–xlii.

5. George Gilmer to Jefferson, July 26 or 27, 1775; Boyd, *Papers*, 1:236–39, notes. This identification of Charles Lewis of Belvoir (and North Garden) is in conflict with an identification made by Sorley in *Lewis of Warner Hall*, pp. 345–46.

6. Dr. Charles Cadwallader Lewis was born at Bel Air, the family home in Franklin County, Virginia. He married Elizabeth Henry Patterson. He was buried in Frankfort, Kentucky. In the next generation the oldest son bore the same name as his father, and also became a doctor. Dr. Charles C. Lewis, Jr. was born in Franklin County, Virginia, died in 1903, and was buried in Owensboro. He married Letitia Anne Barron, who was a direct descendant of George Mason, successor to George Washington's seat in the Virginia legislature, author of the Virginia Bill of Rights, and much of the Virginia state constitution. In the third generation of the Charles C. Lewis family the oldest son was also named Charles Cadwallader Lewis. He married Harriet Bryant, to whom the author is indebted for the above information.

7. Sheriff Nicholas Hamner's Account Book, p. 25, Vi U.

8. Sorley, *Lewis of Warner Hall*, p. 365; personal papers of Mrs. Marilyn J. Martin, Newtown Square, Pennsylvania; *Lewisiana*, book 45, ch. 30, p. 88.

9. Liv. Co. Deed Book DD, pp. 1–7.

10. Power of Attorney Assignment, Charles L. Lewis to Tucker W. Lewis, August 6, 1822, Liv. Co. Deed Book E, pp. 267–68.

11. Liv. Co. Deed Book BB, pp. 143–50.

Appendix 2

1. Jefferson sometimes referred to Anthony Gianinni as Anthony, and at other times as Gianinni. Gianinni should not be confused with Giovanni, a tailor who was self-employed, but who did make clothes for Jefferson and his servants (Bear, *Jefferson at Monticello*, p. 5; Jefferson to Philip Mazzei, April 4, 1780, Boyd, *Papers*, 3:342.

2. Betts, *Garden Book*, p. 81; Marraro, "Unpublished Correspondence," pp. 120, 122.

3. Jefferson to Philip Mazzei, April 4, 1780, Boyd, *Papers*, 3:342.

4. Jefferson to Philip Mazzei, January 7, 1792, Maruzzi Archives, Pisa, Italy, published in Marraro, "Unpublished Correspondence," p. 120.

5. Charles L. Lewis to Jefferson, March 22, 1792. The location and contents of this letter are unknown.

6. Jefferson to Col. Charles L. Lewis, June 4, 1793, ser. r. 87:15050, DLC.

7. Jefferson to Philip Mazzei, May 30, 1795, DLC, published in Marraro, "Unpublished Correspondence," p. 122.

8. Jefferson to Philip Mazzei, May 26, 1795, Ford, *Works*, 8:180.

9. Garlick, *Philip Mazzei*, p. 134.

10. Not trusting banks as depositories, Jefferson, who held Mazzei's power of attorney, had lent himself over six thousand dollars of Mazzei's money. Jefferson paid interest, but was unable to repay the principal, pleading bad business conditions as an excuse (Schachner, *Thomas Jefferson*, pp. 951–52). Other records pertaining to Jefferson's management of Mazzei's estate may be found in Boyd, *Papers*, 16:307–309.

BIBLIOGRAPHY

DISCUSSION OF SOURCES

The most important of the sources that deal directly with the murder of George have been discussed in Chapter 25 (pp. 258–64). Of these four, the Livingston court records appear to be the most reliable. Like the court records, the brief newspaper article in the *Kentucky Gazette,* May 12, 1812, leaves unsaid far more than it reveals. The letter of Rev. William Dickey, written in 1824 and expanded for republication in 1837, is the main source for most of the accounts of the murder that have been published since 1837. Carleton's *The Suppressed Book about Slavery,* published in 1864, contains a one-page description of the murder, but it is a condensed version of Dickey's letter and contributes nothing new to the facts of the story.

It is regrettable that Dickey's letter contains so many questionable allegations mixed in with what are, no doubt, true facts, for those who have subsequently quoted his letter have repeated his errors. Another account of the tragedy, apparently not based on Dickey's letter, is a newspaper feature article by Atlanta H. Taylor Pool, which was published in the *Louisville Courier-Journal* in 1894. Although it is longer than Dickey's letter, and includes some information about the background of the Lewis family, it also contains even more mistakes than Dickey's version of the tragedy. It appears that Mrs. Pool had access to cursory research done in the Livingston court records and in Albemarle County, Virginia. She identified some of her other sources as "veracious elderly men, who received the story from their fathers."

William C. Watts, in his book, *Chronicles of a Kentucky Settlement,* published in 1897, relied almost entirely on local legend and tradition as the source for his fifty-page version of the Lewis tragedy. Watts used pseudonyms, but reasonably accurate keys to the names may be found at the Filson Club in Louisville.

In 1908, Mrs. Martha Grassham Purcell, a west Kentucky local historian, published in the D.A.R. *Souvenir* (Lexington, Kentucky, October 23, 1908), an article about the Lewis tragedy. Like the earlier versions of the story, Mrs. Purcell's article is notable for its errors. Although she made some use of local legends, Mrs. Purcell added little to the Lewis story except a new account of the discovery of George's head. Due to the efforts of Mrs. Purcell, in 1927 the fieldstone markers were removed from the three graves in Lilburne's cemetery and an inscribed gravestone, two feet long and a foot high, was installed there to mark Lucy Lewis's last resting place. Unfortunately, it is almost certain that Lucy is buried two miles away in the graveyard above Birdsville.

After Mrs. Purcell's investigations, which took place before 1908, the sources of verbal history died away. Since that time local versions of the Lewis story have become dependent upon and, in most cases, originated in the inaccurate accounts that had been published by Watts, Pool, Dickey, and Purcell. The newspaper feature articles, published from time to time since 1900, were usually based on Watt's book, or Pool's article, and have done little to correct the mistakes in their sources.

Only one scholarly study of the tragedy has been attempted up to the present time. That is a thirty-page article by Otto A. Rothert, published in *The Filson Club History Quarterly* in October 1936. Mr. Rothert, a distinguished Kentucky historian and secretary of the Filson Club, was limited by time and funds in gathering research material. Although Mr. Rothert made carefully qualified use of Watts, his article is documented by other more reliable sources, and may be credited with keeping alive a fairly accurate outline of the tragedy.

Since Rothert's article in 1936, nothing of historical value has been added to the story in the accounts that have been published on the subject. The incident has received passing mention in the works of J. Winston Coleman, Jr., Jonathan Daniels, and a few other authors.

Two other works, which were not used in the preparation of this book, should be mentioned here. One of them is *The Wedgwood Pitcher* (1944) by Ruby Dell Baugher. The author of this now scarce book said that because she was physically unable to gather research material, she chose to tell the Lewis story as fiction. Her main sources appear to have been the work of Watts and Pool, which she elaborated with romantic imagination, gentle humor, and dignified propriety.

The best known work concerning the Lewis story is *Brother to Dragons* (1953) by Robert Penn Warren. This book is a dialogue in verse. Because of its unique literary and artistic quality it stands alone among other works based on the Lewis tragedy. In

426

regard to the historicity of *Brother to Dragons,* Warren states in the preface: "I am trying to write a poem and not a history, and therefore have no compunction about tampering with facts." Warren succeeded admirably, both in his poem and in tampering with the facts. However, it might be ventured that facts usually do stand in the way of poetic expression and artistic triumph, such as Warren has achieved.

The following works, though not concerned directly with the Lewis tragedy, were found to be extremely helpful in assembling the research material used herein: Julian P. Boyd, *The Papers of Thomas Jefferson*; J. Winston Coleman, Jr., *A Bibliography of Kentucky History*; Wendell H. Rone, Sr., *An Historical Atlas of Kentucky and Her Counties*; Earl G. Swem, *Virginia Historical Index*; Constance E. Thurlow, et al., *The Jefferson Papers of the University of Virginia*. Also of essential help were the editorial control files (sometimes referred to as the "Jefferson checklist") of *The Papers of Thomas Jefferson*, by Julian P. Boyd. These files, which locate and describe briefly all of Jefferson's known letters and papers, have been microfilmed and copies deposited in several of the larger libraries across the country.

NEWSPAPERS CONSULTED

Evansville Sunday Courier and Press (Indiana) 1968
Herrin Egyptian Republican (Illinois) 1926
Lexington American Statesman (Kentucky) 1811
Lexington Kentucky Gazette 1790–1812
Louisville Courier-Journal (Kentucky) 1894
Marion Crittenden Press (Kentucky) 1954
Russellville Farmer's Friend (Kentucky) 1809–1810
Russellville Mirror (Kentucky) 1807–1808
Washington Republican (Mississippi) 1813–1817

WORKS CITED

Acts Passed at the First Session of the Forty-Fourth General Assembly of the Commonwealth of Kentucky. Frankfort: J. H. Holeman, Public Printer, 1836.

Ambler, Charles H. *A History of Transportation in the Ohio Valley.* Glendale, Cal.: Arthur H. Clark Co., 1932.

Anburey, Thomas. *Travels through the Interior Parts of America.* 2 vols. Boston: Houghton Mifflin Co., 1923.

Anderson, Sarah T. L. *Lewises, Meriwethers, and Their Kin*. Richmond, Va.: Dietz Press, 1938.

Arnold, William E. *A History of Methodism in Kentucky*. 2 vols. Louisville: Herald Press, 1935, 1936.

Arnow, Harriette S. *Seedtime on the Cumberland*. New York: Macmillan Co., 1960.

Audubon, John J. *The Birds of America from Drawings Made in the United States and Their Territories*. 7 vols. New York: V. G. Audubon, Roe Lockwood & Son, 1859, 1860.

————. *Delineations of American Scenery and Character*. New York: G. A. Baker & Co., 1926.

Ayres, S. Edward. "Albemarle County, 1744–1770: An Economic, Political, and Social Analysis." *Magazine of Albemarle County History* 25 (1966–1967): 36–55.

Baker, Clauscine R. *First History of Caldwell County, Kentucky*. Madisonville, Ky.: Commercial Printers, 1936.

Banta, R. E. *The Ohio*. Rivers of America Series. New York: Rinehart & Co., 1949.

Baugher, Ruby D. *The Wedgwood Pitcher*. Cynthiana, Ky.: Hobson Book Press, 1944.

Bear, James A., Jr., ed. *Jefferson at Monticello*. Charlottesville: University Press of Virginia, 1967.

————. "Thomas Jefferson's Account Books." Typescript. Monticello, Charlottesville, Va.

Beard, Richard. *Brief Biographical Sketches of Some of the Early Ministers of the Cumberland Presbyterian Church*. Nashville, Tenn.: Southern Methodist Publishing House, 1867.

Bergman, Peter M. *The Chronological History of the Negro in America*. New York: Harper & Row, 1969.

Betts, Edwin M., ed. *Thomas Jefferson's Farm Book with Commentary and Relevant Extracts from Other Writings*. Princeton: Princeton University Press, 1953.

————. *Thomas Jefferson's Garden Book, 1766–1824, with Relevant Extracts from his Other Writings*. Philadelphia: The American Philosophical Society, 1944.

Betts, Edwin M., and Bear, James A., Jr., eds. *The Family Letters of Thomas Jefferson*. Columbia: University of Missouri Press, 1966.

Biddle, Francis. "Scandal at Bizarre." *American Heritage* 12 (August 1961), 10–13, 79–82.

Bishop, Robert Hamilton. *An Outline of the History of the Church in the State of Kentucky*. Lexington, Ky.: Thomas T. Skillman, 1824.

Boles, John B. *The Great Revival, 1787–1805: The Origins of the Southern Evangelical Mind*. Lexington: University Press of Kentucky, 1972.

Book, John David, Jr. "Audubon in Louisville, 1807–1810." *Filson Club History Quarterly* 45 (April 1971), 186–198.

Bowers, Claude G. *Jefferson and Hamilton: The Struggle for Democracy in America.* Boston: Houghton Mifflin Co., Riverside Press, 1925.

Boyd, Julian P., ed. *The Papers of Thomas Jefferson,* 19 vols. to date. Princeton: Princeton University Press, 1950–.

Bradbury, John. *Travels in the Interior of America in the Years 1809, 1810, and 1811.* Liverpool: Sherwood, Neely and Jones, 1817.

Bradford, Gamaliel. *Damaged Souls.* Boston: Houghton Mifflin Co., Riverside Press, 1923.

Branchi, E. C., trans. "Memoirs of the Life and Voyages of Doctor Philip Mazzei." *William and Mary College Quarterly Historical Magazine,* 2d ser. 9 (1929): 161–174.

Breckinridge, Robert J., et al., eds. *The Danville Quarterly Review.* 4 vols. Danville, Ky.: Moore, Wilstach & Baldwin, 1864.

Brown, Alexander. *The Cabels and Their Kin.* Boston: Houghton Mifflin Co., 1895.

Bryant, William C. *The Embargo.* Ed. Thomas O. Mabbott. Gainesville, Fla.: Scholars' Facsimilies & Reprints, 1955.

Burnaby, Andrew. *Burnaby's Travels through North America: Reprinted from the Third Edition of 1798, with Introduction and Notes by Rufus Rockwell Wilson.* New York: A. Wessels Co., 1904.

Campbell, Charles W. *Memoirs of a Monticello Slave: As Dictated to Charles Campbell in the 1840's by Isaac, one of Thomas Jefferson's Slaves.* Charlottesville: University of Virginia Press, 1951. Reprinted in James A. Bear, Jr., ed., *Jefferson at Monticello,* Charlottesville: University Press of Virginia, 1967.

Campbell, Tom W. *Two Fighters and Two Fines: Sketches of the Lives of Matthew Lyon and Andrew Jackson.* 2d ed. Little Rock, Ark.: Pioneer Publishing Co., 1941.

Carleton, George W. *The Suppressed Book about Slavery: Prepared for Publication in 1857, Never Published until the Present Time.* New York: Carleton, 1864.

Cartwright, Peter. *Autobiography of Peter Cartwright, the Backwoods Preacher.* William P. Strickland, ed. Cincinnati, Ohio: Cranston & Curts, 1856.

Casseday, Ben. *The History of Louisville, from its Earliest Settlement till the Year 1852.* Louisville: Hull & Brother, 1852.

Chastellux, Marquis de Francois Jean. *Travels in North America in the Years 1780, 1781, and 1782.* 2 vols. Howard C. Rice, Jr., ed. Chapel Hill: University of North Carolina Press, 1963.

Clark, Thomas D. *The Rampaging Frontier: Manners and Humors of Pioneer Days in the South and Middle West.* Indianapolis: Bobbs-Merrill Co., 1939.

Clift, G. Glenn. *The "Corn Stalk" Militia of Kentucky, 1792–1811.* Frankfort: Kentucky Historical Society, 1957.

_____, comp. *Kentucky Marriages, 1797-1865.* Baltimore: Genealogical Publishing Co., 1966.

Coffman, Edward. *The Story of Logan County.* Russellville, Ky.: Edward Coffman, 1962.

_____. *The Story of Russellville.* Russellville, Ky.: News-Democrat Printers, 1931.

"Col. Charles Lewis." *William and Mary College Quarterly Historical Magazine,* 2nd ser. 2 (July 1922), 194.

Coleman, Ann M. B. (Mrs. Chapman Coleman). *The Life of John J. Crittenden.* 2 vols. Philadelphia: J. B. Lippincott & Co., 1871.

Coleman, J. Winston, Jr., comp. *A Bibliography of Kentucky History.* Lexington: University of Kentucky Press, 1949.

_____. *Famous Kentucky Duels.* 2n ed., rev. Lexington, Ky., Henry Clay Press, 1969.

_____. *Slavery Times in Kentucky.* Chapel Hill: University of North Carolina Press, 1940.

Collins, Richard H. *History of Kentucky.* 2 vols. Covington, Ky.: Collins & Co., 1874. Reprinted, Frankfort, Ky.: Kentucky Historical Society, 1966.

Cossitt, F. R. *The Life and Times of Rev. Finis Ewing, One of the Fathers and Founders of the Cumberland Presbyterian Church.* Louisville, Ky.: L. R. Woods, 1853.

Coues, Elliott, ed. *History of the Expedition under the Command of Lewis and Clark.* 4 vols. New York: F. P. Harper, 1893.

Cramer, Zadock. *The Navigator: Containing Directions for Navigating the Monongahela, Allegheny, Ohio and Mississippi Rivers.* Pittsburgh: Cramer & Spear, 1808. Numerous editions from 1801 to 1824.

Craven, Avery O. *Soil Exhaustion as a Factor in the Agricultural History of Virginia and Maryland, 1606–1860.* Urbana: University of Illinois Press, 1926.

Cuming, Fortescue. *Sketches of a Tour to the Western Country through the States of Ohio and Kentucky.* Pittsburgh: Cramer, Spear, & Eichbaum, 1810.

Dabney, Virginius. "Jack Jouett's Ride." *American Heritage* 13 December 1961): 56–59.

Dabney, William M. "Jefferson's Albemarle: History of Albemarle County, Virginia, 1727–1819." Ph. D. dissertation, University of Virginia, 1951.

Daniels, Jonathan W. *The Devil's Backbone: The Story of the Natchez Trace.* The American Trails Series. New York: McGraw-Hill, 1962.

_____. *The Randolphs of Virginia.* Garden City, N. Y.: Doubleday & Co., 1972.

Dann, John C., reviewer. "The Great Revival, 1787–1805," by John B. Boles. *The Filson Club History Quarterly* 47 (January 1973): 58–59.

D. A. R. Patriot Index. Washington, D. C.: National Society of the Daughters of the American Revolution, 1966.

Dillon, Richard H. *Meriwether Lewis: A Biography.* New York: Coward-McCann, 1965.

Donovan, Frank. *River Boats of America.* New York: Thomas Y. Crowell Co., 1966.

Dos Passos, John. *The Head and Heart of Thomas Jefferson.* Garden City, N. Y.: Doubleday & Co., 1954.

Douglas, Byrd. *Steamboatin' on the Cumberland.* Nashville: Tennessee Book Co., 1961.

Drake, Benjamin. *The Life of Tecumseh and of His Brother the Prophet.* Cincinnati: H. S. & J. Applegate & Co., 1852.

Draper, Lyman C. *King's Mountain and It's Heroes: History of the Battle of King's Mountain.* New York: Dauber & Pine Bookshops, 1929.

Du Roi, August W. *Journal of Du Roi the Elder, Lieutenant and Adjutant, in the Service of the Duke of Brunswick, 1776–1778.* Charlotte S. J. Epping, trans. Americana Germanica, N.S. 15. New York: D. Appleton & Co. for the University of Pennsylvania, 1911.

Durrett, Reuben T. "Early Banking in Kentucky." Paper read at Filson Club, Louisville, Ky., October 4, 1892. Typescript.

Eaton, Clement. *The Civilization of the Old South: Writings of Clement Eaton.* Albert D. Kirwan, ed. Lexington: University of Kentucky Press, 1968.

————. *A History of the Old South.* New York: Macmillan Co., 1949.

————. *The Mind of the Old South.* Rev. ed. Baton Rouge: Louisiana State University Press, Louisiana Paperback, 1967.

Eaves, Charles D. *The Virginia Tobacco Industry (1780–1860).* Lubbock: Texas Technological College Research Publication, 1945.

Elkins, Stanley M. *Slavery: A Problem in American Institutional and Intellectual Life.* 2d ed. Chicago: University of Chicago Press, 1968.

Filson, John. *The Discovery, Settlement and Present State of Kentucke.* Wilmington, Del.: printed by James Adams, 1784. Reprinted, The American Experiment Series. New York: Corinth Books, 1962.

Ford, Paul L., ed. *The Works of Thomas Jefferson.* Federal Edition. 12 vols. New York: G. P. Putnam's Sons, Knickerbocker Press, 1904–1905.

Fuller, Myron L. "The New Madrid Earthquake." *U. S. Geological Survey Bulletin 494.* Washington, D. C., 1912.

Furnas, J. C. *The Americans: A Social History of the United States, 1587–1914.* Vol. 1. New York: Capricorn Books, 1971.

Garlick, Richard C., Jr. *Philip Mazzei, Friend of Jefferson: His Life and Letters.* The Johns Hopkins Studies in Romance Literatures and Languages, extra vol. 7. Baltimore: Johns Hopkins Press, 1933.

Gilmer, George. "The Papers of George Gilmer, of 'Pen Park,' 1775–

1778." *Collections of the Virginia Historical Society* NS 6 (1887): 71–140.

Girardin, Louis Hue. *The History of Virginia; Commenced by John Burk, and Continued by Skelton Jones and Louis Hue Girardin.* Vol. 4. Petersburg, Va: M. W. Dunnavant, printer, 1816.

Greer, William. "Terror of 1910: Halley's Comet." *Evansville* (Indiana) *Sunday Courier and Press,* December 29, 1968.

Groom, Littleton, comp. "Henry F. Delany: Pioneer Lawyer and Minister in Kentucky." Typescript, 9 pp. Princeton, N.J., 1970?

——. "History of the Livingston Presbyterian Church, U.S.A., Caldwell County, Kentucky, 1797–1885." Mimeographed manuscript, 22 pp. Princeton, N. J., 1966.

——. *History of Salem Presbyterian Church, Logan County, Kentucky, 1792–1900, in its Early Years: Also Known as Muddy River Presbyterian Church.* Princeton, N. J.: Littleton Groom, 1969.

Hall, James, *Letters from the West: Containing Sketches of Scenery, Manners and Customs.* London: Henry Colburn, 1828. Reprinted, Gainesville, Fla.: Scholars' Facsimilies & Reprints, 1967.

Hamilton, James. *Observations on the Utility and Administration of Purgative Medicines in Several Diseases.* 5th rev. ed. Edinburgh: Archibald Constable & Co., 1815.

Hamlin, L. Belle. "Peyton Short." *Quarterly Publication of the Historical and Philosophical Society of Ohio* 5 (January–March, 1909), 3.

Harlow, Alvin F. *Weep No More, My Lady.* New York: Whittlesey House, McGraw-Hill Book Co., 1942.

Harrison, Lowell H. *John Breckinridge: Jeffersonian Republican.* Filson Club Publications Second Series, No. 2. Louisville, Ky.: Filson Club, 1969.

——. "Memories of Slavery Days in Kentucky." *The Filson Club History Quarterly* 47 (July 1973), 242–257.

Hartley, Joseph R. *The Economic Effects of Ohio River Navigation.* Bloomington: School of Business, Indiana University, 1959.

Havighurst, Walter. *Voices on the River: The Story of the Mississippi Waterways.* New York: Macmillan Co., 1964.

Haynes, Mrs. C. W., comp. "History of Crittenden County . . . A Niece of Thomas Jefferson." *Marion* (Ky.) *Crittenden Press,* November 19, 1954.

Hening, William W. *The Statutes at Large; Being a Collection of All the Laws of Virginia, 1619–1792.* 13 vols. New York, Philadelphia: R. & W. G. Bartow, 1809–1823.

Hofstadter, Richard. *Anti-Intellectualism in American Life.* New York: Random House, Vintage Books, 1963.

Hopkins, James F. *A History of the Hemp Industry in Kentucky.* Lexington: University of Kentucky Press, 1951.

_____, ed. *The Papers of Henry Clay*. 5 vols. to date. Lexington: University Press of Kentucky, 1959–.

Hulbert, Archer B. "Western Ship Building." *American Historical Review* 21 (July 1916): 720–733.

Ireland, Robert M. "Aristocrats All: The Politics of County Government in Ante-bellum Kentucky." *The Review of Politics* 32 (July 1970): 365–383.

_____. *The County Courts in Antebellum Kentucky*. Lexington: University Press of Kentucky, 1972.

_____. "The Sale of Public Office in America." *Mid America* 52 (October 1970): 262–279.

Jefferson, Thomas. *Autobiography of Thomas Jefferson*. Introduction by Dumas Malone. New York: Capricorn Books, 1959.

_____. *Notes on the State of Virginia*. William Peden, ed. Chapel Hill: University of North Carolina Press, 1955.

Jillson, Willard R. *The Kentucky Land Grants: A Systematic Index*. Filson Club Publications No. 33. Louisville, Ky.: Filson Club, 1925. 1 vol. in 2 parts. Baltimore: Genealogical Publishing Co., 1971.

_____. *Pioneer Kentucky*. Frankfort: State Journal Co., 1934.

Jones, R. R. "The Ohio River, 1700–1914." Cincinnati: U.S. Army Corps of Engineers District Office, 1941. Unpublished manuscript.

Kentucky Adjutant-General's Office. *Kentucky Soldiers of the War of 1812*. Baltimore: Genealogical Publishing Co., 1969.

Kephart, Horace. *Out Southern Highlanders*. New York: Outing Publishing Co., 1913.

Kincaid, Robert L. *The Wilderness Road*. Indianapolis: Bobbs-Merrill Co., 1947.

Kirwan, Albert D., ed. *The Civilization of The Old South: Writings of Clement Eaton*. Lexington: University of Kentucky Press, 1968.

Knox, Barbara R. *Amos Persons, His Forebears and Descendants*. Fort Worth, Tex.: Barbara R. Knox, 1967.

La Rochefoucauld-Liancourt, Duc de. *Travels through the United States of North America in the Years 1795, 1796, 1797*. London: R. Phillips, 1799.

Latrobe, Charles J. *The Rambler in North America; 1832–1833*. 2 vols. London: R. B. Seeley and W. Burnside, 1835.

Latrobe, John B. *The First Steamboat Voyage on the Western Waters*. Fund Publication, No. 6. Baltimore: Maryland Historical Society, 1871.

Leahy, Ethel C. *Who's Who on the Ohio River and Its Tributaries*. Cincinnatti: E. C. Leahy Publishing Co., 1931.

Levin, H., ed. *The Lawyers and Lawmakers of Kentucky*. Chicago: Lewis Publishing Co., 1897.

Lewis, William T. *The Genealogy of the Lewis Family in America*. Louisville, Ky.: Courier-Journal Job Printing Co., 1893.

433

Lewisiana, or The Lewis Letter. A monthly inter-family paper. Lisle, N.Y., 1887–1907.

Lipscomb, Andrew A., and Albert E. Bergh, eds. *The Writings of Thomas Jefferson.* Monticello edition 20 vols. Washington, D. C.: Thomas Jefferson Memorial Association, 1904–1905.

Littell, William. *The Statute Law of Kentucky, with Notes, Praelections, and Observations on the Public Acts.* 5 vols. Frankfort, Ky.: printed by and for William Hunter, 1809–1819.

Littell, William, and Jacob Swigert. *A Digest of the Statute Law of Kentucky: Being A Collection of all the Acts of the General Assembly.* 2 vols. Frankfort: printed by Kendall and Russell, 1822.

Malone, Dumas. *Jefferson the Virginian.* Vol. 1, *Jefferson and His Time.* Boston: Little, Brown & Co., 1948.

Marraro, Howard R. "Unpublished Correspondence of Jefferson and Adams to Mazzei." *The Virginia Magazine of History and Biography* 51 (April 1943): 113–133.

Martin, Vernon P. "Father Rice, the Preacher who Followed the Frontier." *Filson Club History Quarterly* 29 (October 1955), 324–330.

Mathias, Frank F. "Slavery, the Solvent of Kentucky Politics." *The Register of the Kentucky Historical Society* 70 (January 1972), 1–16.

Mayo, Bernard, ed. *Thomas Jefferson and His Unknown Brother Randolph.* Charlottesville: Tracy W. McGregor Library, University of Virginia, 1942.

Mazzei, Philip. *Memoirs of the Life and Peregrinations of the Florentine Philip Mazzei, 1730–1816.* Howard R. Marraro, trans. New York: Columbia University Press, 1942.

McAllister, John M., and Laura B. Tandy, eds. *Genealogies of the Lewis and Kindred Families.* Columbia, Mo.: printed by E. W. Stephens Publishing Co., 1906.

McDonald, Leslie. *Echoes of Yesteryear.* Smithland, Ky.: Livingston Ledger, 1972.

McMaster, John B. *History of the People of the United States from the Revolution to the Civil War.* 7 vols. New York: D. Appleton & Co., 1883–1913.

McMeekin, Isabel M. *Louisville, The Gateway City.* New York: Julian Messner, 1946.

McMurtrie, Henry. *Sketches of Louisville and Its Environs.* Louisville, Ky.: S. Penn, June 1819. Reprinted, Louisville: G. R. Clark Press, 1969.

McVey, Frank L. *The Gates Open Slowly: A History of Education in Kentucky.* Lexington: University of Kentucky Press, 1949.

Mead, Edward C. *Historic Homes of the South-West Mountains Virginia.* Philadelphia: J. B. Lippincott Co., 1899.

Meade, William. *Old Churches, Ministers, and Families of Virginia.* 2 vols. Philadelphia: J. B. Lippincott Co., 1861.

434

Melish, John. *Travels in the United States of America.* 2 vols. Philadelphia: Thomas and George Palmer, 1812.

Mellon, Matthew T. *Early American Views on Negro Slavery: From the Letters and Papers of the Founders of the Republic.* New York: New American Library, Mentor Books, 1969.

Michaux, François A. *Travels to the Westward of the Allegheny Mountains.* London: J. Mawman, 1805.

Miller, John C. *The Federalist Era, 1789–1801.* The New American Nation Series. New York: Harper & Row, Harper Torchbooks, 1963.

Miyakawa, T. Scott. *Protestants and Pioneers: Individualism and Conformity on the American Frontier.* Chicago: University of Chicago Press, 1964.

Moore, Arthur K. *The Frontier Mind: A Cultural Analysis of the Kentucky Frontiersman.* Lexington: University of Kentucky Press, Kentucky Paperbacks, 1957.

Nettels, Curtis P. *The Emergence of a National Economy, 1775–1815.* The Economic History of the United States Series, vol. 2. New York: Harper & Row, Harper Torchbooks, 1969.

North, Douglass C. *The Economic Growth of the United States, 1790–1860.* New York: W. W. Norton & Co., Norton Library, 1966.

Oakes, Edwin S., and George S. Gulick, eds. *American Jurisprudence.* 58 vols. San Francisco: Bancroft-Whitney Co., Rochester, N. Y.: Lawyers' Co-Operative Publishing Co., 1936–1948.

O'Malley, Charles J. *History of Union County, Kentucky.* Evansville, Ind.: Courier Co., 1886.

Padover, Saul K., ed. *A Jefferson Profile: As Revealed in His Letters.* New York: John Day Co., 1956.

Palmer, William P., ed. *Calendar of Virginia State Papers and Other Manuscripts . . .Preserved in the Capital in Richmond.* Vol. 3. Richmond: James E. Goode, printer, 1883.

Parton, James. *The Life and Times of Aaron Burr.* 9th ed. New York: Mason Brothers, 1858.

Pereira, Jonathan. *Elements of Materia Medica and Therapeutics.* 2 vols. Philadelphia: Lea & Blanchard, 1846.

Perkins, Bradford. *Prologue to War: England and the United States, 1805–1812.* Berkeley and Los Angeles: University of California Press, 1970.

Perkins, James H. *Annals of the West: Embracing a Concise Account of Principal Events.* Cincinnati: James R. Albach, 1846.

Perrin, William H. *Counties of Christian and Trigg, Kentucky.* Chicago: F. A. Battey Publishing Co., 1884.

Perrin, W. H., J. H. Battle, and G. C. Kniffen. *Kentucky. A History of the State.* 2d ed. and 3d ed. Louisville: F. A. Battey & Co., 1885, 1886.

Pickard, Madge E., and R. Carlyle Buley. *The Midwest Pioneer: His Ills, Cures, & Doctors.* New York: Henry Schuman, 1946.

435

Pierson, Hamilton W. *Jefferson at Monticello: The Private Life of Thomas Jefferson . . . 1862.* Reprinted, James A. Bear, Jr., ed., *Jefferson at Monticello . . .* Charlottesville: University Press of Virginia, 1967.

Pool, Atlanta H. T. "Tragedies in Livingston." *Louisville Courier-Journal,* June 10, 1894.

Posey, Walter B. *Frontier Mission: A History of Religion West of the Southern Appalachians to 1861.* Lexington: University of Kentucky Press, 1966.

Purcell, Martha C. G. *Lucy Jefferson Lewis . . . Virginia, 1752–Kentucky, 1811.* 24-page brochure. Paducah? Ky.: n.p., 1924.

Quisenberry, A. C. *The Life and Times of Hon. Humphrey Marshall.* Winchester, Ky.: Sun Publishing Co., 1892.

Randall, Henry S. *The Life of Thomas Jefferson.* 3 vols. Philadelphia: J. B. Lippincott Co., 1871.

Randolph, Sarah N. *The Domestic Life of Thomas Jefferson.* 3d ed. Charlottesville, Va.: Thomas Jefferson Memorial Foundation, 1947.

Rankin, John. *Letters on American Slavery.* 2d ed. Newburyport, Conn.: Charles Whipple, 1837.

Ravenswaay, Charles van. "New Madrid Reminiscences." *Missouri Historical Society Bulletin* 4 (January 1948): 93–96.

Rawlings, Mary, ed. "Albemarle County Court, Order Book, 1744–1746." *Papers of the Albemarle County Historical Society* 5 (1944–1945): 7–35.

———. *The Albemarle of Other Days.* Charlottesville, Va.: Michie Co., 1925.

Robert, Joseph C. *The Story of Tobacco in America.* New York: Alfred A. Knopf, 1949.

Robertson, John E. L. "Paducah: Origins to Second Class." *The Register of the Kentucky Historical Society* 66 (April 1968), 108–136.

Rogers, James R. *The Cane Ridge Meeting House.* Cincinnati: Standard Publishing Co., 1910.

Rone, Wendell H., Sr. *An Historical Atlas of Kentucky and Her Counties.* Owensboro, Ky.: Progress Printing Co., 1965.

Rosenberger, Francis C., ed. *Jefferson Reader, a Treasury of Writings about Thomas Jefferson.* New York: Dutton, 1953.

Rothert, Otto A. *A History of Muhlenberg County.* Louisville, Ky.: John P. Morton & Co., 1913.

———. "The Tragedy of the Lewis Brothers: Two Sons of Lucy Jefferson Lewis." *The Filson Club History Quarterly* 10 (October 1936): 231–260.

Schachner, Nathan. *Thomas Jefferson: A Biography.* New York: Thomas Yoseloff, 1957.

Schultz, Christian, Jr. *Travels on an Inland Voyage through the States of New York, Pennsylvania, Virginia, Ohio, Kentucky, and Tennessee.* New York: printed by Isaac Riley, 1810.

Smelser, Marshall. *The Democratic Republic, 1801–1815*. New American Nation Series. New York: Harper & Row, Harper Torchbooks, 1968.

Smith, James. *History of the Christian Church, from Its Origin to the Present Time . . . including a History of the Cumberland Presbyterian Church.* Nashville, Tenn., Cumberland Presbyterian Office, 1835.

Smith, Walter B., and Arthur H. Cole. *Fluctuations in American Business: 1790–1860*. Cambridge, Mass.: Harvard University Press, 1935.

Smith, Zachariah F. *The History of Kentucky.* 4th ed. Louisville: Courier-Journal Job Printing Co., 1901.

Smyth, John F. D. *A Tour in the United States of America.* 2 vols. London: for G. Robinson, 1784.

Sneed, William C. *A Report on the History and Mode of Management of the Kentucky Penitentiary, from its Origin, in 1798, to March 1, 1860.* Frankfort: John B. Major, state printer, 1860.

Snively, W. D., Jr., and Louanna Furbee. *Satan's Ferryman: A True Tale of the Old Frontier.* New York: Frederick Ungar Publishing Co., 1968.

Sonne, Niels H. *Liberal Kentucky, 1780–1828.* Columbia Studies in American Culture, vol. 3. New York: Columbia University Press, 1939.

Sorley, Merrow E. *Lewis of Warner Hall: The History of a Family.* Columbia, Mo.: E. W. Stephens Co., 1935.

Sprague, Stuart S. "The Louisville Canal: Key to Aaron Burr's Western Trip of 1805." *The Register of the Kentucky Historical Society* 71 (January 1973):69–86.

Stampp, Kenneth M. *The Peculiar Institution: Slavery in the Ante-Bellum South.* New York: Random House, Vintage Books, 1956.

Stanard, William G., ed. "Virginia Legislative Papers." *Virginia Magazine of History and Biography* 13 (July 1905): 40–45; 16 (July–December 1908): 170–172; 17 (July–December 1909): 52–60; 18 (1910): 255–258.

Staples, Charles R. *The History of Pioneer Lexington.* Lexington, Ky.: Transylvania Press, 1939.

Starling, Edmund L. *History of Henderson County, Kentucky.* Henderson: 1887. Reprinted, Evansville, Ind.: Unigraphic, 1965.

Sullivan, Mary M. "The Gentry and the Association in Albemarle County, 1774–1775." *Magazine of Albemarle County History* 23 (1964–1965): 35–44.

Swem, Earl G. "Kentuckians at William and Mary College before 1861 with a Sketch of the College before that Date." *The Filson Club History Quarterly* 23 (July 1949): 5–30.

————, comp. *Virginia Historical Index.* 2 vols. Roanoke: Stone Printing and Manufacturing Co., 1934–1936.

437

Tapp, Hambleton. "Three Decades of Kentucky Politics, 1870–1900." Ph.D. dissertation, University of Kentucky, 1950.

Tarleton, Banastre. *A History of the Campaigns of 1780 and 1781, in the Southern Provinces of North America.* Dublin: printed for Colles, etc., 1787.

Taylor, Harrison D. *Ohio County, Kentucky, in the Olden Days.* Louisville, Ky. John P. Morton & Co., 1926.

Thacker, Joseph A., Jr. "The Kentucky Militia from 1792 to 1812." Master's thesis, University of Kentucky, 1954.

Thomas, Joseph. *The Life of the Pilgrim, Joseph Thomas, Containing an Accurate Account of His Trials, Travels and Gospel Labours.* Winchester, Va.: J. Foster, printer, 1817.

Thomas, Samuel W. "William Croghan, Sr. (1752–1822): A Pioneer Kentucky Gentleman." *The Filson Club History Quarterly* 43 (January 1969): 30–61.

Thomas, Samuel W., and Eugene H. Connor. "Henry McMurtrie, M.D. (1793–1865): First Historian and Promoter of Louisville." *The Filson Club History Quarterly* 43 (October 1969): 311–324.

Thurlow, Constance E.; Francis L. Berkeley, Jr.; John Casteen; and Anne Freudenberg. *The Jefferson Papers of the University of Virginia.* Charlottesville: University Press of Virginia, 1973.

Tocqueville, Alexis de. *Democracy of America.* 2 vols. Henry Reeve, trans. New York: Colonial Press, 1900.

Trail, Robert. "Livingston County, Kentucky—Stepping Stone to Illinois." *Register of the Kentucky Historical Society* 69 (July 1971): 239–272.

Turpin, John B. *A Brief History of the Albemarle Baptist Association.* William W. Landrum, ed. Richmond: Virginia Baptist Historical Society, 1891.

United States Bureau of the Census. *Heads of Families at the First Census of the United States Taken in the Year 1790 . . . Virginia.* Washington, D.C.: Government Printing Office, 1908.

Van Deusen, Glyndon G. *The Life of Henry Clay.* Boston: Little, Brown & Co., 1937.

Van Every, Dale. *The Final Challenge: The American Frontier, 1804–1845.* New York: Morrow, 1964.

Viitanen, Wayne. "The Winter the Mississippi Ran Backwards." *The Register of the Kentucky Historical Society* 71 (January 1973): 51–68.

Warren, Robert Penn. *Brother to Dragons: A Tale in Verse and Voices.* New York: Random House, 1953.

Warville, Jaques P. Brissot de. *New Travels in the United States of America, 1788.* Durand Echeverria, ed. Cambridge, Mass.: Harvard University Press, Belknap Press, 1964.

Watlington, Patricia. *The Partisan Spirit: Kentucky Politics, 1779–1792.*

New York: Atheneum, for the Institute of Early American History and Culture at Williamsburg, Virginia, 1972.

Watts, Charles W. "Colonial Albemarle: The Social and Economic History of a Piedmont Virginia County, 1727–1775." Master's thesis, University of Virginia, 1948.

Watts, William C. *Chronicles of a Kentucky Settlement.* New York: G. P. Putnam's Sons, 1897.

Weaks, Mabel C., comp. *Calendar of the Kentucky Papers of the Draper Collection of Manuscripts.* Calendar series, vol. 2. Madison: State Historical Society of Wisconsin, 1925.

Weeks, Elie. "Snowden." *Goochland County Historical Society Magazine* 3 (Autumn 1971): 24–28.

Weir, James. *Lonz Powers: Or the Regulators.* 2 vols. Philadelphia: Lippincott, Grambo & Co., 1850.

Weld, Theodore D., comp. *American Slavery as It Is: Testimony of a Thousand Witnesses.* New York: American Anti-Slavery Society, 1839.

Wertenbaker, Thomas J. "The Rivanna." *Magazine of Albemarle County History* 14 (1954–1955): 1–8.

Westerfield, Thomas W., ed. *Kentucky Genealogy and Biography.* 4 vols. to date. Owensboro, Ky.: Genealogical Reference Co., 1970–.

Whitley, Edna T. *Kentucky Ante-Bellum Portraiture.* Paris? Ky., 1956.

Wilkerson, Marcus M. *Thomas Duckett Boyd: The Story of a Southern Educator.* Baton Rouge: Louisiana State University Press, 1935.

Williams, Samuel C. *History of the Lost State of Franklin.* New York: Press of the Pioneers, 1933.

Wilson, Charles M. *Backwoods America.* Chapel Hill: University of North Carolina Press, 1934.

Wilson, Joseph M. *The Presbyterian Historical Almanac and Annual Remembrancer of the Church, for 1864.* Philadelphia: Joseph M. Wilson, 1864.

Wilson, Major L., ed. *A Letter from the Jackson Committee . . . upon the Subject of Gen. Jackson's Marriage.* Mississippi Valley Collection Bulletin. Memphis, Tenn.: Memphis State University, 1968. Reprinted from *A Letter from the Jackson Committee. . . .* Nashville, Tenn.: Hall & Fitzgerald, printers, 1827.

Woods, Edgar. *Albemarle County in Virginia.* Charlottesville: Michie Co., 1901.

Wyllie, John Cook. "Daniel Boone's Adventures in Charlottesville in 1781." *Magazine of Albemarle County History* 19 (1960–1961): 5–18.

———. "Writings about Jack Jouett and Tarleton's Raid on Charlottesville in 1781." *Magazine of Albemarle County History* 17 (1958–1959): 49–56.

Wynes, Charles E. "Banking in Virginia, 1789–1820." *The Annual Collection of Essays in History* (Corcoran Department of History, University of Virginia) 4 (Winter 1957): 35–49.

439

Young, Bennett H. *History and Texts of the Three Constitutions of Kentucky.* Louisville, Ky.; Courier-Journal Job Printing Co., 1890.

———. *A History of Jessamine County, Kentucky.* Louisville, Ky.: Courier-Journal Job Printing Co., 1898.

Young, Jacob. *Autobiography of a Pioneer: Or, the Nativity, Experience, Travels and Ministerial Labors of Rev. Jacob Young.* Cincinnati: Cranston and Curts, 1857.

fish, in western waters, 112
Fitch, Gideon, 183–85; letter to, from Jefferson, 184–85
Flannery, Elijah, 281n
flatboats, 101–102, 105
Fleming, James J., 132
Fliece (Flease), Enoch, 359–64
flood of Ohio River, 1812, 295
Fluvanna Co., Va., 343
Ford, James, 121, 238
Ford, Judge Jesse, 176, 187–88; background of, 274–77; character of, 415; leaves Livingston Co., 323; presides over circuit court, 281–85, 287
foreign trade, see agriculture, foreign trade
forest fires in Va., 46
Fort Adams, La., 86
Fort, David, 241, 245, 359, 365, 409
Fort Massac, Ill., 136
Frank (aged slave of Randolph Lewis), 222; converted, 208–209; grief of, 264; rented out, 417; sold, 316; value of, 241–42
Frank (slave of Lilburne Lewis), 124, 353, 361, 420
Frankfort, Ky., 106, 396
Frankfort Western World, 148
Fredericksburg, Va., 20
Fredericksville Parish, 4
frontier: abolition movement on, 199–200; banking and finance, 135–36; building homes on, 130–31; discussed, 329–30; medicines in use on, 353–58; moves into Ky., 36; roads, 97; towns, 115–16; violence, 232–33
fruit, see agriculture: crops
Fulkerson, Abraham, 285n
Fulton, Robert, 410
Furnace, Dr., 132

Gallatin Co., Ill., 405
Gallatin Co., Ky., 105, 352, 390–91
Gallipolis, Ohio, 108
Galt, William, 51
Gamble and Temple, firm of, 51
Garfield, James A., 351
Garrard, Gov. James, 186
Garth, John, 361
Gaspar River Church, 191
Gay, James, 126
genetic inheritance: inbreeding in

Lewis and Jefferson families, 320–21, 420. See also mental instability
gentry, see aristocrats
George (slave of Lilburne Lewis), 164–65, 256; head of, discovered, 267–68, 279–80; murder of, effect of on slavery, 338; murdered, 256–64
Gianinni, Anthony, 348–49, 423
Gibson, Jesse, 281n
Gilmer, Dr. (Lt.) George: confiscates English money, 15–16; letters from, to Jefferson, 15, 22, 23; loyalty oath of, 20; organized minutemen, 13; quoted, 9; second march of, 14; speech of, 14
Giovanni (a tailor), 423
Giovannini, 348–50
Given, Judge Dickson: appointed judge, 412; background of, 275–77; character of, 415; death of, 323, distrusts orphans' guardians, 322–23; indicted, 155; presides over circuit court, 281–85. 287; will of, 322–23, 275–77
Given, Esther, 275
Given, Henry, 275
Given, Joseph R., 322
Given, Nancy, 322–23
Gloucester Co., Va., 3
Gooch, John, 272
Goochland Co., Va., 3, 5, 396
Gordon, James, 157–58
Gordon, John, 398
government of counties, see courts: county in Ky.
government officials, see courts, county in Ky.
grand jury, March 16, 1812, 281–83
grand jury, March 18, 1812, 285–86, 285n
grants of land, see land grants
Grasty, 414
graveyard: on farm of Randolph Lewis, 218, 420; gravestones altered in, 426; at Rocky Hill, 163, 218, 320, 420; suicide in, 293–301
Gray, John, 175; as attorney for Lynch Brooks, 174; background of, 230–31; elected senator, 323–24; indicted, 155, indicts Isham and Lilburne Lewis, 258–59; indicts James Ivy, 120; indicts Lilburne Lewis, 283; payment of note to, refused,

Lewis), 163, 307, 344, 347, 420;
boarded out to school, 167–68, 246;
guardian appointed for, 420; as leg-
atee, 293; marriage of, 320, 343
Lewis, Councillor John (the younger,
of Warner Hall), 346, 372
Lewis, Maj. John, 346
Lewis, L. (identity uncertain), 359
Lewis, Letitia Griffin Rutter, 347;
confinement and escape of, 266,
289–91, 307, 332; dower rights of,
308; given slaves from estate, 320;
marries Christopher G. Houts, 320;
marries Lilburne Lewis, 218–219;
mentioned in will, 293–95; pregnancy and childbirth of, 246, 266;
purchases of, at auction, 309, 361–
66; unhappy marriage of, 256, 261,
331; as witness to murder of
George, 260, 264, 289–90
Lewis, Lilburne, 351; acquaintance of,
with Jefferson, 80; aids James Mc-
Cawley, 138; admitted to bail, 288–
89, 415; appointed legal arbitrator,
179–80; appraises brother's estate,
241; as bondsman for Richard Ferguson, 283–84; books of, 366–67;
business affairs of, 87–88, 330; buys
land in Ky., 89, 92–93; career of,
1803–1807, 88–89; character disintegration of, 256, 261, 410; as child,
21; as client of Henry F. Delany,
230; confines wife and slaves, 266;
cursed by James McLaughlan, 243–
44, 264; daughters of, boarded out
at school, 167–68; death of wife,
Elizabeth, 163–64; deeds of,
recorded, 182, 186; deserted by
wife, Letitia, 289–90; early marriage of, 71; estate of, 307–11, 359–
70; as executor of brother's will,
240; family of, broken up, 320;
family records of, 163; final
disgrace of, 292; financial problems
of, 168, 170–74, 215–18; friends of,
141–42, 242; as frontier aristocrat,
123–24; given land by father, 49,
381; grave of, 420; house of, in Ky.,
127, 131; household furniture of,
127; indictment and arrest of, 258–
59, 283–86; indicts James Trimble,
285; indicts William Brown, 282;
jury duty of, 161, 175, 179, 231–32,
245, 398; land of, in Ky., 110, 121,
129–30, 187–88, 343, 365; lawsuits

against, for debt, 168, 173–74, 244–
46, 310–11 (see also Dr. Arthur
Campbell, Lynch Brooks, William
C. Bradburn); letters from, to Dr.
Arthur Campbell, 164–67; loan
from Lynch Brooks, 170–74; marriage of, 48, 71; medical bills of,
166–68, 353–54; mental instability
of, 329–35; militia service of, 146–
47, 180–82, 226, 246, 291, 418;
mortgage demanded from, 291;
partnership of, with father, 48; personal possessions of, 98; plans move
to Ky., 90–91; possessions of, sold at
auction, 308–309, 366–69; probable punishment of, for murder,
272–73; property of, 1798, 48; rejected as justice of the peace, 243;
relationship of, to brother, Isham,
334–35; relationship of, to brother,
Randolph, 243; relationship of, with
John Gray, 231; relationship of,
with slave, George, 256; released
overnight on bond, 284; religious
affiliation of, 195, 197; role of, in
community, 215; resentment
against, 243–44; second marriage
of, 218–19, 331; as second nominee
to county court, 221; sells land at
Buck Island, 88; sisters of, cited for
contempt, 281–82; slaves of, 124,
215–16, 220, 309–10, 332, 361,
368, 420; suicide of, 293–301; takes
census of 1810, 167, 216–17; tragic
end of, discussed, 317–18; trial of,
postponed, 288–89; trip of, to
Bluegrass, 167–68; trip of, to Ky.,
1806, 170, 389; as trustee of Westwood, 216, 245–46; use of alcohol
by, 247, 256–57, 261–63, 329, 332;
will of, 293–96, 301, 307–308; witnesses a deed in Va., 387
Lewis, Lilburne Livingston (son of Lilburne Lewis), 165, 293, 307, 320,
343, 347, 415
Lewis, Lucy B. (Mrs. Washington A.
Griffin, daughter of Charles L.
Lewis), 35, 339, 342, 347; as leg-
atee, 293; letter from, to Jefferson,
223–24; marriage of, 306; scheme
of, to defraud Craven Peyton, 313–
16
Lewis, Lucy J. (daughter of Lilburne
Lewis), 165, 347; boarded out at

Lewis, Robert (of Wales), 3
Lewis, Gen. Robert, 346
Lewis, Robert Randolph (son of Randolph Lewis), 305–306, 342–43, 419, 538
Lewis, Susannah H. (daughter of Randolph Lewis), 305–306, 313, 343, 347, 419
Lewis, Tucker (son of Randolph Lewis), 264, 305, 343, 347, 419
Lewis, Warner (son of Randolph Lewis), 221, 264, 305–306, 319–20, 342–43, 347, 419
Lewisiana, 317–18
Lexington Gazette, 104, 249
Lexington, Ky., 26n, 167
Lexington Reporter, 312
Liberty Hall (school), 190, 204
Lime Kiln Branch, Albemarle Co., Va., 373
Limestone Creek, 373
Lincoln Co., Ky., 392
Lincoln Co., Va., 392
Lindsay, Lt. Col. Reuben, 23
liquor, *see* alcohol
Little Creek, Ky., 226
livestock, *see* animals
Livingston Church, (Centerville), 204–205
Livingston Co., Ky., 110, 402; boundaries of, 1808, 115; census of 1810, taken, 216–17; division of, 159, 392, 398; county seat of, moved, 159–161; Cumberland Presbyterian church, in, 195; flora and fauna of, 111–15; Indian patrols in, 312–13, 419; militia regiment of, 396; parent counties of, 392; population of, 1800, 405; population of, 1810, 217; sale of public office in, 153–54; slavery in, 235–39; tax delinquency of, 397; towns in, 115–22
Livingston Creek, Ford of (Centerville), 159
Livingston Presbyterian Church, 117–18
Logan Co., Ky., 189–90, 392, 402
Logan, James, 158
Louisa Courthouse, Va., 25
Louisiana (ship), 137
Louisville Courier Journal, 317
Louisville, Ky., 108; diseases common in, 354–56; earthquake damage in, 266; falls at, 97, 106–107; financing

a theater in, 254; laws of, 108; steamboat at, 253
Love, William, 232
Lucas, William, 393
Lusk, James, inspection station of, 156–57, 361–62, 398
Lyon Co., Ky., 392, 396, 398, 419
Lyon, Matthew: establishes Eddyville, Ky., 116–17; as jury foreman, 227; urges invasion of Canada, 145–46

McAllister, John M., letter to *Lewisiana,* 317–18, 422
McAmy, Samuel, 139
McCawley, James, 138–42, 215; assaults John Herrington, 324; at auction, hires two slaves, 361, 364; buries Robert Lewis, 320; cares for orphan, Robert Lewis, 307; cruelty of, 238; as friend of Lilburne Lewis, 242; as guardian of Robert Lewis, 325; indicted, 138, 286; jury duty of, 324; mentioned in will, 293–95; posts marriage bond, 394; refuses executorship, 308; removed from coroner's jury, 297; rents slave, 166; tried for perjury, 245; verifies will, 308; wins lawsuit, 231
McCleod, Capt., 25
McDaniel, John, 285, 285n, 414–15
McGee, John, 402
McGee, William, 402
McGready, Rev. James, 190, 195, 205
McKlesky, William, 281n
McLaughlan, James, 243–44, 264
McMaster, John B., 191–92
McMurtrie, Dr. Henry, *Sketches of Louisville and Its Environs,* 354–56
M'Namar (McNemar), Richard, 196
Madison, James, 176, 403
magistrate, *see* justice of the peace
Magruder, Rev. John B., 417
Mahhan, David, 363
malaria (yellow fever), 130, 164–67, 355
Malone, Dumas, 82
manslaughter, legal penalty for, 268–73
Marietta, Ohio, 101, 108; boatbuilding at, 395
Marion, Ky., 351–52, 398, 404; woman's club, 351
Marion Cumberland Wave, 351–52
Marion Crittenden Press, 351–52
Markham & Wirt, firm of, 315

Library of Congress Cataloging in Publication Data

Merrill, Boynton, 1925–
  Jefferson's nephews.

  Bibliography: p.
  Includes index.
  1. Kentucky—History—1792–1865.   2. Lewis,
Isham, d. 1815 (?)   3. Lewis, Lilburn, d. 1812.
4. Lewis family.   I. Title.
F455.M47   976.9'03   76-3267
ISBN 0-691-04640-9